MW00817930

The Many Hands of the State

The state is central to social scientific and historical inquiry today, reflecting its importance in domestic and international affairs. States kill, coerce, fight, torture, and incarcerate, yet they also nurture, protect, educate, redistribute, and invest. It is precisely because of the complexity and wide-ranging impacts of states that research on them has proliferated and diversified. Yet, too many scholars inhabit separate academic silos, and theorizing of states has become dispersed and disjointed. This book aims to bridge some of the many gaps between scholarly endeavors, bringing together scholars who study states and empires from a diverse array of disciplines and perspectives. The book offers not only a sample of cutting-edge research that can serve as models and directions for future work, but an original conceptualization and theorization of states, their origins and evolution, and their effects.

KIMBERLY J. MORGAN is Professor of Political Science and International Affairs at George Washington University. She is the author of two books, *Working Mothers and the Welfare State: Religion and the Politics of Work-Family Policy in Western Europe and the United States* (2006), and co-author of *The Delegated Welfare State: Medicare, Markets, and the Governance of Social Policy* (2011), and is co-editor of the *Oxford Handbook of U.S. Social Policy* (2014).

ANN SHOLA ORLOFF is Professor of Sociology and Political Science, and Board of Lady Managers of the Columbian Exposition Chair at Northwestern University. She is the co-editor of *Remaking Modernity: Politics, History and Sociology* (2005) and the co-author of *States, Markets, Families: Gender, Liberalism and Social Policy in Australia, Canada, Great Britain and the United States* (Cambridge University Press, 1999). Orloff co-founded *Social Politics: International Studies in Gender, State and Society*.

The Many Hands of the State

Theorizing Political Authority and Social Control

Edited by

KIMBERLY J. MORGAN
George Washington University

ANN SHOLA ORLOFF
Northwestern University

CAMBRIDGE
UNIVERSITY PRESS

CAMBRIDGE
UNIVERSITY PRESS

One Liberty Plaza, 20th Floor, New York, NY 10006, USA

Cambridge University Press is part of the University of Cambridge.

It furthers the University's mission by disseminating knowledge in the pursuit
of education, learning, and research at the highest international levels of excellence.

www.cambridge.org
Information on this title: www.cambridge.org/9781316501139

10.1017/9781316471586

© Cambridge University Press 2017

First published 2017

Printed in the United States of America by Sheridan Books, Inc.

A catalogue record for this publication is available from the British Library.

Library of Congress Cataloging-in-Publication Data
NAMES: Morgan, Kimberly J., 1970– editor. | Orloff, Ann Shola, editor.
TITLE: The many hands of the state : theorizing political authority and social control / edited
by Kimberly Morgan, George Washington University ; Ann Shola Orloff,
Northwestern University.
DESCRIPTION: New York, NY : Cambridge University Press, 2016. | Includes
bibliographical references.
IDENTIFIERS: LCCN 2016023227 | ISBN 9781107135291 (hardback) |
ISBN 9781316501139 (paperback)
SUBJECTS: LCSH: State, The–Case studies. | State, The–Philosophy. | Authority–Case
studies. | Authority–Philosophy. | Social control–Case studies. | Social
control–Philosophy. | BISAC: POLITICAL SCIENCE / General.
CLASSIFICATION: LCC JC131 .M333 2016 | DDC 320.1–dc23 LC record
available at https://lccn.loc.gov/2016023227

ISBN 978-1-107-13529-1 Hardback
ISBN 978-1-316-50113-9 Paperback

Contents

List of Figures   *page* vii

List of Tables   ix

List of Contributors   xi

Acknowledgments   xiii

Introduction: The Many Hands of the State   I
Kimberly J. Morgan and Ann Shola Orloff

PART I LOCATING THE STATE:
THE PROBLEM OF BOUNDARIES

1   Reconciling Equal Treatment with Respect for Individuality:
    Associations in the Symbiotic State   35-53
    Elisabeth S. Clemens

2   Beyond the Hidden American State: Classification Struggles
    and the Politics of Recognition   58-75
    Damon Mayrl and Sarah Quinn

3   States as a Series of People Exchanges   81-98
    Armando Lara-Millán

4   State Metrology: The Rating of Sovereigns and the Judgment
    of Nations   103
    Marion Fourcade

PART II STRATIFICATION AND THE
TRANSFORMATION OF STATES

5   Gendered States Made and Remade: Gendered Labor Policies
    in the United States and Sweden, 1960–2010   131-151
    Ann Shola Orloff

v

6 States and Gender Justice   158
   Mala Htun and S. Laurel Weldon

7 The Civil Rights State: How the American State Develops Itself 178
   Desmond King and Robert C. Lieberman

8 Disaggregating the Racial State: Activists, Diplomats,
   and the Partial Shift toward Racial Equality in Brazil   203
   Tianna S. Paschel

   PART III DEVELOPING THE SINEWS OF POWER

9 Democratic States of Unexception: Toward a New Genealogy
   of the American Political   229
   William J. Novak, Stephen W. Sawyer, and James T. Sparrow

10 Performing Order: An Examination of the Seemingly Impossible
   Task of Subjugating Large Numbers of People, Everywhere,
   All the Time   258
   Christian Davenport

11 Fiscal Forearms: Taxation as the Lifeblood of the Modern
   Liberal State   284
   Ajay K. Mehrotra

12 The State and the Revolution in War   306
   Meyer Kestnbaum

   PART IV STATES AND EMPIRES:
   THE TRANSNATIONAL/GLOBAL TURN

13 Imperial States in the Age of Discovery   333
   Julia Adams and Steve Pincus

14 Making Legibility between Colony and Empire: Translation,
   Conflation, and the Making of the Muslim State   349
   Iza Hussin

15 The Octopus and the *Hekatonkheire*: On Many-Armed States
   and Tentacular Empires   369
   George Steinmetz

Index   395

Figures

4.1a Total number and percentage of nations rated by
Moody's, 1918–1948   *page* 109
4.1b Percentage of nations with sovereign ratings by agency,
1975–2013   109
4.2a Standard and Poor's sovereign ratings methodology   112
4.2b Moody's sovereign ratings methodology   112
6.1 Family law index, 2005   166
6.2 VAW index, 1995   170
6.3 VAW index, 2005   171
10.1 Basic states versus challengers (SvC)   265
10.2 Zones of contestation in SvC   266
10.3 States versus challengers as grid   266
10.4 States versus challengers and the Hobbesian balance   268
10.5 States versus challengers and the Rashomon effect   269
10.6 States versus challengers and state control   272
15.1 Oxford University Colonial Services Club, June 1939   383
15.2 Oxford University Colonial Services Club, 1949 (close up)   383

Tables

6.1 Typology of policies to promote gender justice/equality   *page* 164

Contributors

Julia Adams, Sociology, Yale University

Elisabeth S. Clemens, Sociology/Political Science, University of Chicago

Christian Davenport, Political Science, University of Michigan

Marion Fourcade, Sociology, University of California, Berkeley

Mala Htun, Political Science, University of New Mexico

Iza Hussin, Politics, University of Cambridge

Meyer Kestnbaum, Sociology, University of Maryland

Desmond King, Political Science, University of Oxford

Armando Lara-Millán, Sociology, University of California, Berkeley

Robert C. Lieberman, Political Science, Johns Hopkins University

Damon Mayrl, Sociology, Universidad Carlos III de Madrid

Ajay K. Mehrotra, Law, American Bar Foundation/Northwestern University Pritzker School of Law

Kimberly J. Morgan, Political Science, George Washington University

William J. Novak, Law, University of Michigan

Ann Shola Orloff, Sociology and Political Science, Northwestern University

Tianna S. Paschel, African American Studies and African Diaspora Studies, University of California, Berkeley

Steve Pincus, History, Yale University

Sarah Quinn, Sociology, University of Washington

Stephen W. Sawyer, History, American University of Paris

James T. Sparrow, History, University of Chicago

George Steinmetz, Sociology, University of Michigan

S. Laurel Weldon, Political Science, Purdue University

Acknowledgments

This project originated in a series of panels that we organized at the Social Science History Association's annual meeting over the course of several years. We are extremely grateful for the continued vibrancy of this interdisciplinary association and its annual conference and for the intellectual engagement of our authors at each meeting. We also want to express our deep gratitude to the Neubauer Collegium for Culture and Society at the University of Chicago – convened by the "State as History and Theory" project led by Elisabeth Clemens, Bernard Harcourt, and James T. Sparrow – for sponsoring a very fruitful meeting of our group in May 2014. On the introduction, we benefited a great deal from the ongoing conversation with our volume contributors as well as the comments and suggestions made by Tom Chevalier, Marion Fourcade, Henry Hale, Patrick Le Galès, Damon Mayrl, Julia Adams, Talia Shiff, Kathleen Thelen, seminar participants at the Institut d'Etudes Politiques, students in the graduate seminar on "Many Hands of the State" at Northwestern, and two anonymous reviewers for Cambridge University Press. We also thank Alexander Reisenbichler, Elizabeth Onasch, and Jane Pryma for their very helpful research assistance. Finally, we thank Robert Dreesen at Cambridge University Press for so ably shepherding us through the publication process and supporting our project.

Introduction

The Many Hands of the State

Kimberly J. Morgan and Ann Shola Orloff

The study of states over the past three or four decades calls forth a number of paradoxes. First, intensifying interest in studying states has run parallel to the intensifying forces of globalization. The more states seem to be entangled in global economic, social, cultural, and political forces, the more scholars reach for the term "state" in their analyses, even as they eschew the "Westphalian" understanding of nation-states as the only proper unit of analysis. The intellectual focus on states also has spilled over into the policy domain, as actors operating within international organizations such as the International Monetary Fund (IMF) and World Bank – the very agents of globalization – have become fixated on shoring up states around the globe. Although many once advocated shrinking public sectors so as to liberate markets, many policymakers now believe that building up states and improving their "quality" (e.g., governance) is vital for economic development or political stability.[1]

A second paradox is that the drive to focus on the state as an analytic category developed powerfully within U.S. academia, despite the widespread sense of many that the United States has a governing apparatus that operates in fundamentally different ways than what the literature on states – above all in Europe – suggested. Perhaps the state has become an enduring scholarly preoccupation of United States-based scholars because they feel most keenly the disjuncture between the projection of U.S. power around the globe and antistatist political currents back home. The history of U.S. statebuilding also contains a perplexing mix of power and impotence: fragmented decision-making structures, multiple layers of government, and pervasive intertwining of public and private authority, yet also a remarkable capacity to conquer, enslave, surveil, and imprison.

Because the operation of political authority in the United States fits uneasily with the ideal-typical state lurking in the scholarly imagination, there is a growing literature seeking to better understand what "the state" is and means in the U.S. context.[2]

The third paradox lies in the fact that, even as we have seen the waning of debates between "state-centered" and "society-centered" theories of the state, its autonomy (or lack thereof), and its capacities, studies of states have increased and diversified, drawing on novel but more dispersed varieties of theorizing. While earlier analysis of states displayed a high level of theoretical engagement within a relatively narrow set of empirical debates, we now confront a situation of far greater empirical breadth but less theoretical engagement among scholars pursuing different lines of thinking.

A fourth paradox is that continued interest in states has coincided with a widely accepted reading of Foucault that the juridical power of states has been displaced by, or at least supplemented by, diffuse, capillary, or "mobile" mechanisms of power. Real-world events, including the emergence of nonterritorial political forces such as al-Qaeda and the increasing influence of both local and supranational entities, have also challenged the analytic primacy of states. In light of these developments, some counseled us to leave states altogether and investigate instead governance or governmentality.[3] We disagree.

Indeed, calls to disaggregate states into their component institutions and to assess different forms of power have not led scholars to drop the state from their analyses. Since the publication of the germinal *Bringing the State Back In* volume in 1985, the state has remained a central category and topic of analysis, and the academic and policy literature on the state is now vast, transcending disciplines, subfields, methodologies, epistemologies, and geographic areas of study.[4] We see this in the proliferation of modifiers that scholars use to characterize states – ambidextrous, administrative, associational, austerity, capitalist, carceral, centaur, clientelist, competition, consolidation, delegated, developmental, disaggregated, emergency, familial, failed, hidden, hollow, imperial, Keynesian welfare, laissez-faire, layered, migration, motherless, neoliberal, patriarchal, patronal, penal, phantom, polymorphic, predatory, racial, regulatory, rentier, Rube Goldberg, standardizing, straight, submerged, taxing, theatre, uneasy, warfare, welfare, women-friendly, and workfare – to name a few. This proliferation of modifiers reflects a problematic lack of engagement among analysts of states – how do these modifiers actually relate to each other? But it does indicate that the concept of the state, however varied and contested it may be, is indispensable to contemporary scholarship.

This introduction, and the volume as a whole, makes an extended argument for the continuing fruitfulness of studying states; yet we need a better analytic armory. Our collective project emerged out of a desire to reflect upon several decades of exciting and innovative research, veering off in many different directions, that has flowered since the initial move to bring the state back in. Building on this wealth of research, we sought to reconnect with one another on a higher, theoretical plane. This volume culminates the intellectual work of several conferences, in which we grappled with theoretical questions about the meaning, contours, and reach of state power as we presented and critiqued our individual analyses of different elements of states. We found intriguing parallels across areas of interest that have been studied in isolation, such as political conflicts over state stratification that resonate across different forms of inequality, time periods, and geographic locations. Moreover, widening our lens beyond nation-states to include empires and other forms of governance enriches understandings of the multiple levels at which governing authority operates, processes of internal and external boundary formation, and how the "rule of difference" operates in both imperial and state contexts. We have arrived at the conclusion that several interrelated theoretical innovations mark the contemporary study of states.

First, our title, *The Many Hands of the State*, aims to capture the pervasive move away from conceptions of states as unitary actors and toward an understanding of states as encompassing multiple institutions, varying forms of interpenetration with civil society, multiple scales of governance, and multiple and potentially contradictory logics. One implication is that to understand states, we must both disaggregate and reaggregate, being attentive to the variable and shifting components of states without losing sight of that which binds them together. This, in turn, enables us to see states not as static structures of political opportunity, but as sets of organizations developing over time. Gaps between rules and their implementation are inevitable, allowing for endogenous as well as exogenous forms of institutional change, and possibly the transformation of the character of states or their constituent institutions.

Second, cultural and constructivist turns in history and the social sciences have drawn attention to the significance of states as classifying, categorizing, and stratifying organizations, as well as to the importance of cognition and cultural schemas in constituting boundaries, institutions, categories, and subjects. Rather than assuming there is a self-evident separation between "state" and "society" or "economy," analysts argue that the state and its boundaries are shaped by cultural and ideological constructions. This also moves us to regain Weber's insight about the importance of *legitimacy*, without which states cannot maintain a monopoly of violence. State officials seek to construct and preserve monopolies over both material and symbolic force, raising questions about how this has been accomplished or why it has not succeeded.

Finally, there is extensive rethinking of the nation-state as a form and a unit of analysis in historical and globally situated contexts. Indeed, many of the nation-states whose trajectories have been treated as prototypical of statebuilding and state formation are in fact better conceptualized as multinational and spatially expansive, noncontiguous empires. The nation-state is but one historically specific form of rule among myriad others, ranging from empires to regions to city-states. Research in this area can be read as overlapping with the renewed interest in how boundaries are culturally and materially constituted, as these are not only "internal" – vis-à-vis "society" or the result of projects of nation-building on contiguous territories – but "external" – vis-à-vis other states or spatially distinct territories.

Our aim in this introductory chapter – after revisiting the intellectual origins and evolution that brought us to our current moment – is to elaborate on the theoretical innovations in the contemporary study of states, sketched here. Let us note that we do not aspire to impose a single theoretical apparatus, based on a singular definition, for studying states. We see the canonical Weberian definition of the state that is so often cited these days – "a human community that (successfully) claims the *monopoly of the legitimate use of physical force* within a given territory" – as a serviceable enough starting point for theorizing states, but one that proves limiting, if narrowly understood.[5] Some scholars using variants of this definition focus only on forms of material power, lopping off Weber's cultural concerns encoded in his reference to legitimacy. Questioning how states legitimate their rule moves us to investigate how beliefs about the essential rightness of a state's rule emerge and are reproduced, alongside the development and consolidation of control of the means of coercion.[6] Moreover, like many definitions, Weber's offers an idealized portrait of that which is studied; in reality, many of the most interesting questions about states concern all that has challenged this ideal – how states are embedded in multiple levels of governance, their malleable and contested boundaries, and challenges to their sovereignty. Once we appreciate the multiplicity or, to invoke our favored metaphor, "hands" of states, it is difficult to imagine that a single theory could address them all adequately. Indeed, the authors in this volume have each drawn in exciting new ways on different theorists, both classical and contemporary, to understand the diverse elements of states and empires.

STUDYING STATES: INTELLECTUAL ORIGINS AND EVOLUTION

Our interest in states, power, and politics was encouraged by the "sound of marching, charging feet" that was all around us in the 1960s and 1970s, and then by the fallout, political and intellectual, from the decline of those movements and the new challenges of neoliberalism and various political right turns. The 1970s had ushered in a shift within history and the social sciences to consider the *political* significance of *social* arrangements and processes. Traditional approaches toward politics and power had kept scholars focused on formal institutions, elites, and conventional forms of participation. Instead, social science historians and historically oriented social scientists insisted on the significance of politics from below and the social sources of power and interests, particularly as rooted in capitalist relations.[7] Soon after, debates emerged around how "the state" (it was singular in those days) should fit into analysis of politics and power. A number of scholars who many in this volume would call intellectual progenitors – including Skocpol, Tilly, and Evans – addressed the failures of neo-Marxist or, more broadly, class determinist accounts of politics with an approach that highlighted the state as potentially autonomous actor and institution, with varying structures and capacities, drawing on Weber, Tocqueville, and others. Specifically political logics derived from struggles over the means of coercion and administration, and competition in the world system of states. Against the grain of much previous social–historical analysis, scholars argued that politics was not fully determined by economic forces, either in the near term or in the "lonely hour of the last instance."[8] This critical intellectual move is captured in the phrase *Bringing the State Back In*, the title of the 1985 volume that still merits our attention – a move that can be seen in many ways as the epicenter of the scholarly movement Adams, Clemens, and Orloff called the "second wave" of historical social science.[9]

The intellectual movement to "bring the state back in" sparked controversy and debate, with some arguing the state had always been an important topic of scholarly analysis that did not need to be reintroduced.[10] The tendency of scholarship from the 1980s through the early 1990s to conceive of the state as an actor that concentrated and institutionalized political authority proved to be both compelling and contested. It was compelling because it threw off the presumed subordination of the state to dominant economic groups while drawing attention to the weighty influence of states in the lives of the ordinary people who paid taxes, served in the military, and were subject to laws and regulations. The political significance of the state was grounded in the assumption that states could be forces against capitalism, as, for example, when Esping-Andersen wrote about "politics against markets" in social democratic Scandinavia, and U.S. scholars considered the progressive legacies of the New Deal in curbing capitalism.[11] State-centered analysis drew attention to the differing capacities and structures of states, as well as the economic and social powers with which states had to contend.[12] And this approach forged links between too-often separate analyses of domestic and international politics, with the state as the central, sovereign actor that lies between the two.[13]

Yet initial conceptualizations of the state-as-actor were heavily influenced by a particular interpretation of Weber, emphasizing his analysis of the material underpinnings of state power rather than his focus on culture, and building upon only a few archetypal examples – Prussia, France, and Japan. The image of states thus underscored certain qualities – centralization, coherence, and autonomy – as intrinsic features of "strong" states.[14] Other states showed signs of being effective and powerful, but lacked such an administrative apparatus. The United States, for instance, long a paragon of statelessness in the academic literature and the national self-conception, clearly lacked the idealized state architecture emphasized by state theorists as central to the "strength" of states, yet mobilized collective power to conquer and settle a vast geographic terrain while dispossessing indigenous peoples, imposed a violent system of slavery, fought two world wars and a cold one, and projected power across the globe.[15] Turning to the global South, we see governing apparatuses that also differ from the bureaucratic ideal type, yet viewing these non-European states solely through the lens of how they fail to measure up to a Western standard assesses states according to preconceived ideas about what they *should* be rather than analysis of what they are.[16] And the categories of "strong" or "weak" that came out of the scholarly fixation on state capacity, understood as infrastructural power to "penetrate" and order civil society, tend to be too vague to tell us much about how states actually govern.

Another limitation of the initial literature was the small number of actors in these stories of political conflict – capital, the working class, and "the state" or, in somewhat less anthropomorphic lingo, state actors (political or policy entrepreneurs, bureaucrats, political leaders). But as scholars asserted the autonomy of the political, many more potential political actors – women and men as gendered actors; religious leaders; ethnic, racial, and national organizations; sexually categorized groups; colonial officials – entered our analytic frames as relevant for shaping state activities. Outcomes of interest also proliferated, including not only the state policies that preoccupied the earlier state-centered literature, but categories of the census and citizenship, how public/private divides were drawn, legal systems, and the political imaginary of state officials.[17] Yet the state remained quite central, as for example when feminist theorists of the state analogized from "politics against markets" to ask if states could roll back the frontiers of male dominance,[18] and scholars of race examined the role of states in securing white supremacy or beginning to unravel it.[19] This work contributed to a larger rethinking of the political as not merely that which takes place in formal politics, but as an ongoing set of struggles of everyday life, including in voluntary organizations, workplaces, homes, and schools. Here, we see interest in both open political struggles and quieter cultural processes of fixing the very boundaries of the state – defining the "public" and "the private," as many feminist analysts have described.[20]

Perhaps most damning for all conceptions of the state as actor was the charge of reification – that viewing the state as a single actor risks subsuming sprawling, complex concatenations of governing institutions under one presumptively unified bureaucratic apparatus. This obscures the multiple actors and processes at work within the state. In response, scholars have sought to unpack this tightly compacted concept, disaggregating the state into its many functions, organizations, and purposes while complicating the initially sharp boundaries drawn between public and private, state and society.

This disaggregating drive has produced much of the literature that inspired our collective project, starting from the many modalities of state action that a metaphor such as "the many hands of the state" implies. When various theories of the state (singular) predominated, analysts conceived of different functions – legitimation and accumulation, for example – as cohering in some way or betraying some inherent contradiction, but kept their eye, simultaneously, on both.[21] Bourdieu gave us a slightly more useful metaphor of the right and left hands of the state.[22] We have been struck by the metaphorical inadequacy of this concept – instead of right and left hands, we have many hands, functions, and forms of power.²³ Perhaps a better metaphorical representation of our concerns than the Leviathan, wielding scepter and sword, is Kali, the multi-limbed – and many-handed – Hindu goddess of time and death, which are, after all, enduring concerns of historicizing political analysis of states. Alas, her singular embodiment does not yet reflect our interest in boundaries and hybridity; ultimately, we may need to find some science-fictional character to replace Leviathan. But in the meantime, it is our hope that "many hands of the state" will be an inspiring metaphor for scholars seeking to understand states in all their profusion and multiplicity.

STUDYING STATES SINCE *BRINGING THE STATE BACK IN*

The "state-centered" versus "society-centered" debates that character-ized the era in which *Bringing the State Back In* was conceived and written fell, by the late 1990s, into intellectual exhaustion and diminish-ing returns, especially as Marxist influences waned and many in history and the social sciences took multifarious cultural, institutional, and transnational turns. Yet moving past the "state–society" debate has spurred theoretical and empirical innovation and a flourishing of research across a proliferation of sites, historical eras, and policy domains. Given this spreading out of state-focused scholarship and its evolution along transnational lines to encompass empires, colonies, and global systems, we think the time is ripe for people who have been involved in this dizzying array of analyses to enter into deeper intellectual exchange with each other.

Our volume explores four theoretical innovations that shape the grouping of chapters, even though the themes are overlapping and interrelated. First, we examine states as entities whose internal and external boundaries are often shifting and malleable, reflecting political contestation over the state's meaning, purpose, and resources; second, states are assessed as powerful forces for social stratification whose effects are nonetheless subject to negotiation and change; third, we evaluate states as organizations with claims to (legitimate) monopolies over both material and symbolic force, but whose control must be constructed and continually reaffirmed; and fourth, we conceptualize nation-states as one form of globally embedded rule that both has parallels with and often emerged out of empires. Our analysis of these shifts brings us to a series of theoretical observations that can guide further work on states and their indispensible contributions to political authority and social control.

Locating the State: The Problem of Boundaries

Critical to any analysis of the state is an understanding of what the state is and is not. Yet sketching the contours of the state is more complicated than it may seem. The embeddedness of states in international and global relationships is one source of complexity, overlapping sovereignties, and potential blurring of boundaries (as will be discussed in the section on empires that follows). Boundaries are variably clear or blurred in domestic political arenas, too, as states often rely heavily on private agents or difficult-to-classify public–private hybrids to make policies, administer state-funded programs, and deliver services.[24] State authority also operates through multiple levels of government, particularly in federal systems, and some have argued that rescaling processes are pervasive today, with power shifting downward to regional or municipal governments and/or upward toward international and supranational organizations.[25] And, as Risse has argued, many parts of the world are characterized by "limited statehood" – by states that lack full control over at least some part of their territory, having ceded that control to nongovernmental organizations, firms, subnational forms of government, indigenous leaders, warlords and criminal operations, and the like.[26]

Public–private hybridity and blurred boundaries between "state" and "society" are often significant features of states in contemporary and earlier eras, but we must avoid *conceptual* blurring – if all forms of power are viewed as equivalent, we will no longer draw any conceptual distinctions between the state and nonstate realms. In the words of Durkheim, "If the state is everywhere, it is nowhere."[27] Whether justified or not, states are often encrusted in layers of legitimacy and forms of power that help distinguish them from nonstate entities. The latter can be potent, and all the more so to the extent they are financed and supported by states, but the former remains, in most societies, the source from which much legitimate power radiates. If we entirely lose sight of these distinctions we risk losing the state as a theoretically or empirically meaningful category of analysis, and miss a significant element of states' symbolic power.

One way to locate the boundaries of the state – and to comprehend the complex goals and practices of state authorities and other political actors in erecting them or effacing them – is to examine the concrete ways in which states do the work of governing. It is only in examining the real-world practices of governance – the mix of public and private (nonprofit or proprietary) actors charged with implementing policies and the nature of their relationship, the responsibilities of national versus subnational layers of government in program delivery, the role of law in achieving various objectives, and the lived experience of state policies on the ground by those subject to them – that we gain insight into what the state is.[28] One example is the extensive literature on street-level bureaucracy – the sites at which individuals and public authority meet, and where varying degrees of discretion allow public officials and, increasingly, private organizations to implement policies in ways that often diverge considerably from formal policy goals and rules.[29] Focusing on boundaries also draws attention to the political struggles over where state power starts and ends – why some political actors might seek to "hide" the state's power, for example, while others might try to draw attention to it.[30]

We can also draw on insights from the cultural turns in sociology and history, and the constructivist one in political science, about how cultural schemas influence categories and classifications, including those that demarcate boundaries between state and nonstate realms. As Mitchell noted back in 1991, the state is not a thing, hovering above society; instead, its very contours reflect ideological and cultural work shaping how officials portray the lines between state and nonstate and how citizens perceive them. Viewing the state as a "sociocultural phenomenon" highlights that states are not solely constellations of material power, but embody ideas and beliefs about legitimacy, sovereignty, disinterestedness, and coherence.[31] Such an approach also compels us to scrutinize the narratives about the state that officials – and scholars – produce as a set of cultural or ideological products. In his Collège de France lectures on the state, Bourdieu warns against adopting the self-legitimating categories of the state that only deepen its mystifying character:

> The state ... is something that you cannot lay your hands on, or tackle in the way that people from the Marxist tradition do when they say "the state does this," "the state does that." I could cite you kilometers of texts with the word state as the subject of actions and proposals. That is a very dangerous fiction, which prevents us from properly understanding the state ... be careful, all sentences that have the state as subject are theological sentences – which does not mean that they are false inasmuch as the state is a theological entity, that is, an entity that exists by way of belief. [32]

In this view, states profoundly shape the normative order, influencing the very terminology we use to describe them and where we locate their boundaries.

Stratification and the Transformation of States

States can impinge powerfully on social relations. States and their emanations – policies, laws, institutions, and doctrines – define, classify, standardize, and measure the world around them in ways that enable officials to better master and remake it.[33] In striving for greater legibility of the populations and territories that state authorities seek to control, these officials deploy practices and schemas that shape and reshape existing lines of social difference or create new ones, stratifying people along the lines of race, class, ethnicity, religion, gender, nationality, age, and sexual orientation, to name only the most prominent. We see these phenomena in empires, where the "rule of colonial difference" divided rulers from the ruled – their colonial and racialized subjects.[34] The legacies of this rule are found in the racializing institutions of the descendants of metropolitan and settler colonial states of the Global North, including the United States. The power of states to authoritatively name, define, and rank order people raises the stakes of political struggle: capturing some of the varied organs of the state is one important avenue for groups to name themselves, define the content of their identity, and craft policies that promote their interests.[35] States can forcefully remake social relations through their power to surveil and incarcerate people, to draft people to fight in wars, and to relocate or even exterminate populations.[36]

The impulse to characterize states by these kinds of effects has contributed to the large number of "modifier + state" terms that we noted at the beginning of this chapter. Affixing a label to states – the patriarchal state, the straight state, the racial state – is an important way to signal how public actions order political and social relationships. Yet we should be careful of overly aggregated analyses: does the term "patriarchal state," for example, encompass all governing entities, including national and subnational forms of government, all agencies, courts, and the legislative branch? The answer may be yes, but precisely how states stratify – through which actors, institutions, and processes – needs to be fully spelled out.

These totalizing labels also have rather static connotations: if the entire state is patriarchal, how could it ever not be? In practice, many analysts of state-shaped stratification are also investigators of state change, precisely because the hierarchies generated and sustained by state policies often spur social or political movements in response. As Scott has shown, the power of the states to transform society is fearsome, indeed, but people have also displayed considerable ingenuity in wriggling out from under this power or mounting challenges to it, either directly or more subversively.[37] We should therefore think about stratification not as an endpoint but as a process subject to contestation and reform, as in the various movements for civil rights and liberation. Nonetheless, we should also avoid teleologies of inevitable progress, for mobilizations in favor of hierarchy and privilege may bolster the maintenance or even intensification of state stratification, as in the turning back of Reconstruction and reimposition of Jim Crow in the U.S. South.

One way to tackle these complex processes of stratification and change is to draw upon the flourishing institutionalist literature. Institutionalism both paralleled and developed out of the work of state-centered scholars and the various forms of institutionalism have helped counter the overly aggregated portrayals of states that initially marked the literature.[38] Moreover, increasing attention within the institutionalist literature to processes of change dovetails with a larger interest of many scholars in state transformation.[39] Institutionalists have sought to characterize and theorize forms of change, both exogenous and endogenous, in response to criticisms that their own accounts were unduly static. Scholars of states have been similarly interested in processes of state transformation, uncovering the ways in which actors and institutions within states can become agents of reform, remaking lines of division and inequality.[40] Here, research on states as differently configured sets of access points that reformers can enter has been especially fruitful, directing our attention to processes transforming states' operation.[41]

In disaggregating states into their component institutions, however, we do not want to lose sight of that which makes the state distinctive.[42] State institutions are not just like other institutions and our theories of institutional origin, stability, and change must help us to understand states' unique characteristics; the distillation and concentration of power in states, while taking varying forms in different places and time periods, generates a characteristic and often potent organizational form, for reasons both cultural and material.[43] This is why so many theorists have grappled with the state analytically and sought to describe that which separates it from other forms of power: Bourdieu referred to the state as a holder of metacapital, for instance, while Durkheim viewed the state as a form of political consciousness, but "one that is limited but higher, clearer and with a more vivid sense of itself" than political society as a whole.[44] For Weber, it is how states compel obedience that sets them apart from other forms of power. We then come back to the question of how states induce, or force, people to obey.

Developing the Sinews of Power

If states are the distinctively powerful governing structures of our time – the very embodiment of modernity that emerged out of and reinforced capitalism, geopolitical competition, imperial expansion, racial hierarchies, and masculine domination – why and how did this come about? And how are some states able to preserve this power – to maintain order, for example, or to respond to governing challenges – while others are not? These questions have animated a large and ever-growing literature on statebuilding that has helped identify the factors shaping the historical development of states around the globe.[45] One contribution of this work has been to shift our understanding of states away from the Lockean, social contract view of states toward one that highlights the violent, messy, and historically contingent processes by which states are made or unmade.[46] The study of states as works in progress also helps analysts avoid reifying them, eschewing a sharp demarcation of state–society boundaries, for instance, and instead examining the processes by which such boundaries get defined. And a focus on the emergence, development, or decline of specific institutional capacities allows us to better understand the successes and failures of particular state projects, thereby avoiding a common functionalist presumption that the states' projects – or those of political authorities or economically dominant classes – are always successful. Much work has homed in on the specific instruments of statebuilding – taxation, for example – or the development of bureaucratic capacity and autonomy in subparts of the state apparatus.[47]

With intellectual cross-fertilization from the cultural turn, work on statebuilding has transcended the earlier, almost exclusive emphasis on material aspects of statebuilding – a focus on physical force; administrative and extractive powers; and control over borders, resources, and people – capital and coercion, in varying degrees, as Tilly had it.[48] States seek a monopoly not only over the use of physical force, but also over the use of symbolic force.[49] A state's power lies not only in its ability to prevent exit and coerce compliance, but also in its ability to induce agreement – to manufacture categories, standards, and principles of social, economic, and political organization that penetrate deep into individual consciousness.[50] Making sense of state authority thus requires us to examine not just material force but also state structures, ideas, and belief systems that shape how individuals or social groups view themselves and their relationship to states.[51]

Another avenue for thinking about how state power is constructed and maintained is through linking statebuilding and representative politics. An ambiguity of the second-wave historical sociological and political science literature was whether to include legislative branches, ruling parties, and democratically elected executives as part of the state. Initially, many scholars seemed to say no, as the states judged as having greater capabilities were those whose civil servants are relatively insulated from rough-and-tumble democratic politics.[52] Moreover, the very problem of statebuilding in the United States was interpreted by scholars as that of forging bureaucratic autonomy in a porous and fragmented polity subject to the whims of electoral politics.[53] These studies brought important insights about state–society relationships but also contributed to conceptual confusion over state "strength" and "autonomy" and the relationship of states to electoral politics. In part, the confusion stems from a misreading of the European statebuilding experience: In focusing on political centralization and bureaucratic coherence as features of an effective state, some scholars exaggerated these qualities (as in the case of France) and neglected crucial counter-examples, such as Britain, in which the power of the fiscal–military state was furthered, not hampered, by representative institutions that mediated social and political conflict.[54]

The development of governing authority in the United States affords further insights into the linkages between civil society, representative institutions, state power, and statebuilding.[55] An important vein of historical research on the United States has shifted attention from the success or failure of grand statebuilding projects from the center to how actors in the periphery fashioned discrete, disjointed, and highly variable administrative and legal approaches to governing a vast, decentralized nation. Democratic politics – the decentralization and fragmentation of political power and concomitant flourishing of civil society as a preexisting site of governance – is the backdrop here, shaping the many hybrid forms of public–private action and the heavy reliance upon law.[56] As Novak describes it, U.S. governing arrangements that emerged in the nineteenth century represented

... a distinctly new kind of coercive power emerging within popular sovereignties, democratic societies, and modern economies – a power more diffuse, less visible, less clearly identified with a single individual (i.e., the king) or institution (i.e., the church), sometimes private as well as public, woven into the everyday substructure of modern social and economic organization.[57]

But if democracy augmented governing authority in the United States, it did so in complex relation with antidemocratic, coercive aspects of rule, as in the subnational authoritarianisms that, in the slaveholding and later Jim Crow states, were part of a larger political bargain for securing territorial control.[58] Scholars of statebuilding in the United States and in other parts of the world direct us to investigate how political authority is concretely constructed and legitimated through governing practices, routines, and symbols as well as through the raw exercise of power. In so doing we can start to understand not only how states construct their material power but also how they produce, in the words of Abrams, "a managed construction of belief about the state ... [that binds] subjects into their own subjection."[59]

States and Empires: The Transnational/Global Turn

Finally, it is important to situate states in international and global dynamics. Initial work in the state-centered vein emphasized the Janus-faced nature of states vis-à-vis the international arena and domestic sphere;[60] one rationalist version of this understood state actors as playing two-level games, at home and abroad.[61] International relations scholars and others were encouraged to peer inside the black box of the state, rather than to conceptualize states as persons.[62] Similarly, those studying domestic political processes turned to the international, supranational, and global spheres, and the forces of diffusion, interdependence, reaction, and isomorphism.[63] And states necessarily had to be situated within larger divisions of power, including imperial relationships and global divisions of labor. Globalization and the growing international and supranational organizational architecture have only intensified the need to cast our visions both below and beyond the nation-state.[64]

In so doing, one needs to strike a balance between highlighting the global forces that have altered or undermined states to varying degrees and emphasizing the resilience of states as dominant actors in the global sphere. We can see this in the economic realm, where the early rush to proclaim the death of the state was subsequently turned back.[65] Claims of neoliberal convergence featured in sweeping and far-too-generic analyses of the revival of capitalist power in the years since 1980, but these accounts have been powerfully challenged by scholars investigating the complicated nexus between states and economies.[66] Market-oriented reforms in many parts of the world have not necessarily diminished the overall role of the state in the economy but often altered modes of state intervention, producing *expansions* of the public sector in some places to buffer societies against economic liberalization.[67] And while the rise in international regulatory bodies initially created new avenues through which firms could impose their interests, states have pushed to regain at least some control over these entities, generating hybrid forms of governance.[68] Even if the state has not been eclipsed, however, it is not tenable to view states as isolated and fully independent units.

"Returning to empire" is one prominent strand of work taking up the challenges presented by globalization and the complexity of relations between the "West and the rest" over the centuries of their contact, conflict, and exchanges.[69] This research has developed the initial second-wave insights that states were embedded in global contexts – the world system of states in the Hintzean–Weberian approach or the world system in Wallerstein's influential but economically determinist version – while also examining politics from the point of view of the oppressed. Extensive work on revolutions and national liberation struggles against colonial and imperial powers and on the resistance of people of color against white racial supremacy in both the Global North and the Global South revealed relations of domination between global-North states – formerly colonial and imperial powers – and states of the global South that were formerly colonies and dependencies.[70] Currently, analysts are debating how to conceptualize different forms of imperial domination. Steinmetz, for example, suggests a distinction between territorial (colonial) and nonterritorial (imperial) forms of empire, with significant repercussions for the shape of individual metropolitan and peripheral states.[71] Colonialism's profound, complicated, and enduring legacies on states around the globe, and the extent of inequalities of power and resources between global North and global South, underline how strongly international and global forces have impinged upon states.[72]

We also see deeper conceptual linkages between states and empires, such that the study of one can and should enrich the other. Definitions of empire – "a centralized, hierarchical system of rule acquired and maintained by coercion through which a core territory dominates peripheral territories,"[73] for instance, or "relationships of political control imposed by some political societies over the effective sovereignty of other political societies"[74] – bear more than a passing resemblance to many definitions of states. Statebuilding often required a projection of power over hostile hinterlands inhabited by supposedly backward or even barbarian people judged to be in need of civilization.[75] Weber noted that there were continental (e.g., statebuilding) versions of imperialism, found in Russia and America, and "overseas" versions, such as those practiced by England and other European states,[76] while Adams and Pincus emphasize that

"European state formation – in all cases – was a thoroughly imperial project in the early modern period."[77] Power, domination, and racialization featured in studies of empires surely carries over to the study of states (and vice versa).[78]

SUMMARY: THEORIZING STATES

This analysis of the rich and proliferating literature on states and empires and its signal theoretical innovations brings us to several core analytic conclusions that we hope will stimulate conversations across various scholarly divides and promote new lines of research.

First, we reaffirm the state as a foundational concept in the social sciences, one that cannot be replaced with "governmentality" or "governance" or "institution," because states are more than mere institutions and signify forms of power that differ from those found in other arenas. The distillation and concentration of power in states, while taking varying forms in different places and time periods, generates a distinctive and often potent organizational form. States are more than bundles of governing institutions, because of their claim to embody the will of a collectivity, whether this occurs through democratic channels or not; the legitimacy in which officials try to encase their actions; and their recognition in the international arena.

Second, states concentrate and deploy both material *and* symbolic powers. Weber was right to emphasize states' control of the means of coercion in specified geographic territories, but he also highlighted the centrality of legitimacy to any form of rule; neither coercion nor legitimacy is a given – they both must be accomplished. State legitimacy requires more than mere force; states also operate through the pull they have on the public consciousness. The subjective element of state power is of vital importance, as states are not mere arenas in which utility-maximizing individuals satisfy their goals. At the very least, states help define those goals, and some would see states operating at a deeper level in constituting subjects and shaping the forms of knowledge out of which public and private action develop.

Third, states work through varied modes of governance. States often delegate to nonstate and subnational actors; they subsidize private agents to do their work; and they may be subject to strong pressures from external agents, including international organizations, nongovernmental actors, and foreign governments. Although it is important to analyze the blurred lines that may result from this complexity, we must avoid a concomitant conceptual blurring such that all forms of power are viewed as equivalent. State power is legitimized in distinctive ways and states deploy forms of power that are different from those used by nonstate entities. Rather than allow the distinctions between state and nonstate institutions to be dissolved into conceptual murk, we are better off charting the linkages and flow of resources and power between these spheres or investigating where boundaries blur, why that might be the case, and what implications this has for power, authority, and legitimacy.

Fourth, our metaphor of the many hands of the state highlights the complexity and multiplicity of actors and institutions within the state, pushing us to go beyond reifying simplifications that would view the state as a uniform, cohesive entity. Doing so draws attention to contradictory or incoherent forms of state action and also helps us think about processes of state transformation, which most often occur unevenly across institutions. Moreover, it encourages a rethinking of the relationship between states and representative institutions (or the lack thereof), a specific and critical element of the broader range of relationships of states to social actors. Once we give up on simplifying notions of states as unified agents, what next? Our challenge is to disaggregate and reaggregate, dissect and reassemble, always taking into consideration the multiplicity of state forms and functions as we try to understand what in some instances binds those parts together and, in others, subjects them to varied centrifugal forces.[79]

Finally, we should situate states vis-à-vis the international and transnational arenas without assuming that these forces always and everywhere undermine the state. There are many challenges to states posed by the forces of internationally mobile capital, transnational political and social movements, international and supranational organizations, or simply states with more power than others. Yet formal legal sovereignty remains a defining feature of what it is to be a state.[80] States are not being eclipsed, but they are enmeshed in forces operating both below and beyond state boundaries. The study of empires can help us think about how states have been and continue to be situated in global contexts, including how international relations of power – between what we now call global North and global South, or between the metropole and colonies in earlier times – enduringly shape states across the globe.

THE CHAPTERS IN THIS BOOK

For this volume, we sought out work that embodies some of the dominant trends in contemporary research while pushing scholarship in new and exciting directions. Our book covers the four major areas of scholarly interest and activity that are featured as the themes of this introduction.

Part I investigates the ways in which state boundaries are defined, understood, shifted, or maintained. Three of the chapters are reflective of the flourishing literature on the U.S. state that seeks to map its contours, while a fourth chapter situates these boundary questions in the global arena, where states are subject to pressures from international organizations, private entities, and other states. The chapters push forward literatures on these topics by highlighting how contestation over both material and symbolic resources shapes where boundaries are drawn. The dividing line between state and nonstate is not solely a matter of law or physical demarcations, but reflects understandings of what "public" signifies or what the "state" means – designations that are at issue in many political struggles, and arguably are constitutive of politics itself.

We see these struggles in the early twentieth-century United States, when expanding public responsibility for social welfare spurred debates over the relationship between government agencies and charitable organizations. As Clemens' Chapter 1 shows, these debates reveal a scramble for power and resources, but also competing visions about what it means to lodge responsibility in the public or private sector. Reconciling equal but standardized treatment (from the state) with individualized but variable care (from charitable organizations) proved difficult, and rather than definitively resolve this tension, the state–society boundary was subject to continuous political maneuvering. In Chapter 2, Mayrl and Quinn examine similar maneuvering and contestation in the United States today in debates over the significance of the state in supporting and shaping market forces. They argue that these disputes, as well as habituation processes, influence whether people see the state and its many hands by drawing attention to, or obfuscating, its responsibilities and reach. Thus, against the widespread claim that the U.S. state is "hidden" or "submerged," owing to its reliance on tax breaks, regulations, and the delegation of responsibilities to private agents, they forward a more encompassing theory of states, cognition, and classification, contending that the U.S. state is not hidden but is frequently misrecognized.

Lara-Millán's Chapter 3 looks at contestation over institutional boundaries within states, examining how governing agencies with joint responsibilities for disempowered populations – in this case, inmates in Los Angeles county jails – jostle to seize or cede control over people. Faced with overcrowding and budget austerity, county officials battled with each other to shift some of the incarcerated population out of jails and into hospitals, an example of "people exchange." Lara-Millán thus offers us a disaggregated account of the state's power to move and control human populations, one that peers behind the state façade to examine the motivations and behaviors of the agents operating within. Finally, in Chapter 4, Fourcade examines the many hands *on* the state from outside national boundaries through the example of private credit rating agencies that scrutinize and grade countries' credit worthiness. The stakes around these evaluations are tremendous: extensions or denials of credit (and the terms attached to it) affect the well-being of human societies and the profits of investors, but these evaluations also shape the perceived boundary between states and the nations they symbolically represent. Thus, financial market actors often assess not only state capacities but also characteristics of entire societies and economies, placing nations into distinct categories of moral worth.

Part II of the volume offers fresh perspectives on the stratifying effects of states and how these are transformed over time. Our chapters in this section push the large literature on state stratification beyond monolithic understandings of these processes and examine how different state agents and their various "products" – including legal decisions, redistributive policies, regulations, and the rhetoric accompanying these governing acts – create, reproduce, and reshape lines of difference and inequality. In so doing, the authors highlight the uneven and often contradictory nature of stratifying and classifying schemas, underlining how these very schemas can provoke social and political resistance that at times achieve transformations of state institutions, while also identifying some of the institutional sources of resistance to change.

In Chapter 5, Orloff investigates the transformation of state policies in Sweden and the United States from supporting households of breadwinning men and caregiving women to encouraging, or compelling, women's paid work, developing a new understanding of institutional change in gendered labor policies (a "many-handed" concept) as encompassing both the destruction of old policies and the construction of new ones. She situates this analysis of policy transformation vis-à-vis changes in feminist state theories, which have shifted from understandings of states as unitary in logic – patriarchal – to conceptualizing them as incorporating multiple institutional logics, including a potentially gender-egalitarian one. Htun and Weldon in Chapter 6 investigate some of the state's "hands" on gender relations through a typology that captures the multidimensional nature of state action vis-à-vis gender equality, illustrating the uneven international spread of policies to combat violence against women and to reform women's status in family law. Exploring why the adoption of transformative policies is so variable across time and space, they find that both hinge on the power of social forces vis-à-vis states. In the case of family law, the historically entrenched power of religious actors often stymies possibilities for reform, while it is the mobilization of autonomous feminist movements that is vital for action on violence against women.

The problem of empowerment looms large in analyses of states and racial transformation; those with power have few incentives to cede it, creating barriers to challengers of racial hierarchy and the state policies that uphold it. This problem motivates King and Lieberman's assessment in Chapter 7 of how the U.S. state became a force for civil rights advancement, with some institutions changing from oppressor to protector in the span of a generation, even as others continued to promote segregation and inequality. Their analysis develops a disaggregated conceptualization of the state by identifying variation in the American state's stratifying effects with respect to race, as well as shifts in the capacities of activists and reformers versus those who would uphold hierarchy. Paschel's Chapter 8 on the radical shift in Brazil from colorblind to race-conscious policies offers a similarly disaggregated view of the state and its relationship with activists seeking to reform its policies. She locates an array of political opportunity structures not only at the domestic level but also in the international forums in which activists, experts, and diplomats comparatively assessed Brazil's racial arrangements and made moral and political claims. Although the resulting policy shifts have been important and meaningful, Paschel identifies other state policies and practices that contribute to maintaining obdurate racial inequalities.

Part III of the volume investigates questions that are at the heart of the expansive literature on statebuilding: how states construct and preserve their capacities to maintain order and govern. Yet, while much of the literature on statebuilding focuses on the material processes of policing borders and taxing populations, the authors here also examine the sources of symbolic power. As Davenport notes in Chapter 10, states cannot sustainably rely on repression alone, but usually govern through some amount of popular agreement, or at least acquiescence. How order is produced, and legitimacy maintained, is thus central to the existence and persistence of states.

One source of power derives from liberal political institutions. In Chapter 9, Novak, Sawyer, and Sparrow challenge prevailing understandings of how state power operates in the United States – through formal law, laissez-fare government, or the "cold monster" of the bureaucratic state. Instead, they trace an alternative genealogy of American political power, showing how representative institutions have enabled political authorities in the United States to harness and organize social energies by joining some amount of public consent to the use of force. That sense of legitimacy proves particularly important in enabling what Davenport calls, in Chapter 10, the "joint production of coercion." Davenport finds that, given the costliness of repression, those in power often engage in a public performance of order and control, legitimating their own existence while downplaying or undermining challengers to the status quo. Political authorities not only make determinations about how much force to use, given the challengers they face, but also try to influence public perceptions of state power through how their actions are depicted in media accounts and other sources.

Mehrotra's contribution to this volume, Chapter 11, also examines representations of state power – in this case, in the late nineteenth and early twentieth century debates in the United States over the federal government's adoption of a progressive income tax. He argues that these debates helped construct political agreement over a new system of tax-ation, enabling state actors to reach deep into the wallets of the citizenry. However, the aim here was not only to generate needed public resources, but also to forge a new set of ties, both affective and material, between the state and the public. Finally, Kestnbaum's Chapter 12, on what he calls "the revolution in war in the late eighteenth century," examines the move by state officials in Europe and the United States to mobilize citizens behind war-making projects through emotional appeals. As in Fourcade's analysis of the conflation of states with the societies they govern during the recent financial crisis, Kestnbaum charts the growing identification of the population with state power as war became the "business of the people." This revolution spurred changes in the practice of war that reverberate to the present day, including the rise of partisans who volun-tarily fight on the state's behalf and the treatment of civilians as "fair game" for military targeting.

Part IV of the volume situates the study of states in the international arena through a focus on empires. The study of imperialism was curiously absent from the state-centered literature that developed in the 1980s, but since then scholars have developed an exciting line of work on empires past and present, building on earlier research on world systems, depend-ent development, and the dually situated character of state elites. Our authors reveal multiple linkages – theoretical and empirical – between states and empires. The legacies of imperialism and colonial states on contemporary states in both the Global North and Global South are significant and lasting, for example in the instantiation of (colonial) rules of difference in the racializing institutions of modern states. Moreover, bringing an imperial theoretical framing to political history recasts our understanding of the emergence of modern nation-states as encompassing far more than consolidating control across a contiguous space.

Adams and Pincus in Chapter 13 contend that the original transition to modernity in Europe was propelled by and indeed inextricable from colonialism and empire, arguing that "the European empires of the early modern era were part and parcel of state formation projects . . . and vice versa. The many hands of the state were vested in empire." Moreover, intellectual observers, political elites, and subject peoples did not necessarily distinguish between empires and states, but saw both as related forms of political organization heralding a break with what had come before. In Chapter 14, Hussin investigates the actual operation of colonial states by examining how a set of intermediaries – Indian Muslim judges in the British empire – rendered legible the societies and polities that colonial officials were seeking to rule while shaping a specific understanding of Islamic law and religion in Indian institutions. The translative work performed by these intermediaries was critical to the operations of British rule on the ground and has had lasting effects on the nature of the postcolonial successor states to the Raj. Finally, in Chapter 15, Steinmetz connects theorizing about states and empires through revisions to Bourdieu's influential theory of bureaucratic or state fields. Steinmetz applies an amended version of field theory to the imperial sphere, cracking open the colonial state to look within it and view the class struggles among officials that at times had deadly consequences for those living under their rule.

The chapters collected here offer the diverse reflections of theoretically engaged scholars on one of the most contested and indispensable concepts in the social sciences. Taken together, these chapters range impressively over the scholarly terrain of states and empires. Each presents an original analysis of a critical arena while creating new analytic tools for future research. We expect that the next thirty years of research on states and empires will be as rich and creative as the last, and hope that this volume contributes to intellectual work that is, we think, crucial for the necessary political work of harnessing states to the needs and demands of the people of the world.

Notes

1 For a discussion and critique of these efforts, see Bo Rothstein, *The Quality of Government: Corruption, Social Trust, and Inequality in International Perspective* (Chicago: University of Chicago Press, 2011).

2 Richard R. John, "Rethinking the Early American State," *Polity* 40, no. 3 (July 2008): 332–39; Gary Gerstle, "The Resilient Power of the States across the Long Nineteenth Century: An Inquiry into a Pattern of American Governance," in *The Unsustainable American State*, ed. Lawrence Jacobs and Desmond King (New York: Oxford University Press, 2009), 61–87; Desmond King and Robert C. Lieberman, "Ironies of State Building: A Comparative Perspective on the American State," *World Politics* 61, no. 3 (July 2009): 547–88; William J. Novak, Stephen W. Sawyer, and James T. Sparrow, "Toward a History of the Democratic State," *The Tocqueville Review* 33, no. 2 (2012): 7–18.

3 See the discussion of this in Steve Sawyer, "Foucault and the State," *The Tocqueville Review* 36, no. 1 (2015): 135–64; Nikolas Rose and Peter Miller, "Political Power beyond the State: Problematics of Government," *British Journal of Sociology* 43, no. 2 (June 1992): 174; Timothy Mitchell, "The Limits of the State: Beyond Statist Approaches and Their Critics," *American Political Science Review* 85, no. 1 (1991): 77–96.

4 Peter B. Evans, Dietrich Rueschemeyer, and Theda Skocpol, eds., *Bringing the State Back In* (Cambridge: Cambridge University Press, 1985).

5 "Politics as a Vocation," in *From Max Weber: Essays in Sociology*, ed. Hans H. Gerth and C. Wright Mills (Oxford: Oxford University Press [1946] 1958), 78. Emphasis in original.

6 Mitchell, "Limits of the State"; George Steinmetz, "Introduction: Culture and the State," in *State/Culture: State-Formation after the Cultural Turn*, ed. George Steinmetz (Ithaca: Cornell University Press, 1999), 8.

7 Ann Shola Orloff, "Remaking Power and Politics," *Social Science History* 36, no. 1 (2012): 1–21.

8 Louis Althusser, *For Marx* (London, New York: Verso 2005), 113.

9 Julia Adams, Elisabeth S. Clemens, and Ann Shola Orloff, "Introduction: Social Theory, Modernity, and the Three Waves of Historical Sociology," in *Remaking Modernity: Politics, History, and Sociology*, ed. Julia Adams, Elisabeth S. Clemens, and Ann Shola Orloff (Durham: Duke University Press, 2005), 1–72.

10 See Gabriel A. Almond, "The Return to the State," *American Political Science Review* 82, no. 3 (1988): 853–874, and the responses to him in that issue.

11 Gøsta Esping-Andersen, *Politics Against Markets* (Princeton: Princeton University Press, 1985); Margaret Weir, Ann Shola Orloff, and Theda Skocpol, eds., *The Politics of Social Policy in the United States* (Princeton: Princeton University Press, 1988).

12 Alfred Stepan, *The State and Society: Peru in Comparative Perspective* (Princeton: Princeton University Press, 1978); Ira Katznelson, *City Trenches: Urban Politics and the Patterning of Class in the United States* (Chicago: University of Chicago Press, 1981); Martin Shefter, "Party and Patronage:

Germany, England, and Italy," *Politics & Society* 7, no. 4 (1977): 403–51; Skocpol, "Bringing the State Back In: Strategies of Analysis in Current Research," in *Bringing the State Back In*, 3–37; Aristide R. Zolberg, "Matters of State: Theorizing Immigration Policy," *Handbook of International Migration* (New York: Russell Sage, 1999), 71–93.

13 J.P. Nettl, "The State as a Conceptual Variable," *World Politics* 20, no. 4 (July 1968): 559–92; Peter Katzenstein, ed., *Between Power and Plenty: Foreign Economic Policies of Advanced Industrialized States* (Madison: University of Wisconsin Press, 1978); Theda Skocpol, *States and Social Revolutions: A Comparative Analysis of France, Russia and China* (Cambridge: Cambridge University Press, 1979).

14 Nettl, "State as a Conceptual Variable."

15 Stephen Skowronek, *Building a New American State: The Expansion of National Administrative Capacities 1877–1920* (Cambridge: Cambridge University Press, 1982), 19; Novak, "Myth of the 'Weak' American State"; Aaron L. Friedberg, "American Antistatism and the Founding of the Cold War State," in *Shaped by War and Trade: International Influences on American Political Development*, ed. Ira Katznelson and Martin Shefter (Princeton: Princeton University Press 2002), 239–66; King and Lieberman, "Ironies of State Building."

16 Karen Barkey and Sunita Parikh, "Comparative Perspectives on the State," *Annual Review of Sociology* 17 (1991): 523–49; Thomas Risse, "Governance in Areas of Limited Statehood: Introduction and Overview," in *Governance Without a State? Policies and Politics in Areas of Limited Statehood*, ed. Thomas Risse (New York: Columbia University Press, 2011), 1–38.

17 George Steinmetz, *Regulating the Social: The Welfare State and Local Politics in Imperial Germany* (Princeton: Princeton University Press, 1993).

18 Ann Shola Orloff, "Gender and the Social Rights of Citizenship: The Comparative Analysis of Gender Relations and Welfare States," *American Sociological Review* 58, no. 3 (June 1993): 303–28; R.W. Connell, *Gender and Power: Society, the Person, and Sexual Politics* (Stanford: Stanford University Press 1987).

19 Anthony W. Marx, *Making Race and Nation: A Comparison of South Africa, the United States, and Brazil* (New York: Cambridge University Press, 1998).

20 Carole Pateman, *The Disorder of Women: Democracy, Feminism, and Political Theory* (Stanford: Stanford University Press, 1990); Elisabeth S. Clemens, "Organizational Repertoires and Institutional Change: Women's Groups and the Transformation of US Politics, 1890–1920," *American Journal of Sociology* 98, no. 4 (1993): 755–98.

21 See, e.g., James O'Connor, *The Fiscal Crisis of the State* (New York: St. Martin's Press, 1973).

22 "Un entretien avec Pierre Bourdieu: 'Il n'y a pas de démocratie effective sans vrai contre-pouvoir critique,'" *Le Monde*, January 14, 1992.

23 Michael Mann, "The Autonomous Power of the State: Its Origins, Mechanisms and Results," *European Journal of Sociology* 25, no. 2 (1984): 185–213; Michael Zürn and Stephan Leibfried, "A New Perspective on the State: Reconfiguring the National Constellation," in *Transformations of the State?*, ed.

Stephan Leibfried and Michael Zürn (Cambridge: Cambridge University Press, 2005), 1–36.

24 Kimberly J. Morgan and Andrea Louise Campbell, *The Delegated Welfare State: Medicare, Markets and the Governance of Social Policy* (New York: Oxford University Press, 2011); Melani Cammett and Lauren M. MacLean, eds., *The Politics of Non-State Social Welfare* (Ithaca: Cornell University Press, 2014); Brian Balogh, *The Associational State: American Governance in the Twentieth Century* (Philadelphia: University of Pennsylvania Press, 2015).

25 Liesbet Hooghe and Gary Marks, *Multi-Level Governance and European Integration* (Boulder: Rowman & Littlefield, 2001); Patrick Le Galès, *European Cities: Social Conflicts and Governance* (Oxford: Oxford University Press 2002); Roger Keil and Rianne Mahon, eds., *Leviathan Undone? Towards a Political Economy of Scale* (Vancouver and Toronto: UBC Press, 2009); Le Galès, "States in Europe: Uncaging Societies and the Limits to the Infrastructural Power," *Socio-Economic Review* 12, no. 1 (2013): 131–52; Daniel Ziblatt, *Structuring the State: The Formation of Italy and Germany and the Puzzle of Federalism* (Princeton: Princeton University Press, 2006).

26 Risse, "Governance in Areas of Limited Statehood"; see also William Reno, *Warlord Politics and African States* (Boulder: Lynne Rienner, 1998); and Henry E. Hale, *Patronal Politics: Eurasian Regime Dynamics in Comparative Perspective* (New York: Cambridge University Press, 2014).

27 Quoted in Anthony S. Giddens, "Introduction," in *Durkheim on Politics and the State*, ed. Anthony S. Giddens, trans. W.D. Halls (Cambridge: Polity Press, 1986), 6.

28 Elisabeth S. Clemens, "Lineages of the Rube Goldberg State: Building and Blurring Public Programs, 1900–1940," in *Rethinking Political Institutions: The Art of the State*, ed. Ian Shapiro, Stephen Skowronek, and Daniel Galvin (New York: New York University Press, 2006), 187–215; Morgan and Campbell, *Delegated Welfare State*; Akhil Gupta, "Blurred Boundaries: The Discourse of Corruption, the Culture of Politics, and the Imagined State," *American Ethnologist* 22, no. 2 (1995): 375–402.

29 Michael Lipsky, *Street-Level Bureaucracy: Dilemmas of the Individual in Public Services* (New York: Russell Sage Foundation, 1980); Evelyn Z. Brodkin and Gregory Marston, eds., *Work and the Welfare State: Street-Level Organizations and Workfare Politics* (Washington, DC: Georgetown University Press, 2013); Didier Fassin et al., *At the Heart of the State: The Moral World of Institutions* (London: Pluto Press 2015); Armando Lara-Millán, "Public Emergency Room Overcrowding in the Era of Mass Imprisonment," *American Sociological Review* 79, no. 5 (2014): 866–87; Lynne Haney, *Offending Women* (Berkeley: University of California Press, 2010); Vincent Dubois, *La vie au guichet: Relation administrative et traitement de la misère* (Paris: Economica 1999); Alexis Spire, *Accueillir ou reconduire: Enquête sur les guichets de l'immigration* (Paris: Raisons d'agir, 2008).

30 Christopher Howard, *The Hidden Welfare State: Tax Expenditures and Social Policy in the United States* (Princeton: Princeton University Press, 1997); Suzanne Mettler, *The Submerged State: How Invisible Government Policies*

Undermine American Democracy (Chicago: University of Chicago Press, 2011); Damon Mayrl and Sarah Quinn, "Defining the State from Within: Boundaries, Schemas, and Associational Policymaking," *Sociological Theory* 34, no. 1(March 2016).

31 Nettl, "State as a Conceptual Variable," 565; Stephen D. Krasner, "Approaches to the State: Alternative Conceptions and Historical Dynamics," *Comparative Politics* 16, no. 2 (January 1984): 232–33; Bob Jessop, "Bringing the State Back in (Yet Again): Reviews, Revisions, Rejections, and Redirections," *International Review of Sociology* 11, no. 2 (2001): 149–73; Steinmetz, *State/Culture*; Mark Bevir and Roderick Arthur William Rhodes, *The State as Cultural Practice* (Oxford: Oxford University Press, 2010).

32 Pierre Bourdieu, *On the State: Lectures at the Collège de France, 1989–1992*, eds. Patrick Champagne, Remi Lenoir, Franck Poupeau, and Marie-Christine Rivière (New York: Polity, 2014), 10.

33 James C. Scott, *Seeing Like a State: How Certain Schemes to Improve the Human Condition Have Failed* (New Haven: Yale University Press, 1998); Mae M. Ngai, *Impossible Subjects: Illegal Aliens and the Making of Modern America* (Princeton: Princeton University Press, 2004); Mara Loveman, *National Colors: Racial Classification and the State in Latin America* (New York: Oxford University Press, 2014); John Torpey, "Coming and Going: On the State Monopolization of the Legitimate 'Means of Movement,'" *Sociological Theory* 16, no. 3 (November 1998): 239–59.

34 Partha Chatterjee, *The Nation and Its Fragments* (Princeton: Princeton University Press, 1993); Nicholas Wilson, "From Reflection to Refraction: State Administration in British India, ca. 1770–1855," *American Journal of Sociology* 116, no. 5 (2011): 1437–77; George Steinmetz, *The Devil's Handwriting: Precoloniality and the German Colonial State in Qingdao, Samoa, and Southwest Africa* (Chicago: University of Chicago Press, 2007).

35 Jane Jenson, "Mapping, Naming and Remembering: Globalization at the End of the Twentieth Century," *Review of International Political Economy* 2 (1995): 96–116.

36 Loïc Wacquant, *Punishing the Poor: The Neoliberal Government of Social Insecurity* (Durham: Duke University Press, 2009); Amy Lerman and Vesla Weaver, "Political Consequences of the Carceral State," *American Political Science Review* 104, no. 4 (November 2010): 817–33; Dorit Geva, *Conscription, Family, and the Modern State: A Comparative Study of France and the United States* (New York: Cambridge University Press, 2013); Patrick Wolfe, *Settler Colonialism and the Transformation of Anthropology* (London: Cassell, 1999).

37 Scott, *Seeing Like a State*; James C. Scott, *The Art of Not Being Governed: An Anarchist History of Upland Southeast Asia* (New Haven, CT: Yale University Press, 2009).

38 Peter A. Hall and Rosemary C.R. Taylor, "Political Science and the Three New Institutionalisms," *Political Studies* 44 (1996): 936–57; Robert Adcock, Mark Bevir, and Shannon C. Stimson, "Historicizing the New Institutionalism(s)" in *Modern Political Science: Anglo-American Exchanges since 1880*, ed. Shannon C. Stimson, Mark Bevir, and Robert Adcock (Princeton: Princeton University

Press, 2007), 259–89. On specific forms of institutionalism, see Douglass C. North and Barry R. Weingast, "Constitutions and Commitment: The Evolution of Institutions Governing Public Choice in Seventeenth-Century England," *Journal of Economic History* 49, no. 4 (1989): 803–32; Sven Steinmo, Kathleen Thelen, and Frank Longstreth, eds., *Structuring Politics: Historical Institutionalism in Comparative Analysis* (New York: Cambridge University Press, 1992); Elisabeth S. Clemens and James M. Cook, "Politics and Institutionalism: Explaining Durability and Change," *Annual Review of Sociology* 25 (1999): 441–66; John F. Padgett and Walter W. Powell, *The Emergence of Organizations and Markets* (Princeton: Princeton University Press, 2012).

39 Paul Pierson, *Politics in Time: History, Institutions, and Social Analysis* (Princeton: Princeton University Press, 2004); Wolfgang Streeck and Kathleen Thelen, eds., *Beyond Continuity: Institutional Change in Advanced Political Economies* (New York: Oxford University Press, 2005); James Mahoney and Kathleen Thelen, eds., *Explaining Institutional Change: Ambiguity, Agency, and Power* (New York: Cambridge University Press, 2010); Stephan Leibfried, Evelyne Huber, Matthew Lange, Jonah D. Levy, Frank Nullmeier, and John D. Stephens, eds., *The Oxford Handbook of Transformations of the State* (Oxford: Oxford University Press, 2014).

40 Robert C. Lieberman, *Shaping Race Policy: The United States in Comparative Perspective* (Princeton: Princeton University Press, 2005); Mala Htun, *Sex and the State: Abortion, Divorce, and the Family Under Latin American Dictatorships and Democracies* (New York: Cambridge University Press, 2003); Orloff, "Gender and Social Rights of Citizenship."

41 Skocpol, *Protecting Soldiers and Mothers*; Tianna S. Paschel, "The Right to Difference: Explaining Colombia's Shift from Color Blindness to the Law of Black Communities," *American Journal of Sociology* 116, no. 3 (2010): 729–69.

42 This loss can be seen in Schmitter's definition of the state, for instance, as "an amorphous complex of agencies with ill-defined boundaries, performing a great variety of not very distinctive functions," cited in Mitchell, "Limits of the State."

43 Scott, *Seeing Like a State*; George Steinmetz, "Introduction: Culture and the State."

44 Émile Durkheim, *Leçons de sociologie: physique des mœurs et du droit*, 54.

45 Charles Tilly, *The Formation of National States in Western Europe* (Princeton: Princeton University Press, 1975); Max Edling, *A Revolution in Favor of Government: Origins of the U.S. Constitution and the Making of the American State* (New York: Oxford University Press, 2003); Jeffrey Herbst, *States and Power in Africa* (Princeton: Princeton University Press, 2000); Victoria Tin-bor Hui, *War and State Formation in Ancient China and Early Modern Europe* (New York: Cambridge University Press, 2005); Miguel Angel Centeno, *Blood and Debt: War and Statemaking in Latin America* (University Park: Pennsylvania State University Press, 2002); Dan Slater, *Ordering Power: Contentious Politics and Authoritarian Leviathans in Southeast Asia* (Cambridge: Cambridge University Press, 2010); Francis Fukuyama, *The Origins of Political Order: From Prehuman Times to the French Revolution* (New York: Farrar, Straus and Giroux, 2011).

46 Scott, *Art of Not Being Governed*; Reno, *Warlord Politics*; Tanisha M. Fazal, *State Death: The Politics and Geography of Conquest, Occupation and Annexation* (Princeton: Princeton University Press, 2007).

47 Margaret Levi, *Of Rule and Revenue* (Berkeley: University of California Press, 1988); Daniel P. Carpenter, *Forging of Bureaucratic Autonomy: Reputations, Networks, and Policy Innovation in Executive Agencies, 1862–1928* (Princeton: Princeton University Press, 2001); Evan S. Lieberman, *Race and Regionalism in the Politics of Taxation in Brazil and South Africa* (Cambridge: Cambridge University Press, 2003); Slater, *Ordering Power*; James T. Sparrow, *Warfare State: World War II Americans and the Age of Big Government* (New York: Oxford University Press, 2011); Torpey, "State Monopolization."

48 Charles Tilly, *Coercion, Capital, and European States, AD 990–1992* (Oxford: Blackwell, 1992).

49 Bourdieu, *On the State*; Mara Loveman, "The Modern State and the Primitive Accumulation of Symbolic Power," *American Journal of Sociology* 110, no. 6 (May 2005): 1651–83.

50 Benedict Anderson, *Imagined Communities: Reflections on the Origin and Spread of Nationalism* (New York: Verso, 1991); Scott, *Seeing Like a State*; Marion Fourcade, *Economists and Societies* (Princeton: Princeton University Press, 2010).

51 Pierre Bourdieu, *Sur l'État: Cours au Collège de France 1989–1992* (Paris: Seuil, 2012), 204, 212; Philip S. Gorski, "Calvinism and State-Formation in Early Modern Europe," in *State/Culture: State Formation after the Cultural Turn*, ed. George Steinmetz (Ithaca: Cornell University Press, 1999), 147–81; Loveman, "The Modern State"; Lisa Wedeen, *Peripheral Visions: Publics, Power, and Performance in Yemen* (Chicago: University of Chicago Press, 2008); Ajay Mehrotra, *Making the Modern American Fiscal State: Law, Politics and the Rise of Progressive Taxation* (New York: Cambridge University Press, 2013).

52 Bertrand Badie and Pierre Birnbaum, *Sociologie de l'Etat* (Paris: B. Grasset, 1982); Hugh Heclo, *Modern Social Policies in Britain and Sweden: From Relief to Income Maintenance* (New Haven: Yale University Press, 1984); Chalmers Johnson, *MITI and the Japanese Miracle: The Growth of Industrial Policy* (Palo Alto: Stanford University Press 1982).

53 Theda Skocpol, *Protecting Soldiers and Mothers: The Political Origins of Social Policy in the United States* (Cambridge: Belknap Press, 1995); Martin Shefter, *Political Parties and the State: The American Historical Experience* (New York: Cambridge University Press, 1994); Sven Steinmo, *Taxation and Democracy: Swedish, British, and American Approaches to Financing the Modern State* (New Haven: Yale University Press, 1996).

54 Pierre Rosanvallon, *L'État en France de 1789 à nos jours* (Paris: Seuil, 1990), 61–74; Sheri Berman, "From the Sun King to Karzai: Lessons for State Building in Afghanistan," *Foreign Affairs* (March/April 2010); John Brewer, *The Sinews of Power: War, Money, and the English State 1688–1783* (New York: Alfred A. Knopf, 1989). We note that early social science theorizing about states assumed representative politics was important, if not central, to what states are about. Weber includes representative bodies and elected

officials as potentially powerful actors in modern states, while for Durkheim, the essence of the state is its legislative function, as it is in parliaments, and not within the bureaucracies, that the most vital work of states occurs, that of fashioning "collective representations and acts of volition" that will guide the polity. And Dewey's writing on the democratic state was in part directed against Hegel and his intellectual descendants, who sharply demarcated state from society.

55 Carpenter, *Building Bureaucratic Authority*

56 William Novak *The People's Welfare: Law and Regulation in Nineteenth-Century America* (Chapel Hill: University of North Carolina Press, 1996); Brian Balogh, *A Government out of Sight: The Mystery of National Authority in Nineteenth-Century America* (New York: Cambridge University Press, 2009); Clemens, "Rube Goldberg State"; John, "Rethinking the Early American State."

57 Novak, "Myth of a 'Weak State,'" 764.

58 Edward Gibson, *Boundary Control: Subnational Authoritarianism in Federal Democracies* (Cambridge: Cambridge University Press, 2012); Gerstle, "The Resilient Power of the States."

59 Philip Abrams, "Notes on the Difficulty of Studying the State," *Journal of Historical Sociology* 1, no. 1 (March 1988): 68; Nettl, "State as a Conceptual Variable," 565–66.

60 Skocpol, *States and Social Revolutions*; John Brewer, *The Sinews of Power: War, Money, and the English State 1688–1783* (New York: Alfred A. Knopf, 1989).

61 Robert Putnam, "Diplomacy and Domestic Politics: The Logic of Two-Level Games," *International Organization* 42 (1998): 427–460.

62 Alexander Wendt, "The State as Person in International Theory," *Review of International Studies* 30, no. 2 (2004): 289–316.

63 Michael Hanchard, *Orpheus and Power: The "Movimento Negro" of Rio de Janeiro and Sao Paulo, Brazil, 1945–1988* (Princeton: Princeton University Press, 1994); Nitza Berkovitch, *From Motherhood to Citizenship: Women's Rights and International Organizations* (Baltimore: Johns Hopkins University Press, 1999); John W. Meyer, "The Changing Cultural Content of the Nation-State: A World-Society Perspective," in *State/Culture: State-Formation after the Cultural Turn*, ed. George Steinmetz (Ithaca: Cornell University Press, 1999), 123–43.

64 Risse-Kappen, *Governance Without a State?*

65 Peter Evans, "The Eclipse of the State?" *World Politics* 50, no. 1 (1997): 62–87.

66 Jonah D. Levy, ed., *The State after Statism: New State Activities in the Age of Liberalization* (Cambridge: Harvard University Press, 2006); Vivien Schmidt, "Putting the Political Back into Political Economy by Briging the State Back in Yet Again," *World Politics* 61, no. 3 (July 2009): 516–46; Kathleen Thelen, "Varieties of Capitalism: Trajectories of Liberalization and the New Politics of Social Solidarity," *Annual Review of Political Science* 15 (2012): 137–59; Huber, Lange, Leibfried, Levy, Nullmeier, and Stephens, "Introduction: Transformations of the State,"*Transformations of the State*, 1–32.

67 Giandomenico Majone, "From the Positive to the Regulatory State: Causes and Consequences of Changes in the Mode of Governance," *Journal of Public Policy* 17, no. 2 (1997): 139–167; Philip G. Cerny, "Paradoxes of the Competition State: The Dynamics of Political Globalization," *Government and Opposition* 32, no. 2 (1997): 251–274; Marcus J. Kurtz and Sarah M. Brooks, "Embedding Neoliberal Reform in Latin America," *World Politics* 60, no. 2 (January 2008): 231–80; Irfan Nooruddin and Nita Rudra, "Are Developing Countries Really Defying the Embedded Liberalism Compact?" *World Politics* 66, no. 4 (October 2014): 603–40.

68 Walter Mattli, "Beyond the State? Are Transnational Regulatory Institutions Replacing the State?" in *The Oxford Handbook of Transformations of the State*, ed. Stephan Leibfried, Evelyne Huber, Matthew Lange, Jonah D. Levy, Frank Nullmeier, and John D. Stephens (Oxford: Oxford University Press, 2014), 286–301; Daniel W. Drezner, "The Global Governance of the Internet: Bringing the State Back In," *Political Science Quarterly* 119, no. 3 (2004): 477–98.

69 George Steinmetz, "Return to Empire: The New U.S. Imperialism in Comparative Historical Perspective," *Sociological Theory* 23, no. 4 (December 2005): 339–67.

70 See, e.g., Julian Go, *American Empire and the Politics of Meaning: Elite Political Cultures in the Philippines and Puerto Rico during US Colonialism* (Durham: Duke University Press, 2008); Adria K. Lawrence, *Imperial Rule and the Politics of Nationalism: Anti-Colonial Protest in the French Empire* (New York: Cambridge University Press 2013). The influential Birmingham School – where Stuart Hall led the Centre for Contemporary Cultural Studies – took a distinctive culturalist approach to these issues.

71 Steinmetz, "Return to Empire."

72 Crawford Young, *The African Colonial State in Comparative Perspective* (New Haven: Yale University Press 1994); Joel Migdal, *Strong Societies and Weak States: State-Society Relations and State Capabilities in the Third World* (Princeton: Princeton University Press, 1988); Darren Acemoglu, Simon Johnson, and James A. Robinson, "Colonial Origins of Comparative Development: An Empirical Investigation," *American Economic Review*, 91, no. 5 (December 2001): 1369–401; Iza Hussin, "The Pursuit of the Perak Regalia: Islam, Law, and the Politics of Authority in the Colonial State," *Law & Social Inquiry*, 32, no. 3 (September 2007): 759–88; Evan S. Lieberman and Prerna Singh, "The Institutional Origins of Ethnic Violence," *Comparative Politics* 45, no. 1 (October 2012): 1–24.

73 Michael Mann, *Sources of Social Power, Volume 3: Global Empires and Revolution, 1890–1945* (Cambridge: Cambridge University Press, 2012), 17.

74 Michael Doyle, *Empires* (Ithaca: Cornell University Press, 1986), 19.

75 Scott, *Art of Not Being Governed*, ch. 1.

76 Weber, *Economy and Society*, 914.

77 "Imperial States," unpublished manuscript.

78 John Gerring, Daniel Ziblatt, Johan Van Gorp and Julián Arévalo, "An Institutional Theory of Direct and Indirect Rule, *World Politics* 63, no. 3 (July 2011): 377–433.

79 Rosanvallon, *L'État*, 14.
80 Phantom states, which lack such recognition by powerful states, often bitterly resent their diminished status and suffer the consequences of their formal isolation from the international state system. Daniel L. Byman and Charles King, "The Mystery of Phantom States," *Washington Quarterly* 35, no. 3 (Summer 2012): 43–57.

PART I

LOCATING THE STATE

The Problem of Boundaries

Reconciling Equal Treatment with Respect for Individuality

Associations in the Symbiotic State

Elisabeth S. Clemens

In 1930 and 1931, drought gripped much of the United States. While crops failed in as many as twenty-three states, in some places the absence of rain led to a downward spiral of impoverishment, malnutrition, and even famine. In Arkansas, people suffered and, eventually, farm families made their way to small towns and cities in hope of relief. Yet there were calls to resist the turn to relief and, above all, to refuse relief from outside local communities. The prospect of such dependence activated troubled memories of the Mississippi River Flood a few years earlier. A. G. Little of Blytheville was quoted as saying that "acceptance of Red Cross aid in 1927 and 1929 cost us more in the loss of self-respect and manhood than anything before experienced and I hope we shall never see it again."[1] To accept such help, even from an organization that understood itself to be the embodiment of the generosity of the American people, was perceived as a threat to civic dignity by this citizen of Blytheville and many of his neighbors.

Soon, however, it became clear that individual and local resources were unmatched to the scale of need. For the next few years, Arkansas came to depend heavily on the Red Cross and other efforts by organized charity both within and beyond the state. As the crisis persisted, the federal government was eventually drawn in, first through the provision of loans under the Hoover administration and then with the creation of the Federal Emergency Relief Administration during Franklin Roosevelt's Hundred Days. Very quickly, private relief was supplanted by government aid. By February of 1931, an aide to the Secretary of War reported on the "Red Cross machinery" in the drought region, concluding that "Texas, like Oklahoma, is not so 'relief educated' as Arkansas."[2]

At first reading, this seems an odd comment. Surely the drought itself, with the loss of income and shortages of food, should be credited with making Arkansans all too educated with respect to the need for relief. But that military aide meant something different by the phrase. Through the efforts of this voluntary – albeit federally chartered – organization, communities had mobilized to carry out systematic surveys of relief and those needy farmers had learned to fill out forms. A private association had done the work of articulating the specificity of each individual dire situation with the categories and formulae of public relief. Restated in theoretical terms, civil society had worked to transform individual citizens so that they aligned with the requirements for intervention by the national state and its organizational allies. Voluntarism, intentionally or not, had performed a kind of preparatory work for the expansion of the welfare state while also marking off the protected domains of individual autonomy and discretion.

The work done in Arkansas was not particularly novel in this respect. Twenty years earlier, the passage of mandatory schooling and minimum working age legislation in many states had been accompanied by a mass effort on the part of the members of the General Federation of Women's Clubs to fan out through their communities to ensure that every child acquired an official birth certificate.[3] After World War I, Red Cross volunteers in the Home Service would count as one of their central responsibilities helping veterans to fill out the forms required to receive their service benefits from the government.[4] "Trained" volunteers might also serve as institutional guides, helping naïve and inexperienced citizens to navigate a strange new world of large bureaucratic organizations and expert professionals employed by the government.[5] Nor were these efforts limited to middle-class do-gooders. With the "revamping of state welfare programs" in the mid-1930s, the Baltimore People's Unemployment League began "to offer a service to members eligible for categorical assistance which involved aid in filling out forms and getting together proper certificates."[6]

Look closely at American political history and one repeatedly finds this type of arrangement in which private voluntary efforts are charged with articulating the relationship between state and civil society, between government programs and private individuals. Although such symbiotic arrangements can be observed across a great variety of regimes,[7] the governing arrangements in the United States have tended toward the "associational" end of the spectrum rather than conforming closely to a classically Weberian model of public bureaucracy.[8] This regularity, in turn, poses a puzzle. If, as Timothy Mitchell has argued, we should understand *[handwritten margin note, top left:]* boundary work

[handwritten margin note, top right:] public relief seen as weak, so government depend on voluntary efforts

the distinction between state and society "not as the boundary between two discrete entities, but as a line drawn internally within the network of institutional mechanisms through which a social and political order is maintained,"[9] why does the "boundary work"[10] of the American state rely so frequently on the kinds of voluntary effort that are more often assumed to be the antithesis of a powerful government? Why are those civic associations that Tocqueville understood as bulwarks against the expansion of the administrative state so often engaged in efforts to implement state policies? What happens as voluntary practices produce "government-ready" subjects and what does this arrangement make happen in turn?

Although political theory sometimes invites us to imagine state and society – or state, civil society, and market – as separate and delineated domains, this interpenetration of associational activity and state projects highlights pervasive forms of interdependence. Just as some species depend on their entanglement with others to survive, so the administrative arrangements of American governance often rely upon private organizations to deliver services and to manage relationships between formal agencies and the organization of other domains of social life. In this specific sense, the American state is symbiotic, dependent on the organized efforts of private persons and groups to advance its projects and implement public policy.[11] *[handwritten:]* If so dependent on us, can't we have greater influence?

This symbiosis takes many forms, among them the work of reconciling two ways of thinking about the relationship of free and equal democratic citizens to their state. The first foregrounds the recognition of the freedoms and rights of those with full claims to civic standing. The individuality of the citizen, in this first sense, is protected by the uniformity and guarantee of those rights with respect to the intervening power of state authority. For example, universal white manhood suffrage meant that all adult white men are entitled to vote or to be treated in accordance with the law, regardless of their occupation, their religion, or the language spoken at home. Admittedly, such equality of treatment in theory is not always matched in practice, but the principle still matters. Such claims are not recognized – much less honored – for those excluded from full civic standing by reason of race, gender, age, criminal record, immigration status, or any of the other attributes that were used to exclude individuals from full citizenship or locate them within hierarchical, ascriptive relationships to those with complete and unquestioned claims to citizenship.[12] From this vantage point, equality is ensured by the administration of state programs in a manner that is intentionally blind to the full individuality of each citizen.

This blindness to individuality, however, may also do damage to citizens insofar as government policy overrides the distinctive preferences and circumstances of private individuals. Variations in private standing generate expectations of differential treatment that sit uneasily with expectations of equal consideration. The policy landscape is littered with evidence of efforts to finesse this contradiction or surrender in the face of the resulting challenges. Touring the country in 1934 to report on conditions to the federal relief administrator, Harry Hopkins, Lorena Hickok confronted these questions at the point where a federal policy premised on equal treatment met a highly stratified labor market:

We are carrying on relief in Texas thousands of Mexican and Negro families, to whom relief, however low, is more attractive than the jobs they can get. And the question is:

Should we cut these people off relief and force them back to jobs that actually represent peonage in order that we may provide more adequate relief for a class for which present relief standards are much too low – a class which is absolutely unable to get work at ANY wages and which is apt to give us trouble?

Or should we keep them out of peonage and on relief, thereby, unless we spend a whole lot more money, actually forcing the white man's standard of living down to that of Negro and Mexican labor?

We might, of course, set up two standards of relief, one for Mexicans and Negroes and one for whites. (It's actually been done, quietly, in some places.) But I don't see how the Federal Government could go in for that sort of discrimination.[13]

Note the multiplication of conflicting standards: a critique of peonage, a presumption that the federal government should not discriminate, awareness that white workers might "give us trouble" if relief wages were too low, and an acknowledgement (if not necessarily an endorsement) of the reality of profound racial and ethnic inequality in the labor market and with respect to "expected" standards of living. Precisely because Roosevelt's initial emergency relief legislation was unusually broad in its terms – officially available without respect to race or family status or even whether a worker was unemployed because of being on strike[14] – the contradictions were especially stark between policy commitments to equal treatment and the practical reality of a social world organized around multiple inequalities and expectations of respect for the individuality of at least some of those citizens.

One response to these concerns has been to tailor interventions to particular persons, often in ways that are guided by the decisions of experts and authorities rather than the desires of those who are in the process of being individuated for receipt of government services. Yet such interventions also provoke resistance. As Hickok reported from Pennsylvania, "the feeling seems to be that every American should have the right to earn the money he gets for relief, receive it in cash, and spend it as he sees fit. 'These people aren't children,' you hear over and over again. 'They're honest, self-respecting citizens who, through no fault of their own, are temporarily on relief.'"[15] Yet this demand to screen one's private decisions from public policy was sometimes coupled to complaints that policy failed to take into consideration individual circumstances. As an experienced social worker in Utah reported of the men on relief,

> ... they seem to mind most being "regimented." They hate like poison having certain days set when they may visit their case worker in her office. They loathe being investigated all the time. They want to be "on their own," with wages, however little, to spend as they see fit. Those at work are beginning to grumble about the pay – that it is woefully inadequate. Mrs. Stevens thinks this may be largely due to the fact that the budgets were arbitrarily set by the work director without any knowledge of the families' needs.[16]

This pair of expectations, that the democratic dignity of citizens requires *both* consistent treatment across citizens and respect for the individuality of each citizen, frames a challenge felt with particular intensity within the American polity. As Kimberly Morgan and Ann Orloff observe in the Introduction to this volume, the United States represents a configuration in which the development of a strong national identity and great governmental capacity has taken shape in the context of an often antistatist political culture. One solution, however partial and problematic, is found in the distinctively symbiotic character of the American state, in which the meshing of universal policies with the requirements of private citizens is often delegated to associations formed by other private citizens. The defining characteristic of this arrangement of state authority and activity, namely the persistent clustering of private (often voluntary) action in the zone of that internal boundary between state and society, requires us to think about both sovereignty and domination, the power of the federal government and the threat to the democratic dignity of those citizens of Arkansas. How is the claim to the legitimacy of a form of public provision articulated with both the specificity of each individual and the equal treatment taken to be the hallmark of political legitimacy?[17]

A BOUNDARY INTERNAL TO STATE AND SOCIETY

In many respects, the configurations of the modern state – and, specifically, the modern liberal state – are the product of a centuries-long engagement of an ideological project with a world always already full of social organization. As it developed within the tradition of contract theory, this ideological project is centered on the concept of the individual and his (only very much later her[18]) rights in relation to the power of the sovereign, understood either as personified ruler or institutionalized authority. Associations, corporations, and intermediary bodies of all sorts are not easily accommodated within this framework. As a consequence, liberal theorists of this particular variety[19] have stripped relational acts of their relational content,[20] cities have been deprived of their medieval powers of corporate self-government and reconceived as having powers only through delegation from the monarch or sovereign authority,[21] and postrevolutionary governments have struggled with the legality and necessity of private associations.[22]

If the primacy of the rational, self-sufficient individual creates one obstacle to theorizing the role of associations within the American version of a liberal polity, another challenge arises from the way in which contract theorists have envisioned the establishment of sovereign power. The usual solution to the challenge of grounding legitimate rule in the natural rights of individuals lay in the formation of a general will. This "general" will was understood as something different from the aggregation of the preferences of all citizens as individuals. Rather, it was the sum of their deliberations on what would constitute the good for the whole community. Associations that encompassed only some members of the polity would interfere with this process. According to Rousseau,

> If, when the people, being furnished with adequate information, held its deliberations, the citizens had no communication one with another, the grand total of the small differences would always give the general will, and the decision would always be good. But when factions arise, and partial associations are formed at the expense of the great association, the will of each of these associations becomes general in relation to its members, while it remains particular in relation to the state.

He followed by noting that, "if there are partial societies, it is best to have as many as possible and to prevent them from being unequal."[23]

Associations, or any intermediary body, might interfere with the process of discerning what was in the general – as opposed to aggregated – interest of all.[24] The consequences of this tension between liberal democracy and associations varied. In post-Revolutionary France, the suppression of associations was particularly intense, fueled by commitments to a plebiscitarian vision of democratic expression along with hostility to the great power and wealth of the religious congregations, a specific but highly salient subset of associations.[25] In the new nation of the United States, by contrast, there was no national counterpart to the power of the Roman Catholic Church once the British Empire had been expelled. Although specific denominations might be established in one state or another, religious organization played a central part in creating institutions of more general interest, particularly colleges and universities. Consequently, the principled hostility toward association evident in France was replaced by ongoing debates over how to demarcate the powers and privileges of private associations[26] augmented by a Tocquevillian vision of how small associations could sustain both democracy and liberty.[27]

But if theorists such as Rousseau emphasized the capacity of partial or intermediary associations to obstruct the workings of the *democratic* state (see Chapter 9), the role of associations in the *administrative* state has been evaluated quite differently. In an essay that was one of the inspirations for this volume, Pierre Bourdieu used a manual metaphor to help us think about the particular quandaries of the contemporary state. Rather than assuming the state to be a unified actor, Bourdieu drew attention to the different – and differently marked – modalities of state action. Like hands (at least for those of us who are not fully ambidextrous), some parts of the state have greater capabilities than others. And, also like hands, the two sides possess strikingly different symbolic associations: the right as dominant and legitimate; the left as subordinate, suspect, and polluted. Not surprisingly, these categories also tend to map on to the gendered and racial character of the state, with those agencies charged with managing subordinated groups through control of social provision coded as the "left hand." The fiscal–military (and implicitly diplomatic) apparatus, for Bourdieu, was clearly the right hand.

Although Bourdieu used this imagery to reflect on general features of the modern state, his framework illuminates changes that were under way in a very particular state at a very specific time: the French state in the wake of the Socialist regimes of the 1980s. Contrary to what one might expect, these socialist administrations had engaged in significant retrenchment of state programs and opened the door to a development more typically associated with neoliberal projects: the privatization or contracting out of state services. The rationale for this realignment, however, was driven by the convergence of three quite distinct political projects: a reformist critique of bureaucracy and call for decentralization; a call for self-management or *autogestion* inspired by the student movement of 1968; and a wave of concern for the homeless, the excluded, and the impoverished.[28] In their own characterization of this move, however, the

French reformers and socialists used an importantly different but equally *manual* metaphor: nonprofit organizations are the fingers of the state.

What changes when multiple fingers are added to the image of the "many hands of the state"? The most obvious shift focuses our attention on the fine work, the more detailed handling that is associated with nimble fingers as opposed to clumsy thumbs. This "customized" or individualized treatment of citizens, however, is at odds with the defense of equal rights and uniform treatment at the center of the liberal political tradition. It therefore changes the image in more profound ways. The "fingers" are not quite of the same flesh as the explicitly public agencies and programs of the state.

This is the key shift that distinguishes the concept of a "symbiotic state" from analyses of state capture; the presence of organizational capacities drawn from outside formal political institutions is actually constitutive of such a regime. Thus the analytic image becomes, in the fashion of cyborgs and Edward Scissorhands, one of a "leviathan with prosthetics." But these prosthetics may also possess a distinctive life of their own. As military operations and occupations are carried out by private contractors, as publicly mandated and funded services are delivered by private organizations that may be charitable or religious in their character, the identification of "state action" becomes much more challenging.[29] To the extent that state capacity is developed by appropriating organizational resources found in other social domains, misrecognition (see Chapter 2) and incoherence are built into the governing arrangements and help to shape the developmental dynamics of what often appears as a "government out of sight," a "Rube Goldberg State," or delegated governance.[30] These arrangements, however, have an additional significance when viewed as "political theory in practice" in that they address the tensions between expectations for equal treatment and for respect of the individuality of private citizens.

EQUAL TREATMENT AND THE PRACTICAL POLITICS OF DELEGATION

In many circumstances, a strong practical case can be – and has been – made for just such arrangements of delegation and collaboration. In the wake of World War I, for example, the U.S. government gave primary responsibility for the rehabilitation of soldiers to the American Red Cross – itself a decidedly hybrid entity, being a voluntary association with a federal charter and a board that included many representatives of the executive branch. The rationale for this arrangement demanded explanation:

One of the questions frequently asked is why the Government does not do what the Red Cross is doing? The Government is compelled to confine itself to a standardized service, treating all men more or less alike. The Red Cross can go into all the ramifications of the individual case and help the man overcome his peculiar handicaps and obstacles. The Government must stick to the essentials of the job. It has a gigantic and difficult task to accomplish the obvious work, common to the handling of every case of a disabled man. It cannot take infinite pains with every case. What it does for one, it must be prepared to do for all who are eligible whether they need it or not.

The Red Cross, it is noted, "is under no such legal obligation." In the place of the relationship of sovereign state to citizen, "the Red Cross is a combination claim agent, friend, adviser, teacher, and general *fides Achates* [sic] of the disabled man. Such a role would be very difficult, if not impossible, for the Government."[31]

That claim for the hybrid role of the Red Cross was, however, contested. In some cases, there were calls for the mass and uniformly minimalist treatment of those in need. Once again, the rebuttal took the form of a claim to respect the individuality of those receiving support from fellow citizens. Such principles were articulated in support of Red Cross practices to aid victims of the Arkansas drought a decade after veterans had returned home from the European War. As the Chairman of the North Lonoke County Chapter explained to the national convention in 1931,

... there was a lack of appreciation on the part of the public as to the necessity of handling Red Cross work upon the individual case system. It was our policy to deal with the individual case and not attempt mass feeding. Shortly after the work started there was a demand on the part of some plantation owners and landlords that whatever relief was afforded to tenants and sharecroppers should be handled through the commissary of the plantation owner or landlords. This, of course, was contrary to the principles of emergency relief and was not countenanced by the Red Cross. Experience has shown the justice of dealing with the individual case.[32]

Although the specifics of this episode involved pots of soup and canvas tents, the abstract political principles at work are quite clear. In insisting on treating the individual as an individual, even at the point of encounter with large-scale organized relief, the Red Cross was mediating between a subject in need of relief and the complex individual person whose particularity required protection even in a moment of crisis. Inevitably, the organization fell short of this goal in many respects, particularly when it came to reinforcing hierarchies of (dis)respect based on race. The political model underlying this concern for individualized treatment was also contested in ways that illuminate its alignment with expectations of self-sufficiency and independence on the part of citizens of a liberal democracy. In 1936, a former national chairman of the Unemployed Council charged that:

> ... the question of relief was relegated to the private "charity" agencies that operate on the "case work" theory. This theory is that there is nothing fundamentally wrong with our social system, but that some individuals are "somehow" unable to adjust themselves to our "perfect" social order. This means, also, that unemployment and destitution are the fault of the individual and that, therefore, having no one to blame but himself, he has no right to make demands upon the class that profits from, and the government that maintains, the capitalist system.[33]

The sustained critique notwithstanding, this complaint clearly recognized how the individuation of private case work functioned to maintain a liberal vision of political order, by focusing on the steps that would restore an unemployed or disabled individual to conditions of self-sufficiency and economic independence. But however imperfect in practice, the principles articulated in support of services to returned veterans and to victims of the drought were roughly the same. By delegating responsibility for mediating between public programs and private persons, associations such as the American Red Cross, the General Federation of Women's Clubs, and even the Baltimore People's Unemployment League articulated the relationship of government and citizens while acknowledging the particular individuality of each citizen.

This protective function, however, came with its own potential dangers. Because the "fingers" of the state are represented by nonstate organizations, the delegation of public responsibilities to private associations destabilizes the status of those who are served as rights-bearing citizens. A state that contracts out responsibilities to private organizations – whether social service nonprofits or for-profit defense firms – creates a regime characterized by variation in the exercise of sovereignty and the ability of citizens to make rights claims. Thus the civic standing of a member of the armed forces is not the same as that of the employee of a private defense contractor. The governing arrangements thereby come to incorporate diverse models of the relations of ruling and authority. This suggests the need to transform Timothy Mitchell's admonition into a question. If the distinction between state and society is understood "not as the boundary between two discrete entities, but as a line drawn internally within the network of institutional mechanisms," why is the line drawn in one place rather than another? As these examples from

American political history suggest, the answer is frequently that the general lies on one side of that boundary, the particular on the other.

Echoing the explanation for the role of the Red Cross in aiding returned veterans, the answer turns on the question of uniformity: "The Government is compelled to confine itself to a standardized service, treating all men more or less alike." In substantive terms, this standardization typically takes the form of a floor or a minimum. If the level of governmental support is constrained by what is acknowledged as necessary (or, perhaps, appropriate) for all citizens, then the multiplication of private associations at the boundaries of public support has the potential to be additive, enriching the opportunities available to citizens in their identity as private, particular citizens. In the words of one scholar of nonprofit organizations, "a combination of public provision and voluntary provision for public purposes makes it possible to accommodate the views and preferences of a greater range of the community than could public provision alone."[34]

This same insight is evident in the frequent claims by private associations that they will tailor or personalize assistance to go beyond the public standard in ways that are required by the particular circumstances or challenges of a fellow citizen. The response to the combined ecological and economic crisis that would become the Great Depression offers ample evidence of this way of envisioning the division of labor to provide social support and, consequently, the appropriate boundary between public provision and private voluntary effort. Recognition of this relationship appeared quickly among private charities as the federal emergency relief system relieved them of their central purpose early in the New Deal. The response by the voluntary sector was creative, entrepreneurial, and individualizing as well as additive.

In New York City, for example, the venerable Charity Organization Society quickly shifted its fundraising appeals to highlight the importance of the "rehabilitation" model of relief in the face of the New Deal's massive (if still inadequate) expansion of public aid after Roosevelt's inauguration. Acknowledging that the government would now take responsibility for relief for the unemployed employables (a new standardizing category promoted by the Roosevelt administration), private charity would still be necessary not only to support the unemployables but also to address all the particular ills that accompanied unemployment, including psychiatric stress, ill health, and domestic violence. In New York City, the Citizens Family Committee reminded readers that "more than half of the families under the care of private family welfare agencies come for help in family problems and personal concerns," but "in the face of problems like these ... the public relief program is helpless." A celebrity case was invoked to back this argument: "'We aren't Quintuplets, but – we have a right to be kept alive too.' The reason the young Dionnes have survived as healthy, normal babies is that they have had highly specialized care."[35] Throughout appeals for donations to support private relief during the 1930s, these themes recur: the need to go beyond "mere subsistence," to tailor the intervention to the person, to rehabilitate individuals, to "do your neighboring."[36]

Although the material results of this articulation of public relief and private charity were inevitably inadequate given the extent of need during the worst years of the Depression, the arrangement did express a fairly consistent response to the delineation of public and private, state and individual. The common denominator was that the beneficiary of the more privileged federal programs was a citizen understood as adult and employable (very often linked to assumptions of white and male).[37] Even representatives of the business-oriented Community Chests made arguments for the expansion of federal work relief in these terms, calling for "decent care for all those on relief instead of the creation of a doubly underprivileged group representing about 60 percent of the load today who are left to local resources, more than half of whom are employables not distinguishable in any sound way from those on work relief."[38] Heightening their differences from federal relief programs available to those who conformed to this generalized model of the citizen as an economically self-sufficient adult, private relief agencies underscored their central role in addressing particular and individualized needs as well as restoring capabilities to support oneself independently of government assistance.

Although highly limited in terms of the support actually provided to those in need, this division of labor conformed closely to the requirements of a political culture built on presumptions of individual autonomy and self-sufficiency. While the adoption of federal programs of social insurance expanded the forms of support available to working – or formerly employed – citizens, they did so on the basis of prior employment. The relationship was captured in an image that was widely used in publicizing the new federal programs: Social Security as a savings account. Although this was fundamentally misleading for a pay-as-you-go system, it portrayed social insurance in a manner that was generally understood to be legitimate.[39] Private charities combined with state and local aid would do what could be done for the unemployables, often creating new kinds of dependencies on agencies or family in the process of addressing individualized, particular needs.

Considered from this vantage point, further expansion of federal social insurance and programs of social support set in motion an interesting dynamic, one that would redraw the internal boundary between state and society. Inasmuch as demands for further expansion were fueled by calls to support citizens in their full individuality – encompassing special needs, abilities, and opportunities – greater capacity to tailor programs to particularities was required. In theory, this could have taken the form of an expanded public workforce of experts and social workers. But, for reasons that ranged from postwar congressional caps on the federal workforce[40] to the extensive expertise of voluntary associations in performing just this sort of work, the expansion of publicly funded services often took the form of increased delegation to private associations. After the New Deal, the next great wave of *domestic* expansion of federal programs took shape through unprecedented contracting out to nonprofit organizations and community agencies.[41] The turn to delegated governance was informed, at least in part, by the difficulties experienced in incorporating particularized programs into the expectation that federal programs would be uniform and "general."

ROLLING IN "THE CATEGORIES"

Although the relation of equal treatment to the individuality of citizens may seem to be an issue of high theoretical abstraction, it was an immediate practical challenge for American social workers at the end of the 1930s, in that brief moment before the shadow of oncoming war became undeniable. The high legislative drama involved in passing the Social Security Act had occurred in 1935, but each of the new forms of social insurance required both endorsement by a state legislature and an "accumulation period" to build up reserves before benefits could be distributed. So it was only in early 1938 that the first of "the categories" (social assistance for the aged, the blind, and dependent children) began to be put into operation and then only in the states that were among the first to pass enabling legislation.

Leaders in the social work community were keenly aware not only of the civic meanings of general and specialized relief, but also of the distinctive political dynamics that followed from each. Most immediately, the implementation of social insurance for the aged, the dependent, and the disabled required reorganizing a field of charitable relief that had sustained the "unemployables" through services and fundraising tightly coupled to specific infirmities (homes for the aged, the orphaned, and the blind) into encompassing categories of citizens entitled to new forms of federal social insurance. Cities such as New York, reflected one social worker, were "in process of effecting an administrative merger of its one-time emergency relief, social security services and long established department of welfare. Local public assistance, in such cases, faces the proposition, long discredited, in arithmetic books, of 'adding a dog, a cat and an apple' to produce one system which makes long range sense."[42] This practice, known to contemporary social theorists as "commensuration,"[43] threatened to undercut the professional practice at the core of social workers' professional identity and legitimacy: individualized case work.[44]

Recognizing the implementation of "the categories" as a moment of both threat and strategic opportunity, social workers carefully considered the politics that would follow from implementation choices. Some attacked the "compartmentalization of human beings," arguing "that category relief is undemocratic; that it creates classes of greater and less eligibility." These inequalities would be the result of "political manipulation by strong groups such as veterans and the aged."[45] Others argued that a sense of expanded public responsibility, even in the form of category relief, would set in motion a political process that would lift the standards of social support for all, or at least many. "What the public generally had not anticipated, when it accepted the theory of categorical assistance," explained Charles F. Ernst, "was the strengthening of the group consciousness of the people categorized by the system and the competition among them that has resulted." The variations in the scale of support or relief "are acutely felt and have bound the members of each group together in a common purpose to protect and extend what they hold to be their rights. 'Bigger and better' is the motto; organization, the technique."[46] In particular, the political mobilization of the Townsend Clubs for a $200-per-month "revolving" old age pension (one that would require recipients to spend the entire sum within a month, thereby stimulating the economy) was linked to the identity effects of the adoption of a federal system of Old Age Assistance:

Here the hopes and emotions of the Townsend Clubs have been translated largely into a drive for more generous allowances on a wider base of eligibility... With ties of kindred long since broken, and lacking the support of adult children, [unattached older people] naturally look to old age assistance as their one hope of warding off the poor house. Given their history and that of the labor movement in these states it is altogether logical that they should see organization as the effective means of getting and keeping the highest obtainable level of assistance. It follows that since public laws determine the characteristics of this assistance its level can be influenced by political action. Every candidate for public office in these states has found it to his advantage of late years to have in his platform at least one plank dealing with old age assistance.[47]

In fractal fashion, however, the inclusion of each new category of public relief seemed to require another heightening of the contrast with private relief, the forms of social support that were offered outside the circle of civic generality. By 1940, one social worker observed that:

More than one hundred thousand individuals are now regularly receiving monthly federal old-age and survivors insurance payments. Within this year payments will go to a half million or more retired workers, their wives and children and the survivors of deceased workers. Because these persons are the beneficiaries of a social insurance program, not the recipients of direct public aid, the questions arise: Does the manner in which their benefits are paid differ from the way in which payments are made under an assistance program? Are the fundamental differences between social insurance and public-assistance reflected in the administration of the insurance program?

After contemplating this problem across the space of a few magazine pages, the author concluded that "unless the differences [between public assistance and social insurance] can be effectively embodied in administration, social insurance cannot fulfill the purpose for which it was established."[48] The implications of this stance were clear to those "ugly ducklings" who were "unlucky enough to have missed the categories of aid in which the federal government participates." Falling between federal work relief, old age assistance, and others of "the categories," these unfortunates were subjected to shaming and harassment, both informal and legally required through the publication of their names in local newspapers.[49] But even in the administration of local relief, the call for uniformity and equal treatment reappeared. After Congress passed an amendment in 1937 that would protect recipients of aid "under the categories" from publicity or the disclosure of personal information, one social worker asked:

If it is considered desirable to protect from publicity the aged, the blind and children in need of assistance, by what reasoning should such protection be denied persons in need of direct relief? Are they less honest, less sensitive to humiliation? Are their children different from the children of those who "fit" the ADC category? Is the fact that, as the *Milwaukee Journal* said, they have "adjusted" to "similar blows" any reason for inflicting a new one?[50]

Policy discussions struggled with the question of how to reconcile the tendency to equate dignity with generality and stigma with the specialized

categories of public social support or its administration by state and local
rather than federal authorities.[51] Others sought to shift the core concepts
of the discussion in order to reconcile the particularity and individual-
ization (or, at least, categorization) of support with the legitimacy of
governmental authorization and funding.

Tellingly, there was a parallel conversation across these years about the
problem of volunteers: the inability to find meaningful ways of engaging
earnest and intelligent citizens in the administration of public support.
The expansion of public – and, particularly, federally funded – programs
of social support had brought a much larger role for professional social
workers, but at the cost of creating a gap "between the one who is helped
and the one who does the helping."[52] Gone, it seemed, were the arrangements in which volunteers played a role in mediating the encounter of
citizens in all their particularity with the infrastructure of public programs
of support. In combination with the seemingly inevitable stigmatization of
those "ugly ducklings" who were not eligible for more legitimated forms
of social support, even those who qualified would get those benefits only
after a direct encounter with agencies and their required forms, inter-
views, and assessments.

In an effort to think around such stark encounters of bureaucratic
hierarchy and the dignity of individual citizens, some social work professionals began to contemplate new ways of articulating the expanded
administrative state with democratic practice. As the author of a letter
to the editor of *Survey Midmonthly* argued, "the future of private social
work will depend largely upon how genuinely democracy has permeated
it." That democracy, the correspondent hoped, would come through the
growing number of "neighborhood and coordinating councils" that had
been founded to "promote some particular project or to attack some
special danger. That is as it should be. You cannot get a popular organization going on generalities." Ideally, this would generate something like a
general will, at least at the local level:

For a community's social work to be genuinely democratic requires evolution; and
the first stage is not financing [as is true of the Community Chests], but discussion
and planning. In this first stage the rank and file of people should be so stimulated
in their interest in social problems as to be moved to attempts of social action.
Then, having clarified their ideas of how things ought to be improved, and having
learned how difficult it is to improve them and how necessary are time, experience
and money, these laymen should be invited to join in a great cooperative enterprise to finance the work of efficient agencies whose services, they should now
realize, are extremely important.[53]

This politically progressive vision of decentralization and local democracy[54] sought to accommodate the specificity of needs and desires not through a common system of categories but rather by delegating the exercise of democratic deliberation to small-scale communities of territory or affinity, a vision that continues to inspire experiments in participatory governance.[55] Although the exploration of this possibility would be delayed by the onset of war and the predictable expansion of the national state, postwar debates would quickly turn again to the possibilities of revitalizing local and community government as an alternative to a direct transformation of the warfare state into a full-fledged welfare state.[56] While these efforts to decentralize democratic governance would be transient, revived in strength only with President Johnson's Great Society efforts and the mandate for community participation, the years after World War II saw yet another turn to delegated governance with respect to the administrative state. Sharp lines that had been drawn to prevent the flow of federal funds to nonprofit organizations at the beginning of the New Deal were substantially relaxed. New federal programs funded higher education and hospital construction, bolstering two domains that remained bulwarks against the "completion" of an American social welfare state.[57] In time, systems of vouchers and tax credits would further individualize forms of publicly funded support, making it ever more difficult for citizens to perceive the qualities of generality that are central to making legitimacy claims for public support. As Georg Simmel argued in his essay on "The Poor":

A Collectivity which comprises the energies or interests of many individuals can only take into account their peculiarities, when there is a structure with a division of labor whose members are assigned different functions. But when it is necessary to perform a united action, whether through a direct organ or a representative organ, the content of this action can only include that minimum of the personal sphere that coincides with everybody else's.[58]

THE DYNAMICS OF THE SYMBIOTIC STATE

This brief historical sketch of the shifting relationships of private voluntary associations and public social support in twentieth-century American political development points to the importance of a generative tension between the political culture of American liberalism and projects of expanding the administrative welfare state. As is widely recognized, liberal regimes are generally inhospitable to generous systems of direct social provision that are at odds with assumptions of the self-sufficiency and independence of citizens. But that incompatibility also fuels a dynamic shaped by the ongoing encounter of liberal premises with a world of heterogeneous individuals and variegated associations. The liberal project brackets both on a conceptual level with the consequence that the "line drawn internally within the network of institutional mechanisms through which a social and political order is maintained" often runs through a terrain populated by associations and organizations that have no place within that political vision. Associational activity may then swarm the boundary, reflecting multiple and diverse responses to the fraught relationship between individual citizens and the two aspects of the state, democratic and administrative. Associations thus buffer, extend, and mediate this relationship in complex ways that ensure that the organization of "infrastructural power"[59] is not only complicated and indirect but also volatile.

Such dynamics are intrinsic to the symbiotic state as sketched here. "Symbiosis" designates a relationship of coexistence between different living species. At one extreme, parasitism denotes a relationship where the existence of one species comes at some harm to the other, but the broad concept allows for different modes of mutualism. Transposed from biology to political sociology, this family of concepts requires us to ask questions of genealogy as well as of the systematic interactions between domains of activity organized around different principles or relational templates. With respect to genealogy, the image of the symbiotic state suggests that state power is often expanded by the appropriation of capacities and resources mobilized elsewhere in society, sometimes for quite different purposes. In the context of American political development, I have described this process as the construction of a "Rube Goldberg" state,[60] invoking the cartoonist's collection of improbably concocted machines to convey a sense of the pervasive repurposing of social organization within governing arrangements.

As a consequence, the geometry of political struggles over policy outcomes is no longer solely one of mobilized interests – business, labor, and so on – operating to pressure legislative and governmental agencies that are more or less autonomous with respect to civil society. Instead, swathes of public policy operate, at least in part, *as if* they were a piece of the market economy or community organizations or religious communities, interacting in often unexpected ways with the formal political commitments of the regime. In such governing regimes, no central adjective applies, much less a classically Weberian bureaucratic logic. Rather than a monolithic ruling apparatus, or a discrete boundary between state and society, the symbiotic state represents a conjuncture of overlapping fields where politics plays out in the effort to draw that "internal boundary" between formal state institutions and purportedly private organizational capacities. In the process, the contrast between the general rights and duties of all citizens and the specificity of private individuals is drawn and redrawn in layered, sometimes contradictory ways. The resulting configurations define the content of civic equality as well as bounding domains of individuality, dividing what is private and protected from what is diagnosed and managed.

Notes

1 Nan Elizabeth Woodruff, *As Rare as Rain: Federal Relief in the Great Southern Drought of 1930–31* (Urbana and Chicago: University of Illinois Press, 1985), 14.

2 C.B. Hodges to Patrick J. Hurley, (February 17, 1931), Box 62, Herbert Hoover Presidential Library, Presidential Papers, Subject File.

3 Molly Ladd-Taylor, *Raising a Baby the Government Way: Mothers' Letters to the Children's Bureau, 1915–1932* (New Brunswick, N.J.: Rutgers University Press, 1986); Florence Kelley, "The Federal Child Labor Law," *The Survey* (September 1 1917), 484–86.

4 "Helping Men to Vocational Education," *Red Cross Bulletin* (September 29, 1919): 6.

5 "Hospital Service and Recreation" (October 4, 1927), Box 86, 104.51 Volunteer Services, Records of the National American Red Cross, 1917–1934, National Archives and Records Administration.

6 Helen Seymour, *When Clients Organize* (Chicago, Ill.: American Public Welfare Association, 1937), 10.

7 For comparative analyses of the organization of social welfare provision, see Ralph M. Kramer, *Voluntary Agencies in the Welfare State* (Berkeley and Los Angeles: University of California Press, 1981); Jennifer R. Wolch, *The Shadow State: Government and Voluntary Sector in Transition* (New York: Foundation Center, 1990); Robert Wuthnow and Helmut K. Anheier, eds., *Between States and Markets: The Voluntary Sector in Comparative Perspective* (Princeton, N.J.: Princeton University Press, 1991).

8 Brian Balogh, *The Associational State: American Governance in the Twentieth Century* (Philadelphia: University of Pennsylvania Press, 2015).

9 Timothy Mitchell, "The Limits of the State: Beyond Statist Approaches and Their Critics," *American Political Science Review* 85, no. 1 (1991): 78.

10 Thomas Gieryn, "Boundary-Work and the Demarcation of Science from Non-Science: Strains and Interests in Professional Ideologies of Scientists," *American Sociological Review* 48, no. 6 (1983): 781–95.

11 Scholarship on the state – as opposed to the specifically American state – has highlighted how the character of and capacity for state action is shaped by

relationships with social networks and organizations that fall outside the official institutional boundaries of public agencies. See, for example, Peter B. Evans, *Embedded Autonomy: States and Industrial Transformations* (Princeton, N.J.: Princeton University Press, 1995).

12 Rogers Smith, "Beyond Tocqueville, Myrdal, and Hartz: The Multiple Traditions in America," *American Political Science Review* 87, no. 3 (1993): 549–66. See also Gretchen Ritter, *The Constitution as Social Design: Gender and Civic Membership in the American Constitutional Order* (Palo Alto, Calif.: Stanford University Press, 2006).

13 Richard Lowitt and Maurine Beasley, eds., *One Third of a Nation: Lorena Hickok Reports on the Great Depression* (Chicago: University of Illinois Press, 1981), 231.

14 The unusual features – in law if not in practice – of the Federal Emergency Relief Act provisions contrast with the racially "stratifying" logic of much social provision. See Cybelle Fox, *Three Worlds of Relief: Race, Immigration, and the American Welfare State from the Progressive Era to the New Deal* (Princeton, N.J.: Princeton University Press, 2012); Chad Alan Goldberg, *Citizens and Paupers: Relief, Rights, and Race from the Freedmen's Bureau to Workfare* (Chicago: University of Chicago Press, 2007); Desmond King, *In the Name of Liberalism: Illiberal Social Policy in the USA and Britain* (New York: Oxford University Press, 1999); Robert C. Lieberman, *Shaping Race Policy: The United States in Comparative Perspective* (Princeton, N.J.: Princeton University Press, 2005).

15 Lowitt and Beasley, *One Third of a Nation*, 4. On the conflicts around social rights and social case work, see Nancy Fraser, "Struggle Over Needs: Outline of a Socialist-Feminist Critical Theory of Late-Capitalist Political Culture," in *Women, the State, and Welfare*, ed. Linda Gordon (Madison: University of Wisconsin Press, 1990); Mark Peel, *Miss Cutler and the Case of the Resurrected Horse: Social Work and the Story of Poverty in America, Australia, and Britain* (Chicago, Ill.: University of Chicago Press, 2012).

16 Lowitt and Beasley, *One Third of a Nation*, 322.

17 J.P. Nettl, "The State as a Conceptual Variable," *World Politics* 20, no. 4 (1968): 562; Philip Abrams, "Notes on the Difficulty of Studying the State," *Journal of Historical Sociology* 1, no. 1 (1988 [1977]): 76, 64.

18 See Linda Kerber, *No Constitutional Right to Be Ladies: Women and the Obligations of Citizenship* (New York: Hill and Wang, 1998); Ritter, *The Constitution as Social Design*.

19 Liberalism, of course, encompasses a variety of approaches. The variant most closely related to the English tradition of contract theory has been characterized as "rationalist." On the contrast between rationalist and pluralist variants of liberalism, see Jacob T. Levy, *Rationalism, Pluralism, and Freedom* (New York: Oxford University Press, 2015).

20 On the treatment of "the gift" as purely voluntaristic rather than relational by Hobbes and Locke, see Harry Liebersohn, *The Return of the Gift: European History of a Global Idea* (New York: Cambridge University Press, 2011), 27–39.

21 Gerald E. Frug, "The City as a Legal Concept," *Harvard Law Review* 93, no. 6 (1980): 1074–78.

22 Amy Gutmann, *Freedom of Association* (Princeton, N.J.: Princeton University Press, 1998); Pierre Ronsavallon, *The Demands of Liberty: Civil Society in France since the Revolution* (Cambridge, Mass.: Harvard University Press, 2007).

23 Jean Jacques Rousseau, *The Social Contract and Discourses* (New York: E.P. Dutton, 1950), 27.

24 Ibid.

25 Ronsavallon, *The Demands of Liberty*, 35–43.

26 Mark McGarvie, "The *Dartmouth College* Case and the Legal Design of Civil Society," in *Charity, Philanthropy, and Civility in American History*, eds. Lawrence J. Friedman and Mark D. McGarvie (New York: Cambridge University Press, 2003); William J. Novak, "The American Law of Association: The Legal-Political Construction of Civil Society," *Studies in American Political Development* 15 (2001): 163–88.

27 In Tocqueville's account, association proceeds through the linking of "the efforts of divergent minds," though assembly, to representative gatherings on the model of a political party. *Democracy in America*, trans. Arthur Goldhammer (New York: Library of America, 2004), 216–17.

28 Claire Ullman, "Partners in Reform: Nonprofit Organizations and the Welfare State in France," in *Private Action and the Public Good*, eds. Walter W. Powell and Elisabeth S. Clemens (New Haven, Conn.: Yale University Press, 1998), 167.

29 Peter W. Singer, *Corporate Warriors: The Rise of the Privatized Military Industry* (Ithaca, N.Y.: Cornell University Press, 2003); Steven Rathgeb Smith and Michael Lipsky, *Nonprofits for Hire: The Welfare State in the Age of Contracting* (Cambridge, Mass.: Harvard University Press, 1993).

30 Brian Balogh, *A Government Out of Sight: The Mystery of National Authority in Nineteenth-Century America* (New York: Cambridge University Press, 2009); Elisabeth S. Clemens, "Lineages of the Rube Goldberg State: Building and Blurring Public Programs, 1900–1940," in *The Art of the State: Rethinking Political Institutions*, eds. Ian Shapiro, Stephen Skowronek, and Daniel Galvin (New York: New York University Press, 2006); Kimberly J. Morgan and Andrea Louise Campbell, *The Delegated Welfare State: Medicare, Markets, and the Governance of Social Policy* (New York: Oxford, 2011).

31 "What Is the Red Cross Doing for Disabled Service Men? A Comprehensive Article Answering This and Many Correlated Questions and Bearing on the Relationship of the American Red Cross to the Government in Completing the Great War Obligation," *Red Cross Bulletin*, vol. V, no. 14 (April 4, 1921), 2.

32 "Drought Relief a Major Red Cross Venture," 6. Address by Cas. A. Wallis, April 13, 1931 (#34734), Records of the American Red Cross, RG III, Box 89, 104.502.

33 Herbert Benjamin, *The Communist* (June 1935), 529–30, quoted in Seymour, *When Clients Organize*, 14.

34 James Douglas, "Political Theories of Nonprofit Organization," in *The Nonprofit Sector: A Research Handbook*, ed. Walter W. Powell (New Haven, Conn.: Yale University Press, 1987), 45.

35 "Write Your Own Ending . . . What About It?," 6, 7, 14. Rockefeller Archive Center, Box 22, OMR II 2F, Economic Interests, Folder #204. For 1936, the Honorary Chairmen of the organizations were Mrs. August Belmont, James G. Blaine, Walter S. Gifford, Hon. Alfred E. Smith, Felix M. Warburg, and Laurence M. Marks.

36 The Citizens Family Welfare Committee, "A Job Taxes Won't Do," 1934. Rockefeller Archive Center, Box 22, OMR II 2F, Economic Interests.

37 Goldberg, *Citizens and Paupers*; Suzanne Mettler, *Dividing Citizens: Gender and Federalism in New Deal Public Policy* (Ithaca, N.Y.: Cornell University Press, 1998); Julia S. O'Connor, Ann Shola Orloff, and Sheila Shaver, *States, Markets, Families: Gender Liberalism and Social Policy in Australia, Canada, Great Britain and the United States* (New York: Cambridge University Press, 1999).

38 In a sign of the times, this argument was made by Charles Taft of Ohio in conjunction with the Citizens' Committee of the Community Mobilization for Human Needs. "Relief," *Survey Midmonthly*, 74, no. 3 (April 1938): 114.

39 Jerry R. Cates, *Insuring Inequality: Administrative Leadership in Social Security, 1935–54* (Ann Arbor: University of Michigan Press, 1983).

40 Morgan and Campbell, *The Delegated Welfare State*, 62.

41 Smith and Lipsky, *Nonprofits for Hire*.

42 Ruth A. Lerrigo, "The Case of the Category," *Survey Midmonthly* 74, no. 1 (January 1938), 6.

43 Wendy N. Espeland and Mitchell Stevens, "Commensuration as a Social Process," *Annual Review of Sociology* 24 (1998): 313–43.

44 Linda Gordon, *Pitied but Not Entitled: Single Mothers and the History of Welfare, 1890–1935* (Cambridge, Mass.: Harvard University Press, 1995); Peel, *Miss Cutler and the Case of the Resurrected Horse*.

45 The arguments of Miss Colcord (also a regular contributor to *Survey Midmonthly* and a staff member of the Russell Sage Foundation?) as recounted in Lerrigo, "The Case of the Category," 6.

46 Charles F. Ernst, "Clients Aren't What They Used to Be," *Survey Midmonthly* 74, no. 5 (May 1938): 143. Seymour, *When Clients Organize*.

47 Ernst, "Clients Aren't What They Used to Be"; on the Townsend movement, see Edwin Amenta, *When Movements Matter: The Townsend Plan and the Rise of Social Security* (Princeton, N.J.: Princeton University Press, 2006).

48 John J. Corson, "When Claims Are Made," *Survey Midmonthly* 76, no. 8 (August 1940): 234–36.

49 Benjamin Glassberg, "Relief's Ugly Duckling," *Survey Midmonthly* 76, no. 8 (August 1940): 238.

50 Glassberg, "Relief's Ugly Duckling."

51 "Relief," *Survey Midmonthly* 76 (August 1940): 244.

52 Helen Cody Baker, "Grandma Called It Charity," *Survey Midmonthly* 76, no. 11 (November 1940): 316.

53 Albert H. Stoneman, "Democracy in Social Work," *Survey Midmonthly* 74, no. 1 (1938): 27.

54 For a summary of this line of argument, see Frug, "The City as a Legal Concept."

55 For examples of ongoing efforts to promote participatory politics, see Gianpaolo Baiocchi, *Militants and Citizens: The Politics of Participatory Democracy in Porto Alegre* (Stanford, Calif.: Stanford University Press, 2005); Caroline Lee, *Do-It-Yourself Democracy: The Rise of the Public Engagement Industry* (New York: Oxford University Press, 2015).

56 Agnes Meyer, *Orderly Revolution* (Washington D.C.: Washington Post, 1945).

57 Scott M. Cutlip, *Fund Raising in the United States: Its Role in America's Philanthropy* (New Brunswick, N.J.: Rutgers University Press, 1965).

58 Georg Simmel and Claire Jacobsen, "The Poor," *Social Problems* 13, no. 2 (1965): 130.

59 Michael Mann, "The Autonomous Power of the State: Its Origins, Mechanisms and Results," *European Journal of Sociology* 25, no. 2 (1984): 185–213. For exemplary studies of the articulation of state agencies and social organization, see Balogh, *A Government Out of Sight*; John Brewer, *The Sinews of Power: War, Money and the English State, 1688–1783* (Cambridge, Mass.: Harvard University Press, 1988); and the contributions to Carol Nackenoff and Julie Novkov, eds., *Statebuilding from the Margins: between Reconstruction and the New Deal* (Philadelphia: University of Pennsylvania Press, 2014).

60 Clemens, "Lineages of the Rube Goldberg State."

2

Beyond the Hidden American State

Classification Struggles and the Politics of Recognition

Damon Mayrl and Sarah Quinn

INTRODUCTION: THE HIDDEN AMERICAN STATE?

As Morgan and Orloff note in their Introduction to this volume, there is a growing awareness of "the complex, puzzling, and multifaceted operation of political authority in the United States."[1] This distinct style of American statecraft is distinguished by extensive *delegation* and formal *complexity*. Policies and programs that would typically be provided through state bureaucracies in Europe may be run through nonstate channels,[2] organized through quasi-governmental corporations and public authorities,[3] or subcontracted to private companies.[4] For instance, as Ajay Mehrotra shows in Chapter 11, American income tax policy has long relied on corporate cooperation to lessen administrative burdens on the federal government. As a result, American policy often resembles a Rube Goldberg machine, notable for its complexity, tangled design, and quirky formal organization.[5] This complexity has political consequences; according to some scholars, Americans have difficulty recognizing the nature and extent of government activity because so much of what the state does takes place through invisible or obscure channels.[6]

Increasingly, scholars have characterized aspects of this unique style of statecraft as being "hidden." Mettler, for instance, argues that the "submerged" nature of American statecraft means that large swathes of government policy "elude our vision" and "remain largely invisible to ordinary Americans."[7] Howard has characterized the extensive use of tax expenditures to enact social policy as a "hidden welfare state,"[8] while Block describes a "hidden developmental state" that coordinates techno-logical progress.[9] Historians have argued that the "hidden" state reflects longstanding American preferences for "a government out of sight," which, while not governing less, did nevertheless "govern less visibly."[10] In perhaps the clearest summary of the "hidden" state thesis, Sheingate writes, "Americans can't see the state ... because it is hidden in a complex web of public and private organizations linked through contractual relationships that conceal, sometimes by design, the actual role of government in American society."[11]

By calling attention to previously underappreciated modes of government action, these scholars have made significant contributions to our understanding of the contours of American political life. Yet, without denying that Americans frequently misunderstand the role of the American state, there are several reasons the concept of a "hidden" state is problematic. To begin, the language of "hiding" places analytic emphasis on state actors and intentionality. Speaking broadly, the general conclusion of this scholarship is that the state "hides" its action in order to attain goals that might otherwise be politically unpopular or unattainable.[12] But while it is true that in some cases government officials actively attempt to conceal their actions by adopting complex policies,[13] it is not always the case that "hidden" programs were intended to be such, or that the obfuscation of state action actually derives from the specific organization of the policy itself. Examining the reorganization of mortgage policy in the Johnson and Nixon Administrations,[14] we found no evidence that government officials were attempting to hide the role of the government in supporting Fannie Mae, even though the government's guarantees of Fannie Mae constitute a classic example of a "hidden" policy form. Nor is there any guarantee that efforts to "hide" the state will be successful, as the intense scrutiny of military outsourcing following the deaths of four "security contractors" in Fallujah, Iraq, in 2004 attests.[15] This suggests the machinations and maneuverings of state actors are only part of the story.

A second, and larger, problem with the "hidden" metaphor is that, although the "hidden" state thesis typically emphasizes how the design or form of a policy contributes to its invisibility, there are multiple instances where the "visibility" of a program is only loosely coupled with its formal characteristics. Consider workplace regulations. These state policies are often deemed "invisible" by political scientists, although they acknowledge that regulations tend to be more visible to workers since they are "proximate" to their lives and hence affect them in concrete, tangible ways.[16] Yet even to the mass public, these regulations are potentially noticeable. In restaurants, for example, evidence of state regulations is everywhere, from signs in the bathroom that proclaim "Employees must wash hands" to health inspection certificates displayed in restaurant windows. Such visible signs suggest something more complex than hiding is at play.

Indeed, the most eloquent discussions of a hidden state touch upon this paradox of how government programs may be visible but overlooked. Mettler notes that even "obviously" visible government programs – those where the government takes an active administrative role and provides regular, recurring evidence of its role through the provision of checks and services – are not understood by many as forms of government support.[17] Balogh notes that aspects of the federal government are hidden in plain sight; we often fail to see the post office as a government agency because it is so integrated into our lives that it has become "invisible."[18] Sheingate argues that the American state is "Janus-faced": highly visible at the state and local levels but harder to see at the federal level. Americans may also be more likely to overlook programs with which they rarely interact.[19] For example, the apparatus of the "carceral state" may be largely hidden from the suburban middle class, but its presence is highly visible and consequential to minorities and the poor in central cities.[20]

Just as formally "obvious" programs may be ignored, so too can complex or "submerged" programs become hyper-visible. In the late nineteenth century, financial regulations – among the most ephemeral and complex of governmental policies – were the focus of sustained, popular, national attention.[21] More recently, many small, targeted policies have become enormously controversial. The estate tax, for instance, only affects around 2–3 percent of the population. Yet a concerted campaign by conservatives and antitax advocates, prominently featuring the reframing of the tax as a "death tax" – thereby suggesting it applied to far more people than it actually did – transformed a largely uncontroversial and "hidden" policy into an issue of nationwide debate.[22] Similarly, Aid to Families with Dependent Children, a program that only benefited a small number of poor families, rose to national prominence through repeated highlighting by political actors, often in highly racially charged terms, before being eliminated in 1996.[23] These programs, neither of which affected a large constituency, became "visible" and highly salient to the public, not because of any feature of their design, but instead, we argue, through political and symbolic campaigns that highlighted and framed those policies for a broader audience.[24]

The core issue of state visibility, then, is not exclusively ontological, but also cognitive. Organizational form and social distance play a role in the popular elision of the state, but given that people can clearly overlook policies they directly interact with, and that people are capable of seeing even the most complex programs, neither is sufficient to account for the overall misunderstanding about the scope of the state. We should therefore not conflate structural complexity with "hiding." The mystery of the misunderstood state is not simply a question of hiddenness or visibility, social distance or proximity. Instead, what we need is a theory of how people categorize what they see as meaningful or irrelevant, as belonging or not belonging to the state. What we need, in other words, is a theory of classification.

In this chapter, we argue that, while it is certainly complex and often misunderstood, the state is rarely actually hidden. Further, we argue that conceiving of state visibility in terms of this metaphor obscures important cultural and political dynamics that are better captured by the Bourdieusian language of classification, doxa, and misrecognition. We draw inspiration from Gestalt psychology to argue that perceptions of the American state are the product of classificatory acts over a complex, multistable system that is readily categorized in various ways. Like an M. C. Escher print, the American state invites differing interpretations. The apparent visibility or hiddenness of the state, in any facet and at any given point in time, is a product not just of the state's formal properties, but also of classifications and the symbolic (mis)recognition that emerges from related processes of attribution and desensitization. These acts can be studied at moments of struggle when people openly articulate their working assumptions about the state.

CLASSIFICATION AND THE M. C. ESCHER STATE

Our approach starts from the insight that classification is the means and stakes of power, and as such is an integral facet of the modern state.[25] As Bourdieu has argued, the state is the most important classifying organization in contemporary society.[26] We see this insight extended in Lara-Millán's Chapter 3, which shows how "frontline" government employees routinely employ the power of classification to obtain or avoid responsibility for particular populations. But the state is not immune to being classified: as Fourcade shows in Chapter 4, a wide range of private and public agencies also regularly engage in classifying the state for their own purposes.

While there are many ways that the state classifies and is classified, we focus here on one essential facet: the processes by which something comes to be classified as belonging or not belonging to the state. Mitchell notes that the apparent boundary of the state "never marks a real exterior" to state influence; instead, it is the idea of the state – the "state effect" – that organizes how we come to recognize the state as something that exists apart from society.[27] The very idea of "the state," in other words, acts as an essential classificatory rubric that allows citizens to identify state action. Indeed, government actors regularly classify their own actions as either belonging or not belonging to the state, since "the state" is a classification with both practical and moral implications.[28]

Because government action frequently involves private actors, that action may potentially be classified as either private or governmental. In the same whimsically serious spirit of those scholars who have described the convoluted form and structure of American governance as a Rube Goldberg state,[29] we suggest that American governance might also be thought of as possessing the baffling, multistable character of an M. C. Escher print. Multistability is a perceptual phenomenon posited by Gestalt psychology wherein repeated viewing of an object results in subjective changes to the object's apparent characteristics.[30] The phenomenon is familiar to anyone who has spent time examining optical illusions, such as the Necker Cube or the face/vase drawing. For our purposes, what is important about multistable phenomena is that their underlying structure remains constant, but subjective perceptions of them vary over time.

We argue that the American state, like many of M. C. Escher's prints, acts like an optical illusion that may be interpreted in different ways. Consider a baseball stadium such as Milwaukee's Miller Park. Do we see a stadium that is part-owned by and hosts games for the privately owned Milwaukee Brewers, which is sponsored by the private Miller Brewing Company, and where private operators manage concessions and parking? Or do we see the state, which owns 71 percent of the stadium in the guise of the Southeast Wisconsin Professional Baseball Park District, paid over three-quarters of its initial capital cost, and pays millions annually in ongoing subsidies and maintenance?[31] The point is not that one or the other of these interpretations is correct; rather, it is that they are *both* true, if partial, depictions of a complex and multistable phenomenon that invites policymakers and citizens alike to engage in classification struggles.

Classifications render the multistable reality of the state perceptually stable. And classifications of the state, like other classifications, are socially patterned.[32] We are "primed" to notice – or not notice – governmental action based on schemas that structure our interpretations of experience. The ability to "see" the state is enhanced or obscured for particular individuals by such things as personal experience, political or ideological predispositions, and political knowledge.[33] Moreover, people may be more or less likely to classify an aspect of governance as "state" or "nonstate" depending on the way that they interact with it. Scholars have noted that the form, regularity, and structure of our encounters with the state affect our ability to perceive the impact of government policy.[34] Taxes, public schools, and social security all feature regular interaction with state agents that help mark those services as "state." Organizational features such as buildings, offices, uniforms, ceremonies, and borders are all concrete practices that attest to the existence of the state and how certain of its aspects intersect with private lives.[35] We learn what the state is by engaging with it, at least to some extent.

Classifications are not uninterested or apolitical, however. People may enlist classifications that serve their economic interests or that permit them to tell a flattering story about themselves. As others have argued, ideas (including categories) are never dissociated from power relations, but rather interests are refracted and filtered through ideas.[36] Classifications of the state can become sites of contestation and struggle. In general, people bring the state into focus when it is in their perceived interest to do so and when they have the ability to do so. Conservatives may highlight welfare programs in order to help reduce government aid to the poor, while liberals may highlight the state's role in Medicare provision to build support for an expanded state role in health insurance. The political dimension of recognition suggests that scholars should focus on *who benefits* from certain classifications of the state.

From Hidden to Misrecognized

Classification schemes can give the world an air of naturalness and permanence, what Bourdieu terms "doxa." Doxa facilitates misrecognition, whereby existing objective arrangements can come to be seen as something other than what they really are. Because it is the winners of classification struggles whose classifications become doxic, misrecognition tends to naturalize existing power arrangements. Doxa and misrecognition, in other words, lend symbolic strength to the dominant, permitting power relationships to persist. By rendering objective reality beyond the realm of thought, misrecognition allows inequalities to be perceived as natural.[37]

All of this suggests that overlooked government programs are not *hidden* so much as *misrecognized*. Misrecognition operates through at least two processes. The first is *attribution*: a person may fail to recognize

[handwritten margin note: Not hidden, but (intentionally?) Framed as natural as to "naturalize" power structures]

the state because they classify a policy that involves nonstate actors as fully "private." It is this process that the "hidden state" literature has so often observed, replete with its implications for public support of government services.[38] The second is *desensitization*: a person may fail to recognize the state because its presence is taken so much for granted that it fades into the background. In this case, even marked government practices may be misrecognized thanks to their familiarity.[39] Most people who head to work every day on government roads through government stop signs and traffic signals do not notice the government's role in facilitating their commute. Through both attribution and desensitization, socially patterned systems of cognition come to be seen as natural, accurate, and timeless.

Struggles over classificatory schemes can shatter this air of permanence, however. Bourdieu writes, "Politics begins, strictly speaking, with the denunciation of . . . the original doxa; in other words, political subversion presupposes cognitive subversion."[40] Classification struggles, in other words, are the essential precondition for all political struggles because they pull existing arrangements out of the realm of doxa and subject them to political contestation. "Knowledge of the social world and, more precisely, the categories which make it possible, are the stakes *par excellence* of the political struggle . . . In fact, this labor of categorization, of making things explicit and classifying them, is continually being performed, at every moment of ordinary existence, in the struggles in which agents clash over the meaning of the social world and their position in it."[41] When these classification struggles do not take place, the symbolic order is effectively depoliticized, and existing arrangements can settle into doxa.

In these struggles, dominant actors have greater power to impose their classifications on policies. The capacity to call others' attention to the state is the stuff of power,[42] and people with more resources may invest those resources in visibility campaigns that direct attention to government practices. When state policies help disadvantaged groups, dominant groups often act to make that aid visible as a first step toward discrediting it. By contrast, when state policies help advantaged groups, privileged actors may discourage efforts to recognize those policies as a product of the state; thus, not highlighted, they more easily lapse into doxa and escape political opposition. Scholars of racial stratification have shown, for example, how government resources used to promote wealth or absorb risks borne by white families may be coded as entitlements or widely ignored, while programs that do the same for families of color may become embroiled in bitter political struggles.[43]

[handwritten marginalia:] role of social work to reframe or keep "hidden"/misperception, then? I suppose its been safer to keep misperception? That way are get foundation not blowing up their money by this spot and govt money vs us as poor not seeing govt help?

If the design of a policy or government practice is not sufficient to explain understandings of the state, it does not follow that ontology is therefore irrelevant. On the contrary, we have focused on the concept of multistability precisely because we think the complex structure of the government facilitates misrecognition. Similarly, we do not contend that the U.S. government is not complex, or that government officials do not at times make concerted efforts to obscure their actions. Our point is simply that noting complexity itself, or even finding an explicit attempt to hide government, is not sufficient to explain the pattern of understandings of what a state is or does. Instead, the key sociological dynamic to study should be the interaction between cognition and ontology.

In sum, classification struggles and processes of misrecognition govern the apparent "hiddenness" or "visibility" of the state. At its core, much of American governance is a complicated, multistable system whose very complexity invites symbolic struggles to classify certain practices and institutions as "state" or "not state."[44] Classifications mediate our encounters with the state, and we may see the state, fail to see it, or misrecognize it as the private sector or market – even when evidence of its presence confronts us directly. Although the form and structure a policy takes may encourage misattribution, people are also able to misrecognize all kinds of government programs through a process of desensitization. Thus Americans are just as capable of experiencing the post office and Medicare as "nonstate" as they are capable of ignoring tax expenditures or government-backed student loans. The absence of conflict may solidify popular understandings of the state/society divide, which in turn allows for the misrecognition of the state's overall role in society, and thus its apparent "hiddenness." At times when such classifications are contested, however, the role of the state may be rendered "visible." The state, from this point of view, is rarely hidden; it is instead frequently misrecognized. But at the same time, the visibility of the state must be constantly reproduced through classifications.[45]

TWO CASE STUDIES

To demonstrate the utility of this approach, we turn to two illustrative case studies of classification struggles in action. The first, a study of the Healthy San Francisco surcharge, highlights a subtle classification struggle driven by nonstate actors at the local level, while the second, a study of the "You didn't build that" controversy from the 2012 presidential election campaign, illustrates an overt classification struggle waged by political actors at the national level. Both demonstrate the importance of classification struggles in highlighting or eliding the state.

Local Classification Struggles: The Case of Healthy San Francisco

Implemented in July 2007, Healthy San Francisco (HSF) was the first major American city program to provide universal health care.[46] The plan restructured and expanded the city's existing charity-care system of public and city-supported nonprofit clinics, hospitals, doctors, and nurses. Uninsured residents who enrolled in the program were assigned a primary care physician and given access to preventive, urgent, and emergency care.[47] To pay for the program, city officials devised a complex regulatory scheme that incorporated both public and private actors. This scheme included a mandate that businesses with more than twenty employees spend a minimum amount of money on health care for each worker per hour.[48] Businesses could meet this requirement in one of three ways: (1) provide employees with traditional private health insurance, (2) pay the city so that their employees could participate in HSF, or (3) place the money in privately managed health care savings accounts from which employees could be reimbursed for medical expenses.[49]

In an attempt to resist the added cost, the Golden Gate Restaurant Association (GGRA) filed a lawsuit seeking to nullify the employer requirement, but their challenge was ultimately unsuccessful.[50] As restaurateurs faced the implementation of the fee, they moved to make the effects of the ordinance more visible to their customers. Starting in 2008, a number of restaurant owners began to add a "Healthy San Francisco surcharge" – sometimes a flat fee of a few dollars, sometimes a percentage of the total – at the bottom of diners' receipts. These surcharges, which were sometimes also advertised on doors and menus, indicated to diners that the money was being put toward employee health care.[51] Raising revenues through a surcharge, rather than just raising menu prices, made sense for many restaurants because restaurant rent is often calculated as a percentage of their gross. Keeping their baseline prices stable while raising offsetting revenue through a surcharge helped restaurants avoid subsequent rent increases.[52] But surcharges also highlighted the city mandate's role in increasing prices. According to Kevin Westlye, the GGRA's Executive Director, the Healthy San Francisco program was "a significant new cost and has to be passed on somehow."[53]

HSF surcharges quickly multiplied. Though not all restaurants added the surcharge, different sources estimated that anywhere from 27 to

66 percent of the city's restaurants did so.[54] These restaurants often highlighted the state's regulations in unmistakable terms, as "San Francisco Health Care Ordinance" or "SF City Tax."[55] Others explained the surcharge in their menus as a response to the "San Francisco Employer Health Care Security Ordinance," "employer mandates including the San Francisco Health Care Security Ordinance," or "San Francisco Employer Mandates, including Health Care Security, Commuter Benefit, and Minimum Wage Ordinances."[56]

As a result of these surcharges, the state's "hidden" actions became highly visible, confronting diners in restaurant windows, on menus, and on receipts. The visible charge shifted the costs from the owners to the customers, but placed symbolic responsibility for the additional costs onto the state. This was an intended effect; restaurant owners told the *Chronicle* that "they didn't want to simply raise prices to absorb the cost; they wanted a separate surcharge so customers understand exactly why they are paying more."[57] This allocation of responsibility for the cost was not necessarily a move to delegitimize HSF, however, so much as an effort to mark the fiscal demands of the state. Some restaurants handed out cards explaining the surcharge and announcing their support of HSF.[58] These cards communicated a sense of civic pride derived from participation in a government activity, even as it distanced owners from responsibility for associated costs.

Although the imposition of the surcharge provoked a flurry of initial commentary, thereafter it generally went unchallenged and began to settle into doxa.[59] Although the surcharge marked the presence of government and connected it to higher prices, it soon faded from customers' conscious view. By 2010, the surcharge was matter-of-factly mentioned in restaurant reviews without further question or explanation.[60] According to *Chronicle* food critic Michael Bauer, the surcharge had "become so pervasive that I now tend to overlook it."[61]

However, in September 2011, attention to the ordinance skyrocketed with the publication of an exposé by Ben Worthen in the *Wall Street Journal*.[62] Worthen revealed that several high-end restaurants had been pocketing thousands – in some cases, hundreds of thousands – of dollars that had been earmarked for health care on customers' receipts. Restaurants that used the health reimbursement account option were permitted to recoup any money allocated for health care not used by employees for health care expenses at the end of the year. Worthen found that health reimbursement accounts were being aggressively marketed to San Francisco businesses explicitly for this purpose. Although the wording on receipts and menus highlighted the state's regulations, the money, as it turned out, was being managed, and mismanaged, by private actors.

After Worthen's exposé, the city quickly revised the ordinance to close the loophole, requiring any business that applied a health care surcharge to their bill to spend all of that money on employee medical expenses.[63] Yet the legitimacy and meaning of the surcharge itself had already come into question. In June 2012, a civil grand jury report blasted the health reimbursement system, arguing that "a significant number of restaurant owners are benefiting financially from the addition of surcharges that are represented to customers as paying for employee health care."[64] The following January, the City Attorney announced plans to prosecute fifty restaurants for fraudulent use of surcharges.[65]

The controversy over the surcharges altered their meaning. San Franciscans increasingly interpreted the surcharges not as evidence of the hand of government, but instead as evidence of the greed and mendacity of restaurateurs. Food critic Bauer reported that diners' complaints had been growing since Worthen's exposé,[66] and that many viewed the surcharges as a form of gouging.[67] For some, surcharges were evidence that the restaurants were failing at their responsibility to provide health care for their workers. One of Bauer's readers wrote, "what really makes me boil is that the restaurant is essentially telling me it's not their responsibility to provide health care to their workers. Therefore, they will directly charge me for that 'benefit.'"[68] Thus, the restaurateurs' efforts ultimately backfired, for in the process of pointing to the state they ended up highlighting their own interests. Ironically, this shift in meaning served to reduce the visibility of the regulations that prompted the surcharge in the first place. Facing "a financial and public relations mess,"[69] some restaurants opted to drop the surcharge and simply raise their prices.[70] By doing so, the evidence of the HSF ordinance was literally erased from menus and receipts.

In sum, then, San Francisco restaurants, motivated by self-interest and a desire to recoup the additional costs of the new health care ordinance, used advertised surcharges to make state action visible to their customers. Yet a series of scandals over the "clawing back" of funds allocated to health reimbursement accounts led some diners to interpret this as evidence of the greed of restaurant owners. Visibility was produced initially thanks to a political act of classification, and then later thanks to interpretive changes that occurred in light of a scandal. The "visibility" of the state in this arena did not follow from policymaker intent or the policy's complex form, but emerged as an unintended consequence of the ordinance through a new symbol (the surcharge) placed by private actors affected by it. But the way that it was interpreted was filtered through narratives that emerged in the wake of a protracted scandal in ways that ultimately rendered salient both a state policy and the interests of those who opposed it.

National Classification Struggles: The "You Didn't Build That" Controversy

Our second case study, the "You didn't build that" (YDBT) controversy, is drawn from the 2012 presidential race between President Barack Obama and former Massachusetts Governor Mitt Romney. At the heart of the controversy was government's role in facilitating entrepreneurship. The seeds of the controversy were sown in September 2011, when Elizabeth Warren, then a candidate for Senate in Massachusetts, gave a speech offering a rousing defense of the role of government in fostering the success of small businesses:

There is nobody in this country who got rich on his own. Nobody. You built a factory out there? Good for you. But I want to be clear: you moved your goods to market on the roads the rest of us paid for. You hired workers the rest of us paid to educate. You were safe in your factory because of police forces and fire forces that the rest of us paid for. You didn't have to worry that marauding bands would come and seize everything at your factory, and hire someone to protect against this, because of the work that the rest of us did.[71]

Liberals and progressives lauded the speech for its clear and passionate defense of government and Warren's uncompromising tone in identifying the role of the state and defending the "social contract" that government interventions implied and supported. The stakes were high: if the state helped businesses succeed, it morally justified income redistribution through taxation. Warren explained: "Now look, you built a factory and it turned into something terrific, or a great idea? God bless. Keep a big hunk of it. But part of the underlying social contract is you take a hunk of that and pay forward for the next kid who comes along."

Warren's speech showed the potential to motivate the activist base of the Democratic Party, and President Obama quickly adopted these themes in his reelection campaign. On July 13, 2012, Obama gave a speech in Roanoke, Virginia, that concluded with a particularly blunt assessment of the role of government in promoting private success. Echoing Warren, Obama declared, "If you were successful, somebody along the line gave you some help. There was a great teacher somewhere in your life. Somebody helped to create this unbelievable American system that we have that allowed you to thrive. Somebody invested in roads and bridges. If you've got a business – you didn't build that. Somebody else made that happen."[72]

The Romney campaign immediately objected to this characterization, and moved to make YDBT a major campaign issue. Ten days after Obama spoke in Roanoke, the Romney campaign unveiled "We did build it" as a new campaign slogan.[73] Romney appeared at campaign events surrounded by workers wearing T-shirts reading "Government didn't build my business – I did!"; Republican activists welcomed Obama to regional airports with banners reading "We did build this"; and conservative advocacy groups advertised their rallies with traveling buses featuring an image of Obama saying "You didn't build that" on the side.[74] The Romney campaign further enlisted small businesspeople to testify about their own hard work and to criticize Obama for "demonizing" their efforts.[75] In August, the Republican National Convention devoted an entire day to the theme "We built this," with speakers repeatedly mocking Obama for insulting small business owners and failing to understand how the economy actually worked.[76]

In this case, the classification struggle over state action took the form of an explicit discussion about how to classify the role of the state in entrepreneurial success and market outcomes. Obama's visibility campaign attempted to highlight the state's facilitating role in economic success. "When we succeed, we succeed because of our individual initiative, but also because we do things together," Obama said after uttering the fateful YDBT line. He illustrated this claim by listing a series of state initiatives. "That's how we built the Golden Gate Bridge or the Hoover Dam. That's how we invented the Internet. That's how we sent a man to the moon."[77]

Romney and his allies, by contrast, encouraged Americans to classify business success as the product of individual effort. Senator Scott Brown, running for reelection against Warren in Massachusetts, argued that in classifying success, it was not the case that we failed to see the role of the *state*, but that we failed to see the *effort* that went into every small business: "Sometimes they're such fixtures in the neighborhood that it can be easy to forget how much work went into each business. They all began as a risk somebody took, a dream somebody pursued – usually with a lot of cost, worry, and aggravation along the way."[78] At the Republican National Convention, Vice-Presidential nominee Paul Ryan echoed this focus: "if small business people say they made it on their own, all they are saying is that nobody else worked seven days a week in their place. Nobody showed up in their place to open the door at five in the morning. Nobody did their thinking, and worrying, and sweating for them."[79]

Indeed, Republicans urged Americans to classify all kinds of success as the product of individual efforts independent of the state. During a rally in Pennsylvania, Romney declared:

[T]he president's logic ... extends to everybody in America that wants to lift themself [sic] up a little further, that goes back to school to get a degree and see if they can get a little better job, to somebody who wants to get some new skills and get a little higher income ... The president would say, well you didn't do that. You couldn't have gotten to school without the roads that government built for you. You couldn't have gone to school without teachers. So you didn't, you are not responsible for that success.[80]

At the convention's YDBT-themed day, Senator Rand Paul restated this theme in blunt and sweeping terms: "When you say they didn't build it, you insult each and every American who ever got up at the crack of dawn. You insult any American who ever put on overalls or a suit. You insult any American who ever studied late into the night to become a doctor or a lawyer. You insult the dishwasher, the cook, the waitress. You insult anyone who has ever dragged themselves out of bed to strive for something better for themselves or their children."[81] In short, Republicans encouraged Americans to classify success in terms that denied a meaningful role for the state, focusing instead on individual effort, sacrifice, and personal risk. The YDBT controversy, therefore, was fundamentally a struggle over how to categorize the role of the state in entrepreneurial success.

In an ironic twist, however, the more that the Romney camp attempted to empirically demonstrate the irrelevance of the state to individual effort, the more the state's hidden role percolated to the fore. As discussed earlier, one of the major features of Romney's "We did build it" campaign was a series of events and advertisements with small businessmen, which highlighted their personal stories and chastised Obama for claiming the state had anything to do with their success. Yet in event after event, small businesspeople claiming to have built their businesses without government assistance were found to have actually benefited from the hand of the state in multiple ways. For instance, Romney debuted his "We did build it!" slogan in a roundtable with business owners in Southern California in which three participants told Romney that they relied on government contracts for a good portion of their business.[82]

In perhaps the most embarrassing incident, the Romney campaign produced a television advertisement in which New Hampshire metal-shop owner Jack Gilchrist scolded Obama for his YDBT remarks: "Through hard work and a little bit of luck, we built this business. Why are you demonizing us for it?"[83] Yet New Hampshire reporters quickly revealed that the state played a substantial role in Gilchrist's business's success: $800,000 in tax-exempt bonds from the state of New Hampshire, a half-million-dollar loan from the Small Business Administration, matching funds from a federally financed trade adjustment assistance program, and nearly $90,000 in military contracts.[84]

In sum, then, Democratic politicians working on the national stage attempted to make the many hands of the state visible by enumerating the means through which government programs contributed to the economic success of individuals. As a visibility campaign designed to justify the redistribution of resources away from businesses, Republicans challenged it as an illegitimate reclassification that demeaned the hard work and independence of entrepreneurs. Republicans soon found, however, that it was difficult to maintain narrative control of efforts to reassert the misattribution and omission of the government, since the very act of talking about business within the context of state programs undermined the doxic misrecognition of government assistance that they had benefited from.

DISCUSSION AND CONCLUSION

American governance is complex. Instead of parsing this structure into "hidden" or "visible" features of the state, scholars should instead approach the state as a multistable system that invites variable classifications. This multistability is illustrated in our case studies. The HSF program operates through city mandates, employer contributions, an expanded city insurance program, and privately managed health savings accounts. The role of the American government in promoting the economy, at issue in the YDBT controversy, is still more complex, involving private actors and individual initiative alongside a welter of formal government programs, infrastructural capacities, loans, subsidies, and contracts. That citizens and politicians could not agree on how to classify the role of the state in our two cases is not a surprise. Neither side was entirely wrong. The multistable nature of the state leaves it open to interpretation.

Recognition of the state emerges from an interaction between classificatory schemas and policy design. Here, as elsewhere, people filter their experiences through schemas that suit particular interests, and competing interests may give rise to struggles over whether or not a phenomenon derives from the state. When people elide the role of the state in facilitating the success of privileged groups, this naturalizes and thus perpetuates inequalities. Actors may highlight the state in an effort to denaturalize and delegitimize a program, as we saw with the HSF case. By the same token, actors may attempt to build support for a program by asserting the beneficial impact of policies on citizens' lives. Democrats' attempts to associate the state with economic prosperity were of a piece with their efforts to build support for a more activist state – as well as their own policy platforms and personal electoral chances. Struggles to classify particular policies, outcomes, or aspects of governance as "state" or "nonstate" are thus a key tool of power.

Our analysis has three broader implications. First, a focus on classification makes it easier to see how programs can become misrecognized or "hidden" for reasons that have nothing to do with policymaker intent. As the HSF case study demonstrates, "seeing" the state is a collective endeavor, and the politics of that endeavor is not restricted to the policymaking process. Because so many actors engage in classification struggles, visibility follows an unpredictable logic and, frequently, produces surprising and unintended outcomes. Yet the language of a "hidden state" places analytical primacy on that which is observed, rather than on the people doing the observing. A narrow focus on politicians and policymakers threatens to obscure this broader dynamic.

There are further reasons to look beyond policymakers and the programs they design. Our YDBT case study suggests that the apparently "hidden" nature of the state may not emerge from the design of any one specific policy, but also in the aggregate, over time and as an unintended consequence. Consider Warren's and Obama's speeches: Many, if not most, of the aspects of the state they highlighted are features that most Americans would acknowledge as products of state agencies: roads, bridges, dams, schools, police, firefighters, and the space program. The various features of the state that make up government intervention in markets, in other words, are often quite visible, even "obviously" part of the state. Ultimately, therefore, the state may not come to be "hidden" primarily because of program or policy design, but instead because of how policies combine in the aggregate, or because misattribution or desensitization emerge from cognitive dynamics over time.

Second, classification struggles are an important means of promoting the recognition of state action. Calling out the role of the state can produce spillover effects that help highlight additional facets of governance. By raising the issue and directly contesting the classification of something as "state" or "nonstate," political actors encourage journalists and bloggers to go looking for the state – and they often find it. This was clearly illustrated in the YDBT case study: Whether in the form of military contracts, low-interest loans, or trade adjustment assistance, each of these "hidden" state forms was exposed thanks to the classification struggle that YDBT sparked – even though they were not the programs that Obama or Warren highlighted in their speeches. The sensitizing that occurs as a result of these struggles helps reveal the many "hidden" hands of the state.

Finally, our analysis points to new pathways of investigation that promise a deeper synthesis of how specific policy forms interact with schemas of classification. To begin, our critique of "hiddenness" as an organizing metaphor suggests that we would benefit from additional investigations of the conditions under which official attempts to control how their programs are perceived are more or less successful. Second, our Bourdieusian approach directs our attention to how struggles to define the contours of the state are related to other systems of classification. For example, we have much to learn about how normative evaluations of the state or political ideology affect the likelihood that any given person or group of people will perceive government action. Third, our general approach would benefit from further studies of how such classification struggles have unfolded in other historical moments and in other nations. The latter will be particularly useful in helping to determine the conditions under which policy structures and perceptions of state action are closely or loosely coupled, and in furthering dialogue between the revisionist American state literature and more canonical formulations of state theory developed to explain European cases.

Scholars of the "hidden" state have contributed a great deal to our understanding of how the American state works, why policies are designed in particular ways, and why Americans have difficulty recognizing the importance of the state in shaping their lives. Naming these programs is a significant empirical contribution, with political ramifications insofar as revealing the role of the state also challenges doxa. But if we fail to note the classification efforts that help make the state "hidden," we risk obscuring the everyday political struggles that go into making aspects of the state visible and relevant to various audiences. If we neglect the classifications that render governance meaningful, we fail to interrogate one of the most important mechanisms of power. We must point out overlooked aspects of the state without naturalizing the processes through which they came to be seen as hidden in the first place.

If the state is multistable, the question of how the state is rendered "visible" is as important as the question of how the state is "hidden." The ability to recognize the role of government is not something that happens inevitably or automatically; it is instead a product of how shared schemas and classification struggles interact with a given policy form. Denaturalizing the idea that the state is ever obvious or inevitably hidden, and focusing instead on the classificatory struggles that help to produce recognition and misrecognition of the state, can advance the project of understanding how and when citizens encounter the state.

Notes

1 We wish to thank Lis Clemens, Siri Colom, Lynne Gerber, Meyer Kestnbaum, Laura Mangels, Kimberly Morgan, Bill Novak, Ann Orloff, Nick Wilson, and the participants in the "Many Hands of the State" conference (University of Chicago, May 2014) for helpful feedback. Cindy Gudino and Pragya Kc provided excellent research assistance.

2 Jacob S. Hacker, *The Divided Welfare State: The Battle over Public and Private Social Benefits in the United States* (New York: Cambridge University Press, 2002); Colin D. Moore, "State Building through Partnership: Delegation, Public–Private Partnerships, and the Political Development of American Imperialism, 1898–1916," *Studies in American Political Development* 25 (2011): 27–56; Kimberly J. Morgan and Andrea L. Campbell, *The Delegated Welfare State: Medicare, Markets, and the Governance of Social Policy* (New York: Oxford University Press, 2011).

3 Gail Radford, *The Rise of the Public Authority: Statebuilding and Economic Development in Twentieth-Century America* (Chicago: University of Chicago Press, 2013).

4 Jody Freeman and Martha Minow, eds., *Government by Contract: Outsourcing and American Democracy* (Cambridge: Harvard University Press, 2009).

5 Elisabeth S. Clemens, "Lineages of the Rube Goldberg State: Building and Blurring Public Programs, 1900–1940," in *Rethinking Political Institutions: The Art of the State*, ed. Ian Shapiro, Stephen Skowronek, and Daniel Galvin (New York: New York University Press, 2006): 187–215; Morgan and Campbell, *Delegated Welfare State.*

6 Hacker, *Divided Welfare State*; Suzanne Mettler, *The Submerged State: How Invisible Government Policies Undermine American Democracy* (Chicago: University of Chicago Press, 2011); Morgan and Campbell, *Delegated Welfare State.*

7 Mettler, *Submerged State*, 5.

8 Christopher Howard, *The Hidden Welfare State: Tax Expenditures and Social Policy in the United States* (Princeton: Princeton University Press, 1997).

9 Fred Block, "Swimming against the Current: The Rise of a Hidden Developmental State in the United States," *Politics & Society* 36, no. 2 (2008): 169–206.

10 Brian Balogh, *A Government out of Sight: The Mystery of National Authority in Nineteenth-Century America* (New York: Cambridge University Press, 2009), p. 379.

11 Adam Sheingate, "Why Can't Americans See the State?" *The Forum* 7, Article 1 (2009), www.bepress.com/forum/vol7/iss4/art1, 1.

12 E.g., Balogh, *Government Out of Sight*; Mettler, *Submerged State.*

13 E.g., Greta Krippner, "The Making of US Monetary Policy: Central Bank Transparency and the Neoliberal Dilemma," *Theory and Society* 36 (2007): 477–513.

14 Damon Mayrl and Sarah Quinn, "The Practical Boundaries of the State: Partnership Politics in Housing and Education Policy," paper presented at the Annual Meetings of the Social Science History Association, November 2013.

15 P.W. Singer, "Outsourcing War," *Foreign Affairs* 84, no. 2 (2005): 119–32.

16 Joe Soss and Sanford F. Schram, "A Public Transformed? Welfare Reform as Policy Feedback," *American Political Science Review* 101 (2007): 111–27.

17 Mettler, *Submerged State*, 38.

18 Balogh, *Government Out of Sight.*

19 Sheingate, "Why Can't Americans See the State?"

20 Alice Goffman, *On the Run: Fugitive Life in an American City* (Chicago: University of Chicago Press, 2014); Loïc Wacquant, *Deadly Symbiosis: Race and the Rise of the Penal State* (Cambridge: Polity Press, 2009); Vesla M. Weaver and Amy E. Lerman, "Political Consequences of the Carceral State," *American Political Science Review* 104 (2010): 817–33.

21 Gretchen Ritter, *Goldbugs and Greenbacks: The Antimonopoly Tradition and the Politics of Finance in America* (New York: Cambridge University Press, 1997).

22 Michael J. Graetz and Ian Shapiro, *Death by a Thousand Cuts: The Fight over Taxing Inherited Wealth* (Princeton: Princeton University Press, 2005).

23 Martin Gilens, *Why Americans Hate Welfare: Race, Media, and the Politics of Antipoverty Policy* (Chicago: University of Chicago Press, 1999).

24 Political scientists have suggested an important relationship between controversy and visibility. Soss and Schram, for instance, distinguish between "invisible-distant" policies, about which most publics are unaware and unaffected, and which include "obscure domestic policies targeted at small, isolated constituencies"; and "visible-distant" policies, which include "controversial domestic policies with small and/or socially isolated target populations." These types of policies generate divergent effects: the "invisible" ones pass nearly unnoticed, while the "visible" ones become highly symbolically relevant. Soss and Schram make significant strides by focusing on social position and political fights, but a problem remains here: the controversy is already baked into the definition. The important question instead should be: How does a policy geared to a small, isolated constituency become controversial, and thus visible? See Soss and Schram, "A Public Transformed?," 121–22.

25 E.g., Julia Adams, Elisabeth S. Clemens, and Ann Shola Orloff, "Introduction: Social Theory, Modernity, and the Three Waves of Historical Sociology," in *Remaking Modernity: Politics, History, and Sociology*, ed. Julia Adams,

Elisabeth S. Clemens, and Ann Shola Orloff (Durham: Duke University Press, 2005): 1–72; Pierre Bourdieu, *Language and Symbolic Power* (Cambridge: Harvard University Press, 1991); Pierre Bourdieu, *On the State: Lectures at the Collège de France, 1989–1992* (Malden: Polity, 2014); Pierre Bourdieu and Loïc Wacquant, *An Invitation to Reflexive Sociology* (Chicago: University of Chicago Press, 1992); Patrick Carroll, "Articulating Theories of States and State Formation," *Journal of Historical Sociology* 22 (2009): 553–603; Mara Loveman, "The Modern State and the Primitive Accumulation of Symbolic Power," *American Journal of Sociology* 110 (2005): 1651–83; Timothy Mitchell, "The Limits of the State: Beyond Statist Approaches and Their Critics," *American Political Science Review* 85 (1991): 77–96; Nicholas Hoover Wilson, "From Reflection to Refraction: State Administration in British India, circa 1770–1855," *American Journal of Sociology* 116 (2011): 1437–77.

26 Bourdieu, *On the State.*

27 Mitchell, "Limits of the State," 90.

28 Damon Mayrl and Sarah Quinn, "Defining the State from Within: Boundaries, Schemas, and Associational Policymaking," *Sociological Theory* 34 (2016): 1–26; Nicholas Hoover Wilson, "The State as a Moral Rationalization," unpublished manuscript, Department of Sociology, Stony Brook University.

29 Clemens, "Lineages of the Rube Goldberg State"; Morgan and Campbell, *Delegated Welfare State.*

30 Fred Attneave, "Multistability in Perception," *Scientific American* 225 (1971): 62–71; David A. Leopold and Nikos K. Logothetis, "Multistable Phenomena: Changing Views in Perception," *Trends in Cognitive Sciences* 3 (1999): 477–513.

31 Daniel Ferry, "Why Are Sports Franchises on Welfare?" *USA Today*, November 4, 2013, www.usatoday.com/story/money/business/2013/11/04/why-sports-franchises-are-on-welfare/3432789/; Martin J. Greenberg, "The Economics of Miller Park," *Milwaukee Journal-Sentinel*, April 5, 2012; Judith Grant Long, *Public/Private Partnerships for Major League Sports Facilities* (New York: Routledge, 2012).

32 Pierre Bourdieu, *The Logic of Practice* (Palo Alto: Stanford University Press, 1990).

33 E.g., Julianna Koch and Suzanne Mettler, "Who Perceives Government's Role in Their Lives? How Policy Visibility Influences Awareness of and Attitudes about Social Spending," paper presented at the Midwest Political Science Association Annual Meeting, March 2011.

34 R. Douglas Arnold, *The Logic of Congressional Action* (New Haven: Yale University Press, 1990); Hacker, *Divided Welfare State*; Mettler, *Submerged Welfare State*; Soss and Schram, "A Public Transformed?"

35 Joel S. Migdal, *State in Society: Studying How States and Societies Transform and Constitute One Another* (Cambridge: Cambridge University Press, 2001).

36 Elisabeth Anderson, "Ideas in Action: The Politics of Prussian Child Labor Reform, 1817–1839," *Theory and Society* 42 (2013): 81–119; John L. Campbell, "Institutions, Politics, and Public Policy," *Annual Review of Sociology* 28 (2002): 21–38; Wilson, "From Reflection to Refraction."

37 Bourdieu and Wacquant, *Invitation to Reflexive Sociology.*

38 Hacker, *Divided Welfare State*; Mettler, *Submerged State.*

39 Sheingate, "Why Can't Americans See the State?"

40 Bourdieu, *Language and Symbolic Power*, 127–28.

41 Bourdieu, *Language and Symbolic Power*, 235.

42 Bourdieu, *Language and Symbolic Power.*

43 E.g., Ira Katznelson, *When Affirmative Action Was White: An Untold Story of Racial Inequality in Twentieth-Century America* (New York: W.W. Norton, 2005).

44 This complexity is fertile ground for multiple forms of social contestation, both in moments of institutional genesis (see, e.g., Clemens' discussion of the Red Cross in Chapter 1) and over time.

45 Indeed, the dynamics of state hiddenness and visibility may follow a roughly cyclical pattern: familiarity and the structure of policy together combine to promote misrecognition of the American state, which is periodically overturned or uprooted by classification struggles, only to sink back into misrecognition and doxa once the dust settles.

46 Bob Egelko, "Top U.S. Court Backs S.F. Health Care," *San Francisco Chronicle,* February 22, 2008.

47 Heather Knight, "S.F.'s Bold Foray into Health Care Ready to Start," *San Francisco Chronicle,* June 28, 2007; Heather Knight, "Universal Health Care Called S.F.'s Future," *San Francisco Chronicle,* March 12, 2009; Cecilia M. Vega, "S.F. Mayor Urges Health Coverage for All Uninsured," *San Francisco Chronicle,* June 21, 2006.

48 Wyatt Buchanan, "734 Businesses Sign Up for S.F. Health Program," *San Francisco Chronicle,* May 2, 2008.

49 Victoria Colliver, "S.F. Businesses Preparing for Health Care Law," *San Francisco Chronicle,* February 17, 2008.

50 John Wildermuth, "Healthy San Francisco Clears Last Legal Hurdle," *San Francisco Chronicle,* June 29, 2010.

51 Stacy Finz and John Coté, "SF Restaurants Pocketed Health Care Fees," *San Francisco Chronicle,* January 25, 2013.

52 Michael Bauer, "Two Reasons Some Restaurants Add the San Francisco Surcharge," *Inside Scoop SF,* February 19, 2014, http://insidescoopsf.sfgate.com/blog/2014/02/19/two-reasons-some-restaurants-add-the-san-francisco-surcharge/; Paolo Lucchesi, "Why Restaurants Have Surcharges," *Inside Scoop SF,* February 1, 2013, http://insidescoopsf.sfgate.com/blog/2013/02/01/why-restaurants-have-surcharges/

53 Quoted in Wildermuth, "Healthy San Francisco Clears Last Legal Hurdle."

54 Michael Bauer, "Restaurants that Forgo the Healthy San Francisco Surcharge," *Inside Scoop SF,* November 1, 2011, http://insidescoopsf.sfgate.com/blog/2011/11/01/restaurants-that-forgo-the-healthy-san-francisco-surcharge/; San Francisco Civil Grand Jury, *Surcharges and Healthy San Francisco: Healthy for Whom?* (San Francisco: Superior Court of California, County of San Francisco, 2012); Carrie H. Colla, William H. Dow, and Arindrajit Dube, "The Labor Market Impact of Employer Health Benefit Mandates: Evidence from San Francisco's Health Care Security Ordinance," Working Paper no. 17198 (Washington: National Bureau of Economic Research, 2011).

55 Knight, "Not All Restaurants Back Suit"; San Francisco Civil Grand Jury, *Surcharges and Healthy San Francisco, 6.*

56 Michael Bauer, "Diners Really Don't Like the SF Surcharges," *Inside Scoop SF,* May 8, 2012, http://insidescoopsf.sfgate.com/blog/2012/05/08/diners-really-dont-like-the-sf-surcharges/; Michael Bauer, "Are San Francisco Restaurants Really Pocketing the 3–4 Percent Surcharges as the Wall Street Journal Claims?" *Inside Scoop SF,* September 27, 2011, http://insidescoopsf.sfgate.com/blog/2011/09/27/are-san-francisco-restaurants-really-pocketing-the-3-4-percent-surcharges-as-the-wall-street-journal-claims/; Paolo Lucchesi, "Michael Mina and the City Attorney Reach a Settlement Surrounding Health Care Surcharges," *Inside Scoop SF,* April 26, 2013, http://insidescoopsf.sfgate.com/blog/2013/04/26/michael-mina-and-the-city-attorney-office-reach-a-settlement-surrounding-health-care-surcharges.

57 Colliver, "S.F. Businesses Preparing."

58 Knight, "Not All Restaurants Back Suit."

59 Bob Egelko, "Court: City Can Make Firms Pay for Health Care," *San Francisco Chronicle,* October 1, 2008; Knight, "Not All Restaurants Back Suit."

60 E.g., Melissa Waldman, "FARINA Restaurant," *San Francisco Examiner,* October 3, 2010.

61 Bauer, "Restaurants that Forgo the Healthy San Francisco Surcharge."

62 Ben Worthen, "Menu Surcharge Can Be Misleading," *Wall Street Journal,* September 22, 2011.

63 Rachel Gordon and John Wildermuth, "Lee Signs Law Closing Loophole," *San Francisco Chronicle,* November 23, 2011.

64 San Francisco Civil Grand Jury, *Surcharges and Healthy San Francisco,* 1.

65 Stacy Finz and Paolo Lucchesi, "SF Restaurateurs Dispute City Allegations," *San Francisco Chronicle,* January 27, 2013.

66 Michael Bauer, "Park Tavern and La Folie Drop Healthy SF Service Charges," *Inside Scoop SF,* January 26, 2012, http://insidescoopsf.sfgate.com/blog/2012/01/26/park-tavern-and-la-folie-drop-healthy-sf-service-charges/.

67 Bauer, "Diners Really Don't Like the SF Surcharges."

68 Quoted in Michael Bauer, "One Last Word on Healthy San Francisco Surcharges," *Inside Scoop SF,* June 5, 2012, http://insidescoopsf.sfgate.com/blog/2012/06/05/one-last-word-on-healthy-san-francisco-surcharges/.

69 Lucchesi, "Why Restaurants Have Surcharges."

70 Bauer, "Park Tavern and La Folie."

71 Elizabeth Warren, "Elizabeth Warren on Debt Crisis, Fair Taxation," *You-Tube,* September 18, 2011, www.youtube.com/watch?v=htX2usfqMEs.

72 White House, "Remarks by the President at a Campaign Event in Roanoke, Virginia," July 13, 2012, www.whitehouse.gov/the-press-office/2012/07/13/remarks-president-campaign-event-roanoke-virginia.

73 Richard A. Oppel, "Romney Pushes 'Build That' Attack with Business Leaders," *New York Times' The Caucus Blog,* July 23, 2012, http://thecaucus.blogs.nytimes.com/2012/07/23/romney-pushes-build-that-attack-with-business-leaders/.

74 Amy Gardner, "Obama Facing Mounting Questions over 'You Didn't Build That' Remark," *Washington Post*, September 3, 2012; C.J. Hughes, "In Midtown, Taking Aim at Occupy Wall St. and Obama," *New York Times*, September 21, 2012, A26; Ashley Parker, "Romney Returns to His Mainstay: The Economy," *New York Times' The Caucus Blog*, August 22, 2012, http:// thecaucus.blogs.nytimes.com/2012/08/22/romney-returns-to-his-mainstay-the-economy.

75 Trip Gabriel, "On the Trail, Romney Runs into Some Opposition," *New York Times' The Caucus Blog*, July 19, 2012, http://thecaucus.blogs.nytimes.com/ 2012/07/19/on-the-trail-romney-runs-into-some-opposition/; Aviva Shen, "Romney's 'You Didn't Build That' Attack Ad Stars Businessman Who Received Millions in Government Money," *ThinkProgress*, July 23, 2012, http://thinkprogress.org/election/2012/07/23/570621/romneys-you-didnt-build-that-attack-ad-stars-businessman-who-received-millions-in-government-money/.

76 Luke Johnson, "Obama on 'You Didn't Build That': 'Obviously I Have Regrets for My Syntax,'" *Huffington Post*, September 6, 2012, www.huffingtonpost .com/2012/09/06/obama-you-didnt-build-that_n_1861096.html.

77 White House, "Remarks by the President."

78 Scott Brown, "Entrepreneurs Did 'Build That,'" *Politico*, August 1, 2012, www.politico.com/news/stories/0812/79269.html.

79 Paul Ryan, "Paul Ryan RNC Speech (Text, Video)," *Politico*, August 29, 2012, www.politico.com/news/stories/0812/80423.html.

80 Quoted in James Taranto, "You Didn't Sweat, He Did," *Wall Street Journal*, July 18, 2012, http://online.wsj.com/news/articles/SB10000872396390444873 204577535053434972374.

81 Rand Paul, "Rand Paul RNC Speech (Text, Video)," *Politico*, August 29, 2012, www.politico.com/news/stories/0812/80398.html.

82 Arlette Saenz, "Romney Tells California Business Roundtable He's No Career Politician," *ABC News*, July 23, 2012, http://abcnews.go.com/blogs/politics/ 2012/07/romney-tells-california-business-roundtable-hes-no-career-politician/.

83 Quoted in Shen, "Romney's 'You Didn't Build That' Attack Ad."

84 Robb Mandelbaum, "'Yes, I Did Build That,' Says Businessman – But It Turns Out He Got Some Help," *New York Times' You're the Boss Blog*, July 25, 2012, http://boss.blogs.nytimes.com/2012/07/25/yes-i-did-build-that-says-a-businessman-but-it-turns-out-he-got-some-help/.

3

States as a Series of People Exchanges

Armando Lara-Millán

[handwritten annotations: This theoretical framework has utility in understanding how states exercise power in a way they're fragmented, but I'm not convinced that people who exchange occurs to harm/privilege intent to harm certain groups]

Bourdieu and Foucault have inspired a generation of scholars interested in how states acquire and deploy symbolic power toward population management.[1] Bourdieu saw modern states as the primary repositories of symbolic power; in the words of Loveman, "through practices of classification, codification, and regulation, for example, modern states not only naturalize certain distinctions and not others, but they also help constitute particular *kinds* of people, places, and things."[2] Foucault, writing in part about the development of capitalism, remarked upon the parallel "accumulation of men," in which the emergence of concern about the health and physical well-being of the population was one of the key transformations in the late eighteenth century.[3] Thus, schools, census taking, tax lists, land surveys, birth certificates, hospitals, prisons, and welfare institutions, among many others, have all been examined as sites of the state's productive administration of lives, in which a key objective of political power is not to subdue but to create certain types of citizens, workers, and subjects. *[handwritten margin note: symbolic power; counter-point to management & social control?]*

Yet, thinking of states as unified entities that are interested in far-reaching "population management" proves challenging when one considers what states actually look like and do: states are made up of discrete public agencies and political leaders who compete for resources and often pursue disparate goals.[4] While modern democratic states are certainly fragmented, being composed of multiple, overlapping agencies vying for jurisdictional control, even the most centralized governments must coordinate action across disparate organizational bodies.[5] States also rely heavily on nonstate actors to achieve many of their goals.[6] Their fragmentation also is reflected in their varied forms of political leadership, including elected and appointed officials in legislative, judicial, and executive government; the leaders of political parties; and personnel in federal, state, and municipal levels of government.

Indeed, another prominent perspective on state agencies' activities and interests – but one that has not yet been much in dialogue with the tradition of research focused on the state as a population manager – is "public choice analysis," which has institutional fragmentation as its starting point. This paradigm – primarily the domain of economists – views state activity as characterized by discrete institutional entities engaged in competitive and uncoordinated budget-maximizing behavior.[7] All other purported concerns of interest to the state, including health, welfare, or other sites of population management, are secondary to the primary aim of budget maximization and institutional survival. Public choice perspectives would likely charge that Bourdieusian and Foucauldian analyses ignore the extent to which policy actors are located in a competitive and fragmented field.

How can a concern for the use of symbolic power in population management be reconciled with the empirical reality of the fragmented state? Being overly attentive to the discrete institutions that make up states – the myriad loosely coupled public agencies and political actors – risks losing sight of the state as a unique organizational body. States are unique, in part, because they exert coercive power to mobilize people. Thus, the question animating this chapter is: how might we attend to the sprawling, complex, and discrete administrative units that make up states yet still theorize state power and population management?

Here I theorize one dimension of state activity as a series of people exchanges. This approach requires focusing on discrete institutional agencies – including both horizontally and vertically disparate agencies and actors – engaging in struggles either to abdicate or obtain responsibility for people, caseloads, and, often, the public revenue attached to them. Political leaders and frontline workers are in constant negotiation with one another over how to classify ordinary men and women and to determine which agency might best intervene in their lives. The result is not coherent population management, in which the movement of people between state agencies is rationally coordinated. Instead, the exchange of people is a product of distinct agencies acting alone, often in conflict with other state agencies over which one will have responsibility for different categories of people.

In the analysis that follows I outline three forms of people exchanges that characterize state activity. First, I discuss the administrative exchange of populations by political leaders at higher levels of government. Political leaders, including politicians, administrative heads, their staffs, and others in charge of shaping public budgets, mobilize symbolic power to redefine target populations and reroute public funds. I explore both direct exchanges, which involve contractual agreements between agencies, and indirect exchanges, which incentivize populations to seek out different agencies of their own accord. Second, I examine the daily exchange of populations by frontline officials at lower levels of government. These state actors continuously vet individuals for their fit into different types of public agencies and create the possibility for exchanges. Finally, I explore how, in contrast to previous characterizations, frontline workers actually determine many of the possibilities for administrative decision making at higher levels of government. Higher-up political leaders can only exchange populations by relying on frontline actors' expertise, their purported ability to differentiate and classify people, and their capacity to generate budgetary savings.

I discuss these three facets relative to various historical examples, including military drafts, labor migration, and the deinstitutionalization of mental health patients in the United States, but also carry a single case study through the analysis. The case study concerns the exchange of juvenile offenders and foster children in the state of California at the turn of the twenty-first century. Drawing on extensive archival research of higher-level public budgeting of juvenile routing centers and my own research observing general frontline work, I offer examples at two levels of government – administrative policymaking and decisions made by frontline officials. The case aptly illustrates fights for classificatory control over a population and the public money attached to their care.

SYMBOLIC POWER, ADMINISTERING LIVES, AND PUBLIC CHOICE THEORY

I build the theoretical foundations for this perspective by drawing on three ways of thinking about the state and state activity: Bourdieu's analysis of the state's use of legitimate symbolic power, Foucault's work on the administration of people, and public choice theories of uncoordinated budget maximization. This distinctive mix of approaches, and the concepts that arise from it, provides the necessary theoretical tools for empirical analysis of people exchanges.

Much scholarly attention has been paid to the state as the locus par excellence of legitimate "symbolic power."[8] Symbolic power is the ability to make "appear as natural, inevitable, and thus apolitical, that which is a product of historical struggle and human invention."[9] Symbolic power is not to be confused with states' ability to marshal nationalistic ideology to inspire loyalty.[10] Instead, symbolic power operates through misrecognition, or "the appearance that no power is being wielded at all."[11] Thus, when state agencies make claims about their target populations, such claims are treated mostly as truths about those populations rather than as the product of frontline officials' discretion and decision making. Scholars inspired by this framework have studied school systems, census taking, civil registries, tax lists, land surveys, birth certificates, standardized weights and measures, product tests, product rankings, certificates of authenticity, and the law, to name a few examples, as the main vehicles by which states impose "common principles of vision and division."[12] Thus, analyses of state activity, including this one, must be attentive to the states' deployment of symbolic power, including, but not limited to, its ability to name and classify populations, as well as provide a dominant understanding of what populations are.

In dialogue with scholarly interest in the state's control of symbolic power is Foucault's influential treatment of the entry of human life into systems of political power and states' attempts to optimize and administer it. Foucault remarked that alongside the accumulation of capital in Europe in the eighteenth century there occurred a parallel "accumulation of men" in which a key objective of political power became the physical well-being of the population – to modify lives not only to ensure control, but to preserve and maintain them so as to enhance their utility. For Foucault, the state's interest in human life was twofold. One was a focus on the human body, "its disciplining, the optimization of its capability, and the attempt to integrate it into more efficient systems of economic production."[13] The other concerned population control as a whole, "its propagation, birth and death rates, level of health, life expectancy, longevity, and so forth."[14] Foucault's interest in this productive administration of lives – which he called bio-power – guided his own studies, and those of his followers, across a diverse array of sites including the family, the army, schools, and hospitals. Thus, in Foucault's view, scholars must be attentive to how states manage whole populations, and to their investment in aspects of human lives beyond economic utility.

While the ideas of "legitimate symbolic violence" and the "administration of lives" are often co-deployed, I make use of a third type of analysis almost entirely ignored in Bourdieusian and Foucauldian approaches to state power: Public choice analysis. In this approach, political actors, whether they are politicians, lobbyists, or bureaucrats, are motivated mainly by self-preservation and budget maximization, not public goods, collective goals, regulation, discipline, or state violence. Public choice analysts delineate the incentives that confront political actors, such as votes and reelection, the size of budgets under their control, and personal prestige. No matter the public issue or objective under consideration, political actors and agencies are seen as responding to this narrow set of incentives. They call attention to policy shortsightedness, in which political decision makers favor short-run returns over longer-term benefits. Thus, a key assumption in this perspective is that political actors privately make decisions in relation to these incentives, even if they contradict officially stated policy intents.

From the public choice perspective, Bourdieusian and Foucauldian analysts mistakenly assume that state activity is coordinated and long-term in orientation, ignoring the extent to which policy actors are located in a competitive and uncoordinated field. Public choice analysts maintain that state agencies and actors are less concerned about widespread investment in whole populations and more concerned about competing with one another for survival and scarce budget resources. A public choice analyst might charge that any sort of public profession of lofty goals hides privately held goals of self-preservation and budget maximization.

On the other hand, from Bourdieusian and Foucauldian perspectives, public choice analysis ignores the extent to which state agencies are heavily involved in the classification, movement, and administration of populations. State agencies are deeply intertwined with the fates of ordinary men and women, mobilizing them toward war, healthcare, labor, and any number of interventions. Hospitals, jails, militaries, schools, and child protective services are, even if uncoordinated, coherent enough to produce powerful effects on their constituencies' lives, altering life courses and mobilizing people toward particular ends. Moreover, for all their concern about budget maximization, state agencies spend much time strategizing over collective population health, producing research and reports on public health statistics, demography, crime statistics, and many other ways of thinking through population management.

Thus, if we are to propose a theory of state activity and power that takes all of these perspectives seriously, it would need to consider the fragmented nature of states and the interest of state officials in shorter-run goals and budget maximization, but also what appears to be a concern for population management and accumulation of symbolic power. I have labeled such a perspective "people exchanging," in which state actors and agencies compete to abdicate or obtain responsibility for populations and the revenue attached to them. In what follows, I break this theory down into administrative population exchange, daily population exchange, and the relationship between administrative and daily exchanges.

THE ADMINISTRATIVE EXCHANGE OF POPULATIONS

Exchanging populations at higher levels of government refers to the work of political leaders – politicians, administrative heads, their staffs, and others in charge of shaping public budgets and agendas. The evidence for population exchanges often can be found in the minutiae of files, orders, memos, statistics, reports, petitions, and meetings of these officials. Such documents detail how political leaders come to reframe target populations, their political intent, and subsequent strategies.[15]

On this higher plane of policymaking, officials may espouse one of two sets of objectives. On the one hand, there are political leaders who seek to decrease their responsibility for populations, perhaps because they are losing funding and legitimacy, or because a population has proven difficult to manage. Often, in these situations, policymakers find that scrutiny or accountability over the treatment of a population by a particular agency creates legal problems, bad publicity, or too much administrative uncertainty. On the other hand, there are political leaders who seek to increase their responsibilities. These officials seek legitimacy for new policy domains or old ones that have lost it. In these instances, redefinition of particular caseloads, their needs, and appropriate interventions might also come with new sources of public funds. The resulting dynamic between state leaders, some of whom seek to abdicate responsibility and some of whom seek to gain it, propels the exchange or shifting of populations between public agencies. While state leaders may publicly claim they are exchanging a population to bring their treatment in line with the public's conception of deservingness (e.g., to treat deserving clients with more empathy, or to treat unworthy clients more harshly), privately they may simply be motivated by the desire to bolster their reelection chances, renew public budgets through taxation, give new purpose to failing public agencies, or justify public institutions as ends in themselves.

There are numerous telltale signs of population exchanges. Exchanges are normally precipitated by the gathering of experts, the convening of public hearings, and consensus building about how best to characterize a problem population and intervene in their lives. Crisis events that gain media attention may compel political leaders and public agencies to convey that they are thinking about old problems in new ways, when, in fact, they are abandoning or capturing populations. Scholars should locate these instances and delve into the archival record surrounding them. Private memos between politicians, administrators, and staff that discuss strategy about pushing through legislation often reveal political intent that differs from that which is publicly stated. Scholars might also compare public gatherings and committees of experts to see how the rhetoric and framings of populations change as political leaders address the same challenges in new ways. These moments may reveal political leaders in the process of formulating new content with which to frame a population that they aim to exchange.

Administrative exchanges of populations can be documented as direct or indirect exchanges. Direct exchanges involve explicit agreements or contracts and can be detected in public documents. One instructive example is the case of juvenile offenders during the last three decades of the twentieth century in the California juvenile justice system.[16] The case is characterized by the periodic renegotiation of responsibility for juvenile offenders between state and local governments. The exchange of juveniles always required the garnering of political support, trade-offs between state and local politicians, and, at times, legal action by courts to force different public agencies to take responsibility for the often costly and difficult-to-manage population. While the shifting was always accompanied by public proclamations that juvenile offenders could be rehabilitated more effectively in a particular branch or level of government, the private reasons were always the same: political leaders were seeking ways to cut costs or obtain new sources of funding. Occasionally some new funding source for juveniles appeared from federal levels of government or the public became motivated to approve new taxes, and political leaders would become interested in reobtaining responsibility for certain classes of juveniles.

What is crucial to this case is that these private reasons for exchange (i.e., the desire to obtain new funding or to shed the difficult work of caring for juveniles) occurred alongside a much more public discussion of the official classifications of these juveniles, what sorts of risks they posed to the public, and theories of how best to transform them into noncriminal adults. At various times, officials at the state level made claims that this group of juveniles was violent and dangerous, and therefore was better housed in state facilities considered to be more secure and punitive and built to handle a higher grade of offender. At other times, when overcrowding swelled in state institutions and housing such juveniles proved to be too costly, state officials began to claim they would be better off in county facilities that were closer to their homes and loved ones. When public funding arrangements changed, experts could always be reconvened and these arguments could be reversed and used to shift the population back again.

Another instructive case is the recent explosion of contractual agreements between subnational state agencies with regard to the international trafficking of temporary laborers. In these arrangements, one set of state officials essentially agrees to sell the rights to large swaths of people – usually highly contingent workers – and another group of state officials agrees to grant those workers temporary work visas. One example is the delivery of Madagascan workers to various Middle Eastern countries in order to sell their labor to private households. Before a military coup in 2009, Madagascar maintained a productive manufacturing sector, supported by trade agreements facilitated by the International Monetary Fund (IMF) and the United States, which employed a large segment of the Madagascan population. After the coup, these international trade agreements were terminated and Madagascar's unemployment and poverty rates, especially among young women, soared. At a loss for options, the new government in Madagascar facilitated labor agreements with several Middle Eastern countries and thousands of workers, mostly young women, were contracted to employment agencies to work in private homes. Official agreements to exchange this population across international boundaries were only possible once state leaders moved to recast the female workers as more fit for domestic labor than for the manufacturing sector. The negotiation over what to do with contingent workers in Madagascar and other parts of the world continues.[17]

However, more often the exchanging of people between agencies occurs indirectly. Indirect exchanges are difficult to document, as they do not come with explicit agreements between agencies. Instead, state officials act to incentivize populations to seek out other agencies of their own accord. For instance, political decision makers can repurpose public budgets or create new policy domains that encourage populations to act in ways that make them eligible for these new public projects. As a consequence, state officials can indirectly shape lines of action that, over time, will gradually attract populations to these new state projects.

An important example is the closure of long-term mental health facilities in the United States during the 1960s and the later increase of mentally ill inmates in local jails in the 1980s. There was no explicit agreement to directly transfer this group of people between mental institutions and jails. Once released from long-term health facilities at the state level, mentally ill people slowly became attractive targets of criminal justice institutionalization. In some cases, criminal justice leaders, looking to increase their responsibilities and to justify enormous public expenses, advocated thinking about this group of people in new ways. One result was passage of laws that criminalized mental illness. In other places, the explosion of public funding for jails and police patrols at the local level made it more likely that such individuals would be found and incarcerated. In effect, this major population shift was not outlined or planned between two agencies, but evolved as one set of state agents attempted to decrease their responsibilities while others sought to increase theirs.[18]

Another example of indirect exchange is military conscription. As Kestnbaum explores in Chapter 12, the entry of ordinary men and women into war, both as soldiers and logistical support workers and as victims, transformed the nature of modern states. Yet, beyond being catalysts for state-building endeavors, wars might also be interpreted as opportunities for state agents to repurpose problem populations. In the United States in the 1940s, for instance, in the midst of a continuing economic downturn, a military draft offered state agents a new way to think about ordinary men and women – people who, previously, had been seen as dependent on public welfare. State agents created an indirect draw: citizens themselves saw an opportunity in the military, began to impute new attributes to themselves (such as identifying with a war effort), and sought out employment with military agencies. Later, the demobilization of soldiers from war – which required imagination and work on the part of administrators and frontline workers about the types of attributes they could assign to ex-soldiers – led to the expansion of social welfare and other peacetime institutions. Women too were funneled from war industry to domestic work. The full implications of these population exchanges were not foreseen: when a military agency institutes a draft and begins vetting citizens who are fit to soldier, it does so without the knowledge of where such individuals might have otherwise ended up. This vast exchange of people required extensive institution building, involving direct contracting of people into new state projects as well as indirect incentives to attract individuals toward the endeavor of war.[19]

The concept of an indirect exchange departs from public choice theory. What makes an exchange indirect is the lack of coordination between different agencies and domains of the state. In cases where state agencies and leaders seek to abdicate responsibility for a certain group of people, they have little knowledge of where those people might end up. In cases where state agencies and leaders seek to bring more individuals under their purview, they might have a limited sense of which institutions had previously dealt with the population. In other words, the exchanging (or indirect shift) of people between agencies is often not a planned management strategy, coordinated between loosely coupled branches of government. Instead, some agencies seek to renege on their commitments to populations, while others seek to capture new populations.

THE DAILY EXCHANGE OF TARGET POPULATIONS

The daily exchange of populations refers to the work of frontline public employees who "interact directly with individual citizens in the course of their jobs."[20] Police, nurses, welfare caseworkers, property tax assessors, teachers, military recruiters, and thousands more work on a daily basis to vet, classify, and assign public statuses to ordinary men and women so that state agencies might properly act upon them. Examples are numerous: military processing personnel decide which citizens are fit for soldiering; doctors decide which returning soldiers are eligible for ongoing mental health services; police officers decide whether to arrest, to release, or even to send the people they encounter to hospitals; and welfare case workers decide who is eligible for public aid and who is not.

What is it that frontline officials specifically do that results in the exchanging of people between institutions? Does the work of frontline officials have an internal logic and does it vary in significant ways? Sociologists studying "street-level bureaucrats" and "people-processing institutions" in the 1980s are instructive here.

The political work that frontline agents do can be identified in their conversations with, assessments of, and reports about clients. Such conversations and assessments contain much information about the intentions of state policy – what sorts of individual attributes state agencies seek to ignore or emphasize and what those attributes tell us about agencies' goals in exchanging populations. Frontline officials "teach political lessons contributing to future political expectations, as well as socialize citizens to expectations of government services and place in community."[21] Auyero writes, "in their apparent ordinariness, state practices provide the poor with political education or daily crash courses in the workings of power."[22] Empirical focus can and should be placed on these relational practices that link daily state operations with people's lives.[23]

To understand the political work of frontline workers we must examine how they deal with and account for the uncertainty involved in the processing of individuals. Prottas showed that the primary aim of front-line officials is to confer public status upon individuals, assigning to them case characteristics and thus turning them into clients so that state agencies can properly act upon them.[24] When frontline officials encounter individuals they try to summarize the person's complex experience and biography so that others in public agencies can easily interpret them. As such, any assignment of case characteristics to complex individuals necessarily emphasizes certain attributes and omits or deemphasizes others. "Bureaucracies cannot deal with the complexities and ambiguities that go into a complete human being, rather they must categorize a person in terms of a limited subset of attributes or characteristics."[25]

When frontline officials engage in the messy business of classifying individuals for their institutional fit there is a great deal of uncertainty involved. A useful example is the multifarious character of frontline classification in juvenile holding facilities. Juveniles are brought to such facilities by a variety of agencies, including the police, probation unit, family services, welfare agencies, and hospitals. These facilities are staffed by professionals whose job is to assess juveniles' medical and mental health needs, criminal threat, fitness for foster care, relationship to parents and family members, and, among many others, continued risk of victimization. Professionals face the complex task of determining how best to characterize the social problems faced by each of these children: are they in danger, are they a danger to others, are they better off or is society better off if they stay with their family or are placed in a foster family, and are they fit for scarce spots in public institutional facilities? At its core, there is a great deal of uncertainty in the frontline decision-making process. Professionals push individuals to identify the immediate circumstances or contexts that led them to an institutional facility. In contrast, when individuals are willing or able to explain at all, they often convey ambivalent information about their circumstances – in a hypothetical example, a juvenile might describe membership in peer groups, gangs, or families for whom they feel both loyalty and distance, having been victimized but also having received care. Some troubling contexts may also simply be temporary and the professional must determine the type and degree of intervention that is necessary.[26]

One result of the missing information and complex social biographies of incoming juveniles is that professionals often act on the basis of "hunches" or guesswork, and inevitably must employ discretion. Routing outcomes can be affected by the nature of the conversation between a potential beneficiary and the professional, wider societal beliefs or stereotypes about the nature of beneficiaries and other sources of information that contribute to contingent and haphazard outcomes. Institutional resources to house vulnerable populations such as needy juveniles are scarce; there are not sufficient spaces in foster care, juvenile detention camps, or transitional housing with appropriate mental health and therapeutic services. Such scarcity of resources can place pressure on classification officers to come up with alternative characterizations, assigning new kinds of attributes to incoming beneficiaries and making it possible to place them elsewhere. In some cases, for instance, juvenile wards might be temporarily sent to juvenile detention centers that are paid for and run by local probation departments, or they might be sent to transitional housing paid for and run by the health and welfare departments. These routings have major consequences for both the individuals being routed and the public budgets that must pay for them.

Frontline officials are also involved in the direct work of processing transfers of people between nearby public agencies. Emerson describes the work of frontline officials as largely consisting of the continual negotiation and exchange of other people-processing institutions' clients.[27] Key to the process of what he called "referrals" is developing "inter-organizational knowledge" with other public agencies about the acceptable reasons for a referral, as well as building the mutual trust that allows both to accept that those reasons are indeed true. When police bring juveniles they suspect require mental health intervention to a transitional home with mental health services, medical professionals will vet these individuals and either accept them or not. Such points of contact constitute the daily work of people exchange and are sites of political activity. These transfers determine which agencies will be responsible for their care and, most importantly, which agencies will assume budgetary responsibility, paying from their own budgets and collecting any public revenues available for that person's care. Thus, in large part, the work of frontline officials is picking which attributes of people to emphasize or to deemphasize, assigning a public status to those people, and routing them toward some public agency that can appropriately intervene in their lives.

Like higher-level officials, frontline workers also indirectly affect the exchanging of people by assigning enduring characteristics and legal statuses to persons they encounter. These statuses persist even after individuals leave the purview of public agencies. An important example is individuals who are convicted of criminal felonies in the contemporary United States. This legal "mark" carries lifelong consequences that structure their interactions with other public agencies even after being released from correctional facilities. Such individuals are likely to experience limits on their ability to work for public agencies or to vote in elections, and often will be constantly entangled with probation and parole institutions for the rest of their lives. These are not direct exchanges of individuals to other public agencies because they involve no explicit agreements or contracts. When lawyers and judges work to convict individuals of crimes they do not make agreements with welfare institutions over how such individuals will be dealt with in the future. Instead, other public agencies make use of legal statuses in making their own decisions about the provision of services.

THE RELATIONSHIP BETWEEN DAILY AND ADMINISTRATIVE PEOPLE EXCHANGE

Much of what we think about the relationship between political leaders and frontline officials is from Lipsky's early work on street-level bureaucrats.[28] Lipsky argued that frontline officials mattered because they are the implementers of policy, showing that policy developed at higher levels of government is altered a great deal by local officials who decide when and how to enforce rules. Essentially, Lipsky's characterization of this relationship was a one-way street: policy originates from the top and makes its way into local agencies of the state, and then frontline actors implement that policy in ways that ultimately alter it.

In fact, the relationship between frontline officials and higher-level decision makers is much more complicated. Streeck and Thelen point out that "rule-takers" (those frontline implementers of rules) can also force "rule-makers" (those who formulate rules) to change, alter, or create new rules. "[Rule-takers'] continuous probing of the boundary between legal and illegal is part of the interpretative struggle that begins as soon as a rule is laid down: it is one mechanism by which the meaning of a rule is both clarified and modified ('worked out') in practice. Favorable discoveries made by adventurous interpretative entrepreneurs may spread fast among the subjects of a regime, forcing rule makers to revise the law in order to restore it."[29] That is, frontline actors not only alter rules during rule implementation, but they can also push political and administrative leaders into new rule formulations.

Beyond Streeck and Thelen's addendum, the relationship between frontline officials and rule-makers takes on three additional forms. First, people exchanging requires that political leaders make a claim that frontline workers can rationally exchange caseloads on some kind of scientific or objective basis. When high-level political leaders create policy that, directly or indirectly, exchanges a population between agencies, they assert that they can effectively and rationally decide which individuals deserve to be transferred. That is, political leaders must be able to claim that their frontline officials can tell the difference between a patient and an inmate, or a worthy public aid recipient and an unworthy one, or a returning soldier who deserves ongoing mental health care and one who does not. These claims require a belief in the state agencies' capacities to gather "truths" about such individuals and confidence in professional expertise to appropriately assign new truths about them.

The uncertainty and haphazardness endemic to the frontline process of classifying individuals must be obscured and minimized during the process of public budgeting at higher levels of decision making. Political leaders can justify to the public, to courts, and to other interested parties that they are indeed assigning people to appropriate institutions, treating them with the appropriate interventions, and turning away those who are unfit for interventions. They must be able to tell the public they have professional, educated people who can implement rational rules to vet and differentiate populations. These sorts of claims appear whenever political leaders attempt a population exchange. ↓ *discretion is not rational*

Second, people exchanging requires frontline workers to gather specific information about reasonable ways that high-level political leaders can exchange a population in one direction or another. That is, political leaders rely on the real-world organizational knowledge of frontline officials to gather ideas about how populations might reasonably be shifted around. Because frontline actors know the most about the people who need to be repurposed, higher-level officials often request their presence and expertise in planning meetings. Frontline officials often appear in strategy sessions, at committee hearings, and in working groups that study a problem population, and are asked to submit recommendations to leaders about how to better intervene in people's lives. From their practical knowledge about populations, frontline officials influence how political leaders come to create policy that shifts populations toward some other agency. Without the reasonable knowledge of frontline officials in planning meetings, high-level public officials would have no basis for choosing to shift populations in one direction or another.

To return to an example from our case study, consider the role those frontline medical professionals played in budgetary decisions to fund medical treatment of juvenile offenders. In the deliberations between local government and state level agencies about where best to house juvenile offenders, they needed to discover and understand links between mental health and criminal behavior. During each of the negotiations between state and local officials either to capture or to abdicate responsibility for this caseload, officials engaged in internal and public meetings and created planning committees that mobilized the expertise of medical professionals. It was the frontline medical workers directly working with this juvenile population who, in part, provided the argumentative content and practical descriptions mobilized to steer responsibility for the caseload to whatever position suited the respective agency's needs.[30]

Third, frontline work creates conditions for general parsimony or more conservative budgeting at higher-level political decision making. Annually, higher-level officials must make budget projections for staffing, salaries, supplies, and other resource expenditures required to service caseloads. These cost estimates are based on a myriad of predictive and probabilistic numbers including, among many others, projected caseload growth or retractions. Key is that political leaders rely on frontline officials' discretion to produce undercounts of caseloads. Frontline officials – due to budgetary pressure, constraints on their time, and the complex social biographies of potential recipients – normally err on the side of stringent application of qualification rules.[31]

The cost-saving nature of this relationship becomes clear if one considers the way that the haphazardness and discretionary nature of frontline work disappear once it is included in higher-level budgetary decision making. The classification work of frontline officials is often anything but objective. Yet, officials assume that frontline professionals can rationally and accurately tell the difference between those who need or are entitled to a service and those who do not or are not. That is, the budget only has to fund services for those individuals determined to be in need by frontline actors and not those who are victims of the uncertain world of frontline processing. Frontline officials provide the public with the perception that the state is fulfilling its duties while, in practice, they disqualify a non-trivial number of people who, in reality, are not that different from people selected to receive resources. By implication, if the uncertainties of the frontline, daily work of the state were included into budgetary projections, governments would need to fund expanded services in order to account for individuals who slip through the cracks. Instead, political leaders can publicly claim they are fulfilling duties while many individuals go untreated or misallocated. The expansion of diagnostic and classificatory frontline personnel is a telltale sign that higher-level officials are

[handwritten margin note: or that it's not the duty of the state?]

working to shift populations from one arm of the state to another and should be the subject of inquiry.

CONCLUSION: PEOPLE EXCHANGING AND STATE TRANSFORMATION

Conceptualizing the relationship between states and subject populations as a series of people exchanges between the state's component parts implies that states do not, in the first order, seek to punish their populations, to make war, to redistribute wealth, to help business, or to carry on any of their other publicly named activities. Instead, state actors seek to reconstitute their agencies and departments through the exchange of people and then, once they have found a viable exchange, create public framings that justify or rationalize those exchanges post hoc. This is a perspective that, in part, views the public naming of state endeavors as "games" or distractions from the real purpose of exchanging populations in order to reconstitute an agency or department. In short, the efforts of state actors to create differences between soldiers, inmates, and the sick are outcomes of state agencies working to relinquish or to obtain responsibility for people.

How does people exchanging relate to the three theoretical perspectives laid out in the beginning of this chapter? Public choice theory usefully highlights how states are actually made up of competing agencies and actors that seek to maximize their own budgets and resources. It fails, however, to recognize states' vast involvement in the mobilization of populations toward specific ends – a mobilization requiring symbolic power to classify, name, and go largely unquestioned. At higher levels of decision making, people exchanging can take the form of direct, contractual exchanges between agencies or it can take an indirect form – creating conditions that incentivize populations to seek out new agencies of their own accord. Public choice theory makes no room for the latter, an activity that produces unanticipated caseload growth or retraction unbeknownst to political leaders and administrators. Foucault draws attention to the interests of modern states in population control and investment. However, such population management ignores the extent to which exchanges of people largely take place in the contingent, microsociological world of frontline classificatory work. While agencies are in the business of exchanging whole populations, it is frontline personnel who haphazardly emphasize, deemphasize, or assign new attributes to bodies. Ultimately, the outcome of discretionary frontline work trickles its way

[handwritten margin note: Not sure that I buy this]

[handwritten margin note: Wouldn't a viable exchange depend on punishment, accomplishing, redistribution, etc?]

up into the hallways and meetings of higher-level decision makers. These officials must then formulate new post hoc rationalizations, budgetary projections, or other rule changes necessary for the exchange of caseloads. In other words, population management is not achieved through a grand master plan whereby "the state" acts on unified long-term plans, but instead is accomplished piecemeal through unlinked exchanges of people between agencies.

This new way of thinking about state activity is fruitful because it solves some of the pitfalls of each of these three perspectives. On the one hand, we gain leverage on the state's interest in accumulating symbolic power and population management without sacrificing the empirical reality that states are uncoordinated and made up of agencies and actors that are often in competition with one another. In this perspective, state actors, in their efforts to obtain new funds and otherwise compete with other agencies, go about expanding (or sometimes abdicating) symbolic power over caseloads. On the other hand, we complicate and add depth to our collective focus on the state's accumulation of symbolic power and interest in population management. These activities, while important innovations in modern states, are only part of a more complex array of budgetary exchanges between state actors. In short, population control and accumulation of symbolic power are compatible with the public choice perspective that emphasizes uncoordinated and budget-maximizing state agencies.

Much of the present volume and wider scholarship on the state is and has been devoted to studying state transformations. Indeed, in this volume Orloff suggests that policy outcomes themselves are essentially imprints of destructive and constructive social processes. Many of the contributions in this volume focus on transformations in the character of the state itself, such as transitions from empires to nation-states (Chapter 13), the entry of the masses into warfare (Chapter 12), and the shifting boundaries of the state's relationship to private organizations in the first half of the twentieth century (Chapter 1). Others focus on astonishing changes in policy focus, such as shifts in policies toward women's paid labor in the rich democracies (Chapter 5), the shift to explicitly race-based social policy in Brazil (Chapter 8), or the enforcement of African-American civil and political rights in the United States (Chapter 7).

It might be tempting to tie the present analysis to the current and ongoing transformation of the political economy through policy and austerity measures inspired by neoliberalism. Governments across the globe are gutting their public sectors, selling off public goods to private enterprise, and engaging in "structural adjustment" and catastrophic budget cuts. For instance, Peck explores how austerity pressures on state governments in the United States are currently leading to a kind of "de-stateness," in which the contracting out of functions, bleeding of public coffers, and shedding of responsibilities produce a general decline in state authority.[32]

In my view, there are shortcomings in such a characterization of people exchange. When state agencies and actors look to jettison or to obtain responsibility for new groups of people, they assign such groups attributes that make them attractive and eligible for new kinds of interventions. Finding the content of these new attributes – that is, the specific character of a new quality – is an imaginative and deliberative process involving consultation between high-level political leaders, frontline actors, and all manner of technical experts and advisors. Such deliberations often lead to new definitional categories and to new opportunities for state interventions. Ultimately, such exchanges can transform the agencies themselves, changing their missions and organizational identities, altering their responsibilities, or making them replaceable. The seeds of transformation are found within the very mechanism of assigning new attributes to people and caseloads. Over time, when continuously linked together, such exchanges, and the new institutional qualities that emerge from them, can add up to larger transformations in policy focus and state character.[33]

Thus, contained within the elements of people exchange are the ingredients for state change. All the cases of transformation examined in this volume – whether it be upholding civil and political rights for African-Americans, instituting race-based policy, or promoting women's employment and men's care work – require the work of frontline actors generating information about the actual people involved, sharing this information with higher-ups, and figuring out which agencies might be responsible for a sudden flood of people with new identities, attributes, and possibilities for state interventions.

Notes

1 I wish to thank Kimberly Morgan, Marion Fourcade, Damon Mayrl, Sarah Quinn, Elizabeth Onasch, Forrest Stuart, Ann Orloff, Camila Gripp, and the participants in the "Many Hands of the State" conference (University of Chicago, May 2014) for extremely helpful feedback.
2 Mara Loveman, "The Modern State and the Primitive Accumulation of Symbolic Power," *American Journal of Sociology* 110, no. 6 (2005): 1655.

3 Michel Foucault, Blandine Barrett Kriegel, Anne Thalamy, François Beguin, and Bruno Fortier, *Les Machines à Guérir: Aux Origins de l'Hôpital Modern* (Paris: L'institut d'Environnement, 1976); Michel Foucault, "The Politics of Health in the Eighteenth Century," in *Michel Foucault: Power/Knowledge: Selected Interveiews and Other Writings 1972–1977*, ed. Colin Gordon (Brighton: Harvester Press, 1980).

4 Joel S. Migdal, *State in Society: Studying How States and Societies Transform and Constitute One Another* (Cambridge: Cambridge University Press, 2001); Edward O. Laumann and David Knoke, *The Organizational State: Social Choice in National Policy Domains* (Madison: University of Wisconsin Press, 1987).

5 See for instance, the classic description of the civil bureaucracy, the Nazi Party, the armed forces, and the business sector in Germany before and during World War II, Raul Hilberg, *The Destruction of the European Jews* (New York: Holmes & Meier, 1985).

6 Kimberly J. Morgan and Andrea L. Campbell, *The Delegated Welfare State: Medicare, Markets, and the Governance of Social Policy* (New York: Oxford University Press, 2011); Elisabeth S. Clemens, "Lineages of the Rube Goldberg State: Building and Blurring Public Programs, 1900–1940," in *Rethinking Political Institutions: The Art of the State*, ed. Ian Shapiro, Stephen Skowronek, and Daniel Galvin (New York: New York University Press, 2006); Chapter 1.

7 Dennis C. Mueller, "Public Choice: An Introduction," in *Encyclopedia of Public Choice*, ed. Charles K. Rowley and Friedrich Schneider (New York: Kluwer Academic Publishers, 2004); Viktor Vanberg, "Public Choice from the Perspective of Sociology," in *Encyclopedia of Public Choice*, eds. Charles K Rowley and Friedrich Schneider (New York: Kluwer Academic Publishers, 2004); Paul B. Stephan III, "Barbarians Inside the Gate: Public Choice Theory and International Economic Law," *American University Journal of International Law & Policy* 10, no. 1 (1994).

8 Loveman, "The Modern State"; James Scott, *Seeing Like a State* (New Haven: Yale University Press, 1998); Philip S. Gorski, *The Disciplinary Revolution: Calvinism and the Rise of the State in Early Modern Europe* (Chicago: University of Chicago Press, 2003); George Steinmetz, *State/Culture: State Formation after the Cultural Turn* (Ithaca: Cornell University Press, 1999); John Torpey, *The Invention of the Passport: Surveillance, Citizenship and the State* (Cambridge: Cambridge University Press, 2000).

9 Loveman, "The Modern State," 1655.

10 Eric Hobsbawm, *Nations and Nationalism since 1780* (Cambridge: Cambridge University Press, 1990); Anthony Giddens, *The Nation-State and Violence* (Berkeley: University of California Press, 1987).

11 Loveman, "The Modern State," 1655; Pierre Bourdieu and Loic Wacquant, *An Invitation to Reflexive Sociology* (Chicago: University of Chicago Press, 1992).

12 Pierre Bourdieu, "Rethinking the State: Genesis and Structure of the Bureaucratic Field," *Sociological Theory* 12, no. 1 (1994): 13.

13 Andrea Mennicken and Peter Miller, "Michel Foucault and the Administering of Lives," in *Oxford Handbook of Sociology, Social Theory and Organization*

Studies: Contemporary Currents, eds. Paul Adler, Paul Du Gay, Glen Morgan, and Mike Reed (Oxford: Oxford University Press, 2014), 16–17.

14 Mennicken and Miller, "Michel Foucault," 17.

15 The redefinition of target populations is an important part of the policymaking process. Schneider and Ingram define the social construction of target populations as "cultural characterizations or popular images of persons or groups whose behavior and well-being are affected by public policy. These characterizations are normative and evaluative, portraying groups in positive or negative terms through symbolic language, metaphors and stories." Such constructions are important to the political process because they set forth "problems to be solved, goals to be achieved, and identify people whose behavior is linked to the achievement of desired ends." See Anne Schneider and Helen Ingram, "Social Construction of Target Populations: Implications for Politics and Policy," *American Political Science Review* 87, no. 2 (1993): 335.

16 This analysis comes from my reading of archival materials surrounding the fight to open Los Angeles County's MacLaren center – a holding/clearinghouse facility for probation, foster care, and abused juveniles – with county, state, and federal funds to the decision to close the facility in 2003. The materials were taken from the donated papers of a Los Angeles County Board of Supervisor held at the Huntington Library, in Pasadena, CA: the papers of Edmund D. Edelman, 1953–1994 (bulk 1974–1994). The relevant materials can be found in the following boxes and files: 127:5–143:5 (especially 140:2–141:1 concerning the MacLaren Children's Center, 1980–1994); 351:5–351:8; 678:13–679:4; and 1024:4–1025:2. See also John R. Sutton, *Stubborn Children: Controlling Delinquency in the United States, 1640–1981* (Berkeley: University of California Press, 1988).

17 My understanding of the trafficking of Madagascar's workers is taken from Aaron Ross, "Why Are Thousands of Malagasy Women Being Trafficked to Abusive Jobs in the Middle East?" *Nation*, April 15, 2014. Another recent explosion of officially organized and sanctioned trafficking of contingent workers is the case of the fracking oil boom in Texas. See SanJuhi Verma, *Black Gold, Brown Labor: The Legalization of Indentured Work through the Transnational Migration Industry*, PhD diss., Department of Sociology, University of Chicago (2012).

18 There are nationally representative data confirming a relationship between mental health deinstitutionalization and criminal justice institutionalization (see Fred E. Markowitz, "Psychiatric Hospital Capacity, Homelessness, and Crime and Arrest Rates," *Criminology* 44, no. 1 (2006); Bernard E. Harcourt, "From the Asylum to the Prison: Rethinking the Incarceration Revolution," *Texas Law Review* 84, no. 7 (2006)). However, the history of mental health facility closures is complex and there is no clear evidence of direct transfer of the mentally ill into carceral facilities (see David Mechanic and David A. Rochefort, "Deinstitutionalization: An Appraisal of Reform," *Annual Review of Sociology* 16 (1990)).

19 My understanding of how the poor were transformed into soldiers in the United States during World War II is largely drawn from the analysis of

Mettler and Katznelson. The authors also describe the subsequent transition of soldiers into being middle-class citizens upon their return home. See Suzanne Mettler, *Soldiers & Citizens: The G.I. Bill and the Making of the Greatest Generation* (New York: Oxford University Press, 2005); Ira Katznelson, *When Affirmative Action Was White: An Untold History of Racial Inequality in Twentieth Century America* (New York: W.W. Norton & Co, 2005).

20 Michael Lipsky, *Street-Level Bureaucracy: Dilemmas of the Individual in Public Services* (New York: Russell Sage Foundation, 1980), 3.

21 Lipsky, *Street-Level Bureaucracy*, 4.

22 Javier Auyero, *Patients of the State* (Durham: Duke University Press, 2012): 7.

23 Lynne Haney, "Homeboys, Babies, Men in Suits: The State and the Reproduction of Male Dominance," *American Sociological Review* 61, no. 5 (1996): 759–778.

24 Jeffrey M. Prottas, *People Processing: The Street-Level Bureaucrat in Public Service Bureaucracies* (Lexington: Lexington Books, 1979).

25 Prottas, *People Processing*, 85.

26 My understanding of the assessment work of frontline workers is taken from an extensive report and memorandum of understanding between various agencies about the aforementioned Los Angeles County's MacLaren center. The report marvelously details the complex task of processing juveniles that arrive from a variety of agencies (e.g., Department of Children and Family Services, Department of Mental Health, Department of Health Services, probation, and Department of Education) and who have no clear destination. The documents are located in the Yvonne Brathwaite Burke Papers, Special Collections, University of Southern California Library, and in the box/files: 429:13. I have also buttressed this analysis with my own description of frontline workers acting on the basis of hunches, guesswork, and discretion in an overcrowded public emergency department. See Armando Lara-Millán, "Public Emergency Room Overcrowding in the Era of Mass Imprisonment," *American Sociological Review* 79, no. 5 (2014): 875–77.

27 Robert M. Emerson, "Case Processing and Interorganizational Knowledge: Detecting the 'Real Reasons' for Referrals," *Social Problems* 38, no. 2 (1991): 198–212.

28 Lipsky, *Street-level Bureaucracy*. See also Wolfgang Streeck and Kathy Thelen, *Beyond Continuity: Institutional Change in Advanced Political Economies* (New York: Oxford University Press, 2005, 14–15) on rule-makers and rule-takers.

29 Streeck and Thelen, *Beyond Continuity*, 15.

30 Papers of Edmund D. Edelman, 1953–1994 (bulk 1974–1994), as cited earlier.

31 Prottas, *People Processing*.

32 Jamie Peck, "Pushing Austerity: State Failure, Municipal Bankruptcy, and the Crises of Fiscal Federalism in the USA," *Cambridge Journal of Regions, Economy & Society* 7, no. 1 (2014).

33 This perspective is animated by a new strand of historical institutionalism that theorizes endogenous forms of institutional change that takes place gradually

over the course of many years. Scholars of path dependence have mostly conceptualized institutional change as originating from "exogenous shocks" or outside political and economic happenings that upset the balance of power among stakeholders. Such an approach has difficulty explaining change in the absence of exogenous shocks. See James Mahoney and Kathleen Thelen, "A Theory of Gradual Institutional Change," in *Explaining Institutional Change: Ambiguity, Agency, and Power*, eds. James Mahoney and Kathleen Thelen (Cambridge: Cambridge University Press, 2010).

4

State Metrology

The Rating of Sovereigns and the Judgment of Nations

Marion Fourcade[*]

INTRODUCTION: THE MANY HANDS ON THE STATE

As Pierre Bourdieu pointed out in a three-year course at the Collège de France (1989–1992),[1] the state is the single most important institution organizing the most mundane aspects of our everyday existence. Take time and space. It is the state, under its various forms, that regulates basic elements of temporality – the definition of the legal workday, the school calendar, national holidays, winter and summer hours, and expectations about the daily synchronicity of individual lives. Government action shapes meaningful spatial divisions, too. Administrative and legal rules monitor which aspects of our individual life experiences are in fact public and which may remain private. And states also count, measure, categorize, and sort people and things, thereby producing social identities such as occupations or professions, racial or ethnic groups, and classes – to give just a few illustrations.[2] They do so by constituting legitimate categories of actors (state officials) whose *raison d'être* is to recognize, sanction, authorize, and require in ways that are (for the most part) imperative and unquestioned. According to Bourdieu, who was twisting the words of Max Weber and Norbert Elias but really building on the work of Emile Durkheim, the state is the locus par excellence of "legitimate symbolic violence." By eliciting and coordinating forms of affective solidarity, and by providing those who are subject to its rule with a sort of logical and moral compass, the state operates as a powerful instrument of social integration.[3] The school system, the law, and all public rituals are the main vehicles of this imperceptible process by which the state inculcates principles of vision and division of the social world and their associated evaluative (i.e., moral) frames.[4]

Seen from this vantage point, it is sometimes easy to forget that nation-states are also themselves the objects of considerable symbolic violence. The cultural–organizational nebula that Meyer and his colleagues call "world society"[5] has tasked itself with the rationalization of what states "must" be and do in order to be considered legitimate sovereign entities. Universalized ideals of state effectiveness compel countries to expand their extractive capacities and implement budgetary or regulatory policies that sometimes come at a great financial cost. Recognition by peers or admission in some supranational institutions, such as the European Union, is predicated on states guaranteeing certain kinds of rights. Metrics and indicators proliferate as a second-order form of control, arraying sovereign entities along some dimension of economic or social best practice.[6] There are national indicators for human rights, for freedom, for ease of doing business, for transparency, for human development, for rule of law. There are hundreds of aggregated economic, social, political, and environmental measures that flatten qualitative differences and allow for neat country rankings and heat maps. Metrics and commensuration also imply comparisons, that is, rankings and hierarchies. Finally, hierarchies carry implicit moral injunctions: international experts and domestic policymakers express concerns and devise plans for the country to move up the ladder, implicitly accepting the externally imposed symbolic order as an internal guide.

States, in other words, have many hands *on* them. They are labeled, evaluated, classified, graded, ranked, praised, or disciplined from without, by many different kinds of actors with a rationalizing, ideological, or economic purpose – international institutions, experts from various professions, social movements, philanthropies, and private companies. States are not the only targets of metrological and categorizing fevers: the modern economy and society are filled with comparisons, rankings, and certification systems that measure, benchmark, and thereby regulate the behavior and performance of individuals and organizations.[7] Nation-state–level metrics have a different flavor, however, because states "represent" social collectives and thus *stand in* for more than themselves. As Durkheim, again, put it, the state "is not the brain that *creates* the unity of the organism [i.e., society], but it *expresses* it, setting its seal upon it."[8] That is, the state not only *literally* emanates from a social collective through a process of political "representation," it also *stands in, symbolically*, for that collective.

Measures of the state are thus always implicitly gauging society, too, operating a metrological reduction of collective histories and their attendant representations. In short, the rating and scoring of states reflects on society by encoding certain perceived characteristics of the nation into a simplified categorical framework. Consequently, the measures, like all representations, come back to touch society: they enter its very constitution and identification by others. Citizens partake emotionally in the institutionalized representations of the collective, be they names or numbers, and they also share in the consequences of these representations. Thus by assigning positions and comparing states across categorical borders, evaluative institutions also regulate the *collective* experiences of citizens, in both a material and a symbolic way. The metrics are social facts in a Durkheimian sense: they are external and coercive, their effects being felt in all individuals who partake in the collective's destiny.

From a sociological perspective, then, the metrology of the state raises three important questions. First, what is the process by which the relevant measures are produced? Second, who gets to determine what kinds of representations get *encoded*[9] in these measures? Third, how are the measures then *decoded* by the various actors in play, and what are their economic effects? Below I address these three questions through a very particular empirical lens: the production of sovereign credit ratings.

STATES ON THE MARKET

Nowhere, perhaps, is the power of metrics on states more evident than in the realm of sovereign debt. Since the late 1980s, sovereign debt has moved from being centered on private bank loans – the early 1980s debt crisis, for instance, was a crisis of intermediation – to being centered on the bonds market, where debt is traded publicly. States' economic value, so to speak, fluctuates publicly on a daily basis. To support this financial activity and the wide range of actors involved, banks and investor firms have bolstered their research departments; dedicated organizations have expanded their "opinion" business to cover a large number of sovereign issuers; and the financial press keeps a close eye on any information, political or otherwise, deemed relevant to the process of risk evaluation.

Market valuations (in the form of spreads on the bond market or sovereign credit default swaps) and evaluations (in the form of briefs, reports, or credit ratings) thus frame the conditions under which states are incorporated into modern financial capitalism, if at all. But the valuation of government bonds is an extremely complex and uncertain process, vulnerable to the vagaries of domestic and international politics, up and down economic trends, or investment fads and fashions. Most importantly, it depends on a multilayered structure of other valuations: since the state remains the last-resort economic actor, its financial legibility cannot be fully detached from the financial legibility of the rest of the domestic economy, and vice versa. A country's entire banking system, to the extent that it can become a *public* liability (as in Ireland's decision to mop up its banks' losses in 2008–2009), may be relevant to the process of state valuation; the same is true of its auto industry, railroads, or other vital economic sectors. From the point of view of state-gauging actors, "the state" can only be apprehended through a complex process of disaggregation and reaggregation[10] that is attuned to the mutable boundaries between state and society, public and private.[11]

These boundaries are themselves under constant construction. States work on market actors to shape perceptions about the national "economy" through policies deemed favorable to "investors," a hospitable political climate, or broader marketing campaigns.[12] Tax breaks and infrastructural investments, but also weak labor, safety, or environmental laws, may enhance the attractiveness of corporate bonds; tight fiscal policies may be more relevant for sovereign ones. "Contemporary financial knowledge," Zaloom remarks, "is organized around the interplay of reason and affect."[13] Capital must be excited by potentially high yields, and it must feel reasonably safe. In the mid-2000s, it was enticing to invest in the BRIC economies. The Goldman Sachs London bureau had popularized this label to designate the four large emerging economies of Brazil–Russia–India–China. Unsurprisingly, the quartet soon claimed the label for themselves and turned the term BRICs into a proud political banner – with its connotations of rock solid material – performing and spontaneously fitting the category in a sort of "looping" effect.[14] Meanwhile, the financial industry developed it into a lucrative business strategy: BRICs-dedicated investment funds and products flourished, as did consulting, branding, and marketing activities, fueling new sources of profit for investment banks, consulting firms, credit rating agencies, and the financial press. Thus Goldman Sachs, in this case, got to define the principles of vision and division of the economic world, but – and this is the important point – the classificatory act was all at once an economic act, a source of profit. So much is at stake, then, because language is never "just words." Labels, nicknames, letter grades, and scores elicit positive and negative emotions, rally up economic excitement or chill expectations, and create identities. These cultural "mood swings" may be hard to pin down, but they do participate in the financial process, too.

Such stories remind us that the economy cannot exist without morality plays, as actors – individuals, corporations, countries – are apprehended not only through numbers, formulas, and charts aiming at precision, but also through rather coarse moral categories of virtue and vice, good and bad, high and low.[15] In the early 2010s, with the fermentation of the Eurozone crisis, the BRICs suddenly experienced a boost in popularity as operators in the financial markets collectively became more pessimistic about Southern European economies and, correlatively, Southern European states, which had to shoulder the adjustment. Described as "European Tigers" just a few years before, the newly forsaken countries of Portugal, Italy, Greece, and Spain were now lumped together under the inelegant label of "PIGS." Then Ireland joined the club, and it was redubbed the "PIIGS."

Markets are in the relative value business: they depend not on absolute assessments but on *trade-offs*, on evaluative comparisons. The decision is never simply "should I invest in X?" but rather "will I be better off investing in X rather than Y? Is the spread worth the risk?" Second, market judgments are conjectures. To the extent that they must judge a country's *willingness* to repay its debt, rather than simply its *ability* to do so (indeed, it may be difficult to disentangle the two in practice), market evaluators of sovereign risk incorporate their own subjective (if heavily rationalized) assessments about the culture, institutions, and politics of various nations. Third, market judgments are recursive. To the extent that these representations play an active part in the functioning of the financial markets themselves, as the PIIGS and BRICS examples suggest, market actors must also track other actors' evolving confidence in the culture, institutions, and politics of various nations *as they are currently reflected in prices*, that is, risk premia or spreads.

Consequently, being attuned to, or in command of, the symbolic universe that shapes these judgments – such as the division between BRICs and PIIGS – is of enormous practical importance. The distribution of symbolic rewards in the international arena is deeply intertwined with the extraction of material profit, and thus an inherent part of the business of finance. Put another way, the "cultural circuit of capital"[16] – the stories we tell about economies, the categories we construct to account for them, and even, to some extent, the instruments we produce to measure them – are not just an epiphenomenon floating above some real, underlying material structure beneath: the circuit stands at the very heart of the capitalist machine.[17] Markets, too, "see" through classifications, and they act upon them.[18]

The market for sovereign debt has a long history, and judgments about the moral personae of states have always been at stake in it. In earlier eras, economic relations between sovereigns and their creditors were mediated through tightly knit networks of personal relations; the social status of one's bond underwriters essentially certified one's prospects as a sovereign borrower.[19] Today, connections between bond issuers, underwriters, and buyers have become more competitive. The primary market is still heavily concentrated: countries' debt management offices maintain close relationships with a few primary dealers who are in charge of selling government bonds to the rest of the market. But certifying states' economic virtue has become a separate and heavily formalized business. Dedicated private organizations, the credit ratings agencies (or CRAs), are the public face of the sovereigns' evaluation process, which fits into a century-long effort of turning uncertainty about various types of borrowers into calculable risk.[20] Investors, especially large ones, have their own in-house services, too, and also use the services of boutique analysis firms. Finally, actors track the opinions of well-respected analysts at all these institutions, either through formal channels or by word of mouth.

MORAL REDUCTION

Country ratings are an extension of Moody's and Standard and Poor's (S&P's) older business of rating public enterprises and municipal bonds,[21] and today the ratings of states and public agencies continue to co-determine each other. Both companies started rating sovereigns after World War I, though their evaluations were limited to European, North American, and Latin American countries.[22] Grades were implicitly benchmarked against U.S. securities, which stood in a class of their own at the apex of the hierarchy (U.S. government securities were then rated A***** or AAAAA by S&P, a category which has since disappeared). The business then died with the wave of country defaults associated with the Great Depression and World War II, only to restart in the mid-1970s after the abrogation of the Interest Equalization Tax.[23]

Figure 4.1a[24] tracks the percentage of the sovereign bonds rated by Moody's over the long run, while Figure 4.1b focuses on cumulative counts for the post-1975 period only but provides data for the three major agencies.[25] Both figures show the rapid rise of the number of countries rated by the three main agencies after that date. Unsolicited at first, ratings have become standard "market devices"[26] that are routinely incorporated in financial decisions. They also partake in the symbolic and material arsenal of the modern nation-state,[27] a way for

(a) Total number and percentage of nations rated by Moody's, 1918–1948.

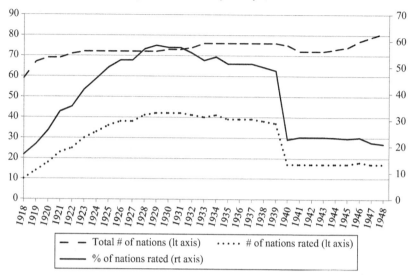

(b) Percentage of nations with sovereign ratings by agency, 1975–2013.

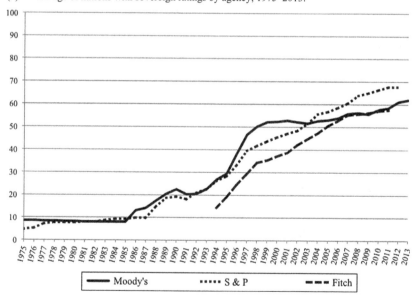

FIGURE 4.1. Historical evolution of sovereign credit rating. (a) Nation-states defined according to CIA World Factbook (www.cia.gov/library/publications/the-world-factbook/). Data for countries rated by Moody's from 1918 to 1948 were generously provided by Norbert Gaillard (see Norbert Gaillard, *A Century of Sovereign Ratings* (Springer 2012), 8). For these years, rated countries are those

states to signal not only borrower status, but also legitimacy as members of the international community. So demand for ratings has increased steadily over time, which has allowed the CRAs to start charging sovereigns for issuing grades.[28]

Credit raters rate by means of letter grades instead of numbers, with only slight variations in the grading schemes used by the main companies. Bizarrely reminiscent of the evaluation system of schoolchildren, ratings begin with a process of *moral reduction*: condensing the moral personality of the political collective as a whole (state *and* nation) and the nature of the social contract between them into a small set of typographical symbols – the rating.[29] How will the state (and its leaders) balance the citizens' interests with those of foreign creditors? Conversely, will the nation be willing to repay debts contracted by its political elites? As Lienau points out, "the current sovereign lending regime finds itself in the uncomfortable situation of functioning without a clear theory of what it means by 'sovereign.'"[30] Practice, as always, is contingent: the political handling of sovereign debts has varied a lot throughout history. In the period immediately following World War I, it was relatively flexible and forgiving. This was due to, on the one hand, high competition in the credit market and, on the other, the growing assertion of a democratic

---

FIGURE 4.1. (*cont.*) with bonds that were denominated in USD or GBP, listed on the NYSE, and assigned a rating by Moody's. (b) Total countries defined by total nation-states at each year according to the Correlates of War database (Correlates of War Project, "State System Membership List, v2011," 2011, http://correlatesofwar.org) and supplemented with author data for 2012–2013. Sovereign ratings data begin in 1975, the year after the repeal of the Interest Equalization Tax (IET) in the United States (see Standard & Poor's, "Default Study"); Moody's original set of thirteen rated countries remained unchanged from 1949 to 1985. Fitch began assigning sovereign ratings in 1994. S&P's began rating sovereign debt issues in the 1920s. However, S&P sovereign rating data prior to 1975 are sporadic and/or incomplete compared with ratings after the repeal of the IET in 1974. Moody's ratings are based on Moody's Sovereign Bond Ratingsand span from 1975 to 2013 (see Moody's, "Sovereign Bond Ratings," September 12, 2013, www.moodys.com/researchdocumentcontentpage .aspx?docid=PBC_157547). Fitch ratings are based on long-term foreign currency ratings for sovereigns and span from the year Moody's began assigning such ratings, 1994, to 2011 (see Fitch, "Sovereign Rating History," August 24, 2012, www.fitchratings.com/web_content/ratings/sovereign_ratings_history.xls). S&P's ratings are based on long-term foreign currency ratings for sovereigns and span from 1975 to 2012 (see Standard & Poor's, "RatingsDirect: Sovereign Rating and Country T&C Assessment Histories," January 3, 2013, www.standardandpoors .com/spf/upload/Ratings_US/TC_Assessment_Histories_1_4_13.pdf).

conception of sovereignty, which made the restructuring or erasing of debts possible in case of war or regime change.[31] The recent period, by contrast, has been marked by the institutionalization of a *statist* conception of sovereign debt, which "assumes the continuity of sovereign obligations across successive regimes and therefore mandates the payment of all debt, regardless of its potential illegitimacy."[32] This shift was propelled, in part, by the growing cohesiveness and institutional power of private credit markets during the last quarter of the twentieth century.

The state may be the contracting party, but the terms of the debt contract incorporate beliefs about the relationship between the country and its outside (i.e., foreign creditors) and between the state and the putative nation that lies beneath it, as well as (I will come back to this point) beliefs about the moral personality of different populations. It is this broad political–cultural compact that is being crystallized in the rating, *as if* the whole nation-state could be treated as a person with a particular character and history.[33]

To identify this character, modern scorecard methodologies rely on a series of weighted criteria, mixing measurable economic attributes – a country's economic position or the fiscal capability of its government – with less clear-cut features, such as "institutional strength" or perceptions about the probability that certain dramatic events (e.g., a banking crisis) will occur. Figures 4.2a and 4.2b offer a simplified representation of the S&P's and Moody's methodologies, as described in their own explanatory material.

In theory, the qualitative dimensions of evaluation, which are essential to the roadmaps reproduced in Figure 4.2, will be collapsed into more quantitative measures in order to enable the smooth ranking of sovereign bonds on a continuous scale. The commensuration process thus feeds on the illusion of "mechanized objectivity,"[34] as the component factors are turned into quantifiable metrics and criteria are homogenized across rated institutions. But as the raters themselves were eager to point out after the 2008 financial crisis, theirs is a business of issuing "opinions." This character is reflected in the adjustment explicitly built into the quantitative methodology, or in the fact that the release of new ratings is always accompanied by a commentary.[35] The commensuration exercise includes the assignment of a "political score" (S&P's) or a score for "institutional strength" (Moody's), which captures, mostly, the CRA's evaluation of the country's *willingness* to pay.[36] The economic score is typically benchmarked against agencies' representations of a functioning free market economy. For instance, looking at the policy record of Latin American nations, Biglaiser and DeRouen[37] demonstrate that trade liberalization

Marion Fourcade

(a) Standard & Poor's sovereign ratings methodology.

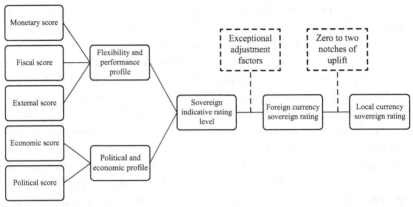

(b) Moody's sovereign ratings methodology.

Broad Rating Factors	Rating	Weighting (toward Factor)	Indicators
Factor 1: Economic Strength	Growth Dynamics	50%	Average Real GDP Growth$_{t-4 \text{ to } t+5}$
			Volatility in Real GDP Growth$_{t-9 \text{ to } t}$
			WEF Global Competitiveness Index
	Scale of Economy	25%	Nominal GDP (US$)$_{t-1}$
	National Income	25%	GDP per capita (PP, US$)$_{t-1}$
	Adjustment Factors	1–6 scores	Diversification
			Credit Boom
Factor 2: Institutional Strength	Institutional Framework and Effectiveness	75%	World Bank Govt. Effectiveness Index
			World Bank Rule of Law Index
			World Bank Control of Corruption Index
	Policy Credibility and Effectiveness	25%	Inflation Level$_{t-4 \text{ to } t+5}$
			Inflation Volatility$_{t-9 \text{ to } t}$
	Adjustment Factor	1–6 scores	Track Record of Default
Factor 3: Fiscal Strength	Debt Burden	50%[1]	General Govt. Debt/GDP$_t$
			General Govt. Debt/Revenues$_t$
	Debt Affordability	50%[1]	General Govt. Interest Payments/Revenue$_t$
			General Govt. Interest Payments/GDP$_t$
	Adjustment Factors	1–6 scores	Debt Trend$_{t-4 \text{ to } t+1}$
			General Govt. Foreign Currency Debt/General Govt. Debt$_t$
			Other Pub. Sector Debt/GDP$_t$
			Pub. Sector Financial Assets or Sovereign Wealth Funds/GDP$_t$
Factor 4: Susceptability to Event Risk	Political Risk	Max. Function[2]	Domestic Political Risk
			Geopolitical Risk
	Government Liquidity Risk	Max. Function[2]	Fundamental Metrics
			Market Funding Stress
	Banking Sector Risk	Max. Function[2]	Strength of Banking System
			Size of Banking System
			Funding Vulnerabilities
	External Vulnerability Risk	Max. Function[2]	(Current Account Balance+FDI)/GDP$_t$
			External Vulnerability Indicator (EVI)$_{t+1}$
			Net International Investment Position/GDP$_t$

*Where a time series is used, historical and forecast data are equally weighted.

[1] These weights can vary.

[2] The aggregation of Political Risk, Government Liquidity Risk, Banking Sector Risk, and External Vulnerability Risk follows a maximum function, i.e. as soon as one area of risk warrants an assessment of elevated risk, the country's overall Susceptibility to Event Risk is scored at that specific, elevated level.

FIGURE 4.2. Sovereign ratings methodology. (a) Standard & Poor's, "RatingsDirect," June 30, 2011. (b) Moody's, "Sovereign Bond Ratings," September 12, 2013.

does, in fact, boost credit ratings, while inflation depresses them. Furthermore, agencies frequently amend their evaluations in light of current events – political disruptions of any kind, including strikes or street demonstrations; government changes; or international tensions. If model predictions yield a grade that seems out of step with these exogenous conditions, CRA boards will "adjust" the rating or its individual components upward or downward, sometimes in very consequential ways (see Figure 4.2a, "exceptional adjustment factors" in S&P's graph, "adjustment factors" in Moody's table, Figure 4.2b). This "arbitrary component of the credit rating" may grow significantly in times of crisis, such as the Euro area sovereign debt crisis at the end of the 2000s[38] or the East Asian crisis at the end of the 1990s,[39] and impact the risk premium paid by the sovereigns.

ENCODING

The murkiness of sovereign ratings and their individual components stands in sharp contrast to the automated character of individual credit scores, which derives from the algorithmic treatment of well-defined quantitative behavioral measures, weighted and collected mechanically over a certain period.[40] It is relatively straightforward to model credit scores from individual-level indicators.[41] By contrast, sovereign ratings are much harder to replicate. In practice, they connect only loosely to standard economic indicators and economic performance measures.[42] CRAs have performed poorly as predictors of crisis, particularly with respect to emerging economies.[43] Part of the problem is technical: rating models do not have enough data to rely upon. As one interviewee at a credit rating agency puts it, "the essential problem is that the world of sovereign borrowers is far smaller than the world of large banks or corporations, and that the number of instances of default in the modern period when we have reasonable national accounts is tinier still . . . So the rating of sovereigns depends more on the art of political economy than on the science of econometrics."[44] To create more data points and sharpen perceptions of a "government's debt payment culture,"[45] countries' records stretch back in time. But are not these records and perceptions themselves the product, rather than the origin, of an existing social structure, with a particular distribution of economic and symbolic capital?

Certainly the argument can be made on an economic level. Small countries and many large countries in the global South are typically unable to borrow internationally in their domestic currency. Marked by what economists call "original sin," these countries experience a systematic and enduring rating disadvantage, *even at rather low levels of debt.* The reason is that "original sin lowers evaluations of solvency because it heightens the dependence of debt service on the evolutions of the exchange rate, which is more volatile and may be subject to crises and crashes."[46] Consequently, lending conditions for these nations tend to be structurally more expensive and more perilous. It is not coincidental that the countries so affected tend to be located at the periphery or semiperiphery of what Immanuel Wallerstein called the "modern world system,"[47] and marred by histories of colonialism or other forms of economic dependency. Looking at a sample of forty-five countries, Eichengreen, Hausmann, and Panizza[48] find that financial centers (United States, United Kingdom, Switzerland, and Japan) suffer the least amount of original sin, followed by Euroland countries. Latin America suffers the most.

On a more symbolic level, and to the extent that it establishes an inequality of status and power between lender and borrower, debt presumes and invites moral comparisons.[49] Representations about a country's history over the *longue durée* – unlike an individual's – are very publicly available for popular consumption, feeding into economic actors' evaluations of its "character." Given that the world's financial system is heavily centered in the global North (primarily the New York–London axis), the social distance between evaluators and evaluated may be considerable.

Common sense as well as expert linguistic categories carry with them all kinds of positive and negative assumptions about different countries and culture. "People," writes Richard Shweder "say yuck at each other all over the world."[50] There is no reason to think that market actors are somehow insulated from this kind of prejudice, and, indeed, Leslie Salzinger's fieldwork suggests that nationality matters, and is consciously marked, on the trading floor.[51] This is not only because social distance is inherent to the business of international finance, but also because everyone expects such distance to inform the politics of sovereign debt more broadly. For instance, the unfolding of the Eurozone crisis provided a useful reminder that enduring myths about North and South always lurk below the surface. These myths have a long history, rooted in popular discourse and longstanding patterns of subordination/domination, but also in pseudo-scientific theories about, for instance, the effect of temperature or geography on moral character. Echoing a central theme of postcolonial theory, Bourdieu identified an elaborate and recurring network of discursive oppositions and equivalences from Montesquieu's climate theory to Ratzel's "anthropogeography": between Northern action and Southern passion, virility and femininity, industriousness and sloth, courage and cowardice, or freedom and servitude/despotism. [52] An analysis of the press coverage of the 2010 Eurozone crisis in Germany, pitting Northern European fiscal saints against Southern European sinners[53] and telling tales of responsibility and irresponsibility,[54] reveals the persistence of such contrasting tropes in more recent times. Once publicly activated, these images may sustain shifts in crowd psychology and herd behavior among market actors.

HARDENING–LOOSENING

The world of finance thus processes all kinds of institutional, cultural, or political information, folding it into its evaluative schemes and asset allocation decisions. Fused and melded into ratings, politics and culture become an economic fact through a process we can call, pace Latour, "hardening."[55] That is, the messy work of the rating's construction is all at once dissolved and hardened, removed from view and projected as an ever-present, objective, real "thing." Via the metric and its echo chambers in the economic press and financial markets, a nation-state's moral standing assumes the objectivity of a social fact.

The methodology is highly elaborated, formalized, and exposed in an effort at legitimation and transparency, as is the ratings' release process. Changes in a country's bond ratings rarely go unnoticed, for instance. The ritual is, in fact, unmistakable. The credit raters make their pronouncements in a highly public manner, defending their grade, methods, and impartiality. Rating changes inevitably prompt statements from heads of state, atonement or self-congratulation from finance ministers, and extensive comments from the business press. Everyone, in short, enacts the collective belief that ratings matter a lot, and does so because everyone else does: after all, *New York Times* columnist Thomas Friedman has called Moody's Bond Rating Service the "second world superpower," after the United States.[56]

Friedman's quote is a vast overstatement: in practice, credit ratings have little influence on finance's *daily* operations. What matters there are the moment-by-moment market positions taken by the real movers of money: banks, hedge funds, dealers. The spread, not the grade, is the real deal. Spreads are determined, primarily, by the asset allocation strategies of financial investors and the risk valuations associated with the issuer. When the latter are high, bonds become objects of speculative practices;

that is, they start trading like equities, and their volatility increases dramatically. John Maynard Keynes likened the practice of "speculation" investment, as opposed to "enterprise" investment, to a beauty contest: "It is not a case of choosing those [faces] that, to the best of one's judgment, are really the prettiest, nor even those that average opinion genuinely thinks the prettiest. We have reached the third degree where we devote our intelligences to anticipating what average opinion expects the average opinion to be. And there are some, I believe, who practice the fourth, fifth and higher degrees."[57] This is when markets see "animal spirits" at work – which Keynes[58] defined as "a spontaneous urge to action rather than inaction, [and not] the outcome of a weighted average of quantitative benefits multiplied by quantitative probabilities."[59]

Excessive market volatility puts the raters in a difficult position, trapping them between their formal role as risk evaluators and their inevitable entanglement in self-fulfilling market dynamics.[60] In practice, ratings changes are often nonlinear, adding – some commentators have argued – to the volatility on the bonds market. Countries can see their grade going from "investment" to "speculative" or "junk" in a matter of months, as happened when Korea spectacularly experienced a 10-notch downgrade in 1997 (from AA– to B+), Greece's grade tumbled 9 notches in 2010–2011 (from BB+ to CC), or Argentina's fell 8 notches in 2001 (from BB– to SD).[61] What is at stake in these speculative episodes is the immediate well-being of millions of people. A sudden shift in confidence, confirmed by a ratings downgrade, can rapidly turn the crisis into a self-fulfilling prophecy.[62]

Though the CRAs are not the markets' primary movers, they are not irrelevant. For one thing, they matter to those outside finance: the existence of a collective belief in the relevance of a categorical system is not something to be dismissed easily.[63] The pithy formula of the rating focuses attention and creates public drama. Second, the CRAs' actions have ripple effects through their embeddedness in the institutional system. Categories, Hacking remarked, truly gain power when they become the unconscious practice of institutions: "all intentional acts are acts under a description. Hence if new modes of description come into being, new possibilities for action come into being in consequence."[64] We must thus investigate which modes of action have come into being with the rise of credit ratings and other types of formal market evaluations. By doing so, we will begin to understand how and why ratings exert their coercive force on states – I refer to these processes as *inscription* and *performativity*.

INSCRIPTION

Hardened ratings may receive a lot of public attention, but they would be toothless if no one used them. Today's credit rating agencies are powerful because states empowered them. Since the 1980s, the practice of embedding public regulation into private ratings has spread globally.[65] In 2004, it was enshrined in the Basel II accords, which decided that the capital reserve requirements for banks would be have to be weighted by the risk of the financial products they hold, and, even more importantly, that evaluations of risk would be made not by regulators, but by approved "external credit assessment institutions."[66] The regulatory use of credit ratings thus became the more direct mechanism determining the desirability of various forms of private and sovereign debt on the financial markets, enhancing the power of the raters vis-à-vis the rated, including states.[67] Indeed, from a chronological point of view inscription was one of the drivers of the generalization of sovereign credit ratings – not the other way around. A rating downgrade and a whole series of organizations can be suddenly deemed unsafe by regulators.

In other words, states, together with central banks and international financial institutions, collectively constructed the hand that placed them under the rule of financial markets. The first step in this process was the financialization of national debts that started in the 1970s. Prior to that, many governments financed public expenditures directly from national savings and the domestic banking circuit.[68] The second step was the state-sponsored delegation of regulatory control to private opinion issuers, seemingly justified by convenience (the ratings were deemed commensurable across nations) and neoliberal ideology. As Bruner and Abdelal put it, "the 'private' authority of the rating agencies is not so private after all. Governments have both valorized and codified their authority. Indeed, governments define the market for ratings and help to determine their influence."[69] The third step was the inscription of raters' authority within the state's machinery itself, both officially (e.g., when rating analysts consult with state officials, or when CRAs utter public statements about a government's strategy) and more insidiously (when state officials incorporate the perceived preferences of portfolio investors in their approach to economic policy, or when they work to improve the country's position on various components of the rating). Anchoring the action of the state in the external necessity of the markets rather than the sovereignty of democratic politics thus outlined a new political logic – the logic of what Linhardt and Muniesa call the state-corporation (*l'État-entreprise*) as opposed to the state-ministry (*l'État-Ministère*).[70] Examples include policy strategies that privilege low budget deficits and inflation,[71] the implementation of performance indicators, or pressures to reform the measurement of national debt, for instance by including off balance sheet commitments to future generations. Such accounting modifications dramatically inflate debt/GDP ratios, provide arguments for fiscally conservative constituencies in their effort to crack down on generous welfare states with high pension levels, and create the conditions of a new domestic politics pitting holders of "financial debt" against holders of "social debt."[72] The Greek case, where national pensions and public sector salaries were slashed in an effort to reimburse creditors (mostly foreign, in this case), possibly gives a taste of the conflicts to come for many Western industrialized countries.

DECODING–PERFORMING

The state's economic value thus fluctuates on the bond markets as a traded commodity. Spreads, in turn, are decoded as reflecting market actors' collective expectations about the future of sovereign bonds as commodities: they might deliver known and dependable cash flows or less dependable cash flows, or the loan's principal might be in question. The CRA's "investment," "speculative," or "junk" grade categories partially overlap with these different potential paths. Market actors' anticipations about the possible futures of existing debt contracts, in turn, determine the terms under which new contracts will be negotiated. The better the quality of the issuer (the higher the rating), and the larger its economy, the more competition to serve it. The more, then, the state can afford to demand from its bankers: better research and placement, more advantageous interest rates and fees, more flexibility in terms of maturity and perfectibility requirements. Conversely, the lowest-quality issuers may find themselves unable to borrow on the public market, and will instead deal privately with institutions lending small amounts at very high costs, in a manner similar to that of individuals obtaining a payday loan.

We may thus ponder the extent to which the relative valuations produced by the financial markets perform not only economic outcomes, but also economic "cultures." The market for sovereign debt takes place within a historically evolved social structure – a social hierarchy of countries – which it both benefits from, in the form of diversified returns, and helps reproduce. Some countries never seem to shake the markets' faith in their good word, no matter how foolish their financial position and domestic politics might look from the outside. With a government *net* debt ratio of 154 percent of GDP but consistently high ratings, Japan is an anomaly, even considering the fact that most of its debt is held domestically. Repeated congressional showdowns over the debt ceiling in the United States – effectively brandishing the threat of default – have had virtually no effect on the country's capacity to borrow, thanks, in great part, to the existence of a reputable lender of last resort (the Federal Reserve).[73] Other countries, on the other hand, have much greater difficulty lifting inherited prejudices about their institutions, and thus remain in a precarious position, plagued by poor reputations and the problem of "original sin." The fact that their debt contracts are more, sometimes much more, expensive, and therefore harder to repay, both materially and politically, in turn further enhances their very precariousness and inability to perform.[74] The chickens often come home to roost in economic slumps. Irving Fisher referred to this as "the great paradox, which is the chief secret of most, if not all, great depressions: *the more the debtors pay, the more they owe.*"[75] This is because in these situations the price of debt (the interest rate) increases more rapidly than the ability of people or institutions to repay it. For some countries, this may amplify the temptation of debt repudiation, either through default or inflation. For others, unfulfilled debt obligations may linger well after default episodes, compounded by arrears, penalties, and expensive litigation costs. The determination, backed by U.S. courts, of New York–based "vulture funds" to obtain full repayment of their portion of Argentina's debt after the 2005 restructuring (debt they had bought at a sharply discounted price) has maintained that country in a precarious political and economic position and threatened restructuring efforts with other creditors.

When, furthermore, debtors come under institutional supervision, the rolling out of austerity policies,[76] the sting of international stigmatization, the sometimes heavy-handed involvement of creditor-country governments (e.g., the United Kingdom with Ireland, Germany with Greece) and courts (in the Argentinian case), and the humiliation of country leaders in debt collection *coups de force* may create the conditions of their own failure by fueling recessions, social conflict, and political instability. Societies, Polanyi reminds us, resist.[77] They also resent. Countries, then, will come to spontaneously fit categories that were seemingly made for them. On the cultural front, institutions will come across as unreformable. And on the economic front, states may just end up aligning with the markets' expectations about them and go into default – a development made all the more likely since the costs of doing so may already have been "priced in."

THE CLASSIFYING AND THE CLASSIFIED: TOWARD A MORAL SOCIOLOGY OF THE STATE

In the eyes of the financial markets, the state is a classifiable entity. To be "in the market" at all, states have to be made legible for market consumption: hence the steady pressure to standardize national accounting and accountability mechanisms in a rational effort to thicken the record, mechanize the evaluation process, and facilitate the assessment of relative value. This is a Sisyphean task: as suggested earlier, the legibility of the state as it pertains to the sale and purchase of sovereign debt extends well beyond the boundaries of public administration, or those of the tax receipts, into public or semipublic enterprises, public–private partnerships, and wholly private institutions that for one reason or another may fall under state purview. Where the state/economy boundary ultimately falls is the outcome of a dynamic process, of the constant ebb and flow of state claims upon society, and society's claims upon the state.[78] In that sense, the state/society divide is both solid and transient: market actors use the distinction all the time, but they must do so in ways that acknowledge its fundamental malleability. That, perhaps, is the meaning of the "structural effect" of the state discussed by Timothy Mitchell:[79] in practice, investors produce such an effect in their own attempts at evaluating and valuing the state as a borrower, projecting their own (and contradictory) readings about its boundaries, making educated guesses and contested bets about the nature of the social contract with citizens and foreigners. In other words, the state in the classifying and investing practice of the financial markets is all at once an actor *and* an arena.[80]

Furthermore, putting "states on the market" presupposes and completes another conflation, a moral one this time, between the state as an economic entity, the government as a political entity, and the country as a cultural one. Notwithstanding efforts at formalizing, quantifying, and standardizing, the process of state valuation cannot be isolated from the history of structural relations between the investors and the invested in, with its attendant prejudices and stereotypes, or from fads and fashions created through and for the benefit of finance. Cultural preconceptions, stigma, and sudden infatuation or disenchantment are not only the unconscious symbolic formation everyone builds upon, but also fair game in the representational manipulations that may enable some actors to gain an edge over their competitors in the financial betting game.

Finally, the very notion of state sovereignty may be itself at stake in the tug of war between countries and their foreign creditors. In the absence of sovereign bankruptcy rules, national assets may suddenly be up for grabs in opportunistic debt collection actions against distressed states, as happened in Africa and Latin America. Some examples include an Argentinian navy ship temporarily impounded in Ghana or the seizure of oil revenues in the Republic of Congo or of debt relief money in the case of Zambia. In these extreme cases, which involve buying distressed bonds for pennies on the dollar *and then* suing countries for the full amount, the law, and not the markets, is the explicit vehicle for generating financial profits. This aggressive enrollment of creditor countries' courts to support "full amount repayment" to holdout creditors is a relatively new and still limited development, and whether it will be strengthened or tamed in the future, no one can say. But it certainly feeds into the perpetuation of stigma and disadvantage, not only by insisting on costly repayments, but also by nourishing the markets' feverish efforts to generate value from historical and present inequalities between states.

Notes

* I am especially grateful to Jonathan Miller, Kimberly Morgan, Fabian Muniesa, and Pierre-Olivier Gourinchas for their close readings and numerous comments on this piece. I also thank Lis Clemens, Martha Finnemore, Bernhard Harcourt, Armando Lara-Millán, Damon Mayrl, Kate McNamara, Ajay Mehrotra, Ann Orloff, Sarah Quinn, Stephen Sawyer, Vivek Sharma, James Sparrow, Josh Whitford, and participants of the Many Hands of the State Conference (University of Chicago, May 2014) for helpful remarks and suggestions. Earlier versions of this chapter were presented at the annual conference of the Social Science and History Association (2013) and at seminars at Columbia University and George Washington University. Finally, Daniel Kluttz provided excellent research assistance, and I am grateful to Dasom Nah for her valuable editorial help.

1 Pierre Bourdieu, *On the State: Lectures at the Collège de France* (Cambridge: Polity, 2014).

2 Paul Starr, "Social Categories and Claims in the Liberal State," *Social Research* 59, no. 2 (1992): 263–95.

3 Emile Durkheim, *The Division of Labor in Society* (New York: The Free Press, 2014)

4 Bourdieu, *On the State*, 162–75.

5 John W. Meyer, John Boli, George M. Thomas, and Francisco O. Ramirez, "World Society and the Nation-State," *American Journal of Sociology* 103, no. 1 (1997): 144–81; John W. Meyer, "The Changing Cultural Content of the Nation-State: A World-Society Perspective," in *State/Culture: State-Formation after the Cultural Turn*, ed. George Steinmetz (Durham, NC: Duke University Press, 1999), 123–43.

6 Sally Engle Merry, "Measuring the World: Indicators, Human Rights, and Global Governance: With CA Comment by John M. Conley," in *Corporate Lives: New Perspectives on the Social Life of the Corporate Form*, eds. Damani J. Partridge, Marina Welker, and Rebecca Hardin, *Current Anthropology* 52, no. S3 (2011): S83–95; Kevin E. Davis, Benedict Kingsbury, and Sally Engle Merry, "Indicators as a Technology of Global Governance," *Law & Society Review* 46 (2012): 71–104.

7 Michael Power, *The Audit Society: Rituals of Verification* (Oxford: Oxford University Press, 1999); Wendy Espeland and Mitchell Stevens, "Commensuration as a Social Process," *Annual Review of Sociology* 24 (1998): 313–434.

8 Durkheim, *Division of Labor*, 282 (my emphasis).

9 Stuart Hall, "Encoding/decoding," in *Culture, Media, Language*, eds. Stuart Hall, Dorothy Hobson, Andrew Love, and Paul Willis (London: Hutchinson, 1980), 128–38.

10 Morgan and Orloff, Introduction.

11 See Clemens, Chapter 1; Mayrl and Quinn, Chapter 2.

12 Incidentally, this is why an entire consulting industry exists around the branding or rebranding of nations, aimed at shoring up legitimacy so that tourists and investors will take their money there. See Melissa Aronczyk, *Branding the Nation: The Global Business of National Identity* (New York: Oxford University Press, 2013).

13 Caitlin Zaloom, "How to Read the Future: The Yield Curve, Affect, and Financial Prediction," *Public Culture*, 21, no. 2 (2009): 245–68.

14 Ian Hacking, *Historical Ontology* (Cambridge, MA: Harvard University Press, 2004).

15 Marion Fourcade, "The Economy as Morality Play, and Implications for the Eurozone Crisis," *Socio-Economic Review* 11 (2013): 620–27.

16 Nigel Thrift, *Knowing Capitalism* (London: Sage, 2005).

17 Marion Fourcade, "The Symbolic and Material Construction of the BRICS," *Review of International Political Economy* 20, no. 2 (2013): 256–67; Leon Wansleben, "Dreaming with BRICS: Innovating the Classification Regime of International Finance," *Journal of Cultural Economy* (2013): 453–71; Samuel Brazys and Niamh Hardiman, "From 'Tiger' to 'PIIGS': Ireland and the use of heuristics in comparative political economy," *European Journal of Political Research* 54 (2014): 23–42.

18 Marion Fourcade and Kieran Healy, "Classification Situations: Life-Chances in the Neoliberal Economy," *Accounting, Organizations and Society* 38 (2013): 559–72.

19 Marc Flandreau, Juan Flores, Norbert Gaillard, and Sebastián Nieto-Parra, "The End of Gatekeeping: Underwriters and the Quality of Sovereign Bond Markets, 1815–2007," in *NBER International Seminar on Macroeconomics*, eds. Lucrezia Reichlin and Kenneth West (2010), www.nber.org/chapters/c11906.

20 Bruce Carruthers, "From Uncertainty toward Risk: The Case of Credit Ratings," *Socio-Economic Review* 11, no. 3 (2013): 525–51; Barry Cohen

and Bruce G. Carruthers, "The Risk of Rating," *Sociétés contemporaines* 1 (2014): 39–66.

21 Rawi Abdelal, *Capital Rules. The Construction of Global Finance* (Cambridge, MA: Harvard University Press, 2007); Richard Sylla, "An Historical Primer on the Business of Credit Rating," in *Ratings, Rating Agencies and the Global Financial System*, eds. Richard M. Levich, Giovanni Majnoni, and Carmen Reinhart (New York and London: Springer, 2002), 19–40.

22 Norbert Gaillard, *A Century of Sovereign Ratings* (New York and London: Springer, 2012); Standard & Poor's, "Default Study: Sovereign Defaults and Rating Transition Data, 2012 Update," (March 29, 2013), www.standardandpoors.com/ratings/articles/en/us/articleType=HTML&assetID=1245350156739.

23 The Interest Equalization Tax (IET) of 1963 taxed investment by U.S. firms in foreign securities – thus making investing in sovereign bonds from other countries unappealing.

24 Gaillard, *Century of Sovereign Ratings*, 8.

25 Standard & Poor's, Moody's (both U.S.-based) and Fitch (U.K.-based).

26 Michel Callon, Yuval Millo, Fabian Muniesa, eds., *Market Devices* (London: Blackwell 2007). On the concept of market "judgment devices," see Lucien Karpik, *Valuing the Invaluable* (Princeton, NJ: Princeton University Press, 2010).

27 Meyer, Boli, Thomas, and Ramirez, "World Society."

28 After the Brady debt restructuration plan of 1989, "countries accepted the policy of paying to be assigned a rating: the most creditworthy governments (e.g., Chile) wanted to demonstrate that their credit standing had recovered from previous crises and middle- and low-income countries preferred a low rating to no rating at all" (Gaillard, *Century of Sovereign Ratings*, 36).

29 This may include the nature of the social contract *between* nations: the sovereign debts of the Southern European nations (and Ireland) were cheap until mounting tensions revealed that the rest of the Eurozone may be unwilling to absorb losses.

30 Odette Lienau, "Who is the 'Sovereign' in Sovereign Debt?: Reinterpreting a Rule-of-Law Framework from the Early Twentieth Century," Paper 594 (Cornell Law Faculty Publications, 2008), 64.

31 Odette Lienau, *Rethinking Sovereign Debt: Politics, Reputation and Legitimacy in Modern Finance* (Cambridge, MA: Harvard University Press, 2014).

32 Lienau, "Who Is the 'Sovereign,'" 66.

33 Alexander Wendt, "The State as Person in International Theory," *Review of International Studies* 30, no. 2 (2004): 289–316.

34 Theodore Porter, *Trust in Numbers: The Pursuit of Objectivity in Science and Public Life* (Princeton, NJ: Princeton University Press, 1995).

35 For instance, in a rating downgrade of Greek sovereign bonds released on April 29, 2015, Moody's explicitly refers to the views of the far left of the Syriza party and the prospect of a referendum on any new financing agreement.

36 CRAs willingly acknowledge the subjective and speculative element in these component scores. According to Standard & Poor's, the political score

"reflects *our view* of how a government's institutions and policy making affect a sovereign's credit fundamentals by delivering sustainable public finances, promoting balanced economic growth, and responding to economic and political shocks. It also reflects *our view* of the transparency and reliability of data and institutions, as well as potential geopolitical risks." (Standard & Poor's, "RatingsDirect: Sovereign Government Rating Methodology And Assumptions," June 30, 2011, www.standardandpoors.com/spf/upload/ Ratings_EMEA/2011-06-30_CBEvent_CriteriaGovSovRatingMethodology AndAssumptions.pdf). In Moody's case, "institutional strength" includes the subcategories of government effectiveness, regulatory quality, rule of law, and control of corruption, all of which are based on the quantification of qualitative assessments.

37 Glen Biglaiser and Karl De Rouen, "Sovereign Bond Ratings and Neoliberalism in Latin America," *International Studies Quarterly* 51, no 1 (2007): 121–38.

38 Manfred Gärtner, Björn Griesbach, and Florian Jung, "PIGS or Lambs? The European Sovereign Debt Crisis and the Role of Rating Agencies," *International Advances in Economic Research* 17 (2001): 288–99.

39 Giovanni Ferri, Li-Gang Liu, and Joseph E. Stiglitz, "The Procyclical Role of Rating Agencies: Evidence from the East Asian crisis," *Economic Notes* 28, no. 3 (1999): 335–55.

40 Donncha Marron, "'Lending by numbers': credit scoring and the constitution of risk within American consumer credit," *Economy and Society* 36, no. 1 (2007): 103–33; Martha Poon, "From New Deal Institutions to Capital Markets: Commercial Consumer Risk Scores and the Making of Subprime Mortgage Finance," *Accounting, Organizations and Society* 34, no. 5 (2009): 654–74; Fourcade and Healy, "Classification Situations."

41 FRB (Federal Reserve Board), *Report to Congress on Credit Scoring and Its Effects on the Availability and Affordability of Credit* (Board of Governors of the Federal Reserve System, 2007).

42 Ricardo Hausmann and Ugo Panizza, "Redemption or Abstinence? Original Sin, Currency Mismatches and Counter Cyclical Policies in the New Millenium," CID Working Paper no. 194 (2010), www.hks.harvard.edu/var/ezp_ site/storage/fckeditor/file/pdfs/centers-programs/centers/cid/publications/faculty/ articles_papers/hausmann/Redemption_or_Abstinence.pdf. Marwan Elkhoury, "Credit Rating Agencies and their Potential Impact on Developing Countries," United Nations Conference on Trade And Development, *Compendium on Debt Sustainability and Development* (2008), 165–89, http://unctad.org/en/docs/ gdsddf20081_en.pdf#page=170. C. Archer and Glen Biglaiser, "Sovereign Bonds and the 'Democratic Advantage': Does Regime Type Affect Credit Rating Agency Ratings in the Developing World?" *International Organization* 61, no. 2 (2007): 341–65.

43 Carmen Reinhart, "Sovereign Credit Rating Before and After Financial Crises," in *Ratings, Rating Agencies and the Global Financial System*, eds. Levich, Majnoni, and Reinhart, 265. Also see Timothy Sinclair, *The New Masters of Capital. American Bond Rating Agencies and the Politics of Creditworthiness* (Ithaca, NY: Cornell University Press, 2005), and Pierre Pénet and Grégoire Mallard, "From Risk Models to Loan Contracts, Austerity

as the Continuation of Calculation by Other Means," *Journal of Critical Globalization Studies* 7 (2014): 4–47.

44 Cited in Andrew Fight, *The Ratings Game* (John Wiley & Sons, 2001), 114.

45 Standard & Poor's, "RatingsDirect," June 30, 2011.

46 Barry Eichengreen, Ricardo Hausmann, and Ugo Panizza, "The Pain of Original Sin," in *Other People's Money: Debt Denomination and Financial Instability in Emerging Market Economies*, eds. Barry Eichengreen and Ricardo Hausmann (Chicago, IL: University of Chicago Press, 2005), 30.

47 Immanuel Wallerstein, "The Rise and Future Demise of the World Capitalist System: Concepts for Comparative Analysis," *Comparative Studies in Society and History* 16, no. 4 (1974): 387–415.

48 Eichengreen, Hausmann, and Panizza, "Original Sin," 13–47.

49 David Graeber, *Debt: The First 5,000 Years* (New York: Melville House, 2010).

50 Richard Shweder, *Why Do Men Barbecue? Recipes for Cultural Psychology* (Cambridge, MA: Harvard University Press, 2003), 177.

51 Leslie Salzinger, "Beneath the Model: From 'Developing Nation' to 'Emerging Market,' Deal by Deal," Annual Conference of the International Sociological Association, August 4, 2012.

52 Pierre Bourdieu, "Le Nord et le Midi: Contributions à une analyse de l'effet Montesquieu," *Actes de la Recherche en Sciences Sociales* 35, no. 1 (1980): 21–25.

53 Matthias Matthijs and Kathleen McNamara, "The Euro Crisis' Theory Effect: Northern Saints, Southern Sinners, and the Demise of the Eurobond," *Journal of European Integration* 37, no. 2 (2015): 229–45.

54 Klaus Armingeon and Lucio Baccaro, "Political Economy of the Sovereign Debt Crisis: The Limits of Internal Devaluation," *Industrial Law Journal* 41, no. 3 (2012): 254–75.

55 Bruno Latour, *Science in Action: How to Follow Scientists and Engineers through Society* (Cambridge, MA: Harvard University Press, 1987). See also Barry Cohen and Bruce G. Carruthers, "The Risk of Rating," footnote 20.

56 Cited in Frank Partnoy, "The Siskel and Ebert of Financial Markets: Two Thumbs Down for the Credit Rating Agencies," *Washington University Law Quarterly* 77 (1999): 620.

57 John Maynard Keynes, *The General Theory of Employment, Interest and Money* (Harcourt, Brace and World, 1965), 156.

58 Keynes, *General Theory*, 162.

59 See Robert J. Shiller, *Irrational Exuberance*, third ed. (Princeton, NJ: Princeton University Press, 2015) and George A. Akerlof and Robert J. Shiller, *Animal Spirits: How Human Psychology Drives The Economy, and Why It Matters for Golbal Capitalism* (Princeton, NJ: Princeton University Press, 2009) for a modern treatment on the subject.

60 Pierre Pénet, "Ratings Reports as Figuring Documents. How Credit Rating Agencies Build Scenarios of the Future," in *Making Things Valuable*, eds. Martin Kornberger, Lise Justesen, Anders Koed Madsen, and Jan Mouritsen (Oxford University Press, 2015), 62–88.

61 These ratings are from S&P's (see Standard & Poor's, "Default Study," www
.standardandpoors.com/ratings/articles/en/us/articleType=HTML&assetID=
1245350156739, 14).

62 Since countries frequently borrow to repay prior debts, a spike in interest rates
can make such borrowing unaffordable, precipitating the crisis.

63 Timothy Sinclair, "Credit Rating Agencies and the Global Financial Crisis,"
European Economic Sociology Newsletter 12, no. 1 (2010): 5.

64 Hacking, *Historical Ontology*, 108.

65 Andreas Kruck, *Private Ratings, Public Regulations. Credit Rating Agencies
and Global Financial Governance* (New York: Palgrave, 2011), 6.

66 Kruck, *Private Ratings*.

67 However, under Basel II rules, banks were incentivized to hold sovereign
bonds denominated in local currency, because states insisted they should be
considered risk-free. An obscure (political) decision by the European Central
Bank at the time of the creation of the euro allowed *any* Eurozone country's
sovereign debt to be considered as the safest kind of asset, usable as collateral
in Eurosystem monetary policy operations. Both of these decisions explain
why sovereign bonds became so attractive to banks, which could borrow from
the central bank at very low cost against these assets and pocket the difference
in yield.

68 For instance, in post-1945 France, banks were forced to hold a certain level of
national treasury bonds, emitted at a fixed price, which allowed the government to finance its expenditures cheaply from domestic savings. A market for
debt existed, but it played a relatively subaltern role compared with what
Lemoine calls the "administrative management of state debt." This administrative system was progressively dismantled in the late 1960s, as French (and
many other) governments began to experiment with the sale of large quantities
of state bonds (whose price now fluctuated) on financial markets. The concern
at the time –coming from economic liberal circles and taking inspiration from
the British system – was to force the state to behave like *any* responsible
borrower. See Benjamin Lemoine, L' ordre de la dette: enquête sur les infor-
tunes de l' Etat et la prospérité du marché. (Paris, La Découverte, 2016). For a
similar evolution in Israel, see Roi Livne and Yuval Yonay, "Performing
Neoliberal Governmentality: An Ethnography of Financialized Sovereign Debt
Management Practices," *Socio-Economic Review* 13, no. 4 (2015).

69 C. Bruner and Rawi Abdelal, "To Judge Leviathan: Sovereign Credit Ratings,
National Law, and the World Economy," *Journal of Public Policy* 25, no 2
(2005): 193. Note that the European Union has sought to contain this influence after the Eurozone sovereign debt crisis.

70 Dominique Linhardt and Fabian Muniesa, "Du ministère à l'agence: Étude
d'un processus d'altération politique," *Politix* no. 95 (2011): 73–102.

71 See Marwan Elkhoury, "Credit Rating Agencies and their Potential Impact on
Developing Countries," United Nations Conference on Trade And Development, *Compendium on Debt Sustainability and Development* (2008), 165–89,
http://unctad.org/en/docs/gdsddf20081_en.pdf#page=170. The policy message,
however, has been more expansionary in times of crisis. As an illustration of
this ambivalence, the following is a statement by the Standard and Poor's

bureau in Germany, accompanying a ratings downgrade for the Southern European countries: *"The current financial turmoil stems primarily from fiscal profligacy at the periphery of the Eurozone."* "In our view, however, the financial problems facing the Eurozone are as much a consequence of rising external imbalances and divergences in competitiveness between the EMU's core and the so-called 'periphery.' As such, *we believe that a reform process based on a pillar of fiscal austerity alone risks becoming self-defeating*, as domestic demand falls in line with consumers' rising concerns about job security and disposable incomes, eroding national tax revenues." (My emphasis, see S&P Frankfurt bureau Standard & Poor's, "Credit FAQ: Factors Behind Our Rating Actions On Eurozone Sovereign Governments," January 13, 2012, www.standardandpoors.com/ratings/articles/en/us/?articleType= HTML&assetID=1245327305715.) Note that most commentators have refuted the "fiscal profligacy" thesis, except in the Greek case; see Mark Blyth, *Austerity: The History of a Dangerous Idea* (New York: Oxford University Press, 2013).

72 Yann Le Lann and Benjamin Lemoine, "Les comptes des générations. Les valeurs du futur et la transformation de l'État social," *Actes de la recherche en sciences sociales* 194 (2012): 62–77; Benjamin Lemoine, "Quantifier et Mettre en Crise la Dette Souveraine: Agences de notation, techniques comptables et constructions privées de la valeur des Etats," *Politique Européenne* 2, no. 44 (2014): 24–51.

73 However, S&P moved the country's rating down one notch, from AAA to AA + in the summer of 2011, owing to "political brinksmanship" in Congress. Moody's and Fitch left the AAA rating standing, only changing their outlook to negative.

74 Guillermo Calvo, "Servicing the Public Debt: The Role of Expectations," *American Economic Review* 78, no. 4 (1988): 647–61.

75 Irving Fisher, "The Debt-Deflation Theory of Great Recessions," *Econometrica* 1, no. 4 (1933): 344.

76 Blyth, *Austerity*.

77 Karl Polanyi, *The Great Transformation: The Political and Economic Origins of our Time* (Boston, MA: Beacon Press, 1944).

78 Clemens, Chapter 1; Mayrl and Quinn, Chapter 2.

79 Timothy Mitchell, "State, Economy and the State Effect," in *State/Culture: State Formation after the Cultural Turn*, ed. Georges Steinmetz (Ithaca, NY: Cornell University Press, 1999), 76–96.

80 For the state as actor/state as arena distinction, see Theda Skocpol, "Bringing the State Back In: Strategies of Analysis in Current Research," in *Bringing the State Back In*, eds. Peter Evans, Dietrich Rueschmeyer, and Theda Skocpol (Cambridge: Cambridge University Press, 1985), 3–37. Also see Novak, Sawyer, and Sparrow, Chapter 9.

PART II

STRATIFICATION AND THE TRANSFORMATION OF STATES

5

Gendered States Made and Remade

Gendered Labor Policies in the United States and Sweden, 1960–2010

Ann Shola Orloff

From the hyper-capitalist United States to social-democratic Sweden and beyond, systems of social provision and regulation – my preferred term for what are often called "welfare states" – increasingly promote maternal employment. This is a striking change in both social policy and the gendered division of labor: gone is the legal and political framework – a mix of positive supports and discriminatory provisions – undergirding men's breadwinning and women's housewifery, primary caregiving, and sometimes paid employment of the last century.[1] These shifts are both consequence and cause of broader and perhaps even more profound transformations of the organization of social life that come with modernity, all of which have been intertwined with the emergence and development of modern states.

Over the course of the last two centuries, women have irrevocably changed their "place," claiming space in public life as workers and political participants, trading second-class citizenship and legal inferiority for full citizenship rights and formal equality. Gender relations have been reshaped as women have been drawn into employment, and legal and social barriers to women's full participation in all aspects of life were challenged and overturned. Women and men expanded the ideas and practices of civic equality, democracy, and universalism to encompass women and other formerly excluded groups, changing the meanings of these concepts for all. Women are now better represented within the polity and the state – foreshadowing, perhaps, a more thoroughgoing transformation in the gendered character of states.

Contemporary changes in the character of gendered divisions of labor, and in the social policies and legal frameworks supporting them, follow from the earlier transformations in culture, technology, education, and labor markets.[2] But women's political mobilization, and that of their allies among men, was critical to achieving suffrage, associated legal reforms, and second-wave feminist victories against discrimination. Moreover, gendered social policies are critical to the sustainability of the economy and larger political structures. Indeed, prominent welfare state analysts insist that completing the "incomplete revolution" is key to women's willingness to engage in the employment and childbearing that will keep welfare states sustainable in terms of fertility, activation, and tax revenues.[3] An optimal equilibrium then depends on promoting women's equality, especially by pushing for men's greater involvement in housework and caregiving. Feminists hope that further reforms would move toward full gender equality, the "redoing" or even "undoing" of gender.[4] The image of an as-yet-unfinished revolution in gender relations is alluring, inviting us to imagine what it will take to finish the job of creating equality between men and women, even though it – rather problematically – is based on the assumption that this change is inevitable, and that we can all agree on what that job will entail. Yet teleologies occlude the uneven, contested political moves that are involved in transforming durable social inequalities and hierarchies.

Whether or not one accepts the teleology of the ultimate, necessary triumph of equality – I don't, even though I certainly want it – or one believes that "undoing gender" is even possible – I say no, again – states, law, and social policies have been at the center of these developments. State institutions and policies may be organized around the logics of patriarchy, gender neutrality, or gender equality; they may facilitate women's domesticity and dependency or women's employment and economic independence, men's breadwinning or their caregiving in addition to paid work. And they may well do a mix of these things, reflecting multiple logics across different arenas of action, although there is some tendency to increasing support for maternal employment; however, it should be noted that such support occurs in connection with otherwise varying configurations of the gendered division of labor. We need to find ways to conceptualize states that account for this multiplicity and the uneven patterns of gendered political change.

This chapter aims to theorize these changes, drawing on the literature on gender and states and my own analysis of gendered policy changes in the United States and Sweden over the last few decades. Beginning with second-wave feminist theorizing and continuing into the current day, the analysis of states, law, policies, and politics was always dual in nature: intellectually focused on understanding the gendered character of major political institutions and politically aimed at changing them. The analytic tools of second-wave feminism were critical to breaking with pervasive liberal conceptions in which the problem of gender inequality was based only in explicit discrimination, and in calling for political efforts aimed at changing relations heretofore thought of as private. Yet these tools were inadequate for understanding how gendered transformations of state institutions might unfold. Thus, I consider more recent, finer-grained, and historically contextualized analyses inspired by moves to re-center the state and by historical institutionalism, which have given us better understandings of the welfare state and laws bearing on gendered labor patterns.[5] In the second part of this chapter, I offer a sketch of changes in what I call gendered labor policies over the last half-century in the United States, with Sweden serving as a shadow case, to illustrate the processes of transformation in gendered states, drawing on the conceptual resources of third-wave feminism and historical social science. Together, employment regulation and family policies – the components of gendered labor policies – affect the levels and quality of mothers' and fathers' employment and unpaid caregiving; the division of domestic and caregiving labor between men and women within and across households, regions, and countries; the links between patterns of labor and men's and women's access to power and valued resources and their capacities for autonomy; and the ways these vary along lines of class, race, and other significant social categories. (My focus on gendered labor policies reflects my effort to "disaggregate the state," in contrast to earlier work, which attempted to analyze the state understood as a whole.) I emphasize the pivotal decades of the 1960s and 1970s, when events led to the replacement of support to men's breadwinning and women's housewifery with backing to employment for all, and the distinctive institutional and political orientations toward maternal employment of the contemporary United States and Sweden were solidified.

I argue that we should conceptualize this transformation as composed of two processes – a destructive one, which eliminates the policy and legal underpinnings for male breadwinner/female caregiver households, and a constructive one, which builds supports for maternal employment (in dual-earner households or households maintained by women alone), contingently and variably linked to gender equality. I draw on recent theories of institutional change as multiple and uneven, and also build on insights originally developed in work with Julia O'Connor and Sheila Shaver on "gender regimes of the liberal welfare states" – ensembles of policies and their specific forms of articulation – a nascent "many-handed" analysis, although we did not use the term.[6] To understand if and how states move from patriarchal to gender-egalitarian logics, we will need eventually to focus on institutional transformations across different arenas, and then reaggregate, with expectations of unevenness and multiplicity rather than uniform transitions from one overarching institutional logic to another.

Why the United States and Sweden?[7] Despite many differences, they are global leaders in promoting women's employment and gender equality, which nevertheless, intriguingly, differ in the means through which this is attempted. While the United States has relied heavily on the regulation of employment practices to eliminate discrimination, especially through the judicial system, Sweden has leveraged family policies both to allow mothers to work for pay and to encourage men's caregiving. Sweden and the United States share certain policy legacies, as well; through the 1970s, they were "weak breadwinner" states, to use Lewis's terms, although this was expressed institutionally in contrasting ways: in Sweden through universalistic support for workers and families and a long tradition of supporting single mothers' employment, in the United States through the absence of public support for working-aged breadwinning men and their economic dependents.[8] Moreover, the processes of destruction and construction unfolded quite differently in the two countries. Sweden's processes of change, particularly in the shift to gender-neutral parental leave, seem to approximate the textbook example of displacement, the simultaneous destruction of the breadwinner/caregiver logic and the instantiation of a logic of maternal employment, while U.S. transformations developed in a far more dispersed way, with the erosion of breadwinner/caregiver and the construction of support for maternal employment and a logic of employment for all happening over a more prolonged period and across different institutions.

Gendered labor policies are not the entirety of the gender order(s) of the state – far from it; they might better be thought of as "two digits" of the "left hand," or one of the "left" hands of the state. I join the other authors in this volume in accepting the premise that the state has "many hands," many functions, which can conflict or dovetail, and have no guarantee of success, vis-à-vis gender relations and other elements of social order.[9] The literature on gender and welfare states, like that of many other subfields of state analysis, often suffers from what, in the introduction, we have referred to as the "modifier state" problem, that is, describing the entire state as characterized by the descriptive modifier emerging from research based in one arena: the "patriarchal" state, the "women-friendly" state, and so forth. But is an entire state thoroughly and evenly "patriarchal" or "women-friendly"? This seems quite unlikely, and in my analysis of gendered labor policies, I attempt to show the uneven processes of change across multiple institutions, from explicitly discriminatory policies toward gender-neutral supports for employment and, to a more limited extent, toward gender equality.

GENDER SHAPING STATES, STATES REDOING GENDER

Feminists have been interested in states from the dawn of the democratic era – when states explicitly institutionalized patriarchal principles – to the contemporary period of formal gender neutrality. State policies and law help to constitute the very categories of gender, kinship, citizenship, and economy that are involved in making political claims around work and family. Feminist theorizing about states, law, and policies emerged from the emancipatory political struggles of the 1960s and after, and aimed toward social transformation. In the midst of passionate political debates, feminists drew on innovative gender analyses and classic political thought to develop understandings that shaped subsequent political projects and campaigns. There were important commonalities across the demands on the state made by feminist movements of different countries but also significant differences of emphasis and political strategy. These reflected the different contours of the polities within which they worked and the varieties of feminist theorizing – liberal, Marxist/socialist, and cultural (or radical) feminisms – that emerged and became dominant in different countries.

I see the following analysis of feminist state theory as helpful in understanding both the political projects and the policy transformations of the 1960s and beyond. Thus, second-wave and later feminisms provide theoretical lenses for understanding policy changes, and also form a crucial part of the political context for these shifts. In particular, I would note the significance of feminist state theorizing that pushed beyond demands for an end to explicit gender discrimination or women's "protection" to problematize the political support for masculine domination in the "private" sphere of family, care, and sexuality – a core component of states' boundary-making processes now garnering our attention. Here are some of the roots of the ensuing radical transformations of gendered labor policies.

[handwritten marginalia: Haley, policing gender]

Second Wave Feminism and States

Both liberal and radical feminists forwarded bracing critiques of de jure and de facto discriminatory legal and policy provisions, highlighting states' support for gender hierarchy and inequality, masculine authority, and strongly differentiated life courses for men and women.[10] Liberal feminists played a pivotal role in transforming gender hierarchies in their political and legal campaigns to end formal discrimination, particularly in the United States, and were a substantial presence even in social-democratic Sweden. They saw gender inequality as rooted in states' deviations from gender neutrality rather than in fully gendered state institutions such as the public/private split. And they were especially effective in targeting explicitly discriminatory laws and policies, including legislation heretofore understood (by labor feminists) as "protective" of women's needs. These began to be reversed in the 1970s, with the support of almost all feminists. By the end of the twentieth century, formally gender-neutral states became the norm, certainly in the United States and Sweden. Still, gender inequalities remained, and many feminists saw further legal and policy changes, along with challenging the deeper gendered character of state institutions, as critical to upending masculine domination.

Liberal feminist projects of the 1960s and 1970s, like their historical predecessors, continuously pressed up against the insufficiency of formal law in dealing with the obduracy of gendered inequalities rooted in long-standing "social" or "cultural" hierarchical relations.[11] A wide variety of radical feminist positions, with intellectual lineages ranging from Marxism to radical democracy, showed that liberal guarantees of state noninterference were and are deeply inadequate in the face of entrenched masculine domination. Instead, they engaged the relationships between states and what was consigned by the mainstream to the "private" sphere: care, reproduction, domestic labor, sexuality. "The personal is the political" is one of second-wave feminism's best-remembered slogans, and for good reason. Women's full social and political participation – as workers, citizens, free individuals – required change beyond ending formal discrimination or developing separate, "protective" provisions for women.

In the heady days of feminist theorizing unleashed in the wake of second-wave activism of the 1960s and 1970s, scholars offered a multifaceted critique of gender relations in the liberal political order, noting women's exclusion from the rights of citizenship, the splitting of "private" and "public" spheres and women's consignment to the former, and the occlusion of the significance of the work of women in raising the next generations of citizens and workers. Path-breaking work examined "women and the state," challenging the masculinist assumptions of politics and political analysis, which took for granted a conception of citizenship based on men's lives and bodies, and later developed into analyses of states as constitutively gendered and of the links between political authority and masculinity.[12] The bourgeois public sphere and the liberal democratic state were constructed on the basis of patriarchal gender relations that were held to be outside the purview of the state – as Carole Pateman put it, the sexual contract preceded and undergirded the social contract. Catherine MacKinnon argued that masculine domination – and gender itself – was produced through sexuality, including sexual harassment at work, which she described as a form of sex discrimination.[13] Socialist or Marxist feminists probed the ways that capitalism and the state depended on daily and generational reproduction, thus on women's reproductive capacities and domestic and caring work.[14] The "patriarchal welfare state" was built around masculine conceptions of independence, which occluded men's dependence on women's care work; social citizenship rights were based on employment or marriage to wage-workers, depriving those who provided socially essential care work of independent recognition.[15]

Second-wave feminist state theorists have provided us with fundamental insights about the ways states, law, and politics sustained hierarchical and unequal gender relations, transcending the bounds of liberal politics and formal inequality. They identified the stakes for political elites and state officials of the organization of reproduction and production, here offering tools for the penetrating critique of mainstream theories of welfare states that emerged in the 1990s, and laying the foundations for contemporary "social investment" advocates' interests in fertility, women's employment, and state social policy.[16] They brought out men's political interests in gender hierarchy and inequalities and in the control of women's bodies, labor, and reproductive capacities. Most critically, we build on their understanding of the constructed character of the public/private split and the political significance of the "private" sphere, care work, and reproduction.[17]

Yet like the masculinist leftist and liberal political analysis they critiqued, second-wave work on states was too often overly abstract and structuralist, leaving few openings for agency, save in the form of women acting on the basis of "objective" interests thought to inhere in their social location. The conception of states as "patriarchal" was too unified, too simplistic, too fixed. Too little attention was paid to the variability of state policies and structures across space, social groups, and state agencies, and over time – in short, this work lacked an analysis of the multiplicity of institutional logics and the unevenness of gendered transformations.

Third-Wave Analyses of Gendered States

By the late 1980s and early 1990s, intellectual work on politics by feminists of a so-called third wave as well as other scholars opened up along many channels. Analysts developed an understanding of states premised on variation, conflict, ambiguity, multiplicity, and contingent and uneven possibilities for change – a set of intellectual shifts that was an important current within what Adams, Clemens, and I have called the third wave of historical or historicizing social science (deploying the wave metaphor for scholarship on politics).[18] Third-wave research on institutions and political power has prospered from disaggregating "the state" into its component parts, tracking the rise, development, and decline of multiple institutional logics. For example, analyses of constitutively gendered states showed the gendered divisions among state agencies, the feminine welfare, educational, and labor agencies versus the masculine coercive and fiscal ones. The insights of historical institutionalism are of particular significance for my analysis of gendered transformations: the multiplicity of institutions and logics, the unevenness in the timing of changes across institutions, the embeddedness of states in informal networks of power, and the different forms of institutional change. In the future, we must reaggregate and engage across scholarship on different state arenas – but there's a great deal of conceptual and empirical work to do in the meanwhile.

Second-wave scholars of politics had a broadly shared vision of "history as a sequence of stages, each relatively distinct and internally coherent" and of "coherent societal types with periods of transition between them."[19] This was reflected in the understandings of change in gender relations as proceeding through "stages," determined by dominant modes of production or technologies. Past revolutions and contemporaneous liberation struggles allowed second-wave feminists and other radicals to imagine women's emancipation as part of a sweeping transformation of the social order, which would require the "overthrow" of the capitalist and/or patriarchal state, and the establishment of a categorically different kind of state that would promote the interests of workers and women in socialized ownership of the means of production and collective responsibility for social reproduction.

Third-wave scholarship on politics conceptualizes change as proceeding unevenly across multiple domains rather than as shifts in overarching systemic logics. There are varieties of transitions, plural. Feminist and other forms of critical political theorizing also shifted in register to less totalizing understandings of change. This parallels changes in the political world: as the flames of revolution died down and popular upsurge ebbed toward the end of the 1970s, activists shifted to the "long march through the institutions."[20] Institutions contain multiple logics, and multiplicity is itself a key source of change, as actors draw upon schema and resources associated with one institution or organization to confront new problems, including those in different institutional arenas – a process of transposition, such as that seen in the 1960s when U.S. feminist activists drew on the politically successful tropes of the civil rights movement to identify some laws as forms of "Jane Crow."[21] Clemens argues: "In a world constituted of diverse elements, lineages and institutions, bricolage – or transposition or recomposition – becomes central to the theoretical imagery of social change."[22] Even where it is difficult to make explicit and authoritative policy decisions leading to the displacement of an old logic, such as the "male breadwinner model," by a new one, such as the "adult worker model," institutions may change gradually through processes of layering, drift, or conversion.[23] Thus, we should expect that gendered political transformations will take place unevenly across institutional domains – quite different from metaphors of total revolution.

Historical analyses leave no doubt that the institutions, laws, and policies of modern states have been built with patriarchal materials and are infused with masculinist logics. Patriarchal principles shaped the emergence of modern programs to address social risks generated by modern capitalism in the late nineteenth and early twentieth centuries. Trade unionists and reform elites, reflecting their own adherence to ideologies of gender difference and the family wage, ensured that the position of breadwinning men was bolstered by the unemployment and old-age insurance programs that formed the fundament of developing welfare states of the twentieth century.[24] Lewis argued that mature welfare systems, at least until the introduction of changes beginning in the 1980s, continued to adhere – in varying degrees – to the logic of the male breadwinner household, assuming and promoting men's privileges in the labor market and social security alongside women's domesticity and economic dependency.[25] Critical feminist reconstructions of the emergence of modern states upend the claims of scholars inspired by

modernization theory that "modern" political forces such as bureaucracy
and capitalism are inevitably gender-neutral and universalizing, and
arrayed against "tradition," especially as it is instantiated in gender-
differentiated households.[26]

Nonetheless, modern states – allowing for the fact that no state is
purely modern, or anything else – appear as a context within which more
foundational changes might unfold, in part because of the enhanced
political participation and public employment of both ordinary and educated women.[27] While democracy at first was defined as masculine, white,
and propertied against the status and participation of women of all races
and classes, men of color, and working men, the initiation of democratic
forms almost inevitably encouraged these "others" to demand entry to
the polity and representation in democratic bodies. Modern bureaucracies
confronted new problems of industrial society and were associated with
the development and regulation of the "social" as a distinctive collective
space, open for political regulation, along with the expansion of state
welfare activities, often staffed by women, whose education and expertise
fitted them for these new duties. This is an originary moment for distinguishing between "left" and "feminine" versus "right" and "masculine"
components of the state. "Right" and "left" may cooperate to reproduce
systems of domination. But they might not.

Second-wave feminist and historical social-science views emphasized
the way elites or dominant groups called upon states, imagined as total-
ities, to reinforce hierarchies and inequalities, and even now many
scholars emphasize the resilience of masculine domination as it changes
form.[28] But increasingly, feminist scholars consider the possibility that
state institutions could instantiate logics of gender equality, imagining
and theorizing states that have been transformed into vehicles for egalitarian projects – or embracing the notion of states as made up of different
institutional orders, in which some parts have been made into such
vehicles, however imperfectly and unevenly. Representative of this line
of thinking was Helga Hernes, social scientist, feminist, and Norwegian
state official, who in the late 1980s famously envisioned the development
of a "woman-friendly" welfare state, based on the trends she observed in
her native Norden.[29] Hernes argued that with the expansion of the public
service sector, women would be spurred to collective action to press for
greater power and more egalitarian policies, which would bring further
political mobilization and increased capacities to shape policy, a virtuous
circle moving societies toward gender equality.[30] This analytic reframing
has gone hand in hand with a reframing of the history of gendered states

("welfare" and otherwise). For example, in the 1990s, feminist scholars rethought the origins of systems of social provision and regulation, excavating first-wave women activists' agency – which was named "maternalist" – in constructing the programs understood by most second-wave feminists as "patriarchal" but now shown to be responsive to the demands of many women.[31]

To summarize: state institutions vary along multiple gendered dimensions, instantiating competing or complementary gendered logics. States have contradictory gendered effects, simultaneously offering support to women and sometimes empowering their political agency while often also reinforcing principles of difference and inequality. This includes the extent to which they promote gender equality projects, diversely defined, from their "defamilizing" qualities to my own concept of "the capacity to form and maintain an autonomous household" – wordy, I admit, but clear about how state social provision can affect the possibilities for women's individual personhood.[32]

Moreover, institutional multiplicity implies that change occurs unevenly, and that shifts toward gender equality in one sphere may be transposed to others. States are not inevitably patriarchal or masculinist, but contingently, historically so. A shift toward greater gender equality is possible.

CHANGING LOGICS IN GENDERED LABOR POLICIES: DESTRUCTION AND CONSTRUCTION

Let us now turn to a brief examination of the processes of change in gendered labor policies in the United States and Sweden over the last half century. Before the 1960s, these institutions supported breadwinning men's privileges in the labor market and social security (albeit somewhat more weakly in Sweden and the United States than in other Western countries) and allowed discrimination against women in the labor market and social security, while providing a modicum of security to some women engaged in full-time caregiving. In the United States, many married women's full-time caregiving was sustained through the support to men's "family wages" that came from employers, the tax system, and, indirectly, through state policies such as the GI Bill, but not explicitly through the welfare state.[33] There was also direct support to full-time caregiving for some single mothers and other caregivers through Aid to Families with Dependent Children (AFDC or welfare), while other single mothers, disproportionately women of color or unmarried women, were considered "employable" and denied access to such benefits.[34] In Sweden, women's full-time caregiving was given backing through family allowances and joint taxation, while the state enabled the employment of poorer and single mothers through child care services and maternity insurance (part of employment-linked sickness insurance).[35] These policies were fatally weakened in both the United States and Sweden in the 1960s and 1970s, as they began to be replaced by legal developments and policies organized around the logic of maternal employment.

These shifts have quite commonly been portrayed as a simple and contemporaneous move from one gender logic to another – "male breadwinner" to "dual earner," or "patriarchal to woman-friendly," for example. Indeed, in the past, I argued that this took the form of a "farewell to maternalism" and turn toward "employment for all."[36] I now believe it is more helpful to conceptualize these policy shifts as unfolding through two analytically distinct sets of changes, one destructive, the other constructive, across many programs and laws, and fueled by distinctive forces. There are the destructive processes: the dismantling of welfare programs organized around the logic of breadwinner/caregiver households, protective legislation that kept women out of certain positions in the labor force, or discriminatory provisions in social security. These also eliminated supports to men's breadwinning and women's full-time, life-long caregiving and domesticity. The constructive processes comprise building policies around the logic of compelling and/or supporting maternal employment, such as public care services or tax subsidies to private services, and the encouragement of mothers' employment through individual taxation, tax credits, training, or affirmative action. In this set of policies, full-time caregiving may be sustained for temporary periods as an element of "work-family reconciliation," through parental leaves or time-limited social assistance. And leaving no alternative to employment implies that mothers are not exempt from commodification.

This conceptual framework makes better sense than the alternatives. There are two especially misleading formulations: first, one that mistakes the destructive shift for the totality of change in gendered labor policies, painting this shift in the terms of neoliberal rollback; second, one that mistakes the constructive shift for the totality of change in gendered labor policies, envisioning this shift as a modernizing, egalitarian promotion of women's employment. My framework takes the timing of change, or lack thereof, seriously; when changes happen shapes what happens. Destructive and constructive processes sometimes have been sequential, but other times have overlapped, and in some cases, constructive moves have preceded "laggardly" destructive ones. Moreover, the historical timing of the processes is critical, as different political–economic contexts come into play – think of the Keynesian 1960s and 1970s in contrast with the neoliberal era following in the 1980s and 1990s, reflecting both worldwide political eras and country-specific political rhythms and factors.

Finally, it is important to note that new policies to support maternal employment are diverse, revealing the imprint of the timing and sequence of destructive and constructive processes as well as long-standing partisan and institutional differences. In other words, there are multiple logics of maternal employment, which reflect different political projects and origins. Support to maternal employment may be coupled with support to men's caregiving in projects of diminishing the gender division of labor – a logic that is often referred to as "dual earner/dual carer." Or they may be modified maternalist logics, aimed simply at making mothers' employment more sustainable, yet still different from fathers' employment. Or they might reflect a logic of "employment for all," a gender-neutral mandate of commodification for men and women alike standing alongside regulatory guarantees of equal treatment in employment and social security.

Gendered Policy Changes in the Second-Wave Era

Let us now take a brief look at the processes of destruction and construction in gendered labor policies in the 1960s and 1970s, focusing on the United States, with Swedish developments presented in extreme summary form to serve as a foil and contrast. Swedish developments are often seen as the paradigmatic case of progressive transformations in gendered labor policies, and the destructive elements are downplayed in favor of the constructive. But, as the following analysis of U.S. developments will show, similar shifts toward support of maternal employment did occur, but with destructive changes happening separately from constructive ones.

Political change was encouraged by social movement mobilization, as second-wave feminism reached its high point. Liberal feminism was predominant in the United States, underwriting an emphasis on regulating employment to prohibit discrimination; in addition, radical feminists focused on regulating sexuality in the workplace. In Sweden, social-democratic feminism was the most significant strain, underpinning a focus on changing divisions of labor through family policies.

Establishment politicians were also concerned with gender inequalities, establishing government commissions to examine women's status, which helped to legitimize political change.[37] In both Sweden and the United States, explicitly discriminatory provisions in social provision and in the regulation of employment were challenged and replaced by gender-neutral provisions; thus, so-called protective legislation was outlawed, equal pay for equal work was mandated, and laws were amended so that employed men and women got the same treatment under social insurance. In this era, one also sees the beginnings of the constructive phase, with new policies to support maternal employment. The divergent political landscapes of the two countries resulted in distinctive sequences and processes of destruction and construction, with significant implications for the character of policy development in the following decades.

In Sweden, employment-linked maternity insurance was eliminated simultaneously with the enactment of the much-heralded gender-neutral, paid parental leave. Benefits were made more generous to encourage men to take leaves. Also in the 1970s, Sweden traded joint taxation for individual taxation, a strong incentive for married women's employment.[38] These initiatives were undergirded by the active labor market policies instituted in the 1950s, initially targeted on men, but soon expanded to encourage women's participation in the labor market.[39] Extensive child care services were also developed to allow mothers to enter employment.[40] Key pillars of support for maternal employment were in place. The destruction of policies organized around the logic of breadwinner/caregiver households came with the construction of policies designed to promote maternal employment and dual-earner households in which – it was hoped – both men and women would have responsibilities for care.

In the United States during the 1960s and 1970s, the destruction of policies organized around the breadwinner/caregiver logic was carried through more completely in the regulation of employment, where the logic of the gender-neutral worker held sway, than in social provision.[41] Feminist activists challenged women's unequal treatment in employment, social security, and all realms of social life.[42] Feminist lawyers such as Ruth Bader Ginsburg, now Supreme Court Justice, were the protagonists of a legal strategy for gaining women's equality, notably in the Women's Rights Project of the American Civil Liberties Union.[43] They brought successful lawsuits on behalf of both men and women victimized by unequal treatment based on "traditional" or "stereotypical" models of gender relations (i.e., the breadwinner/caregiver model and women's economic dependency) institutionalized in the provisions of social security, family, and employment law. Congress passed relatively strong forms of action against discrimination and established the Equal Employment Opportunities Commission (EEOC), which was bolstered for a time by the activism of social movements.[44] Destruction progressed to construction, as outlawing discrimination soon led to "affirmative action" in education and employment, opening many formerly masculine occupations to women.[45] Feminist lawyers, inspired by MacKinnon, also took on "quid pro quo" demands for sex and other unwanted sexual advances at work, as well as sexualized and hostile work environments. By defining "sexual harassment" as a kind of discrimination and making employers vulnerable to lawsuits if they did not take preventive action, they directly contributed to the reshaping of the American state, as regulatory agencies took action against these practices.[46]

The United States had fewer policies supporting women's caregiving than Sweden – there were no family allowances or employment-linked maternity provisions, which could have served as a foundation on which to build new policies for the support of women workers. But the development of constructive policies was also impeded by the difficulties in eliminating policies that supported women's full-time caregiving. AFDC, or "welfare," was an entitlement that had, since the 1930s, given meager benefits (usually supplemented by some form of undeclared work or familial aid), which allowed a limited number of very poor and unpartnered parents, overwhelmingly mothers, to stay at home to care for children. Despite its relatively small budgetary footprint, the program had outsize political importance in symbolically endorsing certain, thoroughly racialized, ideals of motherhood. Until the 1960s, many women of color or unmarried women in the South and Southwest were classified as "employable mothers" and not eligible for benefits, revealing different logics of motherhood and employment for white women and women of color.[47] In the 1960s and early 1970s, civil rights and feminist lawyers successfully challenged these practices, allowing formerly excluded women to gain access to AFDC.

The activism of governments and civil society groups around poverty and inequality are emblematic of the 1960s, but the many reform initiatives often reflected contradictory goals. One aimed to shift AFDC's logic of supporting full-time caregiving for its very poor and limited constituency to mandating and encouraging employment, while another, the Family Assistance Plan (FAP), focused on bolstering the logic of breadwinner/caregiver households by providing new benefits to households "headed" by low-wage and unemployed men, understood as disproportionately men of color.[48] Still another aimed to make AFDC more inclusive and generous, retaining some elements of maternalist logic, while encouraging, but not mandating, employment in the name of rehabilitating welfare mothers.[49] But these all fell afoul of conservative members of Congress trying to restrict welfare in any form and to impose the logic of employment for all, save women "properly" married to wage-earning men – that is, the "traditional" model of male breadwinner/female caregiver and a sexual double standard. Political actors with different agendas vis-à-vis poor, disproportionately minority mothers came to a stalemate. In the end, none of the sweeping reforms proposed under Presidents Johnson, Nixon, or Carter was enacted. Reformers managed only to add ineffectual new work incentives for women on welfare, alongside more substantial new benefits for the poor such as Medicaid.[50]

Reformers did not shift the formal logic of full-time caregiving as appropriate for poor single mothers within AFDC, nor were supports to a wider clientele of employed mothers enacted. President Nixon vetoed a law substantially expanding child care services in 1971, and family leave was not even introduced in Congress in the 1970s.[51] Individual taxation was off limits, although the tax advantages for housewife-maintaining families were "balanced" by dependent care tax credits, thought to assist two-earner households.[52] A relatively unnoticed innovation, the Earned Income Tax Credit, passed in the wake of FAP's defeat; it initially provided very modest benefits through the tax system to employed parents, but was later to play a more important role in encouraging single mothers' employment.[53]

In Sweden, policy reforms of the 1960s and 1970s led to a decisive shift to maternal employment and the emergence of the ideal of "dual earner, dual carer."[54] In the United States, by contrast, changes of the 1960s and 1970s had not eliminated policies reflecting the logic of supporting mothers' full-time caregiving, nor had comprehensive supports to maternal employment been built. The contradictory elements of U.S. gendered labor policies reflected and sustained political, social, and cultural conflicts over ideals of motherhood, as the political parties became increasingly polarized over gender issues, sometimes coded as "culture wars" and entangled with racial inequalities as well.[55]

Gendered Labor Policies in Neoliberal Times

The differing legacies of near-complete destruction and substantial construction in Sweden and incomplete destruction and uneven construction in the United States were consequential for the trajectories of gendered labor policies in the 1980s and 1990s. In Sweden, the legacies of the 1970s directly contributed to the "daddy politics" of the 1990s. When it became clear that simply opening generous parental leave to men was insufficient to unseat deeply entrenched gendered divisions of labor, which left women economically disadvantaged, reformers considered how to further gender equality, and came to the conclusion that changing men would require a more forceful approach. Starting in the late 1970s, academics and government commissions found that women dominated the expanded public sector and disproportionately took up the generous, gender-neutral parental leaves and shorter workdays. This situation reinforced gender segregation in the labor market and the gendered division of household labor, as policies had enabled women to continue, more easily, to perform a disproportionate share of care work as they increasingly worked for pay, while they had far less impact on men's take-up of care work.[56] Swedish feminists and social democrats therefore sought to change men by encouraging their caregiving, authorizing a form of "gentle force" against entrenched gender divisions of labor, as in "daddy quotas," use-it-or-lose-it provisions to reserve a set period of parental leave for the parent not taking the majority of the leave – overwhelmingly fathers.[57]

Yet the step forward on fathers' leave by a center-right coalition government (1991–1994) was accompanied by what social-democratic feminists thought was a step back, the promotion of "choice" in leave policies structured around the reality of mothers' employment, with a "cash for care" program; though initially short-lived, it was revived by a new bourgeois government in the mid-2000s. Here, one sees an attempt, which is ongoing, to shift the logic of gendered labor policies from dual earner/dual carer to something closer to a maternalist logic, allowing for reconciliation of paid work and care for women but not men. Although these programs have been gender-neutral, benefits are low, with no incentives for men to take them up. Greater flexibility has been one hallmark of Swedish forms of neoliberalism, seen also in the right government's gender equality legislation, which prevailed over voluntary agreements in the labor market, pitting gender equality against the principle of self-determination, yet still leaving regulation of discrimination in employment weaker than in the United States.[58] As yet, the cash for care program has not unseated dual earner/dual carer as the prevailing family policy logic, but it does bring greater incoherence to Sweden's gendered labor policies. And support for maternal employment remains uncontested.

In the United States, the successes and failures of gender-egalitarian projects appeared reversed from those in Sweden: women were empowered in the labor market as formal discrimination was broken down but were given little governmental support along the lines of Sweden's family policies. Constructive efforts in the 1980s and 1990s were channeled toward the regulation of employment. Following the Reagan administration's intransigence toward the EEOC and antidiscrimination regulation, the Clinton administration was more supportive of gender equality, and successive laws and court cases expanded the legal remedies available to combat sex discrimination, including sexual harassment. Yet women facing demands for vocational dedication (and intensive mothering) would surely have welcomed public leave benefits and child care services. The Family and Medical Leave Act was passed in 1993, but – reflecting the austerity of the era – was not accompanied by cash benefits.[59] Without income replacement, workers have often found it difficult to claim the rights guaranteed by the law. Private care services have expanded in the years following Nixon's anticommunist veto of public child care, but they are uneven in quality and price, and depend on a labor force disproportionately made up of often-undocumented immigrants whose presence in the United States was facilitated by a lax, employer-friendly immigration policy. Tax credits for dependent care may be marginally helpful to some better-off households, but they are manifestly inadequate to ensure a supply of quality services.[60]

President Clinton pledged to make radical changes in AFDC, requiring mothers to engage in paid employment; his proposal stipulated that jobs could be part-time, and envisioned government jobs being offered if private employment was not available.[61] AFDC's maternalist logic of supporting full-time mothering was out of sync with the logics of other institutions, which were premised on employment for all, including mothers, contributing to mounting pressure to reform welfare. Pushed to the right by the election of 1994, which ushered in Republican control of Congress, Clinton's welfare reform took on a far more conservative cast than even his election promises (the part-time work option and back-up public jobs were gone, with "workfare" – work for the welfare check – as a substitute). The Personal Responsibility and Work Opportunity Reconciliation Act (PRWORA) of 1996 eliminated AFDC, replacing it with Temporary Assistance to Needy Families (TANF), and ended the entitlement of poor single parents, overwhelmingly mothers, to social assistance that allowed full-time caregiving. Thus, the United States shifted from a maternalist logic to a logic of employment for all. Had this shift in logics succeeded in the 1960s or 1970s, it is hard to imagine it would have been such a harsh departure from earlier policies. Softening the blow of welfare reform has been the expansion of the Earned Income Tax Credit, used overwhelmingly by employed single mothers – another instance of institutionalizing the logic of (maternal) employment, but without the paid leave benefits that would address the needs of mothers and others who need "time to care" or the services that guarantee a "right to be cared for" and mothers' capacities to enter employment.[62]

Did welfare reform reinstitutionalize the divergent logics of mothering and employment for white women and women of color that had pre-vailed prior to the 1960s, in that poor women who rely on welfare face employment mandates, while other women have greater "choice" in their life options?[63] In the Social Security system, widows of covered wage earners with young children receive benefits regardless of their own employment status, reflecting the partial retention of the breadwinner/caregiver logic now made gender-neutral – so widowers receive these benefits as well. There are several issues to consider here. To my mind, the most significant is that the vast majority of households – maintained by single mothers or fathers or married couples – may in principle enjoy the possibilities of "choice" with respect to work and care, but in practice face the logic of commodification, or employment for all: there simply are no state programs to offer support to their caregiving work, and they must rely on "private" resources, most often employment. This translates into a logic of employment for all – enforced with sanctions and mandates for those on welfare, by the logic of the market for those outside.[64]

CONCLUSION

And now to come back to the questions with which I began: how shall we characterize the change in the character of gendered labor policies as an element of the remaking of the gendered state? Do shifts toward logics of maternal employment also take us from a patriarchal to a gender-neutral state or, to use Hernes's evocative albeit imprecise term, a "woman-friendly state"? I think not. Asking the question in this way presumes that states are unitary, and reflect a single logic. As I have been arguing, gendered labor policies are only one component of the vast ensembles of units, practices, and effects that we call "states." Moreover, states must be contextualized in broader institutional fields and networks of power where "doing gender" is ubiquitous. But surely there are moments and places in which gendered labor policies have increased women's capacities for economic independence and advancement.

What does the future hold for gendered labor policies? Those who would change these policies face different kinds of political challenges across different polities, including those created by the character, timing, and sequence of the destructive and constructive phases of transformation. The system of social provision feminists and others confronted at the beginning of the 1960s supported some women when the family wage system failed – when their husbands or fathers of their children could no longer be counted on due to death, desertion, or divorce – but it simultaneously created institutional barriers to women as they increasingly entered the paid labor force and sought advancement. With the destruction of many explicitly gender-differentiated programs and provisions, some women the United States and Sweden have done well, benefiting from the end of discriminatory treatment in employment and education and the advances in supporting maternal employment.[65] The risk of politics that destroy old institutional orders is that we do not always know that good replacements will be constructed. This was clearly the case with the 1996 U.S. welfare reform, when support for full-time caregiving on the part of vulnerable populations was dismantled, but supports for employed motherhood and parenthood were never guaranteed. Today, it is those guarantees we still seek.

In Sweden, maternalism was not so fully dispensed with but rather was reworked in an attempt to make men as well as women "encumbered workers," that is, employees also engaged in caregiving. The simultaneous elimination of supports to breadwinner/caregiver households and building of supports to dual-earner households left an open field for the consideration of further family policy reforms that would encourage men's involvement in care and domestic work. But these policies face obstacles: many employers' intransigence, some men's reluctance. With women disproportionately taking leaves and reduced workdays, they continue as "junior partners" in wage earning in coupled households or, when single, suffer from lower living standards. Work, although transformed, has not been rendered entirely compatible with care, as yet. Even with Sweden's decidedly nonliberal willingness to use "gentle force" to change familial divisions of labor, the workplace itself remains in many respects off-limits for gender reforms.

Might new policies supporting maternal employment develop in a more egalitarian direction? Thinking of states as encompassing multiple institutional arenas, with multiple gendered logics, suggests some possibilities. A Gramscian "pessimism of the intellect" leads me to think that gendered labor policies, even with the radical goal of shifting the gendered division of labor, are unlikely to be able to displace the formidable powers of masculine domination still institutionalized in the state's other arms and the vast realms of gendered social life. It is impossible to imagine there could be a truly "woman-friendly welfare state" if other significant elements of state practices and policies reflect logics of masculine domination. (Armies and policing come to mind, despite women's donning the uniforms of the state's coercive agencies.) Yet an analysis based on multiplicity allows us to see the ongoing struggle among competing institutional logics and political forces. Changes in gendered labor policies might contribute to women's empowerment and political mobilization, informing a Gramscian "optimism of the will," the hope that we might yet arrive at a qualitatively different moment in the long and bloody history of states and gender, one bringing succor to the forces of emancipation.

Notes

For reading and giving comments on this paper, many thanks go to Marianne Constable, Joan Fujimura, Robert Gibbons, and Margaret O'Mara, all of whom helped to make my stay at the Center for Advanced Study in the Behavioral Sciences so enjoyable and intellectually stimulating. The members of my Northwestern Sociology writing group – Savina Balasubramanian, Natalia Forrat, Marie Laperriere, Liz Onasch, Jane Pryma, and Talia Shiff – provided compelling suggestions and questions. I received helpful comments from the participants in the SCANCOR colloquium at Stanford University, especially from Mitchell Stevens and Woody Powell. Let me also express my gratitude to Damon Mayrl and Kimberly Morgan, who read multiple versions of this paper – far above and beyond the call of duty. And I benefited tremendously from the discussions at our Many Hands panels at the SSHA and at the Many Hands of the State workshop sponsored by the University of Chicago Neubauer Collegium for Culture and Society project, "The State as History and Theory." Jane Pryma provided excellent research assistance.

1 There are parallels here to arguments about states and racial orders by Paschel (Chapter 8) and King and Lieberman (Chapter 7); states that once institutionalized inequality have been transformed into states that promote equal rights, at least in some arenas, even as they continue to stratify through formally gender or racially neutral mechanisms.
2 Claudia Goldin, *The Quiet Revolution That Transformed Women's Employment, Education, and Family*, No. *w11953* (Cambridge, MA: National Bureau of Economic Research, 2006): 1–48.
3 Gøsta Esping-Andersen *Incomplete Revolution: Adapting Welfare States to Women's New Roles* (Cambridge: Polity, 2009).

4 Analysts disagree as to whether gender can be "undone," or simply "redone," that is, done in different ways; see, e.g., Judith Butler, *Undoing Gender* (New York: Routledge, 2004); Francine Deutsch, "Undoing Gender," *Gender & Society* 21, no. 1 (2007): 106–27; Tey Meadow and Kristen Schilt, *Re: Doing Gender: A Queer Response to Feminist Social Theory* (Berkeley: University of California Press, forthcoming).

5 See, e.g., Ann Shola Orloff, "Gendering the Comparative Analysis of Welfare States: An Unfinished Agenda," *Sociological Theory* 27, no. 3 (2009): 317–43; Julia O'Connor, "The State and Gender Equality: From Patriarchal to Women-Friendly State?" in *Oxford Handbook on Transformations of the State*, eds. Stephan Leibfried et al. (New York: Oxford University Press, 2015).

6 Julia O'Connor, Ann Shola Orloff, and Sheila Shaver, *States, Markets, Families: Gender, Liberalism and Social Policy in Australia, Canada, Great Britain and the United States* (New York: Cambridge University Press, 1999).

7 There is an extensive literature using Sweden and the United States as "most different cases," referencing their differing sizes, positions in the world system of states, legal systems (civil versus common law), religious heritages, and more. I consider these differences and their implications for gendered labor policies more fully in my forthcoming manuscript, *Farewell to Maternalism? Toward a Gender-Open Future? Transformations in Gender, Global Capitalism and Systems of Social Provision and Regulation.*

8 Jane Lewis, "Gender and the Development of Welfare Regimes," *Journal of European Social Policy* 2, no. 3 (1992): 159–73; Ann Shola Orloff, "Markets not States?: The Weakness of State Social Provision for Breadwinning Men in the United States," in *Families of a New World*, eds. Lynne Haney and Lisa Pollard (New York: Routledge, 2003).

9 See also Lynne A. Haney, "Feminist State Theory: Applications to Jurisprudence, Criminology, and the Welfare State," *Annual Review of Sociology* 26 (2000): 641–66; Htun and Weldon (Chapter 6).

10 Linda K. Kerber, *No Constitutional Right to Be Ladies: Women and the Obligations of Citizenship* (New York: Macmillan, 1998); Ruth Lister, *Citizenship: Feminist Perspectives* (New York: New York University Press, 2003); Linda Zerilli, "Feminist Critiques of Liberalism," in *Cambridge Companion to Liberalism*, ed. Steven Wall (Cambridge: Cambridge University Press, 2015).

11 Zillah Eisenstein, *The Radical Future of Liberal Feminism* (Boston: Northeastern University Press, 1993); Susan Moller Okin, *Justice, Gender, and the Family* (New York: Basic Books, 1989); Mary Dietz, "Context Is All: Feminism and Theories of Citizenship," *Daedalus* 116, no.4 (1987): 1–24.

12 Anne Showstack Sassoon, ed., *Women and the State: The Shifting Boundaries of Public and Private* (London: Routledge, 1987); R.W. Connell, "The State, Gender, and Sexual Politics," *Theory and Society* 19, no. 5 (1990): 507–44.

13 Catharine A. MacKinnon, *Toward a Feminist Theory of the State* (Cambridge, MA: Harvard University Press, 1989), and *Sexual Harassment of Working Women: A Case of Sex Discrimination* (New Haven, CT: Yale University Press, 1979); Kathrin S. Zippel, *The Politics of Sexual Harassment: A Comparative Study of the United States, the European Union, and Germany* (New York: Cambridge University Press, 2006).

14 Barbara Laslett and Johanna Brenner, "Gender and Social Reproduction: Historical Perspectives," *Annual Review of Sociology* (1989): 381–404; Heidi Hartmann, "The Unhappy Marriage of Marxism and Feminism," in *Women and Revolution*, ed. Lydia Sargent (Montreal: Black Rose Books, 1981).

15 Carole Pateman, *The Sexual Contract* (Palo Alto, CA: Stanford University Press, 1988), and "The Patriarchal Welfare State," in *The Disorder of Women* (London: Polity, 1989).

16 Nathalie Morel, Bruno Palier, and Joakim Palme, eds., *Towards a Social Investment Welfare State?: Ideas, Policies and Challenges* (Bristol: Policy Press, 2012).

17 Their insights about the political construction and contingent character of the "public/private split" partly anticipated later analysis of state boundaries and borders, and the interpenetration of "public" and "private," as discussed by Mayrl and Quinn, Chapter 2, and Clemens, Chapter 1.

18 Julia Adams, Elisabeth Clemens, and Ann Shola Orloff, eds., *Remaking Modernity: Politics, History, and Sociology* (Durham, NC: Duke University Press, 2005).

19 Elisabeth Clemens, "Afterword: Logics of history? Agency, Multiplicity, and Incoherence in the Explanation of Change," in *Remaking Modernity*, Adams et al., eds. (Durham, NC: Duke University Press, 2005), 495, 500.

20 Mary Katzenstein, "Feminism Within American Institutions: Unobtrusive Mobilization in the 1980s," *Signs* 16, no. 1 (1990): 27–54.

21 On "Jane Crow," see Pauli Murray and Mary O. Eastwood, "Jane Crow and the Law: Sex Discrimination and Title VII," *George Washington Law Review* 34 (1965): 232; on transposition, William H. Sewell, Jr., "A Theory of Structure: Duality, Agency, and Transformation," *American Journal of Sociology* 98, no. 1 (1992): 1–29.

22 Clemens, "Logics of History?," 500.

23 Jane Lewis, "The Decline of the Male Breadwinner Model: Implications for Work and Care," *Social Politics* 8, no. 2 (2001): 152–69. On gradual institutional change, see, e.g., Wolfgang Streeck and Kathleen Thelen, eds., *Beyond Continuity: Institutional Change in Advanced Political Economies* (Oxford: Oxford University Press, 2005).

24 Alice Kessler-Harris, "Designing Women and Old Fools: The Construction of the Social Security Amendments of 1939," in *U.S. History as Women's History: New Feminist Essays*, eds. Linda K. Kerber, Alice Kessler-Harris, and Kathryn Kish Sklar (Chapel Hill: University of North Carolina Press, 1995).

25 Lewis, "Gender and the Development of Welfare Regimes"; Orloff, "Markets Not States?"

26 Robert Max Jackson, *Destined for Equality: The Inevitable Rise of Women's Status* (Cambridge, MA: Harvard University Press, 1998).

27 Denise Riley, *"Am I That Name?": Feminism and the Category of "Women" in History* (London: Macmillan Press, 1988).

28 Wendy Brown, "Finding the Man in the State," *Feminist Studies* 18, no. 1 (1992): 7–34; R.W. Connell, *Gender and Power* (Palo Alto, CA: Stanford University Press, 1987).

29 Helga Maria Hernes, *Welfare State and Woman Power: Essays in State Feminism* (Oslo: Norwegian University Press, 1987), 15; Anette Borchorst, "Gender and State," in *Introduction to Political Sociology*, ed. Benedikte Brinkner (København: Hans Reitzel, 2013), 91–108.

30 Evelyne Huber and John D. Stephens, "Partisan Governance, Women's Employment, and the Social Democratic Service State," *American Sociological Review* 65, no. 3 (2000): 323–42; Barbara Hobson and Marika Lindholm, "Collective Identities, Women's Power Resources, and the Making of Welfare States," *Theory and Society* 26, no. 4 (1997): 475–508; Åsa Lundqvist, *Family Policy Paradoxes: Gender Equality and Labour Market Regulation in Sweden, 1930–2010* (Bristol: Policy Press, 2011).

31 Seth Koven and Sonya Michel, eds., *Mothers of a New World: Maternalist Politics and the Origins of Welfare States* (New York: Routledge, 1993); Pat Thane and Gisela Bock, eds., *Maternity and Gender Policies: Women and the Rise of the European Welfare States, 1880s–1950s* (London: Routledge, 1991); Theda Skocpol, *Protecting Soldiers and Mothers* (Cambridge, MA: Harvard University Press, 1992). For a critique of the literature on maternalism, see Julia Adams and Tasleem Padamsee, "Signs and Regimes: Rereading Feminist Work on Welfare States," *Social Politics* 8, no. 1 (2001): 1–23.

32 Chiara Saraceno, "The Ambivalent Familism of the Italian Welfare State," *Social Politics* 1, no. 1 (1994): 60–82; Ann Orloff, "Gender and the Social Rights of Citizenship: The Comparative Analysis of Gender Relations and Welfare States," *American Sociological Review* 58, no. 3 (1993): 303–28.

33 Suzanne Mettler, *Soldiers to Citizens: The GI Bill and the Making of the Greatest Generation* (New York: Oxford University Press, 2005). These mechanisms disproportionately supported white families. And one must note that Social Security did offer a modicum of economic security to covered breadwinning men when they retired and, to a lesser degree, when they were unemployed. Support to their wives was conditional on the breadwinners' entitlement. But "family wages," family incomes, and women's caregiving were not directly subsidized.

34 Robert C. Lieberman, *Shifting the Color Line: Race and the American Welfare State* (Cambridge, MA: Harvard University Press, 1998); Joanne L. Goodwin, "'Employable Mothers' and 'Suitable Work': A Re-evaluation of Welfare and Wage-earning for Women in the Twentieth-Century United States," *Journal of Social History* 29 no. 2 (1995): 253–74.

35 Celia Winkler, *Single Mothers and the State: The Politics of Care in Sweden and the United States* (Lanham, MD: Rowman & Littlefield, 2002); Lundqvist, *Family Policy Paradoxes*.

36 Ann Orloff, "From Maternalism to 'Employment for All': State Policies to Promote Women's Employment Across the Affluent Democracies," in *The State After Statism: New State Activities in the Era of Globalization and Liberalization*, ed. Jonah Levy (Cambridge, MA: Harvard University Press, 2006), 230–68.

37 Cynthia Harrison, *On Account of Sex: The Politics of Women's Issues, 1945–1968* (Berkeley: University of California Press, 1989); Lundqvist, *Family Policy Paradoxes*.

38 Lundqvist, *Family Policy Paradoxes.*

39 Åsa Lundqvist, "Activating Women in the Swedish Model," *Social Politics* 22, no. 1 (2015): 111–32.

40 Anita Nyberg, "From Foster Mothers to Child Care Centers: A History of Working Mothers and Child Care in Sweden," *Feminist Economics* 6, no. 1 (2000): 5–20.

41 This did not grow out of, nor could it depend upon, active labor market policy – there was none in the United States; see, e.g., Margaret Weir, *Politics and Jobs: The Boundaries of Employment Policy in the United States* (Princeton, NJ: Princeton University Press, 1992). Rather, the regulation of access to and conditions of employment was the institutional route for change in gendered labor policies.

42 Kessler-Harris, *In Pursuit of Equity*, and Nancy MacLean, *Freedom Is Not Enough: The Opening of the American Workplace* (Cambridge, MA: Harvard University Press, 2008); on feminists' legal strategies, see Nicholas Pedriana, "From Protective to Equal Treatment: Legal Framing Processes and Transformation of the Women's Movement in the 1960s," *American Journal of Sociology* 111, no. 6 (2006): 1718–61.

43 Amy Campbell, *Raising the Bar: Ruth Bader Ginsburg and the ACLU Women's Rights Project* (Xlibris, 2003).

44 Nicholas Pedriana and Robin Stryker, "The Strength of a Weak Agency: Enforcement of Title VII of the 1964 Civil Rights Act and the Expansion of State Capacity, 1965–1971," *American Journal of Sociology* 110, no. 3 (2004): 709–60; Kevin Stainback and Donald Tomaskovic-Devey, *Documenting Desegregation: Racial and Gender Segregation in Private Sector Employment Since the Civil Rights Act* (New York: Russell Sage Foundation, 2012).

45 See, e.g., John Skrentny, *The Minority Rights Revolution* (Cambridge, MA: Harvard University Press, 2009), ch. 8; Nancy MacLean, "The Hidden History of Affirmative Action: Working women's struggles in the 1970s and the Gender of Class," *Feminist Studies* 25, no. 1 (1999): 42–78.

46 Frank Dobbin, *Inventing Equal Opportunity* (Princeton, NJ: Princeton University Press, 2009), ch. 8; see also Zippel, *Politics of Sexual Harassment*; MacKinnon, *Sexual Harassment of Working Women.*

47 Lieberman, *Shifting the Color Line*; Goodwin, "'Employable Mothers' and 'Suitable Work.'"

48 Jill Quadagno, *The Color of Welfare: How Racism Undermined the War on Poverty* (New York: Oxford University Press, 1994).

49 Jennifer Mittelstadt, *From Welfare to Workfare: The Unintended Consequences of Liberal Reform, 1945–1965* (Chapel Hill: University of North Carolina Press, 2005); Ellen Reese, *Backlash Against Welfare Mothers: Past and Present* (Berkeley: University of California Press, 2005).

50 Marisa Chappell, *The War on Welfare: Family, Poverty, and Politics in Modern America* (Philadelphia: University of Pennsylvania Press, 2012), and Reese, *Backlash Against Welfare Mothers.*

51 Kimberly J. Morgan, "A Child of the Sixties: The Great Society, the New Right, and the Politics of Federal Child Care," *Journal of Policy History* 13, no. 2 (2001): 215–50; Sonya Michel, *Children's Interests/Mothers' Rights:*

The Shaping of America's Child Care Policy (New Haven, CT; Yale University Press, 1999).

52 Edward J. McCaffery, *Taxing Women* (Chicago, IL: University of Chicago Press, 2007).

53 Christopher Howard, *The Hidden Welfare State: Tax Expenditures and Social Policy in the United States* (Princeton, NJ: Princeton University Press, 1999).

54 In 1989, the widows' pension was eliminated, removing the one remaining program structured along breadwinner/caregiver lines; Jan M. Hoem, "To Marry, Just in Case. . .: the Swedish Widow's-Pension Reform and the Peak in Marriages in December 1989," *Acta Sociologica* 34, no. 2 (1991): 127–35.

55 Christina Wolbrecht, *The Politics of Women's Rights: Parties, Positions, and Change* (Princeton, NJ: Princeton University Press, 2010).

56 Yvonne Hirdman, "The Gender System," in *Moving On: New Perspectives on the Women's Movement*, Acta Jutlandica LXVII:1; Humanities series 66, eds. Tayo Andreasen et al. (Aarhus University Press, 1991), 187–207, and "State Policy and Gender Contracts: The Swedish Experience," in *Women, Work and The Family in Europe*, eds. Eileen Drew, Ruth Emerek, and Evelyn Mahon (London: Routledge, 1998), 36–46; Lundqvist, *Family Policy Paradoxes*, 92–93. Recent work on the so-called "welfare state paradox" highlights the high levels of occupational sex segregation obtaining in the Nordic countries alongside relatively low gender wage gaps and poverty levels. Hadas Mandel and Moshe Semyonov, "A Welfare State Paradox: State Interventions and Women's Employment Opportunities in 22 Countries," *American Journal of Sociology* 111, no. 6 (2006): 1910–49. They are challenged by Walter Korpi, Tommy Ferrarini, and Stefan Englund, "Women's Opportunities Under Different Family Policy Constellations: Gender, Class, and Inequality Tradeoffs in Western Countries Re-examined," *Social Politics* 20, no. 1 (2013): 1–40.

57 Arnlaug Leira, *Working Parents and the Welfare State: Family Change and Policy Reform in Scandinavia* (Cambridge: Cambridge University Press, 2002), 94; Guðný Björk Eydal and Tine Rostgaard, eds., *Fatherhood in the Nordic Welfare States: Comparing Care Policies and Practice* (Bristol: Policy Press, 2014).

58 Lundqvist, *Family Policy Paradoxes*, 98; Laura Carlson, *Searching for Equality: Sex Discrimination, Parental Leave and the Swedish Model With Comparisons to EU, UK & US Law* (Philadelphia: Coronet Books, 2007).

59 Morgan, *Working Mothers*, 151–52; Catherine R. Albiston, *Institutional Inequality and the Mobilization of the Family and Medical Leave Act: Rights on Leave* (New York: Cambridge University Press, 2010).

60 Kimberly J. Morgan, "The 'Production' of Child Care: How Labor Markets Shape Social Policy and Vice Versa," *Social Politics* 12, no. 2 (2005): 243–63.

61 Kent Weaver, *Ending Welfare as We Know It* (Washington, DC: Brookings, 2000).

62 John Myles and Paul Pierson, "Friedman's Revenge: The Reform of 'Liberal' Welfare States in Canada and the United States," *Politics & Society* 25, no. 4 (1997): 443–72; Bruce D. Meyer and Dan T. Rosenbaum, *Welfare, the Earned Income Tax Credit, and the Labor Supply of Single Mothers, No. w7363*

(Cambridge, MA: National Bureau of Economic Research, 1999); on caring rights, see Trudie Knijn and Monique Kremer, "Gender and the Caring Dimension of Welfare States: Toward Inclusive Citizenship," *Social Politics* 4, no. 3 (1997): 328–61.

63 See, e.g., Gwendolyn Mink, *Welfare's End* (Ithaca, NY: Cornell University Press, 1998).

64 In Social Security, change in the formal – and now gender-neutral – breadwinner/caregiver logic has been politically near-impossible, for it would mean taking dependents' benefits away from many people. But changes have occurred through drift, as women increasingly pay for their own benefits in that, even as employment levels and their contributions to the system increased, a retired worker must choose between benefits based on her own employment records and those based on her husband's. Madonna Harrington Meyer, "Making Claims as Workers or Wives: The Distribution of Social Security Benefits," *American Sociological Review* 61, no. 3 (1996): 449–65; Pamela Herd, "Reforming a Breadwinner Welfare State: Gender, Race, Class, and Social Security Reform," *Social Forces* 83, no. 4 (2005): 1365–93.

65 Which groups benefit in each country is subject to dispute; see, e.g., Korpi et al., "Women's Opportunities Under Different Family Policy Constellations"; Marie Evertsson, Paula England, Irma Mooi-Reci, Joan Hermsen, Jeanne De Bruijn, and David Cotter, "Is Gender Inequality Greater at Lower or Higher Educational Levels? Common Patterns in the Netherlands, Sweden, and the United States," *Social Politics* 16, no. 2 (2009): 210–41; Hadas Mandel, "Winners and Losers: The Consequences of Welfare State Policies for Gender Wage Inequality," *European Sociological Review* 28, no. 2 (2012): 241–62.

6

States and Gender Justice

Mala Htun and S. Laurel Weldon

Can the "many hands" of the state be a force for social justice and equal rights? Many activists and international organizations seem to think so. They lobby for public policy changes, call on states to endorse and enforce treaties, and hold state actors accountable for their normative commitments to equality and dignity. At the same time, there are many reasons to be skeptical about states. States are responsible for genocide and other massive violations of human rights, famine, and the large-scale destruction of the natural environment. Their operating procedures and institutions commit everyday violence against the complexity of human practices, cultures, and identities. The state, as Peter Evans notes, is both a source of the problem and part of the solution.[1] It is a cause of, and a remedy for, human suffering.

Our broader research project explores the conditions under which the state's many hands can be harnessed as a force for gender justice. Specifically, we ask: what are the political, historical, and societal contexts associated with state actions to enhance equality and freedom? Which actors and conditions matter in shaping progressive policy? Democracy? Wealth? Secularization? Leftist parties? Active social movements? As Orloff puts it in Chapter 5, scholars have shifted their focus from simply mapping the stratifying and gender-differentiating state to charting the ways in which it can alter the gender (and racial) order. The central questions today, she notes, center on *how* and *through what mechanisms* states can be transformed.

The answer to this question is not one, to paraphrase Simone de Beauvoir, but many.[2] State transformation to promote the rights and dignity of women is far from a simple, linear, or unidimensional process.

As many scholars have pointed out, states can be both progressive and regressive. They can extend greater rights and freedoms to women and men with one hand while taking them away with the other.[3] The "woman-friendly" welfare states of Northern Europe provide generous maternity and parental leave, and some, such as Norway and Sweden, pioneered the "daddy leaves" that encourage greater sharing of caregiving and income-earning between partners. But some of these countries were late to adopt the innovative policies to address violence against women (VAW) that were rapidly spreading across the world. Meanwhile, in the United States, Canada, and Australia – where governments were taking innovative action on VAW and pushing other countries to do the same – state action provided much weaker support for working mothers or even parents more generally. Support varies dramatically across Canadian provinces, Australian women lacked publicly paid parental leave until 2010, and most women in the United States still lack publicly funded parental leave.

Understanding state action vis-à-vis gender demands that we disaggregate and differentiate among the historically different ways that the state has acted to shape the gender order. State action differs across the different dimensions of gender, and follows a distinctive logic in each way that the state attempts to prop up or change this order. To analyze the diversity and contradictions of state action, we develop a typology of gender-related policy that is defined by examining the intersection of gender, class, and nation. This typology suggests fresh insights for scholars seeking to understand why states sometimes take action to combat marginalization, oppression, and exploitation, and at other times tolerate or endorse these relationships.

Like other chapters in this volume, we do not see the state as a single actor but as a constellation of institutions, functions, and purposes. Yet the state is not just *any* set of institutions, as Morgan and Orloff point out in their introductory chapter. The state's access to legitimate coercive force, and administrative and normative power, endow it with a unique capacity and opportunity to craft alternative social relations. The state does not act in the same way with respect to all issues or all groups. Different aspects of the state developed along distinct historical pathways. Its structures simultaneously enable mobilization and access to some groups while denying it to others.[4]

Gender, for its part, is not just an attribute of individual identity or a type of performance, but a collection of institutions: a set of rules, norms, and practices, widely held and somewhat predictable – though not uncontested – about what it means to be and act as a woman and a man.[5] Gender is the mechanism through which "woman" and "man" and "masculine" and "feminine" come to be known as legitimate conceptual categories.[6] Conceptualizing gender as an institutional phenomenon helps account for its structural and historical character: it cannot be reduced to the actions and preferences of individuals and derives much of its weight from its endurance over time. The state's many hands, such as its civil and criminal laws, institutions of organized violence, and social welfare apparatus, help to uphold the institutions of gender (albeit in varying, and often contradictory ways), though other forces, such as the capitalist economy and religious and cultural systems, are also important.[7]

In previous work, we outlined a typology to facilitate analysis of state action to promote gender equality and gender justice.[8] First, we distinguished between those gender issues that touch upon religious doctrine ("doctrinal" issues) and those that do not ("nondoctrinal" issues). Policy change on the former types of issues – including family law (also called personal status law), abortion, and contraception – is often shaped by the institutionalized relationship between the state, on the one hand, and religious groups, clans, and tribes, on the other. Second, we distinguished between issues that advance women's rights as a status group and those that are inflected by class differences. We argued that feminist movements and international norms are frequently important to mobilize awareness and political will for change on "status" issues. "Class" issues touch upon the relative responsibilities of states, markets, and families for social provision, and include publicly funded maternity and parental leave and child care.[9] Whereas feminist movements and international norms may also be important forces for change on "class issues," the ways that left parties and labor mobilization have shaped state–market relations will also matter.

The typology distinguishes between contemporary dynamics of state action. It also differentiates historically distinct pathways through which state action has unfolded. In this chapter, we illustrate the power of analysis that disaggregates these dynamics and pathways by describing patterns of policy change on family law and violence against women. We show that global variation in family law is strongly associated with historical experiences and contemporary institutional arrangements forging certain types of state–religion relations. Yet religious factors are less important for policy development on VAW. Under the influence of autonomous feminist movements and international norms, many countries – including non-Western and less developed ones – took early initiatives to combat VAW.

GENDER AND GENDER EQUALITY

Since institutions of gender disadvantage women in particular ways (and different women in distinct ways), state-sponsored interventions must tackle and address each of these ways in order to promote equality. Following Iris Marion Young, we see gender as comprised of distinct, irreducible subinstitutions, or what Young calls the "basic axes of gender structures": the status hierarchy, the sexual division of labor, and normative heterosexuality.[10] The *status hierarchy* refers to those institutionalized patterns of cultural value that privilege men and the masculine and devalue women and the feminine.[11] By virtue of their low status, women and the feminine are marginalized, rendered "other," lesser beings less worthy of rights and dignity. The *sexual division of labor* refers to the tendency, across most societies, for women to shoulder a disproportionate burden of reproductive and care work. This pattern reinforces economic inequalities, including occupational sex segregation, gender wage gaps, and the scarcity of women in upper management.[12] *Normative heterosexuality* locates heterosexual coupling as the legitimate site of rights, reproduction, and romance. Under the regime of normative heterosexuality, deviations from gender dimorphism and heterosexuality are unintelligible,[13] leading to lack of recognition of same-sex relationships and parenting and transgender expressions, among other phenomena.

Gender equality is one possible configuration of gender institutions, though it exists in no contemporary society.[14] We define it as an ideal condition in which groups constituted by gender – such as men and women – have similar opportunities to participate in politics, the economy, and social activities; their roles and status are equally valued; none suffers from gender-based disadvantage or discrimination; and both are considered free and autonomous beings with dignity and rights.[15] We define gender equality policies as those measures through which government can accelerate or obstruct progress toward this ideal: "Gender equality policy aims to dismantle hierarchies of power that privilege men and the masculine, a sexual division of labor that devalues women and the feminine, and the institutionalization of normative heterosexuality."[16] In the rest of this chapter, we analyze factors associated with progressive state action against the sexual division of labor and status hierarchy, addressing normative heterosexuality in later work.

DISAGGREGATING STATE ACTION

Policies to advance women's rights challenge prevailing patterns of social organization, but in potentially different ways. Progress toward gender justice may question not only the sexual division of labor and institutionalized patterns of cultural value privileging masculinity, but also the authority of religious institutions and the reach of markets. Each issue involves different actors, activates different cleavages, and motivates different types of political conflicts. The movement toward gender equality is varied and even contradictory. Since achieving equality involves modifications in many spheres of life, such as politics, the economy, the family, and civil society, we can better understand and categorize the diverse political conditions under which this occurs by disaggregating policies into different dimensions.

Doctrinal/Nondoctrinal

To promote equality, the state must first have legitimate jurisdiction and authority. Yet in some societies, the state's claim to regulate issues related to kinship and reproduction is recent, incomplete, and contested. Churches, clans, and tribes historically administered such rules, which include provisions on marriage, divorce, inheritance, and registries of birth and death. By regulating how, when, and with whom women and men bear children, kinship rules enabled religious and traditional leaders to control the boundaries of cultural communities.[17] They continue to form a central component of most religious doctrines, as well as the codified traditions of cultural groups, and leaders of such groups are heavily invested in their content.

Other gender issues, by contrast, are not contemplated by religious doctrine and are more removed from the historical authority of ecclesiastical authorities. They concern zones of life rarely touched upon by scripture (such as government versus private provision of childcare) or more modern dilemmas that traditional religions and customs failed to anticipate (such as equality in the workplace). We call the former sets of issues, including family or personal status law and issues concerning reproduction and sexuality (such as abortion and contraception), "doctrinal" issues. We call the latter set of issues "nondoctrinal."

Doctrinal issues are often highly controversial because they are perceived to touch upon not just the position of women but also the public status of religion and cultural groups. Regimes wanting to curtail the influence of religion and marginalize traditional cultures have used legislation on women and the family as an instrument to attack religion. By empowering women, they aimed to break down the influence of traditional authorities. By contrast, religious and cultural groups seeking to enhance their power, or emphasize and maintain their difference, often endorsed rules that subordinated women to the authority of their husbands and fathers.[18] We can therefore expect that the broad context of state–religion relations will go a long way toward shaping the context for policymaking on doctrinal issues.

Status/Class

Institutionalized patterns of cultural value subordinate women as a status group.[19] They deny women the recognition and dignity they merit as human beings by casting men as normative and women as inferior, "other," and lacking in value. We call policies to remedy such harms "status policies." They address those practices and values that render women vulnerable to violence, marginalization, exclusion, and other injustices that prevent them from participating as peers in political and social life.

Other types of injustice are more directly attributable to the reproductive work that women do by virtue of their position in the sexual division of labor, and are experienced differently by women of different class positions. Wealthier women can purchase at least some reproductive work[20] on the market by hiring domestic workers to serve as nannies, cooks, and cleaners, or by exiting the labor market to perform domestic duties. Poor and working-class women find this much more difficult, if not impossible. They are far more dependent on the state for help in alleviating their reproductive responsibilities. We call policies addressing class inequalities among women "class policies." They include paid maternity or parental leave, government-funded child care, and funding for services enabling reproductive freedom, such as abortion and contraception.

Change in status policies involves altering the relationship between the state and particular kinds of bodies. At stake is the status such bodies hold in political life, the degree of autonomy they are afforded (or, conversely, the degree of regulation and invasion of privacy that is acceptable), and the degree to which their security is considered a priority. Changing the social, legal, and political status of a group often requires legal reforms, criminal justice innovations, provision of social services, and the like, but may not involve fundamentally restructuring state–market relations.

TABLE 6.1. *Typology of Policies to Promote Gender Justice/Equality*

		Do the policies challenge the doctrine of religious organizations or the codified tradition or sacred discourse of major cultural groups?	
		Doctrinal	Nondoctrinal
Does the policy advance women's rights as a status group or as a class?	Status	Family law Abortion legality Reproductive freedom	Violence against women Gender parity/quotas Constitutional equality Workplace equality
	Class	Public funding for abortion and contraceptives	Maternity/parental/ daddy leave Public funding for child care

Source: Htun and Weldon 2010 (modified from its original version).

In contrast, change in class policies involves alteration of relations between the state and the market. The pattern of social provision and the degree and kind of market regulation is critical for understanding resistance and innovation in this area.

Table 6.1 depicts our typology of gender-related policy issues. Our classification of some issues as "doctrinal" and others as "nondoctrinal," some as "class" and others as "status," is not a scheme that is fixed for all countries and all points in time. Political struggles involve attempts by actors to reframe issues. What is more, issues that play out as "nondoctrinal" in some contexts – through a dynamic that fails to invoke or involve religion – may be heavily doctrinal in others. For example, though religious authorities failed to oppose measures to combat violence against women in North America, Latin America, and Europe, advocates of VAW policies in some countries in the Middle East and North Africa (MENA) have encountered religiously based opposition. Provisions against marital rape, for example, have provoked objections framed in religious discourse emphasizing a woman's marital duties and a husband's prerogatives.[21]

In the next sections of the chapter, we show how our disaggregated approach helps to account for distinctive patterns of policy development. We discuss examples from two quadrants of our typology: family law (doctrinal, status policy) and violence against women (nondoctrinal, status policy). As this brief discussion of two issue areas shows, the same factors are not associated with progress toward gender justice. As we have suggested earlier, each follows a distinct logic of change depending on the historical context of state action and the broader set of issues and actors the policy invokes.

Institutionalized Religion and Family Law

Family law (also called personal status law) refers to rules regulating marriage, divorce, the rights and obligations of spouses, property, parenting, inheritance, and related issues. A crucial component of women's (and men's) citizenship, family law shapes private rights and relations as well as public autonomy and opportunities. It is a central way that the modern state upholds – or denies – women's rights. Family law was liberalized in most countries of the West during the latter half of the twentieth century, but remains discriminatory in much of the global South, even as international human rights norms and feminist movements have been able to make headway on other areas of women's rights.

Figure 6.1 depicts variation in family law in the seventy countries of our study (blank spaces indicate that the country was not included). Each country's score is based on an index we developed to measure the degree of sex equality in a range of areas.[22] The higher the score, the more egalitarian; the lower the score, the more discriminatory. The vast majority of countries with high scores in 2005 were European (including both Western and post-Communist countries) and Latin American. Most of the lowest scoring countries in 1995 and 2005 were located in the MENA, parts of South and Southeast Asia, and Sub-Saharan Africa.

Our historical and statistical analysis of trends in family law suggests that the degree of sex equality today is strongly associated with institutionalized relations between the state and religion. In countries where political and ecclesiastical power are tightly linked, family law tends to discriminate against women. In contexts with a greater separation of secular and religious institutions, family law tends to be more egalitarian. Why? The reason is not that religions are inherently patriarchal; they are only historically so (as are most secular traditions). Religious doctrine is less likely to evolve and adapt to changing social practices in contexts where ecclesiastical doctrine is upheld by the state. Patriarchal interpretations of religion become frozen and linked to the public status of religion more generally.[23]

It can be hard to reform family law in these contexts. Challenges to the religious interpretations endorsed by state law come to be seen as challenges to the entire institutional configuration binding state power and religious authority. Family law turns into a referendum on the role of religion in the polity and on the public and legitimizing character of

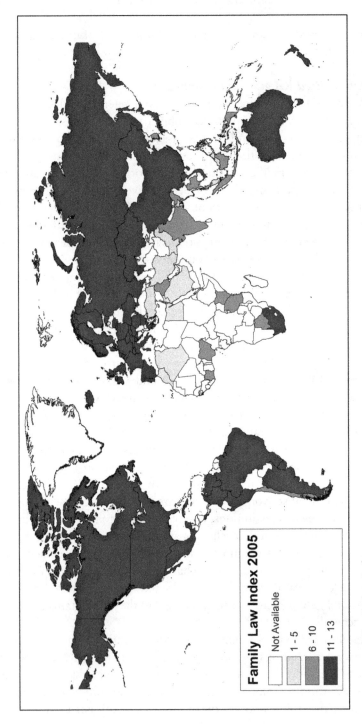

FIGURE 6.1. Family law index, 2005.

religious doctrines. To uphold patriarchal family law is to defend religion's public status; to favor egalitarian reforms is to challenge the relationship between church and state. As a result, critics of family law (and other elements of state power) are often branded as heretics. The greater the degree of political institutionalization of religion, the more likely it is that criticism will be suppressed and critics maligned, thwarting legal changes advancing equality.[24]

Malaysia's experiences with family law reform illustrate this process. The linkage between religious power and family law was established during colonial rule. In treaties that progressively established British power over the Malaysian peninsula, the domain of indigenous Malay rulers was circumscribed to matters of "religion and custom."[25] With British assistance, Islamic law was codified, and bureaucracies to administer it were created. This pattern "placed local rulers at the center of Malay ethnic and Muslim religious identity during the colonial period and made legal codes and institutions a key instrument of their power. Islamic law came to occupy the center of Malay elite legitimacy, and a unified Malay ethnicity and Muslim religious identity became closely identified."[26]

Islamicization measures adopted in the 1980s further bound Malay identity and political legitimacy to religious law.[27] For example, the government expanded and rationalized the Shariah court system and promulgated the Islamic Family Law (Federal Territories) Act of 1984. Though one of the more progressive Muslim personal laws in the world for imposing conditions on polygamy, the husband's right to unilateral divorce, and recognizing the wife's claim to some matrimonial assets, it discriminates against women in multiple ways. Women lack guardianship rights over children, are legally obliged to obey their husbands, and suffer unequal conditions of and consent to marriage and divorce and unequal inheritance rights.

A vocal feminist movement – headed by the group Sisters in Islam (SIS) – began to propose reforms to the discriminatory elements of family law in the 1990s and 2000s. Notably, the group framed its demands in religious discourse and justified its demands with reference to the rich history of *fiqh* (jurisprudence). Yet SIS was branded in the press and by state officials as "traitors" and accused of insulting Islam. The government's religious affairs department (JAKIM) even proposed to ban people they considered to lack adequate knowledge of Islam from speaking in public on Muslim issues.[28]

At the core of debates over women's rights were competing interpretations of Muslim law and who is authorized to supply them. In classical

Islamic traditions, legal opinions (*fiqh*) are inherently flexible and pluralistic, and the product of human agency. *Fiqh* consists of a diverse jurisprudence applicable to changing social relations.[29] Yet the Malaysian state has promoted an alternative view stressing that Muslim law is fixed, uniform, divine in origin, and that only the *ulama* – or Muslim clergy – has the authority to speak on religious matters. The state's view has shaped public opinion, leading to pervasive misunderstandings of the nature of Islamic law and legal theory. As a result, it is easy to convince ordinary people that groups who question the state's laws are undermining Islam.[30]

A similar dynamic holds in other countries where family laws justified in the name of religion continue to discriminate against women. The Sudanese Family Law, for example, codified by the Islamist authoritarian regime in 1991, discriminates against women in multiple ways. A coalition of civic groups and some religious leaders has endorsed reforms to end child marriage, grant women rights to divorce, and eradicate polygamy. As in Malaysia, these advocates frame their positions in religious discourse. Yet reformers are regularly branded as agents of the West and against Islam. The women's rights convention CEDAW has become a virtual "swear word" in public debate.[31]

Though religion – particularly when its provisions are codified and the authority of its leaders upheld by state power – is a crucial factor shaping state action on family law, religion is less important for other areas of gender and women's rights. As we show in the following section, the contours of state policy on other issues is less associated with a religion–state dynamic, but instead turns on the mobilization of autonomous feminist movements calling attention to women's subordinate status and violations of their dignity.

AUTONOMOUS FEMINIST MOVEMENTS AND VAW

Sexual assault, intimate violence against women and girls, stalking, honor killings, sexual harassment, street harassment, and other forms of violence against women are significant barriers to their enjoyment of full rights as democratic citizens. In many contexts, VAW has prevented women from participating in public discussions, voting, and running for public office. Women modify their daily behavior to prevent violence and to feel secure: they curtail their public activities; rely on male escorts to achieve mobility, even in the most advanced democracies; and still find themselves unprotected in the most intimate areas of sexuality and the family.[32]

VAW continues to be pervasive. In the United States, for example, one in six women is sexually assaulted and one in five experiences domestic violence during the course of her lifetime, while in Europe, women are at far greater risk from violence against women than terrorism or cancer.[33] Surveys on U.S. college campuses and in the military reveal that sexual assault is widespread.[34] Yet most violations of women's human rights still go unreported to police or other authorities. VAW is difficult to articulate, especially for victims, as doing so often produces a sense of shame or guilt. The pervasiveness of women's subordination in many societies implies that VAW is often hidden from view, something many citizens do not even acknowledge.

In response to domestic and transnational activism, governments from some 180 countries endorsed, at the Fourth World Conference on Women held in Beijing in 1995, a set of official measures to protect women victims of violence and prevent future occurrences. These measures – such as shelters, counseling, public awareness campaigns, and legal reform – cut across several policy sectors including the administration of justice, public education, and social service provision. As this suggests, combating the scourge of violence against women demands a comprehensive, integrated governmental approach. We measured the extent of state action by developing an index covering legal changes, services, public education, and administrative reform.[35]

State action to combat VAW has been uneven across countries and over time (see Figures 6.2 and 6.3, which depict global variation in our VAW Index for 1995 and 2005). Canada, Australia, and the United States were the earliest countries to act and also enacted the most comprehensive policies on VAW. Latin American countries were also relatively early adopters. Meanwhile, several otherwise progressive states of Europe lagged behind, even in 1995 as the global community agreed to the Declaration on the Elimination of VAW. By 2005, many more states had adopted comprehensive policies to adopt VAW, but not all. Though communist countries were some of the earliest states in the world to reduce religious influence over family law and promote sex equality, for example, they were laggards when it came to VAW.

Our research has examined these intriguing patterns of state policy change to address VAW, patterns that confound traditional ideas about the drivers of policies to advance women's rights. Countries that were the first to take action were not distinguished by having a particularly large proportion of women in the legislature, nor were they countries where left parties were particularly strong or with the most advanced welfare states. Rather, the countries that were early movers and developed the most comprehensive action on VAW were those with strong, autonomous

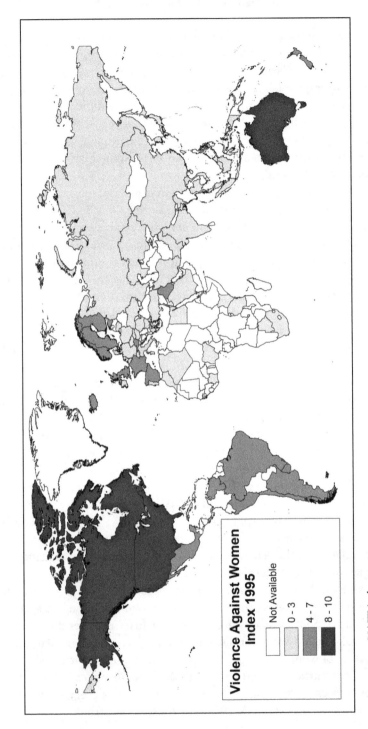

FIGURE 6.2. VAW index, 1995.

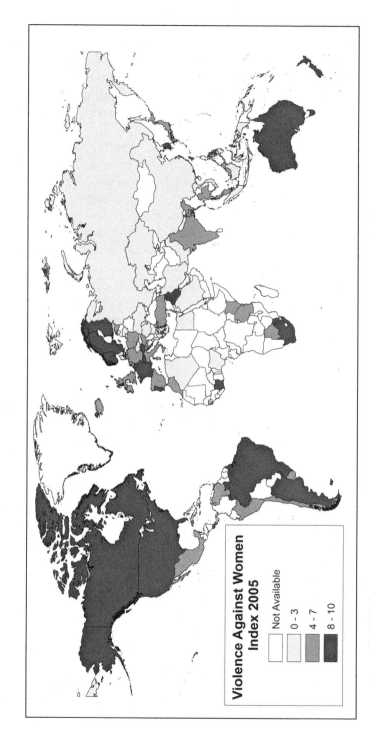

FIGURE 6.3. VAW index, 2005.

feminist movements. When these movements were able to draw on international norms – or, even more powerfully, regional norms and activist networks – state action of VAW accelerated and expanded. The roots of progressive action on women's rights, in this nondoctrinal, status-based policy area, lie in civil society, where social movements and transnational norms drive change.[36]

In countries with less robust civil societies, state action on VAW has been slower to develop. Communist countries historically reduced the influence of religion and promoted sex equality in family law; they also expanded welfare provisions to promote women's employment. In the twenty-first century, countries with historical experiences of Communism were among the most progressive in the areas of sex equality in family law and publicly funded maternity and parental leave.[37] Yet the post-Communist zone is a laggard when it comes to VAW, as Figures 6.2 and 6.3 show, since feminist movements autonomous from the state, political parties, and civic organizations such as labor unions have been slower to develop. Historical pathways that pave the way for action on some gender equality issues create obstacles for progressive change on others.

CONCLUSION

These results highlight the importance of treating both states and gender justice as multidimensional. Given the broad scope of challenges that equality poses, the factors that may help advance women's rights in some areas may very well be unimportant, or even inhibitive, in others. We can better understand the diverse ways the state configures the gender order by disaggregating state actions, though we do not disaggregate into traditional categories such as branches of government, functional specializations, and levels of federalism. Rather, what is important are the distinct ways that the state has historically upheld and enforced norms of gender, and the broader array of actors and issues that have been complicit in – or worked to contest – these diverse trajectories.

Promoting the changes that gender equality involves requires engaging with the particular dynamics of each trajectory of state action. In the case of family law, sex discrimination was closely tied to the development of the historical, institutionalized relations between the state and organized religion. Countries in which political authorities constructed and propped up religious power tended to have more discriminatory family laws into the late twentieth century, even as international norms endorsed equality and reformist coalitions mobilized for change. By virtue of its linkage to the public status of religion more generally, family law proved difficult to change without calling into question the broader contours of state–religion relations and provoking opposition of actors invested in particular arrangements of ecclesiastical power.

The trajectory of state action on VAW adhered to a different logic. Women's organizing as women publicly contested the status hierarchy of female subordination that rendered violence invisible and characterized it as an issue unworthy of concerted action by states and the international community. The power of institutionalized religion was less relevant than the autonomous mobilization of feminist movements, their linkage to international norms and networks, and the ability of local groups to bring global agreements home to matter in local contexts.

We began this chapter by posing the question of whether and how the state can be induced to be part of the solution to entrenched problems of discrimination, marginalization, subordination, and deprivation. Our work suggests that enlisting the state's assistance in a project of social change requires attention to the different historical pathways and multiple mechanisms through which it has helped uphold the gender order(s). The state has been a problem for women's rights, but it has not been a problem in only one way. (Nor has each problem been suffered similarly by different groups of women.) The state's relationship with organized religion, the respective roles of state and market in social provision, and the strength and autonomy of civil society each pose different constraints and opportunities for advancement on women's rights.

Notes

1 Peter Evans, "The State as Problem and Solution: Predation, Embedded Autonomy and Structural Change," in *The Politics of Economic Adjustment: International Constraints, Distributive Conflicts, and the State*, ed. Stephan Haggard and Robert Kaufman (Princeton, NJ: Princeton University Press, 1992).

2 Simone De Beauvoir, *Le Deuxième Sexe* (New York: Random House, 1953).

3 See, e.g., Julia S. O'Connor et al., *States, Markets, Families: Gender, Liberalism and Social Policy in Australia, Canada, Great Britain and the United States* (Cambridge: Cambridge Univerity Press, 1999).

4 Theda Skocpol, *Protecting Soldiers and Mothers: The Political Origins of Social Policy in the United States* (Cambridge, MA: Harvard University Press, 1992).

5 Cf. Ridgeway, who refers to gender as an "institutionalized system of social practices for constituting males and females as different in socially significant ways and organizing inequality in terms of those differences." Cecilia Ridgeway, "Gender, Status, and Leadership," *Journal of Social Issues* 57, no. 4 (2001), 637. Of course, there are a wide variety of approaches to gender, which we do not review here for reasons of space. For an overview and further

discussion, see Mary Hawkesworth, "Sex, Gender and Sexuality: From Naturalized Presumption to Analytic Categories," in *Oxford Handbook of Gender and Politics*, eds. Waylen et al. (Oxford: Oxford University Press, 2013); or the Critical Perspectives on Gender in *Politics and Gender* 1, no. 1 (2005).

6 Judith Butler, *Undoing Gender* (New York: Routledge, 2004).

7 Mala Htun and S. Laurel Weldon, "When Do Governments Promote Women's Rights? A Framework for the Comparative Analysis of Sex Equality Policy," *Perspectives on Politics* 8, no. 1 (2010): 207–16.; Mala Htun, "What It Means to Study Gender and the State," *Politics & Gender* 1, no. 1 (2005): 157–66.

8 Htun and Weldon, "When Do Governments Promote Women's Rights?"

9 Ann Shola Orloff, "Gender and the Social Rights of Citizenship: The Comparative Analysis of Gender Relations and Welfare States," *American Sociological Review* 58, no. 3 (1993): 303–28.

10 Iris M. Young, "Lived Body vs. Gender: Reflections on Social Structure and Subjectivity," *Ratio* 15, no. 4 (2002): 422.

11 Nancy Fraser, "Social Justice in the Age of Identity Politics: Redistribution, Recognition, and Particpation," in *Redistribution or Recognition?: A Political-Philosophical Exchange*, ed. Nancy Fraser and Axel Honneth (New York: Verso, 2003); "Feminist Politics in the Age of Recognition: A Two-Dimensional Approach to Gender Justice," *Studies in Social Justice* 1, no. 1 (2007): 23–35.

12 See, e.g., Victor Fuchs, *Women's Quest for Economic Equality* (Cambridge, MA: Harvard University Press, 1990); Susan Moller Okin, *Justice, Gender, and the Family* (New York: Basic books, 2008).

13 Butler, *Undoing Gender*.

14 Htun and Weldon, "When Do Governments Promote Women's Rights?" 208.

15 Feminist scholarship offers a wide variety of approaches to understanding gender equality. For a few examples, see the special forum, entitled "Inequality Regimes: Refracting Gender, Race and Class." *Social Politics*, 7, no. 2 (2000), especially the article by Joan Acker; Diane Sainsbury, *Gender, Equality and Welfare States* (New York: Cambridge University Press, 1996); Emanuela Lombardo, Petra Meier, and Mieke Verloo, eds., *The Discursive Politics of Gender Equality: Stretching, Bending and Policy-Making* (New York: Routledge, 2013).

16 Htun and Weldon, "When Do Governments Promote Women's Rights?" 208.

17 Cf. Ayelet Shachar, *Multicultural Jurisdictions: Cultural Differences and Women's Rights*, (New York: Cambridge University Press, 2001), and Ayelet Shacar, "Privatizing Diversity: A Cautionary Tale from Religious Arbitration in Family Law," *Theoretical Inquiries in Law* 9, no. 2 (2008): 573–607; Seyla Benhabib, *The Claims of Culture: Equality and Diversity in the Global Era* (Princeton, NJ: Princeton University Press, 2002).

18 Mounira Charrad, *States and Women's Rights: The Making of Postcolonial Tunisia, Algeria, and Morocco* (Berkeley: University of California Press, 2001); Mala Htun, *Sex and the State: Abortion, Divorce, and the Family Under Latin American Dictatorships and Democracies* (New York:

Cambridge University Press, 2003); Gregory J. Massell, "Law as an Instrument of Revolutionary Change in a Traditional Milieu: The Case of Soviet Central Asia," *Law and Society Review* 2, no. 2 (1968): 179–228; Kandiyoti, Deniz, *Women, Islam, and the State* (Philadelphia, PA: Temple University Press, 1991); Maxine Molyneux, "Family Reform in Socialist States: The Hidden Agenda," *Feminist Review* 21 (1985): 47–64.

19 Fraser, "Feminist Politics in the Age of Recognition."

20 We refer not to gestational carriers and egg donation but to the entire range of work needed to reproduce and maintain human life – child care, food production, cleaning, care for the sick and elderly, keeping track of schedules, transportation, household expenses, and the like.

21 Liv Tønnessen, "When Rape Becomes Politics: Negotiating Islamic Law Reform in Sudan," *Women's Studies International Forum*, 44 (2014): 145–53. In addition, religious power was historically important in the development of welfare policies (which we classify here as class-based and nondoctrinal issues) in several European countries. See Kimberly J. Morgan, *Working Mothers and the Welfare State: Religion and the Politics of Work-Family Policies in Western Europe and the United States* (Palo Alto, CA: Stanford University Press, 2006).

22 For more information, see Mala Htun and S. Laurel Weldon, "State Power, Religion, and Women's Rights: A Comparative Analysis of Family Law," *Indiana Journal of Global Legal Studies* 18, no. 1 (2011): 145–65; on the expansion of individual rights vis-à-vis family (for children and women), see also Goran Therborn, *Between Sex and Power: Family in the World 1900–2000* (New York: Routledge, 2004).

23 Mala Htun and S. Laurel Weldon, "Religion, the State, Women's Rights, and Family Law," *Politics & Gender* 11, no. 3 (2015): 451–77.

24 Ibid.

25 Iza Hussin, "The Pursuit of the Perak Regalia: Islam, Law, and the Politics of Authority in the Colonial State," *Law & Social Inquiry* 32, no. 3 (2007): 760.

26 Ibid, 765.

27 Seyyed Vali Reza Nasr, *Islamic Leviathan: Islam and the Making of State Power* (Oxford: Oxford University Press, 2001): 121–29.

28 Jaclyn Ling-Chien Neo, "'Anti-God, Anti-Islam, and Anti-Quran': Expanding the Range of Participants and Parameters in Discourse over Women's Rights and Islam in Malaysia," *Pacific Basin Law Journal* 21, no. 1 (2003): 70. Ironically, few of the officials involved in codifying Malaysia's Shariah court procedures had formal training in Islamic jurisprudence. Moustafa notes that "the Islamization of law and legal institutions in Malaysia was ... more the project of state officials who lacked any formal training or in-depth knowledge of Islamic legal theory rather than the traditional '*ulama*.'" Tamir Moustafa, "Islamic Law, Women's Rights, and Popular Legal Consciousness in Malaysia," *Law & Social Inquiry* 38, no. 1 (2013): 168–88. See also Kikue Hamayotsu, "Politics of Syariah Reform: the Making of the State Religio-Legal Apparatus," in *Malaysia: Islam, Society and Politics*, eds. Virginia Hooker and Norani Othman (Singapore: Institute of Southeast Asia Studies, 2003): 55–79; Maznah Mohamad," Making Majority, Undoing Family: Law,

Religion and the Islamization of the State in Malaysia," *Economy and Society* 39, no. 3 (2010): 360–84.

29 Asifa Quraishi, "The Separation of Powers in the Tradition of Islamic Statehood," in *Constitutionalism in Islamic Countries*, ed. Rainer Grote and Tilmann Röder (New York: Oxford University Press, 2012) and Asifa Quraishi, "Who Says Shari'a Demands the Stoning of Women- A Description of Islamic Law and Constitutionalism," *Berkeley Journal of Middle Eeastern & Islamic Law* 1 (2008): 163.

30 Tamir Moustafa, "Islamic Law"; Chandra Muzaffar, "Tolerance in the Malaysian Political Scene," in *Islam & Tolerance*, ed. Syed Othman Alhabshi and Nik Mustapha Nik Hassan (Kuala Lumpur: Institute of Islamic Understanding Malaysia (IKIM), 1994); Zainah Anwar and Jana S. Rumminger, "Justice and Equity in Muslim Family Laws: Challenges, Possibilities, and Strategies for Reform," *Washington & Lee Law Review* 64, no. 4 (2007): 1529.

31 Samia al-Nagar and Liv Tønnessen, "Family Law Reform in Post-Conflict Sudan: Competing Claims for Gender Justice between Sharia and Women's Human Rights," Paper Presented at conference on Women's Rights and Democratization in Asia and Africa, Bergen, November 2014.

32 Lori L. Heise, Jacqueline Pitanguy, and Adrienne Germain, "Violence Against Women: The Hidden Health Burden," *World Bank Discussion Papers* 255 (New York: World Bank, 1994); S. Laurel Weldon, *Protest, Policy, and the Problem of Violence Against Women: A Cross-National Comparison* (Pittsburgh, PA: University of Pittsburgh Press, 2002); Mona Lena Krook, *Quotas for Women in Politics: Gender and Candidate Selection Reform Worldwide* (New York: Oxford University Press, 2009).

33 R. Amy Elman, *Sexual Equality in an Integrated Europe: Virtual Equality* (New York: Palgrave Macmillan, 2007): 85; U.S. Department of Justice Violence Against Women Office, *Biennial Report to Congress 2010*. Department of Justice (2010), www.ovw.usdoj.gov/docs/2010-biennial-report-to-congress.pdf.; U.S. Department of Justice Violence Against Women Office, *2011 Roundtable on Sexual Violence*. Department of Justice (2011), www .ovw.usdoj.gov/sexual-violence-report- march.pdf.

34 Carol Bohmer and Andrea Parrot, *Sexual Assault on Campus: The Problem and the Solution* (New York: Lexington Books, 1993); Heather M. Karjane, Bonnie Fisher, and Francis T. Cullen, *Sexual Assault on Campus: What Colleges and Universities Are Doing About It* (Washington, DC: U.S. Department of Justice, Office of Justice Programs, National Institute of Justice, 2005). Recent events at the University of Virginia and Columbia University have brought this issue to the forefront of public discussion, and the *New York Times* recently reported on a survey of undergraduates at the Massachusetts Institute of Technology, showing that 17 percent of respondents had been victims of sexual assault. *New York Times*, October 27, 2014. A U.S. Department of Defense survey in 2014 found that 22 percent of active duty women and 7 percent of men reported being victims of sexual assault in the previous year. Available at www.defense.gov/News/News-Transcripts/Transcript-View/Article/607047; David Cantor, Bonnie Fisher, Susan Chibnall, Reanne

Townsend, Hyunshik Lee, Carol Bruce, and Gail Thomas, *Report on the AAU Campus Climate Survey on Sexual Assault and Sexual Misconduct* (Washington, DC: The Association of American Universities, 2015).

35 See Weldon, "Protest, Policy and the Problem," and S. Laurel Weldon, "Women's Movements, Identity Politics, and Policy Impacts: A Study of Policies on Violence Against Women in the 50 United States," *Political Research Quarterly* 59, no. 1 (2006): 111–22; Mala Htun and S. Laurel Weldon, "The Civic Origins of Progressive Policy Change," *American Political Science Review* 106, no. 3 (August 2012): 548–69.

36 For more detail, see Htun and Weldon, "Civic Origins," and S. Laurel Weldon, "Beyond Bodies: Institutional Sources of Representation for Women in Democratic Policymaking," *Journal of Politics* 64, no. 4 (2002): 1153–74.

37 The purpose of communist action on women's rights was less to promote their individual rights or autonomy than to facilitate national development goals, such as full employment, secularization, and fertility control. See, e.g., Maxine Molyneux, "Family Reform."

7

The Civil Rights State

How the American State Develops Itself

Desmond King and Robert C. Lieberman

The study of the politics of the American state has flourished in the last three decades. Galvanized initially by the twin stimulants of Stephen Skowronek's foundational work on the American administrative state and the comparative political sociology project to "bring the state back in," the resultant body of scholarly literature on the American state defies the longstanding conventional characterization of the United States as a "stateless" polity and provides instead a rich seam of empirical and theoretical insights.[1] Scholars of American politics working in a variety of analytical traditions and with different historical foci recognize a plethora of American states, including the hidden state, the submerged state, the litigation state, the activist state, the national security state, the regulatory state, the unsustainable state, the segregated state, the warfare state, and the fiscal state.[2]

Collectively, this body of scholarship demonstrates two particular aspects of the state in American political development. First, its presence is central to the analysis of American government and politics. It is next to impossible, for example, to comprehend the fierce ideological and partisan polarization of American politics without considering current struggles over the state's size and role in the economy and society.[3] Second, this literature increasingly suggests the importance of disaggregation for analysis. Many observers perceive the American state as "weak" or "limited" – for example, advocates of expanded social welfare protection or greater regulation. Others see the same state as excessively strong – defenders of free markets, for example, but also African-Americans during the first two-thirds of the twentieth century, when American state power maintained and protected a segregationist order.

The American state has many different aspects. Decomposing "the state" into a set of primary activities and dimensions helps untangle the various and multiple ways in which the state affects American politics and society. In this chapter we focus on what we call the "civil rights upholding state" as a way of exploring both of these claims – the American state's inescapable presence and its multiplicity and variety – and connecting them to the linked challenges of statebuilding and democratization. This civil rights upholding state is a recent phenomenon and contrasts with the pre-1960s American state, which opposed rather than advanced civil rights. Certainly some parts of the federal government – notably in the Department of Justice from the 1950s – began to develop a civil rights agenda around the right to vote but mostly this activity succumbed to the common view of the American state as weak and overwhelmed by society. The American state's role since the 1960s, by contrast, in which some parts of the executive and even federal courts have advanced racial equality, implies the need for a new conceptualization of the state in the supposedly "stateless" United States, a theme taken up in this chapter.

Disaggregating the state to distinguish its effects on internal patterns of stratification, especially racial hierarchies, is not unique to the American state, as several chapters in this volume illustrate. Tianna Paschel shows that the often-lauded egalitarianism in Brazilian public policies and politics often conflicted with de facto realities and racism. She notes that the scale of racism has prompted the Brazilian state to engage actively in the sort of affirmative action policies from which the American state has distanced itself since the 1980s. Thus both the Brazilian and American states find themselves directly involved in addressing profound patterns of racial inequality despite developing on different trajectories. Significantly for comparative analysis, Paschel locates a similar civil rights grassroots movement driving efforts to get the Brazilian state's policies to be responsive to racial inequality. And she finds also that state engagement is partial, confined to certain key agencies, and vulnerable to shifting pressures and political coalitions. Modern states, it seems, are inherently weak in the role of promoter of racial equality. This fragility or weakness derives fundamentally from the persistence of racial hierarchy in political discourse (the dominance of "colorblind" rhetoric) and the political marginalization of advocates of material racial equality.

NOT STATELESS BUT MULTIDIMENSIONAL

Reacting to early accounts of the American state as a peculiarity in comparative terms – an underdeveloped "Tudor state" that lacked the coercive capacity to maintain order in a modernizing society, as Samuel Huntington argued in the 1960s – the work of Stephen Skowronek demonstrated that American national administrative capacities developed out of America's distinctive political patterns rather than the European model centered around the progressive democratization of absolutism.[4] Subsequent legions of studies have examined the development, peculiarities, and capacities of the American state, placing it at the core of the subfield of American political development.[5] But for Skowronek, as for those who have followed him, the American state was defined by the existence of formal, coercive administrative power lodged with public bureaucracies, and its dimensions – presence, size, strength, autonomy, and the like – measured against the European-derived Weberian model. In this perspective, the American state is regarded as anemic, limited in scale and scope.

This conventional framework derives from a number of characteristics of the American state comparatively and historically, which are usually cited cumulatively as evidence of American statelessness and infirmity. But if we break down these aspects of the American state and examine each closely, we find that such a simplistic weak–strong metric fails to capture the complexities of the American state and the variety of ways in which it accomplishes a distinct set of political and policy purposes even though it does not always look the part. The cumulative effect of looking at the American state in this way is not to observe the weakness of the state but rather to expose the ironies and complexities of the American state that demand explanation. In previous work, we identify a number of dimensions of American state activity, building on J. P. Nettl's valuable 1968 article, that bear on the state's capacity to secure and protect democratic rights.[6] Here we briefly identify five aspects of the American state.

1) *The Administrative State as a Distinct Bureaucracy.* One reason for the absence of the term "state" in respect to the United States is the search for a common bureaucratic form, which has proved misguided and misleading. The quintessential bureaucratic state, considered by the German sociologist Max Weber, was the contemporary Prussian and French forms. In contrast to the professional, elite bureaucrats who presided over centralized power in these countries, American national bureaucracy is fragmented and incapacitated by its ambiguous position in the

governmental structure. But, as Daniel Carpenter has shown, the result of this arrangement is not an incapacitated administrative state but bureaucracy that relies on alternative mechanisms – not formal coercive capacity but networks and democratic roots in civil society – to be effective.[7] This administrative state was entangled with the long and nonlinear evolution of democracy in the United States, acting over time both to limit and to protect democratic rights in a variety of ways. But to identify the absence of a centralized bureaucratic Weberian structure as signaling an absent or impaired American state is no longer tenable analytically. What the United States possesses is a different kind of state.

2) *The Standardizing State.* Both because many central initiatives have been resisted and because the center's institutional capacity is weak comparatively, it is often maintained that the American state's ability to establish and enforce uniform national standards (particularly to enforce democratic rights) for policy and governance is limited.[8] The resistance to national standards and the persistence of localism in policymaking suggest the national state's limits in commanding uniformity in the design and application of policy and the enforcement of rights across the population.[9] Among the principal costs of the devolution of power to small local units and the resulting policy diversity has been the tendency to place policymaking in the hands of oppressive local majorities.[10] This federal–state policy divergence, among other effects, helped to cement the segregationist racial order manifest not only in the ideology of states' rights and the locally rooted policies of Jim Crow but also in patterns of urban residential segregation, local labor markets, and access to local government. It permitted authoritarian enclaves to persist.[11]

Nonetheless, standard-setting by the national state has not been entirely unsuccessful. Federal policies often form a recognizable expression of national authority and policies in ways comparable to those of other countries and thereby create standards that unjustly treated citizens can cite. Those occupying the enduring institutional core of political authority – lawmakers, presidents, and judges – proclaim ends and mobilize support for policy ideas. Implementation, definition of detail, regulation of practices, policing of deviance from identified standards, and renewal of mandates depend critically upon bureaucrats, their allies, and public compliance.[12] Thus, the American state engages continuously in policy formulation, regulation, standard setting, and enforcement, as much as do other states.[13]

3) *The Fragmented State versus Executive Power.* As a consequence of confronting a fragmented polity, scholars of American politics typically

focus separately on the institutions of separated power – the presidency, Congress, the courts, or the bureaucracy. Or they may think about "government" loosely conceived as a package of bureaucratic agencies and the regulations enforced by these agencies. Still others will consider electoral politics or federalism as agents of fragmentation. However, not only has the American state as a whole taken on an ever-increasing role in policymaking and governance since the late nineteenth century, but the state's core institutions have significantly expanded their particular mechanisms of wielding power. The federal courts, for example, have been increasingly inclined to employ constitutional authority to protect civil and political rights (while leaving the other branches substantial leeway to pursue their own policies in other realms).[14] But it is the executive that has grown most dramatically and significantly as an institution that employs state power. The presidency has expanded its power through such strategies as increased use of executive orders and signing statements to augment often-elusive statutory instruments. Like court decisions, executive actions were an important component of the American state's expansion into civil rights protection, and they were key elements of the development of federal affirmative action in the 1960s.[15] There is now little political difference at the center between the Republicans and Democrats about wanting to control the state – though to use it for different ends.

4) *The Associational State: A Strong Nation.* Much analysis, influenced by Tocqueville, emphasizes the strength of American political culture and the country's sense of nationhood, reinforced by an ideology of liberal individualism, a decentralized institutional framework, and the rhetoric of openness to newcomers (a rhetoric frequently compromised in practice). Such a view complements the analytical bias already created by the multiple sites of power. These Tocquevillian assumptions underlie an important tradition that sees civil society as a counterbalance to the centralization of state power and a necessary ingredient for the success of democratic governance.[16]

But these assumptions have not limited an expansion in national state power and remit. A robust civil society is not a substitute for a weak state; rather, civil society can best support democracy when it is aligned with strong political institutions and a functioning state.[17] There is also growing appreciation of the importance of the American state in fostering, sustaining, and renewing the values perceived as intrinsic to U.S. political culture. National state institutions play a major integrative role in the United States, providing central foci around a common vision of the nation that the country's many ethnic, racial, and national groups are invited to share and support (and which most do).

The most fundamental limitation of the Tocquevillian celebration of decentralization and local communities is that the latter proved to be the basis for enduring discrimination and racism in the twentieth century. In practice, localism has meant discrimination and inequities.[18] As we know from many comparative studies of federalism, excessive local powers can become an enemy of civil liberties.[19] This certainly occurred in the United States, where states chose either to implement constitutional safeguards and legislative mandates for segregation in the 1880s and 1890s (in place until the 1960s) or to permit de facto segregated race relations, as in housing and schooling.[20]

5) *The Segregating State*. The American state's deep and complex entanglement with patterns of racial classification, division, and hierarchy is one of the key – and comparatively distinctive – consequences of the dimensions of American "stateness" that we have elaborated.[21] The historic racially constructed differences among the population, which have been central to the structure and processes of American politics, mean that white and black Americans (and, more recently, Latinos, Asian-Americans, and other groups) have experienced the state in very different ways.[22]

The enduring significance of this segregating state has been documented by, among others, political scientist Ira Katznelson in his analysis of how a system of "affirmative action for whites" operated concurrently with the expansion of the American state's organizations and public programs from the 1930s.[23] Katznelson gives the example of how, in practice, the GI Bill widened inequalities since few African-Americans in either the North or the South were beneficiaries. Thus public policy was not neutral but quite partial in its effects, as office holders will have intended.

Race is most commonly associated with state weakness through its effects on such processes as regional differentiation, class formation, and welfare statebuilding. But this weakness is two-faced: weakness is also an expression of strength for those enjoying the benefits.[24] The long-dominant white supremacist racial policy alliance was maintained at key points by the Southern political control of Congress, a control complemented by public policies that ensured the endurance of segregationist racism. However, citing Southern influence insufficiently explains how the federal government accommodated and fostered the segregationist alliance through much of the twentieth century through a wide range of policies and political and administrative practices.[25]

More recently, the state has been the key agent of civil rights advancement, going from oppressor to protector in the span of a generation while still acting as an agent of segregation and inequality in other areas.[26] It is this variation across time and space in the American state's capacity to act as a protector of democratic rights for racial minorities that both creates our central puzzle and offers an analytical opening toward a new conceptualization of the state in the supposedly "stateless" United States.

AVOIDING THE "DEMOCRATIZATION TRAP"

This conundrum has both historical and analytical dimensions. Historically, there are a number of distinct but interconnected explanations for this shift: the emergence and success of a broad social movement among African-Americans to claim rights promised but denied,[27] changing racial attitudes among whites and the diminution of the gap between the American creed of liberty and equality and the country's treatment of racial minorities, the pressures of the Cold War, and the legitimation imperative of state officials in the face of racial violence during the 1960s.[28]

Analytically, the puzzle is a form of what we might call the "democratization trap": the ultimate success of the expansion of democratic rights depends on the state's ability to protect and enforce those rights, but in a society with already-established democratic procedures, those in power must act affirmatively to include the excluded.[29] In order to accomplish this, the state must not only nurture opportunities for political participation and even promote substantive equality but also restrain itself from interfering in the civil liberties necessary for the flourishing of democracy.[30] But if the state is to be at least, in part, the guardian of democratic rights, which depend on freedom from an overbearing state, who (as Juvenal asked) will guard the guardians?[31] Can a democracy, especially one seeking to emerge from a less than fully democratic past, accomplish this without resorting to means that effectively subvert the transparency and popular control that are the hallmarks of democratic policymaking? Moving from one sort of equilibrium, where a state in the hands of the strong preys on the weak, to another, where the state acquires the capacity to protect the weak, is no easy task.[32] As Jennifer Hochschild observes, the tension between integration for an excluded minority and democratic majority rule is a characteristic dilemma of the civil rights era.[33] Nevertheless, this is the path – from segregated state to civil rights state – that the United States followed for a brief but revealing period in the 1950s and 1960s, and that demands explanation. The key questions to consider are how the state participated in this transformation and how the state was, in turn, transformed by this process.

We describe this change in which state power decidedly evolved toward the protection of a vulnerable minority group not to suggest that the process of statebuilding is necessarily linear or progressive or reducible to a single dimension – quite the contrary, in fact.[34] The civil rights–upholding state narrative that we sketch here highlights the political and operational challenges of such a statebuilding transformation. Our multidimensional approach to the state and the processes of statebuilding focuses attention on both the contingency and fragility of such change. The architecture of the civil rights–upholding state was uneven across the state's various domains, and the incomplete triumph of civil rights protection – which cuts against the more conventional triumphalist, movement-centered narrative of the civil rights revolution – made the gains in the state's capacity to protect and promote racial equality especially vulnerable.[35] When juxtaposed with limits to material racial equality and the outright reversal of some active policies aimed at protecting civil rights, notably the growth of the "carceral state" in the decades since the civil rights revolution, our story raises further important questions about the potential reversibility of statebuilding.

MAKING AMERICA'S CIVIL RIGHTS–UPHOLDING STATE

The 1960s mark a key decade in the American state's role in securing rights of citizenship. One of the most basic rights – the right to vote – was the subject of the Voting Rights Act (VRA) in 1965. This legislation created extensive powers of intervention for the U.S. Department of Justice, particularly in some Southern states, which had used egregious measures to exclude black voters from the ballot box.[36] The intervention was the culmination of several decades of protest: despite the slow build up, the intervention nonetheless signaled a firmness of federal purpose backed up with federal marshals that had been previously absent. A temporary measure initially, the VRA was made permanent over four decades. Its first renewal in 1970 barely succeeded as the Republican president Richard Nixon considered vetoing to repay his debt to the Southern segregationist, Strom Thurmond, who had rallied whites to the GOP in 1968.[37] The preclearance trigger mechanism (enabling a

Justice Department assessment of changes in a state's voting rule or reapportionment) remained in place until a 5–4 Supreme Court ruling declaring it unconstitutional in 2013.[38]

The denial of voting rights was a pillar of the segregationist order in place between the 1880s and 1960s. For the most part, the act of illegality in respect to voting rights is measurable: a citizen has rights to be registered to vote and, once registered, is either admitted or denied access to the ballot box on the day of the election. (There are, of course, continuing discrepancies and issues around requiring a photo ID to register; the incorrect compilation of, and illegal excisions from, electoral registers; and the varying status of former felons.) Less easy to measure so categorically and harder to change is discrimination against some citizens because of their race. But the segregationist order rested upon and fanned discrimination against African-Americans in myriad legal and informal ways throughout all sectors of public and private America. Among key areas ripe for federally empowered reform were education, employment, housing, and transportation.

Scholars often speak of the "civil rights revolution" as if it were a single, unified event. But even a cursory glance at the history of race policy and racial inequality in the United States reveals that the expansion of civil rights occurred unevenly and came about through the operation of a variety of often-disconnected events and mechanisms. The civil rights–upholding state was built along each of the dimensions of the American state that we have elaborated, unfolding along each dimension according to distinct logics and temporal patterns. Disaggregating this multidimensional process not only underscores the variability of civil rights progress but also allows us to pose key questions about the development of state power in a democratic context (and see the discussion in Chapter 9).

Civil Rights and the Administrative State

Both voting rights and the ambition to eradicate discrimination drove changes in each of the dimensions of the American state that we have identified. But these changes were uneven, more successful and complete along some dimensions than others.

Before the civil rights revolution, the administrative state was neither equipped nor inclined to enforce equality. The administrative state itself was segregated and a segregator for much of the twentieth century, and there was very little administrative capacity within the state to enforce racial equality. At the federal level, President Franklin Roosevelt, under the threat of mass protest, created a Fair Employment Practices Committee (FEPC) during World War II to investigate racial discrimination by defense contractors, although many critics complained that the FEPC was toothless and ineffectual. Congress refused to make it permanent. During the 1940s and 1950s, a number of states sought to establish their own FEPCs to address employment discrimination. In some states these measures were successful, although they provoked substantial opposition among the business community. (However, in several states the delays in achieving this outcome were striking.)[39]

The Justice Department's Civil Rights Division, created in 1957, has also been a key participant in the state's enforcement efforts. In the wake of the civil rights revolution in law and policy, the paper capacity of the administrative state in civil rights has proliferated, ranging from the active enforcement of voting rights (until the Civil Rights Division and its voting section were gutted by the George W. Bush administration) to the well-documented limitations of agencies, such as the Equal Employment Opportunities Commission(EEOC) and Housing and Urban Development (HUD)'s Office of Fair Housing and Equal Opportunity.[40] There remains a great deal of variability and uncertainty in the state's capacity to enforce racial equality; here the transformation seems limited.

Constructing the policies and agencies and appointing the personnel to take forward the antidiscrimination civil rights agenda was bound to be a complex process. From numerous studies we now know that several unanticipated processes and decisions drove it. For example, the emerging practice of "affirmative action" was extended and given authoritative force by the Nixon White House under the Philadelphia Plan and, as John Skrentny documents, the secretary of labor found himself defending an expansive conception of the policy to a highly skeptical Senate.[41] Although the Nixon administration soon lost interest in pursuing an affirmative action agenda forcefully, this period installed a crucial definition of the policy and some of the instruments – in particular, minority hiring on federal contracts – that helped reduce discrimination in labor markets. Another well-documented stream of civil rights enforcement mechanisms is the "strength of the weak state" strand of research, which demonstrated how regulatory tools could in fact be employed for enforcement and transformative purposes. This useful phrase, coined by sociologists Frank Dobbin and John Sutton, conveys how the apparent weakness of new regulatory powers lodged in the administrative state to eradicate discrimination in labor markets proved to be powerful tools of transformation. Fearful of litigation from federal agencies empowered to impose tough measures on firms, the executives at corporations choose to establish Human Resources departments drafting appropriate antidiscrimination and prodiversity rules and procedures.[42] Dobbin demonstrates the two complementary trajectories of internal reforms within corporations. First, personnel managers responded to changing circumstances and tried to anticipate future pitfalls in their hiring and promotion arrangements, and second, external dynamics principally motored by a Supreme Court that for a brief period embraced affirmative action and the ambitious standard of testing for "disparate impact" handed down in the famous 1971 case *Griggs v. Duke Power Company*.[43] Absorbing the implications of this external force again fell to the personnel experts central to Dobbin's narrative. According to Dobbin, "personnel experts convinced executives that formal systems could stem discrimination and keep them out of court... By 1979 some two-thirds of top corporate executives favored government affirmative action efforts."[44]

Civil Rights and the Standardizing State

Where the transformation to the civil rights–upholding state really expanded the American state's presence was in its role as an agent of standardization. Standardizing democratic rights as implied and indeed guaranteed in the 1964 and 1965 laws (aided by subsequent laws, such as the 1968 Civil Rights Act) required mobilizing this dimension of American state activity.

The American state had guaranteed a standard of "separate but equal" between 1896 and 1954, a practice legitimated by the Supreme Court.[45] This standard, ironically, revealed the failure of the national state as a standardizer. The Court's decision in *Plessy* signaled, and in fact validated, the federal government's withdrawal from the civil rights field after its attempts to standardize citizenship (through the Fourteenth Amendment) and voting and other practices (through a series of civil rights laws and ultimately unsuccessful "force" acts) in the second half of the nineteenth century. In effect, then, it was the lack of standard enforcement of the "equal" half of the *Plessy* formula that was the most salient feature of the state's civil rights stance in the first half of the twentieth century, until the NAACP Legal Defense Fund's litigation strategy and the direct action of the civil rights movement revealed its hollowness as a standard.[46] As conflict over the enforcement of civil rights standards escalated in the 1950s and 1960s, the federal government was reluctant and its leaders hesitant even as it gradually entered the field.

Richard Neustadt famously interpreted President Eisenhower's unenthusiastic commitment of federal troops to oversee the integration of Central High School in Little Rock as a failure of presidential power.[47] John and Robert Kennedy were equally reluctant to bring visible federal power to bear in defense of the Freedom Riders and the black students who sought to enroll in southern state universities. This same American state now was expected to enforce the right to effective federal antidiscrimination laws and treatment promised by a new standard of democratic rights. The United States was democratizing. But the mechanisms for this process of standardization were underspecified – if specified at all – in the key acts of Congress.

Somewhat inconsistently, the federal courts have played a positive and key role in advancing the standardizing project in civil rights. This connection is found, for example, in Paul Frymer's work on the National Labor Relations Board.[48] Successful litigation against a handful of large employers for failing to meet equal opportunity best practices prompted other corporations to revise their internal personnel codes to preclude being sued. Dobbin records this change: "in 1975 the Supreme Court, in *Albemarle Paper Company v. Moody*, signaled that employers found guilty of discrimination would routinely pay the kinds of mammoth back-pay awards seen in the consent decrees. Personnel experts now advised all sorts of firms to put in equal opportunity 'best practices' to inoculate themselves. At the same time, a change in the character of discrimination suits piqued executive interest in bureaucratizing promotion."[49] Similarly, in higher education, the Supreme Court has played a role in the convergence of admissions standards on a rationale ("diversity") and a means ("holistic admissions") for considering race as a factor in university admissions[50] (criteria the Court chose not to review in 2012 but to return it to the relevant federal court[51]). However, in both of these areas the Court subsequently retreated.

Civil Rights and the Fragmented State

The fragmentation of the state before and after the civil rights revolution is familiar. Fragmentation is a factor both within the federal government and between the federal government and states and municipalities. Fragmentation enabled opponents of civil rights to conduct their campaign on multiple fronts, using the courts, on the one hand, to challenge the legality of executive decisions and, on the other hand, challenging the jurisdictional power of agents of the federal government in their state or local domains. For instance, the Little Rock crisis in 1957 arose from the decision of the local school district board to implement the Supreme Court's 1954 desegregation judgment. But the school board rapidly lost control of the situation as the state governor entered the fray spearheading his challenge to the Court's ruling and disregarding Justice Department compliance orders. The school integration struggle, despite occurring in a global media storm, was distinct from efforts to tackle discrimination preceding the legislation of the 1960s. But fragmentation did effectively compel centralized and authoritative executive leadership to transcend coordination problems for the key decision of deploying national guards to protect African-American children.

Institutional fragmentation requires action in pursuit of civil rights enforcement at multiple sites of governance. In principle, a department such as Justice, with its established Civil Rights Division, could take the lead to coordinate civil rights enforcement across numerous areas of American society. In practice, however, discrimination in housing and in employment relations are issues confronted in the relevant dedicated departments or agencies such as HUD and the National Labor Relations Board, respectively. Also, state governments have increasingly pursued their own race policies, whether on their own initiative (such as California's Proposition 209, the 1996 state constitutional amendment that prohibits affirmative action in state government activities, including public universities) or in the face of court challenges (as in the Texas 10% plan, implemented as a work-around after a federal appeals court limited race-conscious admissions to the University of Texas).[52] Multiple sites make for complexity, particularly given the ambition to impose common standards. Furthermore, the pursuit of antidiscrimination measures implies more than simply regulating behavior; it also implies imposing standards to rectify historical injustices.

Civil Rights and the Associational State

Finally, the associational connections between the state and nonstate actors constitute another dimension that has undergone a substantial transformation over the last half-century. Through the mid-twentieth century, associational connections and the effective delegation of state power to private actors empowered segregationist and white supremacist groups and essentially enlisted them as co-enforcers of Jim Crow in the South, through groups such as the Ku Klux Klan and the White Citizens' Councils, which were instrumental in maintaining the Southern racial order through violence as well as other means. In the North, groups of private citizens performed similar functions; realtors, neighborhood associations, and labor unions, among others, all contributed to the maintenance of residential and workplace segregation and of a distinctively racialized industrial political economy.[53]

After the civil rights revolution, the state was administratively ill equipped to enforce emerging norms of colorblindness and equal treatment. This has been the common predicament of the American state. Whether through deliberate design or the political exigencies of legislating under separated powers, the American state often lacks the coercive authority that would allow it to live up to the expectations of governance that are typically embedded in major policy innovations. Such, at least, was the case after the Civil Rights Act, which outlawed discrimination across a wide swath of social and economic relations but withheld from the national state the regulatory tools to enforce this prohibition. This is, in many ways, the crux of the American statebuilding dilemma.

At the same time, the period in which the American state was called upon to significantly expand its upholding of democratic rights for a group of its citizens – well over 10 percent of the population – coincided with a declining trust in the government's capacity to "do the right thing." Referring to American National Election Studies opinion survey data, Donald Moynihan and Patricia Ingraham report that "by the late 1960s and increasingly in the 1970s, trust in government went into a freefall."[54] Consequently, those responsible for designing and expanding the civil rights state were compelled to develop subtle, nonintrusive means to achieve this end that generally involved partnerships with nongovernmental groups, whose resources could be deployed to further public ends that were beyond state's direct reach. Much of the civil rights enforcement agenda – the substitution of group-based, race-conscious antidiscrimination practices ("affirmative action") for a more colorblind and individualistic approach, for example – was achieved through public–private associational arrangements; associational connections, as much as coercive authority, helped launch and consolidate the state's expanded enforcement role.[55]

MULTIPLE DIMENSIONS, MULTIPLE LOGICS

As a moment for expanding the American state's role as an upholder of democratic and other civil rights and locating the multidimensional transformation of the state, the mid-1960s seemed propitious. Each of these dimensional transformations occurred in its own time and unfolded according to its own logic, but the 1960s was a moment when each converged.[56] The logic of each dimension differed because of the distinct historical formation in such areas as the administrative or associational state. Parts of the administrative state derived from the founding of the republic and there were some key nineteenth-century developments – such as the demonstrated power of the federal level to transform the circumstances of Native Americans.[57] Likewise, the strong nation underpinning the American state changed during the middle of the nineteenth century when a civil war exploded about the meaning of its membership parameters.

These logics were manifested throughout the 1960s. For example, the culmination of the civil rights movement's demands in the 1960s signaled fundamental change in the associational state's conception of who made up the nation, imploding a narrow and often whites-only conception. This transformation continues as the parameters of America's multiracial demography expand and recognition of that expansion is more widely appreciated.[58] Labor market and housing discrimination also gained increased salience during this time, as social protests and legislative debate galvanized attention. The logic of these changes was both endogenous to the U.S. polity – maintaining a white segregationist order was unsustainable – and exogenous as racial discrimination received extensive foreign coverage. Similar forces structured the dismantling of the segregated state.

The New Deal years, but especially World War II and the 1950s, inspired increasing public confidence in the competence of the federal government's bureaucratic capacities and the appositeness of using such capacities to standardize. Moynihan and Ingraham characterize these decades as the state's "administrative heyday – a time when government and administration were held in high popular esteem, trusted, and enjoyed bipartisan support. While defining administrative epochs is an inexact practice," they continue, "the beginning of the New Deal in 1932 represents a reasonable starting point for this period, while the political repudiation of the Great Society in 1968 represents an endpoint."[59] Between the late-1950s and mid-1960s when voters were asked if the government could be trusted to act appropriately, over 70 percent of respondents affirmed either "just about always" or "most of the time."[60]

But there are three flaws in this analysis. First, the American state and government, which voters applauded, was a segregating one. Both among the bureaucratic employees and in the bureaucratic agencies' direct presence through program delivery in society, strict segregation between whites and African-Americans was entrenched and reproduced.[61] Second, during this period of "administrative heyday," the American state was called upon to implement judicial decisions after the 1954 case abrogating "separate but equal" arrangements. It initially proved faint-hearted. In October 1957, a reluctant President Eisenhower deployed federal national guards to enforce a desegregation order at a school in Little Rock, Arkansas, to admit nine African American children to a formerly whites-only high school. This intervention produced only short-term relief. This episode – of global, not just national, significance and media coverage – just precedes the opinion data cited by Moynihan and Ingraham finding high voter trust in government action, which might therefore reflect endorsement of the Eisenhower court enforcement. Third, the American state's mechanisms or instruments for enforcement were historically underdeveloped. Because the state developed primarily as an agent of regulation and policing rather than standardization and enforcement, the challenge presented by new enactment of civil and voting rights pushed the American state into uncharted territory.

CONCLUSION: MOVING AMERICAN STATE THEORY FORWARD

How does the burgeoning scholarly literature in both American political development and comparative politics help shed light on the American state and its core activities? In this chapter, we identified the parameters of America's civil rights state and argued that it furthers our understanding of the American state in two ways. First, the concept of the civil rights state at least suggests a fundamental transformation in the American state's pre-1960s role as an upholder of segregation. This transformation therefore provides a case with which to understand endogenous institutional reconfiguration and change. Second, realizing that the civil rights state was built in a piecemeal fashion across a range of agencies dealing with different spheres of discrimination permits a nuanced account of this process. Such an account therefore acknowledges the persistence of subnational authoritarian enclaves.

At the same time, the civil rights state has come unraveled in many ways in the decades since the 1960s. Material racial inequality remains entrenched in many spheres of American society and public policy, and in many cases the state and public policy are important factors in reproducing inequality rather than mitigating it.[62] Voting rights, which were at the core of the civil rights revolution, are currently under attack through laws requiring photo identification in order to vote and attempts to restrict early voting, efforts that tend to suppress turnout and particularly target minority voters.[63] The 2013 decision *Shelby County v. Holder* fired a nearly fatal hole in the VRA's preclearance powers.[64] The contemporary political impasse over taxation and government spending limits the state's capacity to address economic challenges that disproportionately affect African-Americans and other minorities.[65] The conservative majority of the Supreme Court is diluting hard-won judicially administered rights and protections, including public school integration and, more recently, affirmative action. And over the last few decades the United States has developed a vast, punitive, and decidedly race-laden "carceral state" that has imprisoned and disenfranchised a large and disproportionate share of young black men, with disastrous consequences for racial equality in economic opportunity and political empowerment.[66]

These apparent reversals in the path of the American state's development raise a set of critical questions about the dynamics of statebuilding. If political development is characterized, as Orren and Skowronek put it, by "*durable* shifts in governing authority," what do we make of the seeming reversibility of some key facets of the civil rights state? Under what conditions is statebuilding particularly susceptible to reversals? The often partial, halting, and incomplete transformation of the civil rights state suggests that a multidimensional perspective on American statebuilding offers useful insights into these questions. This analytical portrait of the state embraces multiple elements that are not always consonant with each other, a potential source of variation – across time, policy areas, and other variables – that can help build a more comprehensive account of the development of state power in the United States. As with the construction of state power, its decay and redeployment can often be understood as a process of endogenous institutional change that results from friction or dissonance among different institutional elements, and policy and statebuilding reversals often follow their own logic and depend on specific configurations of institutional structure and development.[67]

The civil rights state is, in many ways, a distinctively American phenomenon – in terms of both substance (racial division as constitutive of politics and citizenship) and institutional form (its characteristically disjointed and indirect modes of governance). But the connection between the long civil rights struggle and the structure and operations of the American state suggest several important lines of inquiry that perhaps extend beyond the particular case of the American civil rights state. Understanding the curious transformation of the civil rights state sheds important light on the American state's multidimensionality, which in turn points toward potentially fruitful insights about state developments more generally in a wide range of comparative settings, especially in the face of transnational forces that not so long ago seemed to herald the state's demise.

Comparatively, this conclusion sits with important recent scholarship about states and civil rights, notably Chapter 8 in this volume and Edward Gibson's book, *Boundary Control: Subnational Authoritarianism in Federal Democracies*, a comparative study of how hard it is to forge democratic institutions across federal systems which contain authoritarian enclaves. Where, in Chapter 8, Paschel writes about Brazil, Gibson's empirical focus is Mexico and Argentina with an illuminating comparative foray into the U.S. federal system. Gibson documents a boundary control conflict structuring politics when a democratic national polity coexists with authoritarian undemocratic enclaves, a key feature of the United States before the 1970s. Establishing democratic boundary control in this setting is taxing and helps explain the scale of challenge facing the transformation of the American state into a serviceable civil rights state.[68]

Notes

1 Stephen Skowronek, *Building a New American State: The Expansion of National Administrative Capacities, 1877–1920* (Cambridge: Cambridge University Press, 1982); Peter B. Evans, Dietrich Rueschemeyer, and Theda Skocpol, eds., *Bringing the State Back In* (Cambridge: Cambridge University Press, 1985).

2 Among the relevant literature, see Kimberley S. Johnson, *Governing the American State: Congress and the New Federalism, 1877–1929* (Princeton: Princeton University Press, 2007); Paul Pierson and Theda Skocpol, eds., *The Transformation of American Politics: Activist Government and the Rise of Conservatism* (Princeton: Princeton University Press, 2007); William J. Novak, "The Myth of the 'Weak' American State," *American Historical Review* 113 (2008): 752–72; Brian Balogh, *Government Out of Sight: The Mystery of National Authority in Nineteenth-Century America* (Cambridge: Cambridge University Press, 2009); Paul Frymer, "Racism Revisited: Courts, Labor Law, and the Institutional Construction of Racial Animus," *American Political Science Review* (2005) 99: 373–87; Lawrence Jacobs and Desmond King, eds., *The Unsustainable American State* (Oxford: Oxford University Press, 2009); Daniel Carpenter, *Reputation and Power: Organizational Image and Pharmaceutical Regulation at the FDA* (Princeton: Princeton University Press, 2010); Sean Farhang, *The Litigation State: Public Regulation and Private Lawsuits in the American Separation of Powers System* (Princeton: Princeton University Press, 2010); Sven Steinmo *The Evolution of the Modern State* (Cambridge: Cambridge University Press, 2012); Adam Sheingate, "Why Can't

Americans See the State?," *Forum* 7 (2009), www.bepress.com/forum/vol7/iss4/
art1; Garry Wills, *Bomb Power: The Modern Presidency and the National
Security State* (New York: Penguin Press, 2010); Suzanne Mettler, *The
Submerged State: How Invisible Government Policies Undermine American
Democracy* (Chicago: University of Chicago Press, 2011); James T. Sparrow,
Warfare State: World War II Americans and the Age of Big Government
(Oxford: Oxford University Press, 2011); and Kimberly J. Morgan and Andrea
Louise Campbell, *The Delegated Welfare State: Medicare, Markets, and the
Governance of Social Policy* (New York: Oxford University Press, 2012). For
the widened appreciation of the importance of studying the U.S. state in the
political science discipline, see the essays in *Forum*, 2010.

3 See Pew Research Center, 2012, "Partisan Polarization Surges in Bush, Obama
Years," June 12, p. 164. Available at www.people-press.org/files/legacy-pdf/
06-04-12%20Values%20Release.pdf.

4 Samuel P. Huntington, *Political Order in Changing Societies* (New Haven: Yale
University Press, 1968), chap. 2; Skowronek, *Building a New American State*;
Barrington Moore Jr., *Social Origins of Dictatorship and Democracy: Lord
and Peasant in the Making of the Modern World* (Boston: Beacon Press, 1966);
Michael Mann, *The Sources of Social Power*, vol. 2, *The Rise of Classes and
Nation States, 1760–1914* (Cambridge: Cambridge University Press, 1993);
Martin Shefter, "Party and Patronage: Germany, England, and Italy," *Politics
and Society* 7 (1977): 403–52.

5 Daniel P. Carpenter, "The Multiple and Material Legacies of Stephen
Skowronek," *Social Science History* 27 (2003): 465–74; Karen Orren and
Stephen Skowronek, *The Search for American Political Development*
(Cambridge: Cambridge University Press, 2004). For two recent outstanding
studies in American political development showing how the American state
shaped African-American inequalities, see Megan Ming Francis, *Civil Rights
and the Making of the Modern American State* (New York: Cambridge
University Press, 2014), and Daniel Kato, *Liberalizing Lynching: Building a
New Racialized State* (New York: Oxford University Press, 2015).

6 See Desmond King and Robert C. Lieberman, "Ironies of State Building:
A Comparative Perspective on the American State," *World Politics* 61 (2009):
547–88. See also J. P. Nettl, "The State as a Conceptual Variable," *World
Politics* 20 (1968): 559–92.

7 Daniel P. Carpenter, *The Forging of Bureaucratic Autonomy: Reputations,
Networks, and Policy Innovation in Executive Agencies, 1862–1928*
(Princeton: Princeton University Press, 2001). See also Robert C. Lieberman,
"Civil Rights and the Democratization Trap: The Public-Private Nexus and the
Building of American Democracy," in *Democratization in America:
A Comparative Historical Analysis*, ed. Desmond King, Robert C. Lieberman,
Gretchen Ritter, and Laurence Whitehead (Baltimore: Johns Hopkins
University Press, 2009).

8 See, for example, Margaret Weir and Theda Skocpol, "State Structures and the
Possibilities for 'Keynesian' Responses to the Great Depression in Sweden,
Britain, and the United States," in *Bringing the State Back In*, ed. Evans,
Rueschemeyer, and Skocpol.

9 Though, as the present economic and fiscal climate shows, "localism" is highly dependent on national/federal funding, many states and local governments presently face extreme difficulty because of reduced federal aid.

10 William H. Riker, *Federalism: Origin, Operation, Significance* (Boston: Little, Brown, 1964); Grant McConnell, *Private Power and American Democracy* (New York: Alfred A. Knopf, 1966).

11 Robert Mickey, *Paths Out of Dixie: The Democratization of Authoritarian Enclaves in America's Deep South, 1944–1972* (Princeton: Princeton University Press, 2015).

12 Richard Rose, "Giving Direction to Government in Comparative Perspective," in *The Executive Branch*, ed. Joel D. Aberbach and Mark A. Peterson (Oxford: Oxford University Press, 2005).

13 Desmond King and Marc Stears, "How the U.S. State Works: A Theory of Standardization," *Perspectives on Politics* 9 (2011): 505–18.

14 Charles R. Epp, *The Rights Revolution: Lawyers, Activists, and Supreme Courts in Comparative Perspective* (Chicago: University of Chicago Press, 1998); Thomas M. Keck, *The Most Activist Supreme Court in History: The Road to Modern Judicial Conservatism* (Chicago: University of Chicago Press, 2004).

15 Kenneth R. Mayer, *With the Stroke of a Pen: Executive Orders and Presidential Power* (Princeton: Princeton University Press, 2001); William G. Howell, *Power without Persuasion: The Politics of Direct Presidential Action* (Princeton: Princeton University Press, 2003); Hugh Davis Graham, *The Civil Rights Era: Origins and Development of National Policy, 1960–1972* (New York: Oxford University Press, 1990); Eric A Posner and Adrian Vermeule, *The Executive Unbound* (New York: Oxford University Press, 2010).

16 Robert D. Putnam, *Making Democracy Work: Civic Traditions in Modern Italy* (Princeton: Princeton University Press, 1993).

17 Sheri Berman, "Civil Society and the Collapse of the Weimar Republic," *World Politics* 49 (1997): 401–29; Theda Skocpol, *Diminished Democracy: From Membership to Management in American Civic Life* (Norman: University of Oklahoma Press, 2003).

18 McConnell, *Private Power and American Democracy*; Jennifer L. Hochschild, *The New American Dilemma: Liberal Democracy and School Desegregation* (New Haven: Yale University Press, 1984); Mickey, *Paths Out of Dixie*.

19 Nancy Bermeo, "The Merits of Federalism," in *Federalism and Territorial Cleavages*, ed. Ugo Amoretti and Nancy Bermeo (Baltimore: Johns Hopkins University Press, 2004); Michael Hechter *Containing Nationalism* (Oxford: Oxford University Press, 1995).

20 *Parents Involved in Community Schools v. Seattle School District No. 1*, 551 U.S. 701 (2007).

21 For some comparative context, see Anthony W. Marx, *Making Race and Nation: A Comparison of South Africa, the United States, and Brazil* (Cambridge: Cambridge University Press, 1998); Melissa Nobles, *Shades of Citizenship: Race and the Census in Modern Politics* (Stanford: Stanford University Press, 2000); Robert C. Lieberman, *Shaping Race Policy:*

The United States in Comparative Perspective (Princeton: Princeton University Press, 2005); and Chapter 8.

22 Desmond King and Rogers M. Smith, "Racial Orders in American Political Development," *American Political Science Review* 99 (2005): 75–92.

23 Ira Katznelson, *When Affirmative Action Was White: An Untold History of Racial Inequality in Twentieth-Century America* (New York: W. W. Norton, 2005). See also Suzanne Mettler, "Bringing the State Back In to Civic Engagement: Policy Feedback Effects of the G.I. Bill for World War II Veterans," *American Political Science Review* 96 (2002): 351–65; Margaret C. Rung, *Servants of the State: Managing Diversity in the Federal Workforce, 1933–1953* (Athens: University of Georgia Press, 2002).

24 V. O. Key Jr., *Southern Politics in State and Nation* (New York: Alfred A. Knopf, 1949); Ira Katznelson, *City Trenches: Urban Politics and the Patterning of Class in the United States* (New York: Pantheon, 1981); Robert C. Lieberman, *Shifting the Color Line: Race and the American Welfare State* (Cambridge: Harvard University Press, 1998); Deborah E. Ward, *The White Welfare State: The Racialization of U.S. Welfare Policy* (Ann Arbor: University of Michigan Press, 2005).

25 See, for example, Desmond King, *Separate and Unequal: African Americans and the U.S. Federal Government* (Oxford: Oxford University Press, 2007); Kenneth T. Jackson, *Crabgrass Frontier: The Suburbanization of the United States* (New York: Oxford University Press, 1985); Douglas S. Massey and Nancy A. Denton, *American Apartheid: Segregation and the Making of the Underclass* (Cambridge: Harvard University Press, 1993); Michael B. Katz, Mark J. Stern, and Jamie J. Fader, "The New African American Inequality," *Journal of American History* 92 (2005): 75–108; Desmond King and Rogers M. Smith, *Still a House Divided: Race and Politics in Obama's America* (Princeton: Princeton University Press, 2011).

26 Jennifer L. Hochschild, "You Win Some, You Lose Some: Explaining the Pattern of Success and Failure in the Second Reconstruction," in *Taking Stock: American Government in the Twentieth Century*, ed. Morton Keller and R. Shep Melnick (Washington DC: Woodrow Wilson Center Press; Cambridge: Cambridge University Press, 1999); Fredrick C. Harris and Robert C. Lieberman, eds., *Beyond Discrimination: Racial Inequality in a Postracist Era* (New York: Russell Sage Foundation, 2014).

27 Tomiko Brown-Nagin, *Courage to Dissent: Atlanta and the Long History of the Civil Rights Movement* (New York: Oxford University Press, 2011); John Dittmer, *Local People: The Struggle for Civil Rights in Mississippi* (Urbana: University of Illinois Press, 1994); Adam Fairclough, *Race and Democracy: The Civil Rights Struggle in Louisiana* (Athens: University of Georgia, 1995); Hasan Kwame Jeffries, *Bloody Lowndes: Civil Rights and Black Power in Alabama's Black Belt* (New York: New York University Press, 2010); Charles M. Payne *I've Got the Light of Freedom: The Organizing Tradition and the Mississippi Freedom Tradition* (Berkeley: University of California Press, 2007); Jeanne F. Theoharis and Komozi Woodward, eds., *Freedom North: Black Freedom Struggles outside the South, 1940–1980* (Houndmills:

Palgrave, 2003); Stephen Tuck, *Beyond Atlanta: The Struggle for Racial Equality in Georgia, 1940–1980* (Athens: University of Georgia Press, 2001).

28 Taylor Branch, *Parting the Waters: America in the King Years, 1954–63* (New York: Simon and Schuster, 1988); Taylor Branch, *Pillar of Fire: America in the King Years, 1963–65* (New York: Simon and Schuster, 1998); Taylor Branch, *At Canaan's Edge: America in the King Years, 1965–68* (New York: Simon and Schuster, 2006); David J. Garrow, *Bearing the Cross: Martin Luther King, Jr., and the Southern Christian Leadership Conference* (New York: William Morrow, 1986); Gunnar Myrdal, *An American Dilemma: The Negro Problem and Modern Democracy* (New York: Harper & Brothers, 1944); Howard Schuman, Charlotte Steeh, Lawrence Bobo, and Maria Krysan, *Racial Attitudes in America: Trends and Interpretations*, rev. ed. (Cambridge: Harvard University Press, 1997); Gary Gerstle, *American Crucible* (Princeton: Princeton University Press 2001); Benjamin I. Page and Robert Y. Shapiro, *The Rational Public: Fifty Years of Trends in American Policy* (Chicago, IL: University of Chicago Press, 1992); Mary L. Dudziak, *Cold War Civil Rights: Race and the Image of American Democracy* (Princeton: Princeton University Press, 2000); Thomas Borstelmann, *The Cold War and the Color Line: American Race Relations in the Global Arena* (Cambridge: Harvard University Press, 2001); John David Skrentny, *The Ironies of Affirmative Action: Politics, Culture, and Justice in America* (Chicago: University of Chicago Press, 1996).

29 Lieberman, "Civil Rights and the Democratization Trap."

30 Robert A. Dahl, *Polyarchy: Participation and Opposition* (New Haven: Yale University Press, 1971). See also Francisco E. González and Desmond King, "The State and Democratization: The United States in Comparative Perspective," *British Journal of Political Science* 34 (2004): 193–210.

31 "Quis custodiet ipsos custodes?" Juvenal, *Satires* 6.347–48.

32 Barry R. Weingast, "The Political Foundations of Democracy and the Rule of Law," *American Political Science Review* 91 (1997): 245–63; Robert C. Lieberman, "Ideas, Institutions, and Political Order: Explaining Political Change," *American Political Science Review* 96 (2002): 697–712.

33 Hochschild, *The New American Dilemma.*

34 For a comparable understanding of multidimensionality in American state development in respect to penal policy, see Michael C Campbell and Heather Schoenfeld, "The Transformation of America's Penal Order: A Historicized Political Sociology of Punishment," *American Journal of Sociology* 118, no. 5 (2013): 1375–423.

35 Garrow, *Bearing the Cross*; Branch, *Parting the Waters.*

36 Alexander Keyssar, *The Right to Vote: The Contested History of Democracy in the United States* (New York: Basic Books, 2000); Richard M. Valelly, *The Two Reconstructions: The Struggle for Black Enfranchisement* (Chicago: University of Chicago Press, 2004); Desmond King, "The American State as an Agent of Race Equity: Shock and Awe in Domestic Policy," in *Beyond Discrimination*, ed. Harris and Lieberman.

37 Ari Berman, *Give Us the Ballot* (New York: Farrar, Straus & Giroux, 2015).

38 Desmond S. King and Rogers M. Smith, "The Last Stand? Shelby County v. Holder, White Political Power and America's Racial Policy Alliances," *Du Bois Review* 13, no. 1 (2016): 25–44.

39 Anthony S. Chen, *The Fifth Freedom: Jobs, Politics, and Civil Rights in the United States, 1941–1972* (Princeton: Princeton University Press, 2009).

40 Nicholas Pedriana and Robin Stryker, "The Strength of a Weak Agency: Enforcement of Title VII of the 1964 Civil Rights Act and the Expansion of State Capacity, 1965–1971," *American Journal of Sociology* 110 (2004): 709–60; Lieberman, "Civil Rights and the Democratization Trap"; Christopher Bonastia, *Knocking on the Door: The Federal Government's Attempt to Desegregate the Suburbs* (Princeton: Princeton University Press, 2006).

41 Skrentny, *Ironies of Affirmative Action.*

42 Frank Dobbin and John R. Sutton, "The Strength of a Weak State: The Rights Revolution and the Rise of Human Resources Management Divisions," *American Journal of Sociology* 104 (1998): 441–76; Frank Dobbin, *Inventing Equal Opportunity* (Princeton: Princeton University Press, 2009).

43 *Griggs v. Duke Power Company*, 401 U.S. 424 (1971).

44 Dobbin, *Inventing Equal Opportunity*, 130.

45 *Plessy v. Ferguson*, 163 U.S. 537 (1896).

46 Mark V. Tushnet, *The NAACP's Legal Strategy against Segregated Education* (Chapel Hill: University of North Carolina Press, 1987); Richard Kluger, *Simple Justice: The History of Brown v. Board of Education and Black America's Struggle for Equality* (New York: Alfred A. Knopf, 1975).

47 Richard E. Neustadt, *Presidential Power: The Politics of Leadership* (New York: Wiley, 1960).

48 Paul Frymer, "Race, Labor, and the Twentieth-Century American State," *Politics and Society* 32 (2004): 475–509.

49 Dobbin, *Inventing Equal Opportunity*, 103–04; *Albemarle Paper Company v. Moody*, 422 U.S. 405 (1975).

50 *Regents of the University of California v. Bakke*, 438 U.S. 265 (1978); *Grutter v. Bollinger*, 539 U.S. 306 (2003). *Fisher v. University of Texas at Austin*, 631 F.3d 213 (5th Cir. 2011).

51 The *Fisher* case had the potential to end affirmative action in university admissions but the Court blinked on its first hearing. However, *Fisher* was reviewed by the Court in 2016. In *Fisher v. University of Texas*, No. 14-981, the justices decided to leave the decision of the lower court permitting the University of Texas's affirmative action program to remain in place, a major victory for supporters of affirmative action in university admissions. This unlikely outcome reflected the death of the ardent color-blind advocate Justice Scalia, leaving the court with eight justices (one of whom recused herself from the case). Justice Anthony Kennedy, previously unenthusiastic about affirmative action schemes, sided with the majority and wrote the majority opinion. Justice Samuel Alito wrote a strong dissent denouncing the Court's majority decision. Alito delivered his dissent from the bench to signal the intensity of his opposition.

52 *Hopwood v. Texas*, 78 F.3d 952 (5th Cir. 1996); Marta Tienda and Teresa A. Sullivan, "The Promise and Peril of the Texas Uniform Admission Law,"

in *The Next Twenty-Five Years: Affirmative Action in Higher Education in the United States and South Africa*, ed. David L. Featherman, Martin Hall, and Marvin Krislov (Ann Arbor: University of Michigan Press, 2009).

53 Thomas J. Sugrue, *The Origins of the Urban Crisis: Race and Inequality in Postwar Detroit* (Princeton: Princeton University Press, 1996); Dorian Warren, "The American Labor Movement in the Age of Obama: The Challenges and Opportunities of a Racialized Political Economy," *Perspectives on Politics* 8 (2010): 847–60.

54 Donald P. Moynihan and Patricia W. Ingraham, "The Suspect Handmaiden: The Evolution of Politics and Administration in the American State," *Public Administration Review* 70 (2010): S231.

55 Lieberman "Civil Rights and the Democratization Trap"; Quinn W. Mulroy, "Public Regulation Through Private Litigation: The Regulatory Power of Private Lawsuits and the American Bureaucracy" (PhD diss., Columbia University, 2012).

56 Lieberman, "Ideas, Institutions, and Political Order"; Orren and Skowronek, *Search for American Political Development*; Paul Pierson, *Politics in Time: History, Institutions, and Social Analysis* (Princeton: Princeton University Press, 2004).

57 Gary Gerstle, *Liberty and Coercion: The Paradox of American Government from the Founding to the Present* (Princeton: Princeton University Press, 2015).

58 Jennifer Hochschild and Vesla Mae Weaver, "'There's No One as Irish as Barack O'Bama': The Policy and Politics of America's Multiracialism," *Perspectives on Politics* 8 (2011): 737–59.

59 Moynihan and Ingraham, "Suspect Handmaiden," S230.

60 Ibid., S231.

61 A point Daniel Carpenter recognizes in his review of the American bureaucracy's development. Daniel P. Carpenter, "The Evolution of National Bureaucracy in the United States," in *The Executive Branch*, ed. Joel D. Aberbach and Mark A. Peterson (Oxford: Oxford University Press, 2005).

62 Harris and Lieberman, *Beyond Discrimination*.

63 Melanie J. Springer, *How the States Shaped the Nation: American Electoral Institutions and Voter Turnout, 1920–2000* (Chicago: University of Chicago Press, 2014).

64 King and Smith, "The Last Stand?"

65 See Theda Skocpol, "Targeting Within Universalism: Politically Viable Policies to Combat Poverty in the United States," in *The Urban Underclass*, ed. Christopher Jencks and Paul E. Peterson (Washington: Brookings Institution, 1991); William Julius Wilson, *When Work Disappears: The World of the New Urban Poor* (New York: Alfred A. Knopf, 1996); Andrea Louise Campbell, "Paying America's Way: The Fraught Politics of Taxes, Investments, and Budgetary Responsibility," in *Reaching for a New Deal: Ambitious Governance, Economic Meltdown, and Polarized Politics in Obama's First Two Years*, ed. Theda Skocpol and Lawrence R. Jacobs (New York: Russell Sage Foundation, 2011).

66 Naomi Murakawa, *The First Civil Right* (New York: Oxford University Press, 2014); Vesla M. Weaver and Amy E. Lerman, "Political Consequences of the

Carceral State," *American Political Science Review* 104 (2010): 817–33; Marie Gottschalk, *The Prison and the Gallows: The Politics of Mass Incarceration in America* (Cambridge: Cambridge University Press, 2006); Loïc Wacquant, *Punishing the Poor: The Neoliberal Government of Social Insecurity* (Durham: Duke University Press, 2009).

67 Lieberman, "Ideas, Institutions, and Political Order"; James Mahoney and Kathleen Thelen, "A Theory of Gradual Institutional Change," in *Explaining Institutional Change: Ambiguity, Agency, and Power*, ed. James Mahoney and Kathleen Thelen (Cambridge: Cambridge University Press, 2010); Paul Pierson, *Dismantling the Welfare State? Reagan, Thatcher, and the Politics of Retrenchment* (Cambridge: Cambridge University Press, 1994).

68 King and Lieberman, "Ironies of State Building." Edward L. Gibson, *Boundary Control: Subnational Authoritarianism in Federal Democracies* (New York: Cambridge University Press, 2013).

8

Disaggregating the Racial State

Activists, Diplomats, and the Partial Shift toward Racial Equality in Brazil

Tianna S. Paschel

INTRODUCTION

Political leaders, ordinary citizens, and visitors to Brazil long held it as a racial paradise of sorts. As one diplomat underscored in a speech delivered before the United Nations in 1978, "even though there is a multiplicity of races that live within our borders, racial problems simply do not exist in Brazil."[1] According to these observers, Brazil's high degree of miscegenation acted as both the cause and the indicator of Brazil's transcendence of race and racism. Indeed, Brazilian state officials promulgated the view of the country as a racial paradise, and thus a model for race relations in the world, well into the 1990s. Many scholars also have suggested that, unlike the United States, Brazil was not weighted down by its racial past of colonization and slavery, perhaps because the country had not institutionalized racial exclusion in the same way as the segregationist state of the United States or the apartheid state of South Africa.[2] Such comparisons began as early as the late nineteenth century; in the 1930s such accounts gained sawy as historians began to compare slavery in the United States and Brazil, with some concluding that slave systems were more benevolent in the latter and more rigid and oppressive in the former.[3]

More recently, however, scholars have questioned these earlier accounts of "cordial slavery" in Brazil.[4] At the same time, they showed how formal egalitarianism never quite translated into real equality, and how critiques of racism were largely silenced in that context.[5] These scholars also found parallels between the inherent contradictions of racial democracy in Brazil, with similar discourses of colorblindness in the contemporary United States.[6] In these accounts, Brazil implicitly serves as a cautionary tale for the United States: doing away with formal racial exclusion does not necessarily mean doing away with racism. In fact, some argued the lack of Jim Crow or official apartheid in Brazil actually mystified racial inequalities, making them more durable.

While this archetypical Brazil–United States comparison did prove useful, recent changes in the former have turned it on its head. Beginning in the 1990s, Brazil took an unexpected turn as various actors within the state began to radically shift their discourse around questions of race and nation. Rather than reproduce the idea of Brazil as a "racial democracy," bureaucrats, politicians and diplomats began to talk about the "myth" of racial democracy. In so doing they also painted a picture of a contemporary Brazilian society plagued by systemic racial inequalities and racism. This transformation of racial discourse by state officials is perhaps best embodied in the figure of former president Fernando Henrique Cardoso. A sociologist who himself had done extensive research on racial inequality in Brazil before becoming president, he said the following in a speech at the end of his second term as president:

We lived boxed into the illusion that this here was a perfect racial democracy, when it wasn't, and it still isn't today. But our democracy does have some elements that allow for greater malleability and flexibility, but those elements, if they aren't worked on, if there isn't a conscious fight for equality and against discrimination, we will not advance.[7]

Yet rather than a mere symbolic shift in state discourse, this period also marked the beginning of radical changes in the Brazilian state's policies around race. Most notable was the adoption of a plethora of policies under the umbrella of the "promotion of racial equality." In addition to the highly publicized affirmative action policies in prestigious state universities and in public service, the Workers' Party-led federal government also mandated the teaching of the history of Africa and of Afro-Brazilians in public school curricula and mainstreamed racial equality in broader social welfare policies.

How do we make sense of this shift in Brazil and what can it tell us about how we understand the racial state? In this chapter, I use ethnographic and archival data to examine the causes and consequences of the Brazilian state's adoption of race-based policies over the last two decades. I make two arguments. First, Brazil's radical shift from colorblindness to racial equality happened as a result of the strategic action of black activists in the context of a convergence of domestic and international openings in something I call political field alignments. Second, while this constituted a reconfiguration of the Brazilian state, it did not amount to a fully coherent or holistic shift toward racial justice. Instead, these changes were located in specific spaces within the state and, as such, they were partial, contingent, and also in contradiction with the many other hands of the state – much like the processes of state transformation found in other contexts (Chapters 5, 6, and 7). In part because of these tensions, the very elements of the Brazilian state that were supposed to ensure racial equality were extremely limited in their actual influence. Ultimately, the Brazilian state's shift from colorblindness to color consciousness underscores the need to move toward a disaggregated theory of the racial state that also considers states' embeddedness in a broader global field of politics.

TOWARD A DISAGGREGATED CONCEPT OF THE RACIAL STATE

Since the invention of the modern nation-state, one of the primary functions of the state apparatus has been to manage all kinds of difference.[8] Given this, scholars have argued that race was inherent to the construction of the modern nation-state. Yet while this racial character of the state was explicitly institutionalized in legal institutions in places such as the United States and South Africa, the role of the law in racialization processes was much more complex in Brazil, and in Latin America more generally.[9] These states did not institutionalize racial exclusion and rather than see race mixture and integration as a serious threat to the nation, Brazilian elites and citizens alike would eventually embrace the idea of racial democracy, or the notion that Brazil's unique mixture of "blood" and "culture" was, in fact, its strength.[10]

Many accounts have upheld this idea of Brazil as a "racial democracy," a term that was introduced to describe the country's unique brand of racial egalitarianism, mixture and harmony. Still, others have cast serious doubt on this characterization. First, creating the mixed nation did not mean transcending race so much as institutionalizing a particular kind of racialized national subject, a racially mixed one. Moreover, as scholars of Brazil and Latin America have highlighted, the very idea of privileging mixture was not only inherently a racial and gendered project, but it was one that relied heavily on cultural and biological essentialism.[11] Indeed, rather than being a nonracial nationalist project, racial democracy could be said to be hyper-racial in that it hinged on very fixed ideas of the "African," "Indian," and "European" elements of the mixed nation. Nationalist thinker Gilberto Freyre's idea of the "Brazilian race" or the "new hybrid tropical race" captures well this inherent tension between transcending and reifying ideas of race.[12] It was these contradictions that led Goldberg to characterize Brazil as a quintessential case of a "raceless racial state."[13]

Second, both symbolic and material ethno-racial hierarchies persisted. A plethora of scholars has shown how blackness and indigeneity, if included at all in the narrative of the mixed nation, were relegated to the past, while the European contributions to the nation were more often seen as important for the present and future of the nation.[14] This symbolic racial order was, of course, a reflection of the period in which Latin American nations actually sought independence, one in which the very idea of the modern nation-state was bound up with ideas of science, modernity, and race.[15] The symbolic hierarchy also mapped directly onto persistent patterns of material inequalities.[16]

Finally, scholars raised fundamental questions about the very casting of Brazil's citizenship regime as formally colorblind. In this, they argued that formally race-blind policies often existed alongside ones that were explicitly racial, if not racist. For example, in her comparative work on the politics of race and national censuses, Loveman showed how Brazilian nationalist thinkers and state officials made explicit and public calls for the need to "de-blacken" the population.[17] Accordingly, Brazil was the only Latin American country to consistently include an ethno-racial question on the national census, in part to measure if they were moving toward the racial horizon they envisioned.[18] Relatedly, a central feature of Brazil's modernization project was whitening policies (late 1800s, early 1900s), which sought to whiten the population by attracting European immigrants, often through subsidies and other incentives to migrate.[19]

The characterization of the Brazilian state as formally colorblind also tends to focus exclusively on state policy at the national level. However, racialized logics also seeped into other types of state policies and at different levels of the state apparatus. Subnational governments throughout Brazil adopted a number of policies that, while not always explicitly racial, did have racial overtones.[20]

As Borges suggests, "a wide range of imperial and republican social policies – regulation of prostitution; sanitation of ships, factories, and barracks; licensing of domestic servants; sports and physical education; universal military service – were also justified in terms of protecting the race from contamination or regenerating its health."[21] In that period, issues of health and degeneracy were inseparable from pseudo-scientific ideas of racial difference.[22]

Goldberg's conception of the racial state is insightful here. He insists that states are "racial" because of their "modes of population definition, determination, and structuration."[23] Thus, processes of racial hierarchization and exclusion are intrinsically bound up with the project of making the nation-state. Goldberg's call to look at the meanings and effects of state practices – rather than their intent or formal language – is particularly useful, underscoring how the formally racial egalitarian emphasis of most of Brazil's legal code did not mean that such legal institutions did not have a racial, or even racist, character. The implications of this approach are that, rather than looking exclusively to Brazil's formal citizenship regime, we should be asking more contextual questions about the effects of state practices. Ultimately, emphasizing Brazil's formal egalitarianism tells us very little about the ways that the state may have been complicit in the reproduction of racial hierarchies or, alternatively, how specific state practices may have worked to undermine such hierarchies.

When we interrogate rather than reify the state, what emerges is a picture that is far from monochromatic. It is one that forces us to move beyond the idea that Brazil is/was *either* a racial paradise or racial hell, that slavery there was *either* benevolent *or* harsh, or that the Brazilian state was *either* committed to racial egalitarianism *or* it was racist. Such thinking also mirrors debates about the nature of Brazilian society, such as race is *either* always salient *or* not salient at all in the everyday lives of ordinary Brazilians. At the center of such debates are strict dichotomies that fall apart upon closer inspection.

A more useful way to think about Brazil's nationalist project is as a fundamentally contradictory one, not in the sense that there was a contradiction between a coherent national myth and reality, but that the internal logic of the Brazilian state's racial project was multiple and contradictory. Political scientists have long seen the state as fragmented and punctuated by splits and contestation between elites situated in different spaces within state institutions. Other social scientists also have moved beyond theories of the "the state" as a singular actor, instead analyzing states as sites of contestation and meaning making.[24] As Morgan and Orloff's Introduction to this volume aptly notes, "viewing the state as an actor risks subsuming sprawling, complex concatenations of governing institutions under one presumptively unified bureaucratic apparatus."

How we conceive of the racial state affects how we understand recent changes in state discourse in Brazil. Scholars of race in the United States and Latin America have shown how specific arms of the state participate in processes of racialization. Among other things, they have pointed to the significant role of the coercive arms of the state in producing and reproducing the racial order through the criminal justice system,[25] as well as through agencies charged with enforcing immigration and labor policy.[26] Yet even more seemingly benign institutions within the state, such as ministries of culture and education, often promulgate exclusionary ideas of the imagined nation.[27] Statistics agencies do the same through the construction of racial categories.[28] As James Scott reminds us, such activities are an inherent feature of statecraft and serve to make legible the illegible.[29]

Despite these multiple functionings of the state as a racial actor, scholars of the United States have tended to highlight the coherence of racial projects,[30] whereas scholars of Latin America have tended to reveal the more fragmented, and even ambivalent, character of the racial state.[31] It is precisely these idiosyncrasies that make Latin America – and Brazil in particular – an interesting site for thinking through broader questions about the relationship between the state and racialization. They force us to ask more specific questions about what it means to say that the state has a racial character, to which we may expect varying answers. Indeed, the recent explosion in ethno-racial legislation in Brazil, and throughout this region, presents a number of interesting puzzles about variation historically and across countries in racial policies.[32] Why did these states adopt racial policies after nearly a century of denying that ethno-racial problems existed? How do we understand these changes in state discourse and policies? What have been the consequences of these changes?

GLOBAL ALIGNMENTS AND RACIAL EQUALITY POLICY IN BRAZIL

The only way to understand the making of racial equality policies in Brazil is to take as a point of departure the idea that the social movements that helped to bring them about, like many movements around the world, operate within the material and discursive boundaries of two fields of contestation: the field of national politics and something I call the global ethno-racial field. These fields (a term I borrow from Bourdieu) are composed of local and global discourses of race, nation, and rights as well as a plethora of political actors including state officials, academic "experts," environmentalists, international human rights and development workers, and other social movement actors. Elsewhere I argue that black activists in Brazil were able to successfully pressure their respective governments to adopt ethno-racial reforms because they acted strategically in the context of changes in domestic politics and the consolidation of a global ethno-racial field oriented around multiculturalism, indigenous rights, and eventually antiracist struggle.[33] By mobilizing around these political field alignments, black activists overcame significant ideological and material odds to transform entrenched state discourses of colorblindness and race mixture. This racial alignment began to take shape in the late 1990s and early 2000s.

It is nearly impossible to talk about the adoption of affirmative action policies in Brazil without discussing the Third World Conference against Racism, Racial Discrimination, Xenophobia, and Related Intolerance in Durban. In fact, nearly all legislation related to promoting racial equality cites Durban as legal justification. One of the many examples of this is Decree 4886 of 2003, which instituted Brazil's National Policy for the Promotion of Racial Equality. The law also alluded to statements made by Cardoso throughout the late 1990s as another legal rationale: "considering that in order to finally break from the limits of rhetoric and solemn declarations, it is necessary to implement affirmative action, and create an equality of opportunities, translated into tangible, concrete and well articulated measures."[34] In this sense, Durban was the needed bridge between symbolic rhetoric and actual policy reforms.

Although the importance of the Durban Conference was not immediately apparent to those involved,[35] it would prove vital in shaping recent reforms. As one activist summed it up, "There is before Durban and after Durban... [F]rom there, everything changed."[36] Nearly all of the activists I interviewed talked about Durban as a "critical juncture" or, as one activist put it, as a moment that "divided the waters." Scholars have also argued that Durban was an extremely important event.[37] Yet neither participants nor scholars have fully explained why the event was so significant. In order to understand the magnitude of the Durban Conference, we must situate it in the context of the Brazilian government's decades-long investment in being the model of race relations in the world, particularly within the United Nations.

Brazil's image as a model of race relations dates back to the late nineteenth century, when scholars from around the world began to visit Brazil and wrote about what they saw as more harmonious race relations. Many African Americans, including prominent theorist of race relations W. E. B. Du Bois, found that Brazil did not suffer from the same burden of racism as the United States.[38] But beyond affirmations by foreigners, the image of Brazil as a racial paradise was also consciously produced and reproduced by Brazilian state officials and intellectuals close to political power. As an emergent leader in the global South, Brazilian officials had high hopes that their leadership in the United Nations in a number of areas including race relations would lead to a permanent seat on the UN Security Council.[39] This goal was part of the Brazilian government's broader strategy to be seen as a leader of the global South.[40]

One of the first examples of Brazil's racial project within the UN came before the UN began working systematically to promote antiracism.[41] In 1950, UNESCO commissioned a large multicity study on Brazilian race relations to be carried out by prominent social scientists from Brazil and elsewhere. The goal was to offer a more harmonious model of race relations to a world plagued by Jim Crow, ethnic cleansing, and apartheid, and one still scarred by the Holocaust and World War II. However, scholars researching São Paulo and Rio de Janeiro concluded that there was a de facto racial hierarchy and pervasive racial inequality, while those researching the Northeast largely reaffirmed ideas of racial democracy.[42]

In September 1952, UNESCO reported the study's findings in their internationally circulated magazine, the *Courier*. Despite the uneven findings, the general tone of the report was still that Brazil was a harmonious multiracial society. The issue featured an article by the father of "racial democracy" himself, Gilberto Freyre, that concluded: "Brazil remains an exemplary nation, destined because of this to play an important role in the building of a world in which mutual respect between races will become an established universal."[43] So while these studies were circulated in Brazil as evidence that racism and racial inequalities did in fact exist, internationally, the findings were packaged to prove that Brazil was *the* model of race relations to be followed by other nations with sordid racial pasts. Brazil's history of colonization and slavery, which it was thought to have overcome, was key to its appeal as a model for countries with similarly sordid pasts. As such, in many UN meetings on antiracism, Brazil was constantly juxtaposed with the racist, intolerant, and cruel regime of apartheid in South Africa.[44]

Brazilian diplomats also actively promoted the country's image as a racial democracy to the world. In so doing, rather than paint Brazil as an organic racial democracy, diplomats often emphasized both the racially mixed and egalitarian nature of Brazilian culture as well as the Brazilian state's proactive approach to combating racism. This was especially true after the adoption of the article criminalizing racism in the 1988 constitution. This dual nature of Brazil's message about its racial character was clear in a UN meeting on November 30, 1999, in which diplomats

discussed the approaching Durban Conference. "Under Brazilian legislation, racism is a crime for which there is no bail or statute of limitations.
Any kind of racial discrimination is punishable by law ... Brazil is proud
to be a melting pot of cultures, all of which has contributed to building a
tolerant, multi-ethnic society."[45] Indeed, diplomats not only emphasized
the inherent features of Brazilian culture and social relations that underpinned racial egalitarianism, but also highlighted the government's leadership in criminalizing racism and ensuring formal equality in the country

In this sense, Brazilian officials did not erase slavery from their recount-
ing of Brazil's racial transcendence, but rather acknowledged that the
country "still *had* to cope with a legacy of social problems largely
resulting from injustices perpetrated during colonial times and the early
stages of independence."[46] Yet, even though Brazilian diplomats acknowledged historic injustices, they often failed to recognize that ongoing
racism and discrimination was a problem in Brazil. Instead, statements
like these, as well as many others made well through the 1990s, painted
the picture of a multiracial, multiethnic society that, as one diplomat put
it, "had always been at the forefront of the struggle against racism and
racial discrimination."[47]

Brazilian diplomats were also extremely active in the UN's antiracism
efforts, participating in monitoring compliance with the Convention on
the Elimination of Racial Discrimination (CERD) and being leaders in
the UN Decade against Racism campaign. Moreover, Brazil was one of
the first countries to speak at the UN about the importance of a Third
World Conference against Racism. In one meeting, a Brazilian diplomat
said that the government planned to take an active role in convening
such a conference because Brazil was proud of its "harmonious coexistence among people of difference religious, racial and cultural back-
grounds."[48] Yet while the Brazilian government's interest in leading
antiracism efforts within the UN may have been rooted in its members'
genuine belief that Brazil was a model of racial tolerance, it may also have
been motivated by geopolitics. In this same period, the Brazilian government was seeking a permanent seat on the UN Security Council, which
put more of a spotlight on Brazil as preparations for the Durban Conference developed.[49]

Fully aware of the image diplomats projected about Brazilian race
relations and their ambitions within the UN, Afro-Brazilian activists
began to mobilize around the conference relatively early. In many ways,
this was exactly what the movement needed to exert pressure on the
Brazilian state to make good on its promises dating back to at least

1995 with the failed efforts of Inter-Ministerial Working Group (GTI) on black populations. As Htun notes, the conference also reenergized Afro-Brazilians working within Cardoso's administration, many of whom had lost momentum and hope on implementing race-based policies.[50]

As a result, in March 2000, Brazil initially agreed to host the Regional Conference of the Americas, the first of four regional preparatory conferences held around the world in preparation for the 2001 Durban Conference. However, the Brazilian government rescinded its offer after scandals emerged around the country's quincentenary (500-year anniversary) "discovery" celebration in April of that year. In a series of confrontations, Brazil's military police violently repressed peaceful protestors, among them students as well as indigenous and black activists; images of this violence flooded the national and international media.[51] In the international press, this state violence was juxtaposed with the popular image of Brazil as a racially mixed and harmonious society. So even as Brazilian diplomats cited a lack of financial resources as the reason Brazil would not host the regional conference, activists speculated that they withdrew because they feared more protest and unwanted international attention.[52] These events signaled to Afro-Brazilian activists that, for Brazilian state officials and the political elite, much was at stake in upholding the country's image as a racial paradise in the international arena.

SANTIAGO, TRANSNATIONALISM, AND THE RISE OF BLACK NGOS

In the absence of Brazil's leadership, the Chilean government agreed to host the regional meeting of the Americas. In October, just two months before the regional conference, the Chilean government held a small meeting in Santiago, Chile, in which twelve experts on discrimination and intolerance presented background papers to help frame the regional conference and Latin America's participation in the Durban Conference. Edna Roland, founder of the black feminist organization Fala Preta ("Speak Black Woman!"), presented the background document on Afro-descendants in the Americas that painted a picture of sharp racial inequalities and racism in Brazil and the region as a whole. This was one of the many moments in the preparations for Durban when Brazilian diplomats had to face black activists contradicting the picture of race relations they had painted for decades. For example, when the Brazilian government highlighted the important work the Inter-Ministerial Working

Group (GTI) was doing to address racial inequalities in the country, Roland disagreed: "while positive changes have taken place in Brazil, the government has not been able to implement many of the recommendations of the GTI and particularly those that would have a real impact on the living conditions of Afro-Latinos."[53] Afro-Brazilian activists offered accounts that were radically different from those of their white diplomat compatriots that were often backed up with solid statistics.[54] In sum, the presence of Afro-Brazilian activists in these elite transnational spaces made it nearly impossible for Brazilian officials to maintain the harmonious and egalitarian picture of race relations in their country. This gave activists an unprecedented opportunity to negotiate with high-level government officials.

Their efforts were successful at the Santiago Regional Conference of the Americas in December 2000. Brazil was one of thirty-five Latin American governments that signed onto the final Santiago Program of Action, which recognized that "racism" and "institutionalized discrimination" were problems in their countries. Among other things, the Santiago declaration called for "strategies, programs and policies that can include affirmative action measures to favor the victims of racism, racial discrimination, xenophobia and other forms of discrimination that impede the effective enjoyment of civil and political rights." Because of both the specificity of the Santiago conference to the Latin American experience and the actual nature of the language in the document, many Afro-Latin American activists see the Santiago Declaration as even more important than the Durban conference in shifting racial policies in Brazil and elsewhere in Latin America.

Upon returning from the Santiago Conference, Cardoso signed a Presidential Decree creating the National Committee charged with preparation for the Third World Conference against Racism in Durban. The Committee included a number of government officials, including Afro-Brazilian Senator Benedita da Silva as well four black activists from established black NGOs. Roland acted as a quasi-member of the committee. In the end, high-level government officials were willing to listen to the recommendations of activists in the National Committee, and in some cases they even charged them with formulating the Brazilian government's position and policies. Roland, for instance, represented the Brazilian delegation in negotiations with other countries in Durban.[55] The Brazilian government's official statement in Durban included binding language and references to specific policies, which contributed to the further development of policies aimed at racial equality in Brazil and other countries in Latin America. Alberti and Araujo show how the inclusion of one phrase in the document that became the Brazilian delegation's official statement at the Durban conference – "quotas in the university for blacks"– set the ball rolling for affirmative action policies approved by the state legislature of Rio de Janeiro in 2001 and in a number of other Brazilian states.[56]

Transnational activism by black NGOs, especially black feminist ones, also profoundly affected the Brazilian government's final position in favor of "affirmative measures" to address racial inequality.[57] Brazilian state officials had already signed on to the Santiago document and sponsored meetings throughout the country, including the National Meeting on Racism and Racial Discrimination with 1,700 participants.[58] Moreover, as the state delegation embarked upon its trip to South Africa, it expressed its intent to exert diplomatic pressure on other governments to include the language of "reparations," "affirmative action," and statements acknowledging the transatlantic slave trade as a "crime against humanity" in the Durban Program of Action.

Somewhat ironically, in responding to pressure by black activists, Brazilian state officials were eventually able to reinforce the country's image as a leader in the struggle against racism both at home and globally. Minister Gregori recounted to me a moment in Durban when Brazilian diplomats and activists were cloaked in a Brazilian flag singing the national anthem; he explained: "We worked a lot on the Durban Conference for reasons that don't have to do with Brazil, exactly ... It helped us, Brazil, emerge in that world of people, with everybody happy, everybody singing, everybody understanding each other, in the context of this dispute between Palestinians and Jews, those things that almost foreshadowed 9/11." By promising to adopt concrete policies to ameliorate racial inequality and discrimination, Brazilian officials were also showing the world that Brazil, in contrast to so many other countries, was a happy, tolerant democracy.

Beyond symbolic gestures, in the days leading to and the months after Durban, the Brazilian state began to adopt what would be an avalanche of racial equality policies. Just days before Durban, officials announced the creation of the first government affirmative action program in the Ministry of Agriculture. Upon returning from Durban, Cardoso announced an affirmative action program for the Foreign Service. The eventual adoption of affirmative action and racial equality policies happened under President Lula through a process that was largely decentralized, happening in some cases through resolutions passed by university-level councils, and in others through state legislation, as was the case with the first affirmative policy at the State University of Rio de Janeiro (UERJ) in 2001. Even so, in the early 2000s, affirmative action policies spread like wildfire and by 2008, 62 of Brazil's 236 public universities had adopted some form of racial and/or class-based quotas.[59]

RECONFIGURING THE STATE, RECONCEPTUALIZING THE NATION

Durban is remembered in most of the world as an ineffective and highly controversial conference; however, in Brazil, it helped initiate a domino effect of historic racial equality policies. Black activists within the Workers' Party also played an important role in shifting the Brazilian state's orientation toward racial issues through the executive branch. Many activists close to Lula's administration had dedicated decades to assuring that racial issues would be at the forefront of the administration's policy. It was, in part, because of these relationships that when Lula took over the presidency, he signed a number of presidential decrees aimed at moving toward racial equality in nearly every area of state policy (e.g., health, education, and social welfare). This reorientation included the construction of a racial equality apparatus.

The Racial Equality Apparatus

On March 21, 2003, the International Day for the Elimination of Racial Discrimination, President Lula announced the creation of the Special Secretariat for the Promotion of Racial Equality (SEPPIR). SEPPIR marks a turning point in the shift toward racial equality policies: unlike previous entities charged with rectifying racial inequality, SEPPIR was a permanent federal agency with ministerial status and its scale was unprecedented. SEPPIR borrowed from the experience of a similar institution within the Workers' Party (PT) – the National Secretariat to Combat Racial Discrimination – that black activists in the party had helped create. After Lula's election in 2003, a number of influential black activists within the PT joined Lula's transitional government.[60] High-level discussions around having a Ministry to deal with issues of racial inequality were already underway within the PT, yet there was much debate within the transitional government about whether this was necessary and if it might present political problems for the PT. In the end, as Flavinho Jorge, a leader in the Workers' Party and the National

Confederation of Black Entities (CONEN), explained in an interview, "the creation of SEPPIR was the result of two factors: Durban and the work of blacks within the PT."[61] Mainly due to his personal relationships with his black PT comrades, Lula had become committed to an antiracism agenda well before he assumed the Presidency. However, it was the weight of Durban, and Fernando Henrique Cardoso's endorsement of affirmative action, that laid the foundation upon which the PT institutionalized racial equality policy within the state.

The heads of SEPPIR tended to be members of the PT's rank and file, while independent black activists were within the lower ranks of the state agency. While some activists did hold state positions prior to Lula, the rise of the PT gave activists unprecedented access to the state apparatus. I asked Ivair Augusto Alves dos Santos, a black activist and member of both the Cardoso and Lula administrations, if there were differences in the political climate around ethno-racial issues within the state under the two presidents. He responded as if the answer was obvious. The differences were "huge," he explained:

First, they had a lot more people. In my day in the administration of Fernando Cardoso, we had, in government positions, five to ten people, max. They had fifty to sixty. It was a colossal difference! In my time [in the government] we couldn't have even imagined that. They had people in different areas with lots of power, power that we didn't even dream to have during the Cardoso period. People outside of the government have no idea how many more influential black people there are than in my day. And the resources they were dealing with, they were way more than we had. The only time we managed a lot of resources was during Durban, something like five or six million reals [two million dollars] ... you can't even compare this [to what they manage under Lula]. They had way more resources and more people to do more effective work.[62]

Though, for Ivair, it was not simply the number of Afro-Brazilians within Lula's administration that was new, but the power they had within the party and state apparatus. This power was particularly important since Brazil's presidential system afforded the executive an incredible amount of power in making legislative and presidential reforms.[63] In fact, most of the legislation aimed at racial equality in Brazil has happened through presidential decrees.

When SEPPIR began operations in 2004, it employed about forty people and managed a budget of roughly $10 million, and the funds allotted to the agency steadily increased.[64] SEPPIR's ministerial status and relationship to the Office of the President – both structural and personal – also made it well positioned to push for affirmative action and other policies within the upper echelons of the Brazilian state.

However, in practice, SEPPIR faced both political and infrastructural challenges. Although the agency's budget far exceeded the budget for racial equality initiatives under Lula's predecessor, it was still abysmal compared with the two other special secretariats that Lula created around the same time. Whereas the 2015 budgets of the Special Secretariat of Fishing and Agriculture and the Special Secretariat of Policies for Women were 254 and 182 million reais, respectively, SEPPIR's was only 39.5 million reais.[65] SEPPIR's budget was the equivalent of just less than 9 million U.S. dollars.[66] SEPPIR also lacked the authority and infrastructure to implement policies or to effectively pressure other ministries to change their policies. This struggle was especially acute with bureaucrats from the Ministry of Education, which had shown strong resistance to affirmative action. As Matilde Ribeiro, SEPPIR's first minister, explained, "the work of that SEPPIR and the Ministry of Education was disjointed. It wasn't like we were holding hands, doing everything together. So sometimes we would go after things, take the risk, try to do it alone, other times we would go and propose things, which sometimes did lead to action."[67]

In addition to SEPPIR (at the national level), Brazil's racial equality apparatus consisted of some 600 special coordinators, secretariats, and offices on the promotion of racial equality at the state and municipal levels.[68] All of these agencies were officially charged with coordinating public policy implementation with the different secretariats and ministries that made up these various levels of government. Like SEPPIR, these local state institutions lacked the mandate to implement policies themselves, and as a result their level of effectiveness depended heavily on the configurations of power within the local political field. Although SEPPIR did face political and budgetary difficulties, especially in the early years, the racial equality apparatus at the state and municipal levels often had even less adequate budgets and more precarious relationships with other local government agencies.

Despite these limitations to Brazil's racial equality apparatus, racial equality policies are now on much stronger footing. In 2012, Brazil's Supreme Court considered a landmark affirmative action case and voted unanimously that such policies were, in fact, constitutional. The decision came at a time when the federal government was also shifting toward a more aggressive stance on racial policy under President Dilma Rousseff and SEPPIR Minister Luiza Bairros. Beyond being more vocal about racism, there were substantive changes in racial policy under this new PT administration. Most notably, in August of 2012, Rousseff signed the

Law of Quotas that had been held up in Congress for over a decade. This was a major feat considering that professors at Brazil's prestigious federal universities had been among the most vehement opponents to affirmative action. The Law of Quotas required all of the country's fifty-nine federal universities and thirty-eight technical institutes to reserve 50 percent of their seats for poor and working-class students. The law also mandated that these same universities guarantee that the racial makeup of those reserved seats match that of the state where the university is located. While federal universities had until 2016 to comply with this mandate, most of them had already done so by the end of 2012.[69]

Rolêzinhos and the Other Side of the Brazilian State

Although Brazil's racial equality apparatus was officially charged with managing racial questions, it did not have a monopoly on this area. When we consider the management of race and inequality by other arms of the Brazilian state, we find many contradictions. On the one hand, the Brazilian state has expanded social welfare policies in ways congruent with its racial equality agenda. On the other hand, the practices of the coercive arm of the Brazilian state are in direct contradiction to racial equality policies.

This fragmented nature of Brazil's racial state was revealed in particularly acute terms in early 2014 when antiracist youth began to flood public spaces throughout the country, including shopping malls and parks, in something they called *rolezinhos*. The word translates literally to "little strolls," but the events were akin to the flash mobs that have become commonplace in the United States in recent years. Unfolding in major cities throughout Brazil, these *rolezinhos* were typically made up of hundreds and sometimes thousands of mostly black and brown youth from favelas and poor neighborhoods. Many of these events did not start off as violent, but ranged from less-coordinated *rolezinhos*, in which youth simply went to the mall to socialize in big groups, to highly coordinated ones where they sang and even did large-scale dance choreographies. The Brazilian state's response included violent repression by the military police. In part to justify their harsh actions, state officials, the police, and mall security also repeatedly portrayed the *rolezinhos* as violent riots of thugs looking for trouble.

Just a year earlier, massive groups of mostly white, middle-class Brazilians had staged protests, and many observers noted obvious differences between how the military police treated the mostly brown and black participants of the *rolezinhos* and these previous protestors.[70] As the youth involved in these events experienced increased state repression, they became more politicized. In São Paulo, for example, after police used rubber bullets and tear gas to break up a *rolezinho*, the event quickly shifted to a protest against racism, classism, and state violence. Black university students and political organizations joined them with a more explicit message against racial discrimination. As they did so, many malls around the country decided to close their doors in anticipation of these events.[71]

While these events were momentary, this arguably marked the first time that the poor, nonwhite masses engaged in such a creative form of disruptive protest on a massive scale. Just a year later, in August of 2015, Brazil would also see some of its biggest mobilizations around racism and policing when Campaign Reaja o Sera Morto (React or Die) organized thousands of people in cities throughout Brazil to protest the "genocide of black youth."[72]

The *rolezinhos* and the Reaja Campaign give us important insights into how different hands of the Brazilian state manage race in the post–affirmative action period. Most notably, they demonstrate the need to take seriously the contradictory role that different state actors and agencies play in the contestation over race, nation, and equality. At the height of state violence against mall-goers throughout Brazil, President Dilma Rousseff called in the Minister of Racial Equality Luiza Bairros, herself a long time black activist, to mediate the situation of the *rolezinhos*. Instead Luiza spoke candidly in a number of media outlets in support of the youth. She also called out both government officials and mall administrations as "racist" and referred to those involved in the rolezinhos as representing an "awakening of black youth."

Debate ensued over the following weeks between Bairros (broadly representing the federal social welfare apparatus) and the military police (representing the state-level coercive arm of the state), which underscore the fragmented nature of the Brazilian state, and of states more generally. Ultimately, while bureaucrats within Brazil's racial equality apparatus were willing to make symbolic statements about racialized state violence, these questions never quite made it to the table of top-level policy discussions. This inability or unwillingness of Brazilian state actors to seriously address the issue of the disproportionate violence against poor black Brazilians compels us to resist simple narratives of the Brazilian state as working under a singular mission to promote racial equality.

CONCLUSION

Over the last two decades the official discourse of the Brazilian state has gone from a disavowal of the existence of racism and racial inequality to a formidable state-led campaign to eradicate these issues. Among other things, this change in the state's orientation toward racial issues entailed the creation of new state agencies explicitly charged with promoting racial equality. What is more, these changes in state discourse and institutions have also prompted an intensification of ideological battles among Brazilians around collective identity and over competing characterizations of Brazilian society. These political and ideological shifts in Brazil offer important insights into how we theorize the role of the state in processes of racialization.

First, the Brazilian state's trajectory from formal colorblindness to the politicization of race must be understood as happening within a global field of politics. The Third World Conference against Racism in Durban offered an unprecedented opening that Brazil's black movement was only able to effectively leverage because state elites had invested decades in projecting Brazil's image as a racial paradise abroad. These international dynamics, and particularly geopolitical factors, have always been important to struggles for racial equity and justice. To be sure, if we scan history, we find many examples of global fields profoundly shaping domestic racial politics, including the antiapartheid struggle in South Africa and the Cold War's impact on black movements in the United States and Cuba.[73] Yet while the global has undoubtedly played a central role in domestic struggles over race and nation, examining these dynamics requires some care. Rather than assume the flow of influence would necessarily be from North to South,[74] I have uncovered a more complex web of relationships that led to the adoption of racial equality policy in Brazil.

Second, this case suggests we move beyond understanding the racial state as a monolithic or coherent socio-political actor. Despite dominant accounts, the Brazilian state of the early twentieth century was not fully racially egalitarian, either in its formal structures or in its informal practices. Instead, it was an amalgamation of different policies, institutions, and individuals that sometimes had conflicting logics around questions of race and nation. The same is also true of the twenty-first-century Brazilian state. Recent reforms in Brazil have been important at the same time that they have been piecemeal, and in some ways have only scratched the surface.

When Brazil's contemporary black movement emerged at the national level in the late 1970s it was primarily in response to the case of Robson Silveira da Luz, a black worker accused of stealing fruit from a market and who was later murdered by the police. Such state violence, which is at once about race and about class, has been virtually unchallenged in this new moment in Brazil. This is in part because the recent transformations of the Brazilian state around race happened through the construction of new arms of the state charged with managing such issues. As such, they have not altered the fundamental character of the very state agencies that were historically complicit with the reproduction of racial hierarchy, most notably the coercive arm of the state.

Consequently, rather than speak of a singular racial state, we must examine how race has figured into the practices of particular actors within it. Such an approach also requires a serious examination of the structure of power within the state, as well as an analysis of the dynamics that compel state actors to make substantive changes. In this case, Brazil's presidential system, the close relationship between the executive and black cadres within the Workers' Party, and the geopolitical dynamics surrounding Durban were all crucial for understanding the shift toward the "promotion of racial equality." Yet, just as actors within the Brazilian state were mounting a racial equality apparatus, other arms of the state continued business as usual.

Thus, when we examine the state as a racial actor, or more accurately as a set of actors, layered and less parsimonious conceptualizations of the state are particularly useful.[75] While a "racial state" may be reasonably coherent across its various institutions (i.e., apartheid South Africa), more typically racial states are deeply divided, ambivalent, and even contradictory around questions of race and nation. This is, in part, because of the institutional multiplicity of the state – its many hands. Indeed, it is precisely when we disaggregate, rather than reify, the state that we gain a more accurate and complex understanding of it. It is only then that we can show how the state functions to construct, reproduce, or undermine the racial order or, more likely, how it does all three simultaneously.

Notes

1 Brazilian Diplomat, Committee on the Elimination of All Forms of Racial Discrimination, 1978.

2 Anthony W. Marx, *Making Race and Nation: A Comparison of South Africa, the United States, and Brazil* (Cambridge: Cambridge University Press, 1998); David Theo Goldberg, *The Racial State* (Oxford: Blackwell Publishers, 2002);

Eduardo Bonilla-Silva, *Racism without Racists: Color-Blind Racism and the Persistence of Racial Inequality in America* (Lanham: Rowman & Littlefield Publishers, 2009); Howard Winant, *The World Is a Ghetto: Race and Democracy since World War II* (New York: Basic Books, 2001); Robert Lieberman, *Shaping Race Policy: The United States in Comparative Perspective* (Princeton: Princeton University Press, 2011).

3 Gilberto Freyre, *The Masters and the Slaves: A Study in the Development of Brazilian Civilization* (Berkeley: University of California Press, 1933); Frank Tannenbaum, *Slave and Citizen* (New York: Alfred A. Knopf, 1947).

4 Carl Degler, *Neither Black nor White: Slavery and Race Relations in Brazil and the United States* (Madison: University of Wisconsin Press, 1971).

5 Michael George Hanchard, *Orpheus and Power: The" Movimento Negro" of Rio de Janeiro and Sao Paulo, Brazil 1945–1988* (Princeton: Princeton University Press, 1994); France Winddance Twine, *Racism in a Racial Democracy: The Maintenance of White Supremacy in Brazil* (New Brunswick: Rutgers University Press, 1998).

6 Goldberg, *The Racial State*; Bonilla-Silva, *Racism without Racists*.

7 Speech by Fernando Henrique Cardoso, December 19, 2001.

8 Benedict Anderson, *Imagined Communities: Reflections on the Origin and Spread of Nationalism* (London: Verso Books, 2006); Goldberg, *The Racial State*.

9 For this analyses on the United States, see: Ian Haney-Lopez, *White by Law: The Legal Construction of Race* (New York: New York University Press, 2006); Evelyn Nakano Glenn, *Unequal Freedom: How Race and Gender Shaped American Citizenship and Labor* (Cambridge: Harvard University Press, 2004). On Latin America, see: Peter Wade, *Race and Ethnicity in Latin America* (London: Pluto, 1997); Marx, *Making Race and Nation*; Edward Telles, *Race in Another America: The Significance of Skin Color in Brazil* (Princeton: Princeton University Press, 2004); Mara Loveman, *National Colors: Racial Classification and the State in Latin America* (New York: Oxford University Press, 2014).

10 George Reid Andrews, *Afro-Latin America, 1800–2000s* (New York: Oxford University Press, 2004).

11 Marisol De la Cadena, *Indigenous Mestizos: The Politics of Race and Culture in Cuzco, Peru, 1919–1991* (Durham: Duke University Press, 2000); Kia Caldwell, *Negras in Brazil: Re-envisioning Black Women, Citizenship, and the Politics of Identity* (New Brunswick: Rutgers University Press, 2007).

12 Freyre, *The Masters and the Slaves*.

13 Goldberg, *The Racial State*.

14 Peter Wade. *Race and Ethnicity in Latin America* (London: Pluto Press, 1997); Andrews, *Afro-Latin America*.

15 Nancy Stepan. *The Hour of Eugenics: Race, Gender, and Nation in Latin America* (Ithaca: Cornell University Press, 1991); Loveman, *National Colors*.

16 Carlos Alfredo Hasenbalg and Nelson do Valle Silva. *Estrutura social, mobilidade e raça*, vol. 7 (Rio de Janeiro: Instituto Universitário de Pesquisas do Rio de Janeiro, 1988); Andrews, *Afro-Latin America*. Telles, *Race in Another America*; Edward Telles, *Pigmentocracies: Ethnicity, Race, and Color in Latin*

America (Chapel Hill: University of North Carolina Press, 2014). It is important to note that these scholars do argue that notwithstanding these real inequalities, there is still a great deal of racial fluidity in identity and social relations in Brazil

17 Loveman, *National Colors*; Andrews, *Afro-Latin America*. Antonio Sérgio Alfredo Guimarães, *Classes, Raças e Democracia* (São Paulo: Editora 34, 2002);

18 Melissa Nobles, *Shades of Citizenship: Race and the Census in Modern Politics* (Stanford: Stanford University Press, 2000); Telles, *Race in Another America*; Loveman, *National Colors*.

19 Stepan, *The Hour of Eugenics*; Andrews, *Afro-Latin America*.

20 Celia Maria Marinho de Azevedo, *Onda negra, medo branco: o negro no imaginário das elites–século XIX* (São Paulo: Annablume, 1987); Dain Borges, "'Puffy, Ugly, Slothful and Inert': Degeneration in Brazilian Social Thought, 1880–1940," *Journal of Latin American Studies* 25, no. 2 (1993): 235–56.

21 Borges, *Puffy, Ugly, Slothful and Inert*, 249.

22 Degler, *Neither Black Nor White*.

23 Goldberg, *The Racial State*, 104.

24 James Ferguson, *The Anti-Politics Machine: "Development," Depoliticization, and Bureaucratic Power in Lesotho* (New York: Cambridge University Press, 1990); Elisabeth Clemens and James Cook, "Politics and institutionalism: Explaining Durability and Change," *Annual Review of Sociology* (1999): 441–66; Michel Rolph Trouillot, "The Anthropology of the State in the Age of Globalization 1: Close Encounters of the Deceptive Kind," *Current Anthropology* 42, no. 1 (2001): 125–38.

25 Loic Wacquant, "From Slavery to Mass Incarceration: Rethinking the 'Race Question' in the U.S.," *New Left Review* 13 (January–February 2002): 41–60; Michelle Alexander, *The New Jim Crow: Mass Incarceration in the Age of Colorblindness* (New York: The New Press, 2012); Christen A. Smith, *Afro-Paradise: Blackness, Violence and Performance in Brazil* (Urbana: University of Illinois Press, 2016).

26 Evelyn Nakano Glenn, *Unequal Freedom: How Race and Gender Shaped American Citizenship and Labor* (Cambridge: Harvard University Press, 2009); David Scott FitzGerald and David Cook-Martín, *Culling the Masses* (Cambridge: Harvard University Press, 2014).

27 De la Cadena, *Indigenous Mestizos*; Jerry Dávila, *Diploma of Whiteness: Race and Social Policy in Brazil, 1917–1945* (Durham: Duke University Press, 2003); Isar Goudreau, *Scripts of Blackness: Race, Cultural Nationalism, and U.S. Colonialism in Puerto Rico* (Urbana: University of Illinois Press, 2015).

28 Nobles, *Shades of Citizenship*; Loveman, *National Colors*; G. Cristina Mora, *Making Hispanics: How Activists, Bureaucrats, and Media Constructed a New American* (Chicago: University of Chicago Press, 2014).

29 James C. Scott, *Seeing Like a State: How Certain Schemes to Improve the Human Condition Have Failed* (New Haven: Yale University Press, 1998).

30 Michael Omi and Howard Winant, *Racial Formation in the United States* (New York: Routledge, 2014).

31 Telles, *Race in Another America*; Alberto, *Terms of Inclusion*; Loveman, *National Colors.*

32 Juliet Hooker, "Indigenous Inclusion/Black Exclusion: Race, Ethnicity and Multicultural Citizenship in Latin America," *Journal of Latin American Studies* 37, no. 2 (May 2005): 285–310.

33 Tianna S. Paschel, "The Right to Difference: Explaining Colombia's Shift from Color Blindness to the Law of Black Communities." *American Journal of Sociology* 116, no. 3 (2010): 729–69.

34 Ibid.

35 While I had a series of questions about the Durban Conference on my interview schedule, in most cases, interviewees mentioned Durban before I had the chance to.

36 Interview, Ivair Alves dos Santos, May 2010.

37 Mala Htun, "From 'Racial Democracy' to Affirmative Action: Changing State Policy on Race in Brazil," *Latin American Research Review* 39, no. 1 (2004): 60–89. Telles, *Race in Another America.*

38 David J. Hellwig, *African-American Reflections on Brazil's Racial Paradise* (Philadelphia: Temple University Press, 1992). Hellwig does argue that Du Bois later changed his position on this.

39 Telles, *Race in Another America.*

40 Peter Dauvergne and Déborah BL Farias, "The Rise of Brazil as a Global Development Power," *Third World Quarterly* 33, no. 5 (2012): 903–17.

41 The UN Convention on the Elimination of all Forms of Racial Discrimination (CERD) was not adopted until 1965 and the CERD Committee was not yet constituted.

42 Telles, *Race in Another America.*

43 August–September 1952 of UNESCO magazine, Courier.

44 This was the case in many of the UN records I analyzed.

45 Official UN record of the 54th session, 22nd meeting 10/25/1999 October 1999, document A/C.3/54/SR.22.

46 Official UN record, October 18, 1991. Emphasis mine. It is not clear, in the translation of this statement to English (by UN officials), if the Brazilian representative meant to say that they had to deal with this in the past, or if they still had to confront it in the present.

47 Official UN record of the 43rd session, 12th meeting on CERD, 10/18/1988, document A/C.3/43/SR.A2.

48 Official UN record of the 54th session, 22nd meeting 10/25/1999, October 1999, document A/C.3/54/SR.22

49 Telles, *Race in Another America.*

50 Htun, "From Racial Democracy to Affirmative Action."

51 In a cursory search of English-language newspaper articles about Brazil in April 2000, I found dozens of articles on these events.

52 Interview, Ivanir dos Santos; interview, Ambassador Gilberto Sabóia, March 2010.

53 Taken from the UN "Report of the Latin American and Caribbean regional seminar of experts on economic, social and legal measures to combat racism with particular reference to vulnerable groups."

54 Telles, *Race in Another America.*
55 Interview, Edna Roland, May 2010, and interview, Minister Gregori, March 2010. In addition, after the Durban Conference, Roland was chosen by the UN to be one of the five eminent experts charged with monitoring Durban follow-up around the world.
56 Verena Alberti and Amilcar Pereira, "A defesa das cotas como estratégia política do movimento negro contemporâneo," *Estudos Históricos* 1, no. 37 (2006): 143–66.
57 Activists helped to draft a substantial amount of the text of the Santiago document from Brazil and throughout Latin America.
58 Sabóia and Porto, 2001.
59 Marcelo Paixão and Luiz M. Carvano, *Relatório Anual das Desigualdades Raciais no Brasil, 2009–2010* (Rio de Janeiro: Editora Garamond, 2010).
60 This included Flavinho Jorge (head of the Perseu Abramo Foundation); Matilde Ribeiro, the first Minister of SEPPIR; and Matevs Chagas.
61 Interview, Flavinho Jorge, May 2010.
62 Interview, Ivair Augusto Santos, October 2010.
63 Scott Mainwaring and Matthew Soberg Shugart, *Presidentialism and Democracy in Latin America* (Cambridge: Cambridge University Press, 1997).
64 Taken from SEPPIR's website.
65 Portal Orçamento Senado Federal. www12.senado.gov.br/orcamento/documentos/loa/2015/elaboracao/parecer-preliminar/relatorio-preliminar/view, accessed September 28, 2015.
66 On October 2, 2015, President Dilma Rousseff announced the closing of SEPPIR; its functions were to be part of a new joint ministry along with those of the Special Secretariat for Policies for Women and the Secretariat for Human Rights.
67 Interview, Matilde Ribeiro, May 2010.
68 STF abre debate sobre cotas raciais nas universidades, March 3, 2010.
69 http://gemaa.iesp.uerj.br/dados/mapa-das-acoes-afirmativas.html, accessed November 22, 2015.
70 João H. Costa Vargas, "Black Disidentification: The 2013 Protests, Rolêzinhos, and Racial Antagonism in Post-Lula Brazil," *Critical Sociology* (2014): 1–15.
71 http://sao-paulo.estadao.com.br/noticias/geral,shopping-de-luxo-de-sp-fecha-as-portas-apos-protesto-em-apoio-a-rolezinho,1120043.
72 Smith, *Afro-Paradise.*
73 Mary L. Dudziak, *Cold War Civil Rights: Race and the Image of American Democracy* (Princeton: Princeton University Press, 2011); Mark Sawyer, *Racial Politics in Post-Revolutionary Cuba* (New York: Cambridge University Press, 2006); John David Skrentny, *The Minority Rights Revolution* (Cambridge: Harvard University Press, 2009).
74 Pierre Bourdieu and Loïc Wacquant, "On the Cunning of Imperialist Reason." *Theory, Culture & Society* 16, no. 1 (1999): 41–58.
75 Also see Chapter 7.

PART III

DEVELOPING THE SINEWS OF POWER

Democratic States of Unexception

Toward a New Genealogy of the American Political

William J. Novak, Stephen W. Sawyer, and
James T. Sparrow

Extemporize all government.

Ralph Waldo Emerson

Post–1989, social commentary on the arc of modern American history trumpeted the end of the Cold War with paeans to American exceptionalism, neoliberalism, and the end of history. Post–9/11, such assessments lost none of their audacity, but shifted attention to a darker, more dangerous national trajectory: from exceptionalism to exception; from civil society to executive decision; from economic and political liberty to necessity, emergency, security, and empire. Both discourses are one with their present rather than histories of the present.

But exceptionalism and exception also share another common denominator: both modes of analysis turn on deceptively conventional renderings of American law and statecraft within an essentially liberal tradition. Despite the huge differences that separate the exceptionalism and state of exception frameworks, in the American context, the interpretive baseline remains largely the same. The concept of law in most such renderings is abstract, doctrinal, and "formal," featuring a stark separation of law from politics, legislative from executive power, and the rule of law from democracy. Similarly, the concept of the state as it figures in both exceptionalism and exception modes remains ineluctably "bureaucratic" – in a word, "Weberian." The prevailing rendering of the state "brought back in"[1] through such interpretations depicts the kind of state predominant in nineteenth-century continental Europe – centralized, administered, rational, official, and monopolistic vis-à-vis the "legitimate use of force within a given territory."[2] In both exceptionalist and exception literatures, administration remains something of the "sine qua non of modernity,"[3] and Max Weber's "legal authority with a bureaucratic administrative staff" the archetype of a modern state transcending democracy.[4] Finally, such a formal concept of the state and law meshes only too well with a narrowly conceived liberal understanding of the American political tradition. In both its 1950s consensus and 1980s neoliberal manifestations, an emaciated reading of liberalism valorizing individual rights, negative liberty, constitutional limitations, and laissez-faire economics undergirds both exceptionalist and exception paradigms. What Louis Hartz dubbed "the master assumption of American political thought," namely, the "reality of atomistic social freedom," continues to frustrate efforts to come to terms with the actual nature of collective social power in modern American democracy.[5] Together, the concepts of formal law, bureaucratic state, and classical liberalism make for a formidable synthesis of the modern political imaginary. But it is a synthesis that consistently insulates the American political tradition from the more robust and comparative history and theory of the state that is one of the collective goals of this volume.

Indeed, reigning interpretations of American exceptionalism and exception have often had more in common with ideology than historical sociology. On the right, of course, new legal formalism and market fundamentalism cut their teeth on opposition to bureaucratic state planning and interventionism, resuscitating the optimistic and orthodox dream of a classical and minimalist liberal state as simply a "neutral site" or night watchman.[6] On the left, deployment of some of the same tropes yields an equally powerful portrait of imperial administrative bureaucracy and executive emergency power underpinning everything from new social and cultural policing at home and abroad to the mechanics of the modern carceral state. Here the conception of governance and statecraft is much in sync with the liberal state's pessimistic alternative – what Michel Foucault talked about as Friedrich Nietzsche's "negative idealization" of the state as a "cold monster."[7] In his final lectures, *On the State*, Pierre Bourdieu notably rejected both the classical liberal theory of a neutral or beneficent state and what he called the "pessimistic functionalism" of the Marxist tradition's mirror image of a "diabolical state."[8] In the end, economic, political, and legal renderings of the American liberal tradition – both for and against – rely on overly simplistic visions of the state emphasizing bureaucracy, police, and an extractive central state apparatus.

Despite the surface attractiveness of such figurations, the problem with these conventional portraits of law, statecraft, and liberalism is that they simply do not represent anything that ever really existed in the American past. They are and always have been essentially ideological rather than historical constructs – bolstered by national myths rather than rooted in historical investigations or empirical reality. And surely, at the end of the day, the basis for judgment must remain grounded in experience. Following Ralph Waldo Emerson, Oliver Wendell Holmes Jr., John Dewey, and Charles Merriam, the critical tradition of American pragmatism, broadly construed, recommends an assessment of exceptionalism and exception in sync with actual historical experience. This essay begins that reassessment by insisting upon a more realistic history and theory of the democratic state.[9]

In contrast to such a realistic approach, prevailing ideas of exceptionalism and exception are primarily products of theory rather than history. Two of the most well-known theorists of exception, Carl Schmitt and Giorgio Agamben, did attempt to ground their theories in actual historical events. But those histories consisted primarily of highly stylized, generalized, episodic – and mostly conventional – historical renderings of very specific constitutional moments. For Schmitt's *Political Theology*, the historical *locus classicus* was 1919, both in terms of the significance of Article 48 of the German Constitution and in terms of the more general "crisis in parliamentary democracy" that he dated from the very same year.[10] In the era of Bush and Cheney, Agamben profitably Americanized this essentially continental European focus without flagging the friction between Anglo-American common law/constitutional experience and his own Roman law analytical vocabulary. Jumping from Lincoln's Civil War to Wilson's World War I to Franklin Roosevelt's "National Recovery Act" (sic) to September 11, 2001, and its aftermath, Agamben tacitly underscored the degree to which the state of exception was a creative theoretical construct rather than a useful historical referent. In line with too much theorization of the American past, such renderings of exception (as well as exceptionalism) rest on an inadequate conceptualization of the American state – in particular: an overly formal theory of law, an overly bureaucratic theory of the state, and an overly liberal theory of politics.

The rest of this chapter takes issue with the history and theory of exception along these three lines. The first section offers a critique of the idea of law at the heart of the theory of exception. By taking a closer look at the history and theory of law in early nineteenth-century America, it offers an alternative reading of the role of exception in Emerson's America – a place and time in which the exception in law was anything but exceptional. The second section offers a critique of the idea of state and sovereignty at the heart of the theory of exception in the early twentieth century. In place of Schmitt's concept of the political, it offers a reconsideration of John Dewey's more democratic conception of "the public" and its problems, where again the exception is an unexceptional part of an everyday and agonistic democratic politics. The third section moves us further into the twentieth century, challenging the suzerainty of both liberal and neoliberal characterizations of exception and totalitarianism in that ideologically charged period. Here, Charles Merriam's ideas about new democracy and new despotism provide an alternative reference point for thinking about the exception, its antidemocratic dangers, and its democratic possibilities.

In the context of a revitalized theory of the nature of power in democratic states, the exception does not appear so exceptional. Indeed, when viewed from the perspective of democratic state history, the exception may be one of the most common ways that democratic states exercise power every day. Evaluating the state of exception from the critical perspective of the modern democratic state exposes the limits of the notions of formal law, bureaucratic statecraft, and liberal politics that so frequently preoccupy discussions of exception and emergency governance. Those rather profound limitations suggest the need for an alternative genealogy of the political. In the theories of law, state, and politics in the writings of Emerson, Dewey, and Merriam, this essay proposes a tentative new genealogy of the modern American political – where democracy is not a problem but a solution and where the exception is not exceptional but one of the most quotidian ways of exercising power in agonistic modes of self-government.

EMERSON, POLICE POWER, AND THE ROOTS OF AMERICAN ANTIFORMALISM

The epigraph in Giorgio Agamben's *State of Exception* bespeaks the centrality of the role of law in his theory of exception: *Quare siletis juristae in munere vestro?* (Why are you jurists silent about that which concerns you?) But, of course, jurists and political theorists have hardly been silent about the exception. Rather, in the actual treatises and texts of Western jurisprudence, Agamben's exception is actually quite the norm in law – the thing always discussed, whether explicitly or implicitly – the question always in play, constantly deliberated, frequently contested. To borrow Richard Rorty's resonant phrase, exception might indeed be the legal "conversation of mankind."[11]

This basic disconnect is a product of Agamben's highly formalist conception of law. Agamben's short theory of exception is built directly upon the fundamental, baseline distinction between "law" and "politics" – placing "the state of necessity, on which the exception is founded" precisely at the "limit" or "intersection" or "border" or "no man's land" between the legal and the political. That is, Agamben's conception of the uncommented-upon exception takes coherent form only through his own deployment of a rigid separation of "public law" from "political fact" and "juridical order" from "life." That foundational bifurcation then opens the interpretive and textual space for the place-ment of necessity and exception in the jural universe as that "point of imbalance" or that "ambiguous, uncertain, borderline fringe" between the rule of law and the world of the political.[12] And while Agamben would have us believe that this space, this no man's land, reflects some-thing like real world circumstance, it is mainly a product of his aesthetic and highly formal rendering of the rule of law – a bit out of sync with the actual history of Western legal experience.[13]

Indeed, the last century and a half of work in law and social science has taken special issue with just such formalist separations of law and politics, juridical order and life. Whether taking the form of historical and sociological jurisprudence, legal pragmatism, legal realism, legal instrumentalism, legal functionalism, law and society, critical legal stud-ies, or socio-legal history, the verdict is essentially the same – that a modern, antiformalist, nonfoundational, postmetaphysical understanding of law confounds the very idea of separating law from politics and/or society. Oliver Wendell Holmes's brilliant deployment of the perspective of the "bad man" in his critical realist "Path of the Law" turned as early as 1897 on confounding the formalist inside/outside or law/outlaw dis-tinction.[14] John Dewey, too, viewed law as "through and through a social phenomenon; social in origin, in purpose or end, and in application." Without investigating law in society as an irreducibly social and political activity, there were "scraps of paper or voices in the air but nothing that can be called law."[15] Dewey's antiformalist critique was echoed by Karl Llewellyn's legal realist indictment of the "myth, folderol, and claptrap" that permeated so many formalist discussions of law and jurisprudence. Llewellyn's *Bramble Bush* exploded the law/politics, legislative/executive distinction: "The doing of something about disputes is the business of law. And the people who have the doing in charge, whether they be judges or sheriffs or clerks or jailers or lawyers, are officials of the law. What these officials do about disputes is, to my mind, the law itself. And rules through all of this are important so far as they help you see or predict what officials will do. That is all their importance, except as pretty plaything."[16] In short, the American legal pragmatic and legal realist tradition was born in fundamental revolt against exactly the kind of abstract legal formalism that haunts Agamben's exceptional categories of law and exception.[17]

But, of course, coming to terms with Agamben's theory also requires a return to Schmitt's authoritative account in *Political Theology*, which opens with the memorable sentence: "Sovereign is he who decides on the exception."[18] Schmitt's theory too was predicated on a rather idiosyncratic conception of the political[19] as well as a construction of state and sovereignty at odds with liberal constitutionalism: for example, "the old liberal negation of the state vis-à-vis law" where it "is not the state but law that is sovereign" and where "the state is confined exclusively to producing law."[20] Consequently, Schmitt's rendering of exception and emergency stands outside and apart from law:

> What is argued about is the concrete application, and that means who decides in a situation of conflict what constitutes the public interest or interest of the state, public safety and order, *le salut public*, and so on. The exception, which is not codified in the existing *legal order*, can at best be characterized as a case of extreme peril, a danger to the existence of the state, or the like. But it *cannot be circumscribed factually and made to conform to a preformed law*.[21]

While Agamben's and Schmitt's theories of exception and emergency have a certain appeal for the critical leverage they appear to give one on highly abstracted understandings of the liberal rule of law, the fact of the matter is that those abstracted and ideological renderings of legalism and liberalism do not reflect what is actually going on in law. And here the American experience is especially instructive.

A classic case in point concerns the American doctrine of "police power" – defined by one commentator as "the inherent plenary power of a State... to prescribe regulations to preserve and promote the public safety, health, and morals, and to prohibit all things hurtful to the comfort and welfare of society."[22] The police power is perhaps the closest American approximation to Schmitt's notion of deciding who decides "what constitutes the public interest or interest of the state, public safety and order, *le salut public*, and so on." The police power was distinctly bound up in determining exactly those things in American public law. Moreover, it had something of the "illimitable-ness" and "open-endedness" associated with Schmitt's notion of "a borderline concept" – "pertaining to the outermost sphere."[23] As Justice Hugo Black once put it, "We deal in other words with what traditionally has been known as the police power. An attempt to define its reach or trace its outer limits is fruitless."[24] In sync with Schmitt's notion of *le salut public* (and thereby his gesture to the French Revolution, the Committee of Public Safety, and the Terror), the common law maxim that undergirds the police power is *salus populi suprema lex est* – the people's welfare (or the safety of the people) is the highest law. The links between the police power and necessity and emergency and exception run deep. William Packer Prentice's *Police Powers: The Law of Overruling Necessity* (1894) drew an explicit connection between police power and emergency and defense: "For the commonwealth a man shall suffer damage as for the saving of a city or a town ... when we raise bulwarks for the defense of the realm ... Such bulwarks are raised by the police laws, but often the line of their defenses is met before the subject is aware of them, or recognizes the dangers to be faced."[25]

The point here – opposite Agamben, Schmitt, and conventional renderings of exception – is that the police power decidedly does not stand outside or apart from law in some borderland intersection of law and politics or some "no man's land between public law and fact" or "juridical order and life." Contra Schmitt, the police power is indeed "codified in the existing legal order," originating in and conforming to a "preformed law." Contra Agamben, the jurists have been anything but silent about police power in the United States. To the contrary, the history of the police power (in its broadest manifestations) encompasses almost the entirety of early American law – the subject of endless pages of cases and commentary. It is thus emblematic of the operation of power and law in a democratic state – where the separation of the political and the jural, police and law, the exception and the norm is anything but a clear-cut matter of formal definitions.

But it is precisely a reliance on overly formalist renderings of law that leads many to separate out police, policy, administration, necessity, emergency, and executive power as somehow distinct from the general operations of law. In their work on police and *Polizei* in American law, both Christopher Tomlins and Markus Dubber underscore just such separate spheres. [26] For Dubber, especially, police is always linked to exceptional sovereign coercive power – overruling necessity – the inherently unlimited, extraconstitutional, discretionary prerogative of the sovereign to act quickly and expediently to eliminate threats to the public health, safety, and security.[27] Philip Hamburger similarly uses formalist conception of the "rule of law" so as to posit much of executive administration as somehow beyond the pale of legality per se.[28] Such ideas draw on a deeply rooted juristic mythology that falsely sees law (or *recht* or *ius*) as the antithesis of power, sovereignty, coercion, violence, and police.

Contrary to the general trend of theorizing police, administration, and exception as transconstitutional or extralegal decisionist and political forces that know no law, they are better understood as part and parcel of the legal history of democratic states. Indeed, far from being strange bedfellows, law and police, constitutionalism and sovereignty, and the juridical and the administrative have been frequent fellow travelers in the history of American law and statecraft. Police power originated and was legitimated in law – in the formal delegations of state prerogative in the charters of the municipalities, villages, corporations, and subsidiary associations that reflected the intimate interrelationships of the state, the law, and the legitimate power to regulate, expropriate, and punish. The official development of police power as a legal doctrine was inseparable from the story of the rise of the judiciary and the common law and American constitutionalism. Indeed, the original phrase "police power" comes from none other than the Chief Justice of the U.S. Supreme Court John Marshall. And the concept was most fully worked out by the equally influential Massachusetts Supreme Court Chief Justice Lemuel Shaw.[29] In short, though it is common to separate the jural state and the police state, the norm and the exception, the actual legal history of the American version of the modern democratic state suggests a close interconnection and interpenetration of sovereignty, necessity, police, and the rule of law.

Ralph Waldo Emerson was among those nineteenth-century Americans especially attuned to the ever volatile, fluid, antiformal, and open-ended character of lawmaking in nascent democratic states. And indeed, the bond linking norm and exception, freedom and necessity in the everyday agonistic experience of democracy was one of the great themes of the "American Renaissance" in general.[30] Though Emerson did not write much on the rule of law per se, the constant interplay of law/politics in democracy was one of his eternal tropes. As he mused rather profoundly in his *Journals*:

America is the idea of emancipation. Abolish kingcraft, Slavery, feudalism, black-letter monopoly, pull down gallows, explode priestcraft, tariff, open the door of the seas to all emigrants. Extemporize all government, California, Texas, Lynch Law. All this covers self government. All proceeds on the belief that as the people have made a govt. they can make another, that their Union & law is not in their memory but in their blood. If they unmake the law they can easily make it again.[31]

Here Emerson captured the degree to which the norm is not a no man's land between law and life, legal and political fact, but is rather bound to the exceptional in democratic states. The exceptional becomes imminent in everyone's claim and impulse to self-rule and self-govern in a democracy, for better or worse. It opens up a limitless horizon of political projects that can range from the abolition of slavery to the reimposition of Jim Crow's "Lynch Law."

In his critique of Daniel Webster and the Fugitive Slave Act of 1850, Emerson's essential democratic antiformalism resonated most fully. There, Emerson decried the law's effects whereby "the learning of the universities, the culture of elegant society, the acumen of lawyers, the majesty of the Bench, the eloquence of the Christian pulpit, the stoutness of Democracy, the respectability of the Whig party are all combined to kidnap [runaway slaves]." Laws were instruments and tools – distinctly subordinate to and drawing their obligation from the larger spirit of the "substantiality of life." Like his friend Henry David Thoreau, Emerson recommended civil disobedience to this "immoral" and "contravened" statute that "enacts the crime of kidnapping." "The law," he claimed, "was suicidal, and cannot be obeyed." Holding the United States to be "a real and *not a statute union*," Emerson criticized a textual adherence to the letter of the law and a formal adherence to law in the books, asking: "What is the use of courts, if judges only quote authorities, and no judge exerts original jurisdiction, or recurs to first principles." Here is the life rather than the logic of the law: "The gravid old Universe goes spawning on; the womb conceives and the breasts give suck to thousands and millions of hairy babes formed *not in the image of your statute*, but in the image of the Universe."

For Emerson, the life of the law was life – experience – and it was a life that belonged to the living and to the future. He reserved his harshest words for a man like Webster, "a man who lives by his memory" and who clung to old law with the dead hand of the past:

He believes, in so many words, that government exists for the protection of property. He looks at the Union as an estate, a large farm, and is excellent in the completeness of his defence of it so far. *He adheres to the letter.* Happily he was born late, after the independence had been declared, the Union agreed to, and the constitution settled. What is already written, he will defend. Lucky that so much had got well written when he came. For he has no faith in the power of self-government; none whatever in *extemporizing a government.*

Emerson's law was a law in action. It was thoroughly democratic and unexceptionally exceptional: "Power ceases in the instant of repose; it resides in the moment of transition from a past to a new state, in the shooting of the gulf, in the darting to an aim."[32] In contrast to this exceptional and exuberant democratic power of a self-governing people, Daniel Webster's formalist legal arguments in support of the "filthy law" made no more impression than "the spray of a child's squirt against a granite wall."[33]

Emerson's spirited critique of formal law shared some key characteristics with Karl Marx's similarly timed (and equally spirited) critique of Hegel's formal and bureaucratic notion of the State. For the early Marx, democracy was "the solution to the riddle of every constitution," for "in it we find the constitution founded on its true ground: real human beings and the real people." The constitution was thus posited as the people's own creation – "the free creation of man." Hegel's error was that he proceeded "from the state," whereas democracy proceeded "from man." For Marx (as for Emerson), "Man does not exist for the sake of the law, but the law exists for the sake of man, it is human existence" rather than "legal existence." Marx concluded, "Democracy relates to all other forms of state as its Old Testament."[34]

Emerson's work suggests that the interpretation of texts and the rule of law in early America refused to conform to the kind of formal separations of law and politics, constitution and democracy, that frequently populate literatures on necessity, emergency, and states of exception. It underscores the reality that some considerations of American law in the first years of the democratic republic insisted on its antiformalism – as bold, experimental, rebellious, and unpredictable as the people making up the continent. From this perspective, the jurists were far from silent on the question of exception. Rather, they were too busy noisily implementing it all the time – from the laws of necessity that allowed mayors to pull down houses in times of great fire calamity to the local legal traditions of the *posse comitatus* in the policing of crime, emergency, and epidemic. Outside the law? Only by envisioning law through a highly intellectual, formalist, and antidemocratic lens that does not reflect actual legal experience.

CARL SCHMITT MEETS JOHN DEWEY

As suggested earlier, coming to terms with the complex articulation between state and exception requires a reckoning with Carl Schmitt's authoritative account of the political and the problem of the decision – as well as with some of Schmitt's most important interlocutors.[35] While Emerson early on challenged some reigning notions of the relationship between norm and exception, he was hardly alone in the American tradition. In the early twentieth century, Dewey continued in this mode, specifically building on ideas of antiformalism and experience in his effort to devise a more democratic theory of state power. Through his move beyond pluralism, his rejection of a singular source of power, and his emphasis on effect over essence, Dewey's theory of the state embraced the exceptional capacities of democracy while providing a profound alternative to Schmitt's formalistic decisionism. Thus, Dewey's political philosophy can still be read as an effective response to what Chantal Mouffe dubbed "the challenge of Carl Schmitt," embracing a fundamental critique of liberalism while providing a profoundly different response.[36] He therefore deserves to be read as part of an important line of thinkers, along with Emerson, Merriam, and many others, who sought to establish the foundations of a democratic state by embracing the exceptional capacities of popular rule.

While Schmitt's theory of the state of exception reached its most canonical form in his *Political Theology*, almost a decade later he further elaborated his theory in "State Ethics and the Pluralist State."[37] Schmitt opened this essay with what might be referred to as *the challenge of pluralism*, citing Ernest Barker's 1915 essay "The Discredited State" (an essay that also influenced Dewey's writings on the state in the years to follow). Pluralists such as Barker and Harold Laski, Schmitt insisted, had summarily dismissed the state of the early twentieth century. Defining the state as one power among many, such pluralists also revealed the contradictions involved in the predominant liberal conception of the state. In Schmitt's view, the pluralist dissolution of the state into its constitutive parts revealed that there were no metaphysical grounds for sovereign authority. Thus, he insisted, sovereign authority could only be made by a sovereign decision.

Within this critique of the pluralist state was a larger Schmittian attack on pragmatism more generally. "If pluralist social theorists such as Cole and Laski adhere mainly to the empirical," Schmitt argued, "they do so as pragmatists and thereby remain consistent with their pragmatic philosophy ... [transposing] the pluralist world view of the philosophy of William James to the state."[38] "In the system of 'political theology,'" Schmitt contended, "the pluralism of James's world view corresponds to the age of today's democratic national states, with their pluralism of peoples who are disposed towards the state on the basis of their nationhood."[39] For Schmitt, James – and pragmatism more generally – was guilty of invoking a political theology because his pluralism was rooted in the nation or the political unity of the people without considering the foundations of this unity or the national state's legitimacy.

What is surprising in his critique, however, is that Schmitt did not criticize the pluralist perspective as such, but rather argued that pluralists did not fully recognize the consequences of this position.

The state really does appear to be largely dependent on various social groups, sometimes as a victim, sometimes as the outcome of their agreements, an object of compromise between social and economic power groups, a conglomerate of heterogeneous factors, parties, interest groups, combines, unions, churches, etc. reaching understandings with one another. In the compromise of social powers, the state is weakened and relativized, and even becomes problematic, as it is difficult to determine what independent significance it retains.[40]

The state in this pluralist theory, Schmitt argued, is relativized, weakened, and possibly dead. The Schmittian challenge to pluralism, then, may be understood in the following terms: if the state is one among many powers and yet it legitimately governs, then either one explains the foundation of such legitimacy or one does not. If the latter, then one may rightly be accused of a "theology" because one is merely assuming that nation-states are unified and governed by some natural, godly purpose. In short, pluralism pushes the moment to its crisis by showing that there is no absolute transcendent foundation for political action at the level of the state. If, therefore, one examines the "concrete" foundations of state unity, instead of taking them for granted, one comes to the conclusion that this unity may only be established by a specific act or decision – for Schmitt, this is why the state of exception is permanent in a context of popular sovereignty.

Central to this claim is that the stuff of the state – the political – unlike the stuff of other social associations, does not have a substance. "Among pluralist theorists of the state as nearly everywhere, an error prevails that generally persists in uncritical unconsciousness – that the political signifies a specific substance, next to the substance of other 'social associations.'" For Schmitt, however, a political association differed from all others because unlike a union, for example, it has no specific purpose. For this reason Schmitt insists that "The political more accurately describes the degree of intensity of a unity"[41] because "the political has no specific substance, the point of the political can be derived from any terrain, and any social group, church, union, business, or nation becomes political, and thus related to the state."[42] A study of the political in this theory becomes then the search for the concrete moment when unity may be established in order to overcome the fissiparous tendencies of pluralism.

Thus, Schmitt's challenge to pluralism contained three essential elements. First, it was radically relativist to the extent that it embraced the fact of the social and political pluralism of modern states. Second, it was rooted in the "concrete" to the extent that it insisted that any attempt to resurrect the authority of the state in such a context without theorizing the decision was a pure theology. And third, since the thing or activity binding the sovereign community – the political – lacked a consistency of its own, it must instead be understood on a spectrum of intensity in which the sovereign decision established unity for the whole.

In *The Public and Its Problems*, Dewey also built his theory of the state on a critical embrace of liberal pluralism as a radical relativism, a response to concrete problems, and a nonsubstantial vision of the political. Moreover, opening with his own critique of a kind of political theology, Dewey wrote: "That the state should be to some a deity and to others a devil is another evidence of the defects of the premises from which discussion sets out."[43] Dewey's refusal to establish a stable foundation for the state, therefore, led to a pursuit that paralleled Schmitt's critique of pluralism until the final moment – the moment when Schmitt sought to establish unity through decision. Dewey looked in another direction in search of the overlapping, direct, and indirect interests and consequences that empirically brought any public into existence, one that built on the antiformalist tradition introduced by Emerson and continued by Charles Merriam.

Like Schmitt, Dewey embraced the plurality of social groupings and the social individuals who inhabited them. Furthermore, he concurred that the plurality of interests and associations did generate an organization that superseded them, but he understood this larger interest as "the public" and not "the people." The public was a product of those interests that spread beyond any one private group, yet it was distinct from other associations. Similarly to Schmitt, Dewey argued it did not have an essence because it was formed through consequences. The public therefore could not act in itself but needed a third party – the political state – to manage the consequences emerging from the conflicts and problems of its common interests. "This public is organized and made effective," Dewey argued, "by means of representatives who as guardians of custom, as legislators, as executives, judges, etc., care for its especial interests by methods intended to regulate the conjoint actions of individuals and groups. Then and in so far, association adds to itself political organization, and something which may be government comes into being: the public is a political state."[44]

Like Schmitt, then, Dewey also argued that the unity of the political state was generated instead of being a natural preexisting condition, but instead of being the product of *a* decision, it emerged in a given moment out of a given public. The radical nature of Dewey's theory resided in his claim that even the state itself was the product of the public's problems and only existed as long as the problem existed: "Special agencies and measures must be formed if they are to be attended to; or else some existing group must take on new functions."[45] The state as organized public could, of course, act to preserve the public interest: "From this point of view there is nothing extraordinary in the preeminence of the claims of the organized public over other interests when once they are called into play."[46] The state could therefore hypertrophy and atrophy in keeping with the specific needs of the people. In other words, unity was a problem and a consequence, not the state's principle of existence. In this way, Dewey overcame "the temptation to generalize from these instances" and also refuted the pluralist conclusion that "the state generically is of no significance," removing any essence of or substance to the state while maintaining its power to act. "There is no a priori rule which can be laid down and by which when it is followed a good state will be brought into existence. In no two ages or places is there the same public. . . The formation of states must be an experimental process."[47] Problems emerged and the public organized itself, and thus formed a state, to manage these problems.

The similarities with Schmitt's framing of the problem of state power are striking. The state – the political, overarching, preeminent power transcending any particular institutions – did not have an essence: "The State must always be rediscovered. Except, once more, in a formal statement of conditions to be met, we have no idea what history may still bring forth. It is not the business of political philosophy and science to determine what the state in general should or must be."[48] At the same time, states were all-inclusive of all the smaller associations that make them up. Moreover, when problems emerged, from sewage to civil war, the public organized itself in order to act. In this sense, both Schmitt and Dewey embraced the decision as the foundation of the political.

But Dewey disagreed rather profoundly with Schmitt about the conclusions to be drawn from this assessment of the modern political. Schmitt insisted that "the issue itself, [was] the problem of a people's political unity"[49] and, in this way, surmised that the only way to reestablish a coherent theory of sovereignty within the pluralist paradigm was to ground the political in he "who decides on the exception." Dewey turned in a decidedly different direction – from "the people" to "the public." Dewey refused to build his state out of a presupposed unity of the people.

Rather, he embraced an even more radical position, jettisoning sovereignty and the people as a principle of political unity. Dewey turned to the quotidian, singular, and often-exceptional problems confronted in the process of self-rule. Thus, instead of the sovereign deciding the exception, Dewey reversed the proposition: "General theory might indeed be helpful; but it would serve intelligent decision only if it were used as an aid to foreseeing factual consequences, not directly per se."[50]

Schmitt established the decision in exceptional circumstances as the only legitimate foundation for the polity. This position was seductive and powerful both for its intellectual coherence and for its political applicability in a moment of crisis. However, this theory also signed the death warrant of democratic life by shutting down the possibility of a democratic state and arguing that any mode of organization outside of the decision of a singular unifying will was a mere shell game of self-deception. So how might we understand attempts during the same moment to build a theory of the democratic state on the political that did not undermine the possibility of maintaining democratic politics? In other words, Dewey asked the question: what would a regime look like that placed the inherent conflict of modern democratic society and the institutional processes of politics necessary for managing those conflicts at the center of its understanding?

Through his critical response to pluralism, Dewey provided at least a partial response to questions like these. Pushing quotidian problems to the fore while denying the power of the unique decision, Dewey's "search for the public" was a search to bring politics and the political together while avoiding the Schmittian trap of fetishizing sovereignty and *the* decision. Weaving politics and the political together as a foundation for the democratic state meant multiplying the moments and wills that served as arbiters for negotiating the serial challenges that emerged in popular rule. From this perspective, Dewey challenged assumptions that found their ways back into our histories and theories of the state, especially those informed by Weber since the 1970s.

First, elections and bureaucratic institutions are a notable absence in Dewey's theory of the democratic state. By placing the public at the heart of the modern democratic polity, Dewey placed a "problem" – a disagreement, a conflict, an impediment – as the defining feature of democratic life. In other words, the political – those elements of the polity such as plurality, debate, and the dissensus that structured the very possibility of a state – took center stage in his analysis. By invoking the public's everyday problems as the root of the democratic state, Dewey diluted the political from those high-intensity moments that Schmitt considered essential for determining the foundation of the polity. Such an approach blurred the distinction between politics and the political. One might suggest that he quotidianized the exceptional nature of democratic life so as to make the exceptional relativism of every particular decision and institutional solution the source of legitimacy without establishing the personal decision as the only legitimate form of rule. The democratic state, then, was the means of responding (however temporarily) to dissensus at various levels of intensity.[51]

Second, Dewey shunned bureaucracy as the quintessential response to the dangers of mass politics that had been formulated just a decade and a half earlier by Max Weber. Indeed, Dewey's theory of a democratic state involved a rather deep critique of the reigning theories of Weber and Robert Michels. Dewey's focus on the public and the state-as-consequence made office-holders an epiphenomenon of the state as process. Bureaucracy was no longer the state's essence but a sign of the state's emergence: "The obvious external mark of the organization of a public or of a state is thus the existence of officials."[52] In this sense, there is a profoundly anthropological quality to Dewey's interpretation of the state. In this view, the state does not acquire its essential characteristic of a monopoly over legitimate force by establishing a core of officials who serve the state. Instead, the state forms around a set of specific problems as the sign that a public exists and has problems that must be settled. The bureaucratic structure is no longer inherent in the state, making it the thing that must be studied; rather, it is a mere indicator or indexical marker that says *something statelike is happening here.* Half a century before Foucault, Dewey urged critical theorists of politics to look for state effects rather than "the state."

Similarly, and consequently, the oligarchic tendencies of democracy, as Michels put it, are not inherent in the democratic state, even if they may obviously emerge within it. Dewey argued that this tendency could be consistently challenged through an understanding of the state as organized public:

> The new public which is generated remains long inchoate, unorganized, because it cannot use inherited political agencies. The latter, if elaborate and well institutionalized, obstruct the organization of the new public. They prevent that development of new forms of the state which might grow up rapidly were social life more fluid, less precipitated into set political and legal molds. To form itself, the public has to break existing political forms.[53]

The state then can only hug the social terrain by consistently breaking with the previous modes of state development instead of creating a "ruling class." Dewey suggests that what happens through revolution would happen as an almost natural development if "the power and lust of possession" did not prevent constantly new state formations. The state, Dewey insists, "is ever something to be scrutinized, investigated, searched for. Almost as soon as its form is stabilized, it needs to be re-made."[54] A generation before Schumpeter celebrated his narrowly framed "creative destruction" – restricted to the liberal domain of economics, and conceived to restrain any competitive creativity by the state within that sacrosanct realm – Dewey recognized that the fluidity and creativity at the center of the modern project were inseparable from the dynamism necessary to sustain the ongoing experiment in self-government.[55]

Dewey's anthropology of the state found an echo in Pierre Clastres's observation almost a half-century later that if the political "can be conceived apart from violence; the social cannot be conceived without the political." As a result, Clastres concludes, "it is not evident to me that coercion and subordination constitute the essence of political power at all times and in all places."[56] Such observations are useful for gaining perspective on Dewey's critique of Schmitt, Weber, and Michels. Dewey refused the idea of independent officials who would be constituted as a distinct group with their own individual interests because his theory of the democratic state was organized precisely against the idea of state autonomy. Conflict created the state and, in turn, in some cases it employed coercion and subordination, but power was generated from the bottom up. As a result, a monopoly of coercion on the part of specific officeholders was antithetical to the state's very origins. Dewey dissolved the essence of the state to such a degree that it became possible to consider moments in which the state was not by some inherent essence a coercive power but might emerge as a coercive power acting on society at specific moments when such power is necessary. In Dewey's theory, *democratic states do not put an end to power relations or coercion, but they do initiate the process of challenging the autonomy of those who have it.*

CHARLES MERRIAM: DEMOCRACY, DECISION, AND DIFFERENTIAL EXCEPTION

The high stakes of the positions articulated by Schmitt and Dewey in the aftermath of the Great War grew even more dire over the course of the 1930s, as the economic crisis of the Great Depression and the geopolitical upheavals it spawned highlighted the need for decisive action. By the late 1930s a new term, "totalitarianism," had been coined to classify together the authoritarian regimes whose embrace of unbridled decisiveness and unlimited political will had placed democracies around the world on the defensive. In American intellectual life, what might be called a "totalitarian synthesis" conflated mortal enemies such as Nazi Germany and the Soviet Union by positing their underlying similarities in the "total" domination of society by an unlimited state whose modernity allowed excesses exceeding those of even the worst despotisms of old. As intellectuals shrank back in horror from purges, outrages, and brutal repressions that rapidly remade the face of politics, they also retreated from the radical relativism on which pragmatic thought had rested. Many simultaneously took refuge in a chastened liberal repudiation of the democratic state – particularly as it mobilized mass constituencies for large-scale social engineering projects. The Colloque Lippmann, Hayek's *Road to Serfdom*, and the Chicago School's early postwar search for an "American road" out of Hayek's dismal highway to hell – these were just some of the many efforts to rethink liberalism beneath the clouds of total war, genocide, and totalitarianism.[57]

Against these headwinds Charles Merriam, a disciple of Dewey's, dispatched the goblins of mass politics and tyrannical majorities, decisionism and authoritarianism, that sent most of his contemporaries running into the arms of a chastened liberalism. Merriam's long education and leadership within progressive politics and political thought largely built on the tradition of antiformalism and democracy that had animated Emerson and Dewey. Facing the fascist assault on democracy head-on, he continued their charge against an emaciated liberalism, even as liberal theorists began to gain ground in their attempts to evacuate the state of democratic accountability. Merriam was one of the central figures associated with the progressive formulation of democratic emergency in the age of "exception." Where Dewey had articulated his theory of the democratic state from outside public office, and in opposition to the poisonous disillusionment with democracy articulated by Walter Lippmann, Merriam advanced his influence and honed his ideas a decade later from within the New Deal, still doing battle with Lippmann's caustic skepticism that was newly amplified by the crisis of democracy in Europe.[58]

In *The New Democracy and the New Despotism* (1939), his major contribution to political theory, Merriam nonetheless confronted the problem of totalitarianism head-on.[59] Rather than opposing state and society, as Lippmann and his followers did, Merriam structured his argument around an opposition between democracy and its historical antagonist, "mastery and slavery" – which had a tendency to "disappear" once "consent of the governed" gained a footing in politics.[60] Divided into discrete sections devoted to the two kinds of politics, the treatise articulated their opposition by working outward from their organizing principles: the "dignity" and "perfectibility of mankind," "consent of the governed," and "consciously directed and peaceful social change" assumed by the "new democracy"; and the "economic inequality," the nobility of "the few," and the heroic charisma of "the Superman" (which was nothing more than a new "Caesarism") on which "the new despotism" fed.

Merriam anatomized the new despotism in a pithy fifty-page section organized around its elitist, antidemocratic principles. These he traced back to the death of absolutism and the transition from *Machtstaat* to *Rechtstaat*, which over the course of the nineteenth century inspired an organized "antidemocratic movement" that was grounded in the ideas of Nietzsche, Spengler, Mosca, and Pareto, and was driven by the actions of modern autocracies. Although his quarry included some obvious targets, he devoted special attention to seemingly undespotic liberal types such as Pareto, who on closer inspection proved hostile to the very possibility of democratic self-government, as reflected in his claim that "We need not linger on the fiction of 'popular representation' – poppy-cock grinds no flour."[61] Decisionists and other critics of self-government made a straw man of democracy's putative dissipation, fractiousness, slowness, and irresolution, while cultivating a fetish of political will and decision. Indulging fantasies of the man on horseback, they overlooked the vulnerabilities of his singular military genius while wrongly discounting the strengths of a democratic structure of power that harnessed many strengths flexibly. "The jurists may call this 'authoritarian,'" he observed dryly, "but the historian may say 'futilitarian.'"[62]

The jest reflected a conviction that for all its martial glory, the new despotism was at root weaker than the new democracy. The bulk of Merriam's treatise drew out the philosophical and political implications of this position, devoting a full (and fulsome) 180 pages to outlining the full breadth of the democratic prospect in the modern world. Contrary to the caricature of corruption, decadence, and enervation applied to it by its despotic enemies, democracy was quite competent to meet the demands of the modern world, whether characterized by emergency or not. Contrasting the failure of the Kaiserreich with the success of the democracies in the previous world war – particularly the rapid and effective U.S. mobilization – he observed that decisiveness was not a quality reserved only for exceptional individuals. Indeed, in the case of Napoleon, it could be seen as a liability. (This certainly would prove equally true of Hitler, whose military "genius" lost its luster in its logical culmination in Operation Barbarossa – a revealing repeat of Napoleon's tragic folly.) Rather, true decisiveness depended on the precise features of social organization, and so was as much "a matter of special social tension and unity of community purpose at a particular time, as it is of particular forms of organization."[63]

At the heart of the problem, and in the crosshairs of Merriam's critique, was the simplistic conceptualization of "exception" and its relationship to emergency. The Continental notion of exception, Merriam recognized, was simply a modern updating of a very old metaphysic of divine right that did not in fact implicate genuine democracy of any variety, whether driven by parliamentary or mass politics.[64] Although the fascists draped themselves in demagogic vestments that seemed to invoke the general will, in fact both their words and their actions revealed their determination to shut down democracy in order to create a new ruling class of Supermen that repudiated the very notion of equality at all levels, from the racial to the ideological and spiritual.

Rather than shrinking from democratic power, as the emerging totalitarian synthesis demanded, Merriam embraced it, arguing that only an amplified demos could meet the challenge of the day. This was apparent in how he situated the problem of "decision," which fell not within the "new despotism" at all, as one might expect, but rather at the very heart of his democratic theory. Indeed, he took up the problem of "Democracy and Decisionism" in a chapter titled "Validation of Democratic Assumptions," which itself was the crux of the "New Democracy" section's central concern, "The Consent of the Governed." Far from representing the outer limit of democratic self-government or its Achilles heel, emergency and exception were at its heart – in the ever-unsettled, evolving, open field of contestation within which citizens resolved their plural and unlimited differences. If citizens could overcome the prospect of civil war then they could face any emergency without suspending the terms of their self-government.

There was nothing special about emergency in the democratic state. It certainly was not the fountainhead of politics, nor was it the negative specter haunting the very prospect of democracy. In this sense, Merriam shared Dewey's critical embrace of pluralism. Precisely because it was not bound to a monolithic conception of the state, he recognized the power of a democracy to act in situations of emergency. A democratic state did not require the cabining of executive power, either. Indeed, all of Merriam's thought and experience had taught him that executive power was absolutely "necessary to make democracy work under modern conditions."[65] The real danger lay in the invitation emergency provided to an "anti-democratic politics" indulged by elites determined to reinvigorate aristocratic politics for Nietzschean Supermen by way of one-party politics. In other words, the threat lay not in some totalitarian *state* but rather, as Franz Neumann would argue in his classic study of the Nazi state, in an overflowing of the political through polarization and one-party domination of society.[66]

If one properly recognized the nature of the threat posed by totalitarianism, all the techniques of democratic problem-solving were available to ensure the survival of democratic self-government and secure the conditions under which its distinctive mode of social power thrived. This explains Merriam's decision to place his treatment of "Democracy and Decisionism" immediately after a crucial section on public administration (which crystallized the larger practice and philosophy of public utility)[67] and right before a crucial section on "plan-making" (centering on the ideas of Laski and Merriam's beloved National Resource Council) and its critics (Hayek, Pigou, and Burns). His approach was in contrast to the totalitarian synthesis, which followed the Austrians and the realists in positing the axiomatic impossibility of social planning. His discussion of public administration, the essence of modern democratic statecraft, presented an extended argument for delegation and the science of administration, which together allowed the "unified and intelligent action" so necessary to meet the challenges of the modern world. Indeed, a refusal to plan or even neglect of planning placed democracy at a disadvantage relative to totalitarianism, since planning was so crucial to institutional efficacy in the modern world.[68] Perhaps the democracies could not afford to plan their societies, as Hayek argued, but their enemies certainly could, and had already demonstrated the effectiveness of their planning with devastating logic.[69]

Like Dewey, Merriam's critique of decisionism and the concept of exception from which it flowed were rooted in his abiding skepticism of sovereignty. Since the beginning of his career, Merriam had argued that the very notion of sovereignty itself was the supreme antidemocratic geist whose final exorcism from the state was necessary to complete the banishment of arbitrary, hierarchical, categorical authority from modern society.[70] This skepticism of any arguments positing even the momentary necessity of absolute power, or of a pure monopoly on its exercise through violence, made him immune to the elisions of the totalitarian synthesis. Seen from the pragmatic point of view, it was Merriam who was the realist. Indeed, one could argue that antitotalitarian thinkers from reformed progressives such as Walter Lippmann to reformed radicals such as James Burnham were themselves captured by the totalizing and mystifying move made by Schmitt and the theorists of total war. They were, in a sense, terrorized into accepting the awesome, Leviathan-like image of unlimited sovereign force and all-penetrating social control that the Nazis, Fascists, and Communists projected. Consequently, they presumed that only its opposite – the "limited states" – could be its antidote.[71]

Such a view ultimately rested on an inverted, monstrous fantasy of popular sovereignty, rather than a historical, measured, discerning understanding of how self-rule had actually operated within American society. The fantasy rested on reifications of political violence that were themselves the mirror image of liberal order grounded in "timeless" human nature. "Both Marx and Mussolini overemphasize the role of violence as a contributory factor in modern advancement," Merriam concluded, and proceeded to develop a democratic response to their violent overflowing of the political. Yet the solution he devised was emphatically *not* to place the state in a liberal or even utilitarian straight-jacket. If politics need not flow from the arbitrary decision, neither did it have to be neutered. In the long run far more power *and* liberty could be generated through a graduated, nonviolent, provisional adjustment of policy to societal requirements as directed by the hurly-burly of popular rule and mixed government within equal freedom.

If, as Neumann would observe a few years later, the Nazis had seized power by *hollowing out* the German state and supplanting it with a parallel party structure that progressively infused German society with principles of domination and decisionism, then the United States could only respond by *suffusing* the state with democratic social power and collaborative problem-solving, much as Merriam's beloved Tennessee Valley Authority summoned all the hydraulic force of an entire watershed by harnessing even the remotest and most capillary tributaries at the headwaters of the Appalachians.[72] Of course, precisely *how* this exercise in social engineering was accomplished would be of great consequence to the nature of the victory over fascism. But not only was it possible within a democratic framework, it was essential to the survival of democracy within America and throughout the "free world."

The core question for Merriam was not whether a democratic state could respond successfully to emergency but rather how effectively the "organization of violence" could be balanced against the "organization of consent."[73] Violence in itself did not generate power. Quite the contrary: a society operating on the principle of unlimited aggression or domination would remain quite feeble, as the constant conflict among myriad warring parties would prevent any combinations of a scope sufficient to canalize social power very far beyond the clan. "Violence," he observed, is "most useful . . . in a world where some operate on the principle of violence and others on that of persuasion and reason." This was just as true of a society characterized by law and order, which implemented its physical coercions judiciously and with unwavering regularity, as it was of a fascist world in which even the total application of violence could not coerce everyone all the time.[74] But where fascist political theory posited a total foundation of exception for state power that fit perfectly with its monistic conception of political will, a democratic political theory required a suppler understanding of the place of violence and decision within the production of political power. "Violence in this sense is not a rule of uniform action," Merriam observed, "but a rule of *differential exception*" (emphasis added).[75]

The solution to the crisis of democracy was more, not less, democracy. The "reign of violence" could only end through the effective use of the democratic stand-by, counterforce. Unlike liberals who were even then fleeing from the demos out of fear of the totalitarian state, Merriam did not abandon the general will. Only the "full development of the popular machinery," not its curtailment, could guarantee a decisive response to the new despotism.[76] That required acting on the recognition that "democracy is prior in importance to [any] particular mechanism of government," rather than reifying, fetishizing, or prioritizing particular democratic institutions such as the legislature or the judiciary, or democratic practices such as the rule of law. All of these techniques, not just a liberal subset, were needed to summon democratic social power safely and with fullest force.[77]

If the great threat to democracy was not emergency or exception, but rather an imbalance of coercion and consent within the democratic state, how could the essential equipoise be guaranteed? What was crucial, according to Merriam, was the existence of "clearly defined channels" where executive and popular will could meet and communicate, as Lincoln and Wilson had done, and flexible, multiply reinforcing, even competitive sources of review and insight – such as from businessmen and labor, multiple branches of the military and civilian administration, and policy-oriented politicians. The history of democratic governance suggested this was eminently possible. The American Civil War, Merriam noted, provided a powerful example of how a "democratic army" could be organized that was equal to the direst emergency.[78] Indeed, the long history of democracy itself could not be separated out from the history of constitutionalizing executive power and demarcating with ever-greater precision the boundaries between civilian and military authority.

It was this underlying principle of expanding the conditions for self-government that explained why the democratic state's resemblance to other, antidemocratic governments was ultimately superficial. The crucial difference lay in the principles operating to balance coercion and consent, with democracies always seeking ways to minimize violent conflict and maximize techniques of cooperation or bounded competition in service of equal freedom, while the new despotisms did the reverse. Categorical inequality and hierarchy provided the first principle for fascism, which relied entirely on violence to articulate an extrinsic racial order and an intrinsic party hierarchy to structure its power. Categorical equality and collective obeisance provided the first principle for Communism, but an equally axiomatic adherence to terror made everyone (except, perhaps, Stalin) equally unfree as sacrificial candidates for the strategic and even tactical needs of the Party. If a balance between liberty and equality could be established, however, the counterpoint of coercion and consent could proceed with a muscular efficacy limited only by the degree of its democratization, and would be perfectly equal to the necessity of any emergency.[79]

CONCLUSION

Merriam was right; the democratic state did prove, in the end, to be more powerful than its competitors who grounded their political principles in the notion of exception. Decisionism provided no advantage in the long run. Yet his differential exception did not provide all the answers any more than Emerson's antiformalist conception of law or Dewey's critique of popular sovereignty, the state, and bureaucracy. They did, however, open a door to reconsidering the nature of power in modern democratic states. To date, such a history and theory remains largely underdeveloped as scholars and theorists continue to run almost instinctively to reigning interpretations highlighting formal law, bureaucratic statecraft, and liberal politics. An alternative genealogy of the political that takes American legal and political theory seriously is necessary. And despite some of their own limitations, Emerson on law, Dewey on the state, and Merriam on politics at least point in the direction of a new and more realistic interpretive horizon. Indeed, we have tried to suggest here the way in which each of their insights into the nature of democratic power improves upon reigning theories of exception and emergency, while excising the rather unrealistic assumptions about law, state, and politics that so frequently animated them.

All of this is not to say that the contemporary obsession with exception and emergency is misguided. To the contrary, these might be the definitive intellectual and political challenges of our time. But such obsessions remain misconceived and disoriented insofar as they posit the state as inherently despotic, a tendency fed by a largely mythological vision of the American political tradition and amplified by an equally mystifying fascination with old Continental theories of the state and the political, most notably Schmitt's. Such perspectives simply cannot account for the real democratic pressures that have been able to mobilize within these developments. The problem ultimately lies in a failure to recognize the democratic components of the state and to articulate a conception of emergency that can do justice to the distinctive promise and perils of democratic social power. So long as we continue to think of the state as a cold monster, quintessentially bureaucratic, an authoritarian leviathan, or the product of an unending state of exception, we will misunderstand the nature of our greatest threats, which lie within our democratic politics – not beyond them – and yet can only be solved by them.

Notes

1 Theda Skocpol, "Bringing the State Back In: Strategies of Analysis in Current Research," in Peter B. Evans, Dietrich Rueschemeyer, and Theda Skocpol, eds., *Bringing the State Back In* (New York: Cambridge University Press, 1985), 3–37.

2 Max Weber, "Politics as a Vocation," in H.H. Gerth and C. Wright Mills, eds., *From Max Weber: Essays in Sociology* (New York: Oxford University Press, 1946), 77–129, 78.

3 Theodore J. Lowi, *The End of Liberalism: The Second Republic of the United States*, 2nd ed. (New York: W.W. Norton, 1979), 21.

4 Max Weber, *Economy and Society*, Guenther Roth and Claus Wittich, eds., 2 vols. (Berkeley: University of California Press, 1968), I: 217. For a critique of this perspective, see William J. Novak, "Beyond Weber: The Need for a Democratic (not Aristocratic) Theory of the Modern State," *Tocqueville Review/La revue Tocqueville*, 36, no. 1 (2015).

5 Louis Hartz, *The Liberal Tradition in America: An Interpretation of American Political Thought since the Revolution* (New York: Harcourt Brace Jovanovich, 1955), 62.

6 See, e.g., Robert Nozick, *Anarchy, State, and Utopia* (New York: Basic Books, 1974)

7 Michel Foucault, *Security, Territory, Population: Lectures at the Collège de France, 1977–1978* (New York: Palgrave Macmillan: 2007), 109; Friedrich Nietzsche, *Thus Spoke Zarathustra: A Book for All and None*, ed. Robert Pippin (Cambridge: Cambridge University Press, 2006), 34.

8 Bourdieu, *On the State*, 5–6.

9 For earlier efforts to build a history and theory of the democratic state, see James T. Sparrow, William J. Novak, and Stephen W. Sawyer, eds., *Boundaries of the State in U.S. History* (Chicago: University of Chicago Press, 2015), esp. introduction; Sawyer, Novak, and Sparrow, "Beyond Stateless Democracy," *Tocqueville Review/La revue Tocqueville*, 36, no 1 (2015); Novak, Sawyer, and Sparrow, "Toward a History of the Democratic State," *Tocqueville Review/La revue Tocqueville*, 33, no. 2 (2012).

10 Carl Schmitt, *Political Theology: Four Chapters on the Concept of Sovereignty*, trans. George Schwab (Chicago: University of Chicago Press, 2005), 11; Carl Schmitt, *The Crisis of Parliamentary Democracy*, trans. Ellen Kennedy (Cambridge: MIT Press, 1988), 19.

11 Richard Rorty, *Philosophy and the Mirror of Nature* (Princeton: Princeton University Press, 2009), 389.

12 Agamben, *State of Exception*, 1.

13 See, for example, Donald R. Kelley, *The Human Measure: Social Thought in the Western Legal Tradition* (Cambridge: Harvard University Press, 1990); Oliver Wendell Holmes, Jr., *The Common Law* (Boston: Little, Brown, and Company, 1881); Karl N. Llewellyn, *Jurisprudence: Realism in Theory and Practice* (Chicago: University of Chicago Press, 1962).

14 Oliver Wendell Holmes Jr., "The Path of the Law," *Harvard Law Review* 10 (1897): 457–478

15 John Dewey, "My Philosophy of Law," in Julius Rosenthal Foundation for General Law, *My Philosophy of Law: Credos of Sixteen American Scholars* (Boston: Boston Law Book Co., 1941), 73–85.

16 Karl N. Llewellyn, *The Bramble Bush: Some Lectures on Law and Its Study* (New York: Author, 1930), 3–5. For a similar sociological and realist view of law and sovereignty, see John R. Commons, *A Sociological View of Sovereignty* (New York: A.M. Kelly, 1965).

17 See Morton White, *Social Thought in America: The Revolt against Formalism* (New York: Viking, 1949).

18 Schmitt, *Political Theology*, 5.

19 Carl Schmitt, *The Concept of the Political*, trans. George Schwab (Chicago: University of Chicago Press, 1996).

20 Schmitt, *Political Theology*, 21–23.

21 Schmitt, *Political Theology*, 6.

22 Lewis Hockheimer, "Police Power," *Central Law Journal* 44 (1897), 158; William J. Novak, *The People's Welfare: Law and Regulation in Nineteenth-Century America* (Chapel Hill: University of North Carolina Press, 1996).

23 Schmitt, *Political Theology*, 5.

24 *Berman v. Parker*, 348 U.S. 26 (1954), 32.

25 W.P. Prentice, *Police Powers Arising under the Law of Overruling Necessity* (New York: Banks & Brothers, 1894), iii; W.G. Hastings, "The Development of Law as Illustrated by the Decisions Relating to the Police Power of the State," *Proceedings of the American Philosophical Society* 39 (1900): 359–554; Ernst Freund, *The Police Power: Public Policy and Constitutional Rights* (Chicago: University of Chicago Press, 1904).

26 Christopher L. Tomlins, *Law, Labor, and Ideology in the Early American Republic* (New York: Cambridge University Press, 1993), 45.

27 Markus D. Dubber, "Criminal Police and Criminal Law in the Rechtsstaat," in Markus D. Dubber and Mariana Valverde, eds., *Police and the Liberal State* (Palo Alto: Stanford University Press, 2008), 92–109; Novak, "Police Power and the Hidden Transformation of the American State," in Dubber and Valverde, 54–73.

28 Philip Hamburger, *Is Administrative Law Unlawful?* (Chicago: University of Chicago Press, 2014). For a blistering critique of this law/nonlaw perspective, see Adrian Vermeule, "No," *Texas Law Review*, 93 (2015), 1547–66.

29 *Brown v. Maryland*, 12 Wheat. 419 (U.S., 1827); *Commonwealth v. Alger*, 7 Cush. 53 (Mass., 1851); Leonard W. Levy, *The Law of the Commonwealth and Chief Justice Shaw* (Cambridge: Harvard University Press, 1957).

30 F.O. Matthiessen, *American Renaissance: Art and Expression in the Age of Emerson and Whitman* (New York: Oxford University Press, 1941); Robert D. Richardson, Jr., *Emerson: The Mind on Fire* (Berkeley: University of California Press, 1955).

31 Ralph Waldo Emerson, *Journals of Ralph Waldo Emerson, 1820–1872* (Cambridge: Riversode Press, 1912), 8: 232.

32 Emerson, "Self-Reliance," 217.

33 Emerson, "The Fugitive Slave Law," in *The Complete Works of Ralph Waldo Emerson*, vol. 11.

34 Karl Marx, "Critique of Hegel's Doctrine of State," in *Karl Marx: Early Writings*, trans. Rodney Livingstone and Gregor Benton (New York: Vintage, 1975), 87–88.

35 Julia Adams and George Steinmetz, for example, have recently sent us back to Schmitt to look for a renewal of sociological approaches to the state and politics. In their account, Schmitt's decisionism provides a way forward beyond the Weberian sociologies of the state that were spawned in 1970s. As this section articulates, Dewey offered an equally potent and radical transition out of Weberian autonomous state-centeredness, but one that also overcame the pitfalls and dangers in the Schmittian response. Instead of rooting decision in sovereignty, Dewey rooted decision in a deeply sociological conception of the public. In this sense, not only was Dewey's conception of the state more sociological, it was also more democratic. Adams and Steinmetz adopt Schmitt's position that returning to a form of agency or decisionism requires a return to thinking about sovereignty. However, Dewey's response to Schmitt (and Weber) suggests not only that this is not necessarily the case, but that a more productive response may be found by jettisoning sovereignty as the foundation for decision. Adams and Steinmetz, "Sovereignty and Sociology: From State Theory to Theories of Empire," *Political Power and Social Theory* 28 (2015): 269–85.

36 Chantal Mouffe, ed., *The Challenge of Carl Schmitt* (London: Verso, 1999)

37 Originally published in *Kant-Studien*, 1930. All references to this article are from Arthur Jacobson and Bernhard Schlink, eds., *Weimar: A Jurisprudence of Crisis* (Berkeley: University of California Press, 2000).

38 Jacobson and Schlink, *Weimar*, 302.

39 Ibid., 311.

40 Ibid., 303.

41 Ibid., 307.

42 Ibid., 308.

43 John Dewey, *The Public and Its Problems* (New York: Henry Holt and Company, 1927), 24.

44 Ibid., 33.

45 Ibid., 25.

46 Ibid., 26.

47 Ibid., 31.

48 Ibid., 32.

49 Schmitt, "Ethics," 307.

50 Dewey, *Public and Its Problems*, 225.

51 On this point, see Vincent Azoulay's critique of Schmitt's conception of the political in the Greek polis. "Repolitiser la cité grecque, trente ans après," *Annales. Histoire, Sciences Sociales* 3 (2014): 689–719.

52 Dewey, *Public and Its Problems*, 25.

53 Ibid., 29.

54 Ibid., 30.

55 Joseph A. Schumpeter, *Capitalism, Socialism, and Democracy* (New York: Harper & Brothers, 1942), 83.

56 Pierre Clastres, *Society against the State: Essays in Political Anthropology*, trans. Robert Hurley and Abe Stein (New York: Zone Books, 1989), 13.

57 On the retreat from pragmatism and rediscovery of the democratic faith, see Edward Purcell, *The Crisis of Democratic Theory: Scientific Naturalism and the Problem of Value* (Lexington: University of Kentucky Press, 1973). On totalitarianism, see Ben Alpers, *Dictators, Democracy, and American Public Culture: Envisioning the Totalitarian Enemy, 1920s–1950s* (Chapel Hill: Univeristy of North Carolina Press, 2003); David Ciepley, *Liberalism in the Shadow of Totalitarianism* (Cambridge: Harvard University Press, 2006). On the (neo)liberal revival, see Angus Burgin, *The Great Persuasion: Reinventing Free Markets since the Depression* (Cambridge: Harvard University Press, 2012).

58 Robert Westbrook, *John Dewey and American Democracy* (Ithaca: Cornell University Press, 1991); Barry Karl, *Charles E. Merriam: An Introduction to the Man and His Papers* (Chicago: University of Chicago Library, 1975); Barry Karl, Charles E. *Merriam and the Study of Politics* (Chicago: University of Chicago Press, 1974); Walter Lippmann, *An Inquiry into the Principles of the Good Society* (Boston: Little, Brown,1937); Ronald Steel, *Walter Lippmann and the American Century* (Boston: Little, Brown, 1980).

59 Charles Merriam, *The New Democracy and the New Despotism* (New York: McGraw-Hill, 1939).

60 Merriam, *New Democracy*, 6.
61 Quoted in Ibid., 210.
62 Ibid., 136.
63 Ibid., 137; 132–45 *passim*.
64 Ibid., 191–242.
65 Ibid., 127.
66 Franz Neumann, *Behemoth: The Structure and Practice of National Socialism* (New York: Oxford University Press, 1942).
67 William Novak, "The Public Utility Idea and the Origins of Modern Business Regulation," in *Corporations and American Democracy*, ed. Novak and Naomi Lamoreaux (forthcoming, 2017).
68 Merriam, *New Democracy*, 127, 132–35.
69 Merriam, *New Democracy*, 179.
70 This was the topic of his dissertation: Charles E. Merriam, *History of the Theory of Sovereignty since Rousseau* (New York: Columbia Studies in the Social Sciences, 1900).
71 Walter Lippmann, *The Good Society* (Boston: Little, Brown and Company, 1937); James Burnham, *The Managerial Revolution* (New York: John Day, 1941).
72 Neumann, *Behemoth*, esp. part I, ch. 1.
73 Merriam, *New Democracy*, 340–45.
74 It is here that we see the advantages of the pragmatic/democratic approach over that of Foucault, for it accounts for coercion without reducing it always to domination, discipline, or governmentality, thus opening conceptual room for citizenship, agency, and self-possession. On the biographical origins of Foucault's totalized (and totalizing) power scheme in his boyhood experience of Vichy France, see Mark Mazower, "Foucault, Agamben: Theory and the Nazis," *Boundary* 2 35, no. 1 (Spring 2008): 23–34.
75 Merriam, *New Democracy*, 345.
76 Ibid., 179.
77 Ibid., 181.
78 Ibid., 140; 133.
79 Ibid., 183–86.

Performing Order

An Examination of the Seemingly Impossible Task of Subjugating Large Numbers of People, Everywhere, All the Time

Christian Davenport

How do states establish and maintain control over those within their territorial jurisdiction? Many would argue that the answer to this question lies in the Weberian definition of the state whereby political authorities claim control and the legitimate use of force; one of the many hands of the state is the coercive one. This points in the right direction but it ignores the fact that the key to understanding political order lies in investigating the actions of government *as well as* the actions of challengers. Hobbes makes this point a bit more directly, arguing that it is the relative balance of state to nonstate coercive behavior that establishes the foundation upon which citizens make decisions about what they will do regarding the relevant political authority. Hobbes has a particular take on the issue, however, as he is concerned with actual government behavior on the ground. I maintain that while this is important, the key to understanding how states establish and maintain control over their territorial jurisdiction resides more in the minds of their constituents than in observing behavior enacted on the streets and hills of the polity.

This is useful to acknowledge because states are severely outnumbered in terms of the number of people working in and for them, relative to the size of the total population. Additionally, for a variety of different reasons, political authorities do not use the full arsenal of weapons at their disposal against those under their care, as it would destroy the very thing that they are trying to preserve/protect/exploit. Awareness of this situation assists us in understanding a fundamental truism regarding the modern context: there are not enough state agents in any nation-state to monitor, intimidate, sanction, and/or kill every citizen, at least not in a straight confrontation or fight.[1] Given this reality, it is crucial for states to try some other means to maintain control over those in the territorial jurisdiction lest the majority discover the true nature of the relationship between the state and the governed and set off challenges throughout the population.

Consistent with the narrative and cultural turn discussed throughout the current volume, this chapter argues that a perception of order is created – I call this "functional order" – through a well-crafted performance put forward by political authorities and directed toward the mass public within the relevant territory. The performance is composed of two actions: (1) coercive behavior undertaken against the status quo (challenges) and (2) coercive behavior undertaken in favor of the status quo (suppression). By considering these two dimensions at the same time, a viewer can assess the amount of political order that is believed to exist as well as the overall legitimacy of the relevant political authorities. In particular, when behavioral challenges are believed to be low and suppression is high, states are believed to have the upper hand in terms of the relevant amount of coercion being jointly produced. When challenging behavior is believed to be high and suppression is low, challengers have the upper hand and the overall legitimacy of the relevant political authorities is limited. When both behavioral challenges and state coercion are believed to be high or low, then neither actor is believed to have the upper hand, but in very different circumstances; the former might be referred to as "armed conflict" or "civil war" whereas the latter might be referred to as "peace."

Although the different positions in the two-dimensional space identified here are important, I maintain that political order is generally viewed as existing when the responses of challengers and authorities are proportional. Here, state behavior largely matches the behavioral challenge being put forward in terms of lethality and/or scope; that is, for every behavioral challenge one sees comparable amounts of state suppression. Deviations here are crucial. When states "overproduce" coercion relative to challengers (contexts of political strength/invulnerability), there will potentially be fear and quiescence, supporting the status quo (a form of functionality – at least for leaders). When states underproduce coercion relative to challengers (contexts of political weakness/vulnerability), however, there will potentially be cascades of increasing doubt and resistance among the public, threatening the status quo (a form of dysfunctionality).

How does or should one study the topic of interest? Historically, diverse sources such as newspapers and state/NGO reports have been used to identify as well as analyze the actual positions of states and challengers within the two dimensions. Interestingly, even for a single challenger–state dyad, there may be multiple points in the relevant space for a specific dyadic interaction (i.e., the actual number of challenging to suppressive events), as different actors have different access to and interest in specific dyads. Although one could suggest that the different opinions emerge because of differential access to and interest in the challenger–state dyad of interest, I would suggest that coverage of these realities and perceptions is largely influenced by the state. Specifically, states can shape how challenges or repression are depicted through various means, including the suppression of alternative opinions, the production of information about the coercive capacity of both the state itself and its challengers, or the explaining away of unwanted deviations, and they can use reports of behavioral challenges and the requirements for suppression to establish legitimacy. The result is a characterization of order that generally favors political authorities and generates mass acquiescence, if not willing obedience.

In this chapter, I outline why this topic has been largely ignored by conflict studies, discuss the joint production of political order as well as the predominant position that states hold in this production, and then provide some examples of how the conceptual model functions. The conclusion lays out some of the implications of this research and points to potentially fruitful future directions.

CONFLICT STUDIES AND ORDER (OR THE LACK THEREOF)

What do states do and how well do they do it? Although many tasks appear to be within their purview, both legitimately and illegitimately, perhaps the one that has been the most fundamental concerns the establishment and maintenance of political order: the relative balance of state coercive behavior compared with nonstate coercive behavior.[2] Unfortunately, existing research has been unable and/or unwilling to address the topic sufficiently. The biggest limitation concerns the inability to address both the state and the challengers at the same time. Since the late 1960s, there have been four notable efforts to make state–challenger interactions central to the study of political conflict, but each has been limited, although in different ways, and thus they have been unable to address the topic effectively. I briefly discuss them chronologically in the following, before turning to my own suggested approach.

The Conflict–Repression Nexus

Largely building on the research agendas of Eckstein, Gurr, Tilly, and the founders of modern domestic conflict studies (see Zimmerman[3] for a good discussion), the first effort is commonly referred to as the "conflict–repression nexus" (e.g., Lichbach[4]). This work concerns itself with behavioral attempts at influencing political order through contentious politics and state repression. Operationally, this involves considering the influence of repression on dissent (e.g., Muller, Ziegenhagen, Francisco, Moore[5]), the influence of dissent on repression (e.g., Davenport, Davenport et al., Moore[6]), or the influence of repression and dissent on each other (e.g., Hibbs, Shellman[7]) – all variables here are measured directly (as events) with some source such as a newspaper article. As the guiding logic here is one of equilibrium – once perturbed by some actor's behavior (dissent for authorities and repression for challengers), the other side responds with some action (respectively, repression and dissent). The work here is also is noteworthy because it situates these dynamic interactions within a broader political-economic-cultural context such that some contexts lead to greater interactions or lethality and some reduce these dimensions.

Through these investigations numerous advances have been made in conceptualization, measurement, research methodology, and theory, but there have been some important limitations as well. For example, while the sheer amount of attention on the topic has been significant, there has been uneven attention across topic areas. The influence of repression on dissent has received by far the greatest amount of attention. The amount of work relevant to the influence of dissent on repression has increased significantly in the last ten years. And the dynamic interaction between dissent and repression is still generally neglected in large part because of the difficulties with modeling the relationship of interest. Additionally, existing work is generally investigating political conflict that is lower in lethality than civil war, armed conflict and human rights violations, such as protest and the policing of protest; thus, many do not believe it to be relevant for more deadly forms of political conflict and violence. This has been extremely detrimental to the development of the literature on lesser violent behavior.

Internationally Oriented Domestic Conflict Scholarship

Beginning in approximately the late 1980s and early 1990s, researchers traditionally interested in interstate conflict – war – shifted their attention to topics defined as "domestic politics," such as civil war (e.g., Fearon and Laitin), terrorism (e.g., Li), and some mass killing (e.g., Valentino et al.[8]). This work concerns itself with behavioral attempts to undermine political order, generally through some challenging activity undertaken by a non-state actor. Scholars in this area claim that an armed opponent to the state must exist, as well as have a capacity to inflict (physical) damage on political authorities; they occasionally mention political objectives. In contrast, repression is not viewed as a "problem" for political order but, rather, is viewed as the "solution" for it. Historically, this has involved considering the influence of diverse structural characteristics on behavioral challenges (e.g., economic development, population, and democracy), so that the research question becomes "under what circumstances do citizens within a national territory come together to successfully challenge their sovereign state in a highly violent manner?"

While largely neglectful of the founders of modern domestic conflict studies mentioned here, it is nevertheless clear that internationally oriented domestic conflict scholars have drawn upon their insights. In one of the most influential pieces in the literature, Fearon and Laitin argue that civil war is likely to emerge when states are not able to identify, monitor, constrain, and/or eliminate behavioral challengers. Thus, they put forth an argument that fails to acknowledge its debt to the literature on the conflict–repression nexus.[9] Their theory is directly relevant to placing state–challenger interactions at the core of the explanation for civil war. Moreover, this work provides an important reinterpretation of political conflict that moves away from largely static political–economic structural factors noted earlier and offers a rigorous test of relevant propositions.

Unfortunately, there are some important limitations with this research that directly relate to its lack of engagement with the broader literature on conflict and violence. For example, while incorporating an important component of the conflict–repression nexus (i.e., the influence of states on behavioral challenges), the other component is ignored (i.e., the influence of behavioral challenges on states). In addition, there is no consideration of related highly lethal forms of conflict, such as genocide, that frequently co-occur with civil war. But perhaps the biggest limitation is the lack of a direct measure of repression or pre–civil war mobilization – the core element of the explanation. Instead, reverting back to the practice of traditional international relations scholars, these authors operationalize the key elements of their arguments with GNP per capita – a variable shown to have a limited impact on state repression within examinations specifically dedicated to the topic.[10] With this work, it was clear that some greater attention needed to be given to dynamic interactions. This is precisely where the field started to go but only in certain ways and with specific forms of conflict: civil war – the vortex that appears to have subsumed political conflict/violence studies.

The Logic of (Some) Violence in Civil War (Sometimes)

In another important work in the field, Kalyvas maintains that to understand civilian-directed violence during civil war one must focus on the dynamic interaction between challengers and states as they fight for territorial control.[11] The work is innovative in that it moves away from the more structurally oriented examinations that preceded it. Introducing a five-zone conception, he argues that the greater the control of either side over specific territory, the lower the likelihood of civilian-oriented violent behavior. Differing from Fearon and Laitin, but very much like the conflict–repression nexus – which again is not explicitly acknowledged – Kalyvas's argument includes a dynamic interaction between challengers and states at the core of political conflict, representing an important contribution. Despite the advancement, however, there are some limitations – in part because of the neglect of the conflict–repression nexus.

First, the topic of civil war is viewed as being distinct from both less-lethal state–citizen interactions, such as protest and protest policing, and related more-lethal citizen–state interactions such as genocide and revolution. This hinders our ability to gauge similarities and differences across types of political violence and to analyze (de)escalation. It also seems to violate some of the principles articulated by Kalyvas himself, such as the acknowledgement that the motives and activities of conflict behavior vary according to local contexts. Why would it not follow that the forms of conflict might also vary as the local motives and activities concatenate in distinct ways? Second, while state–challenger interactions are central to the discussion, the work is not really about these actors or actions; one loses a sense of the overall contest, its dynamics and, most importantly, its aftereffects. What is violence against civilians during civil war but an outcome of state–challenger dynamics? To understand these dynamics, however, one would need to ground such a discussion in the conflict–repression nexus and not in a critique of civil war studies. Third, and related, Kalyvas does not provide measures of the core concepts and, indeed, avoids the topic of measurement, as he seems to believe it is not easy to do.[12] Instead, he draws on mass remembrances of what took place a number of years after the conflict of interest. While consistent with some research in social movements (e.g., Opp and Roehl[13]), this approach is not generally advocated because of a host of problems, such as recall bias.

Dyadic Interaction: It Really Does "Take Two," Doesn't It?

Initially drawing upon the interstate war literature but then moving beyond it, there have recently been some attempts at exploring citizen–state dyads (e.g., Harbom et al., Buhaug et al., Cunningham et al.)[14] This research again places those who challenge states and political authorities as central to the topic at hand, acknowledging that national-level aggregations are probably not the best unit of analysis to analyze what takes place during violent political contests. This topic is explored through direct consultation of diverse news records as both challengers in state behavior are measured. Here, some important insights have emerged about how best to model and to conceive of state–challenger interactions, for example, the importance of considering within-group factionalization, decision-making processes, and tactical variation across challengers in the same territorial units.

Although beginning to move in line with the most advanced research on state–challenger interactions found in the conflict–repression nexus, the research here is still limited. For example, once again distinct forms of political conflict are held as unrelated to one another, precluding investigation of commonality/difference, substitution, escalation, and generalizability (but see, e.g., the work of Cunningham and Lemke[15]). The work has been much better at taking interactions apart than considering how the diverse components fit together to explain socio-political order writ large. For instance, how does the behavior of one actor influence the behavior of another? Relatedly, how does the persecution of one challenger influence the persecution of another? What types of actions are related to other actions within as well as between actors? This body of scholarship is not alone in neglecting the co-production of order or violence, as similar limitations afflict research on the conflict–repression nexus as well as Kalyvas's work. The former appears to be more interested in understanding variation in actor response to particular activities (in a specific place/time) than in understanding generally who wins state–challenger interactions. The latter appears to be more interested in understanding variation in citizen harassment than in understanding which way the civil war goes, although it is clear that the two are related. Regardless, one is left wondering what else is connected: terrorism–counterterrorism, protest–protest policing, petitions, strikes, torture, boycotts, curfews, and so on. There needs to be some way to bring these various forms together and explore the broader meaning for order. I pursue this in the following section.

STATES, CHALLENGERS, AND POLITICAL ORDER

My view of conflict studies begins with simply joining two axes of behavior (Figure 10.1). On the left (the *y*-axis) lies repressive lethality, which ranges from low-level conflict activity such as surveillance to high-level conflict behavior such as mass killing.[16] Along the bottom (the *x*-axis) lies challenger lethality, which also ranges from low coercive action, for example everyday forms of resistance, to higher-level action such as mass killing. The juxtaposition is important for guiding our thinking. For example, within this framework, conflict outcomes are understood as jointly produced since one is led to pinpoint precisely where particular interactions exist on the two-dimensional space – that is, one can tell where a country is by identifying where a particular dyad is located on the grid. One need not think of this exclusively as a single point. It may be preferable to identify a range of discrete interactions (i.e., points) within the space. Here, one could take the average in an effort to summarize a collection of interactions.

The space itself can be divided as a function of the precision of the data being employed. In the most constricted scenario (displayed in Figure 10.2), if one were just to use Fearon and Laitin's civil war data (zone 2), Harff's[17] data on genocide (zone 1), and Goldstone's data on revolution (zone 3), one could identify three distinct forms of activity that could take place individually or concurrently.

In the least constricted scenario (Figure 10.3), one could identify a wide range of "zones." Unfortunately, we will not be able to get to this

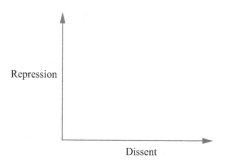

FIGURE 10.1. Basic states versus challengers (SvC).

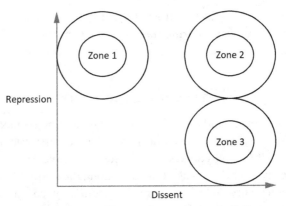

FIGURE 10.2. Zones of contestation in SvC.

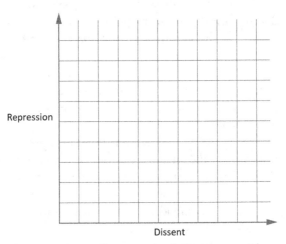

FIGURE 10.3. States versus challengers as grid.

for quite some time, because we do not yet have the granularity in the data (i.e., detailed data on all challenger–state dyads within a particular time and space). Nevertheless, it is useful to imagine the possibility and it is useful for those who employ other, less restrictive methodologies.

Within both of the scenarios presented here, researchers could identify, monitor, and examine placement in the relevant space at one point in time, across time, and/or across contexts, allowing them to explore topics of escalation/deescalation, substitution, and trajectories in new ways.

Adopting this framework, the key to understanding placement is to clarify how much lethal violence is generated by each of the "two sides" of a conflict (I will relax this assumption in the following). In the tradition of contentious politics as studied by Tilly,[18] underlying the juxtaposition of actors is a political contest between those that have an interest in establishing and maintaining a particular political economic order (political authorities) and those that have an interest in changing or replacing it (challengers). Each side marshals forces toward their specific ends, which involves inflicting costs on the relevant opponent in terms of wages, human capital, or favorable opinion from the population. In this framework, the greater the lethality, the greater the potential cost imposed on the other actor.

While an important initial step, it is not simply the joining of the two dimensions but exactly how they fit together that proves to be even more important. For example, the juxtaposition links ancient to modern conceptions of the field. In his now-legendary discussion of coercion (noted at the beginning of the chapter), Hobbes maintained that individuals should defer to a central authority when it is able to vanquish any challengers in the relevant territorial domain that also wield coercive power. If a state could do this, he suggested that individuals should acquiesce and accept the legitimacy of the central authority. If states could not do this, however, he argued that individuals should rebel and replace the impotent political entity because it "under-produces" political order (i.e., it engages in coercive action that falls far below nonstate political coercion). Not all productions of coercion were acceptable to Hobbes. He maintained that if the central authority is able to vanquish challengers but does so at such a high level that it coercively dominates the relevant territorial unit, this presents a different problem but leads to a similar solution as the under-production problem: here, again, Hobbes suggested that individuals rebel and replace the excessive political entity because it "over-produces" coercion (i.e., it engages in coercive action that far outpaces nonstate political coercion). This suggests that there is an acceptable zone of engagement within which individuals should evaluate joint coercive interactions.

Indeed, this approach suggests that there is a balance that must be maintained between state and nonstate coercive action (on the diagonal of Figure 10.4). This I refer to as the Hobbesian balance. This conception is important because it orients most discussions about coercive interaction, either implicitly or, occasionally, explicitly. As such, it serves as a barometer by which all forms of political conflict can be evaluated, as I demonstrate in the following.

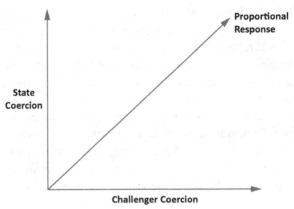

FIGURE 10.4. States versus challengers and the Hobbesian balance.

Studying the Topic

Historically, people have studied political conflict through a systematic evaluation of different sources: newspapers (in conflict studies frequently the *New York Times*), newswires (such as Reuters), NGO or state reports (such as Amnesty International Country reports and the State Department Country Report, respectively), or, more recently, Twitter feeds. Once coded to identify what happened as well as who did what to whom, this information yields either a distinct point in the two-dimensional space above (representing an overall characterization of a conflict – for example, coding a particular case as a revolution, civil war, or terrorism) or an array of points (representing a series of individual events – for example, the number of protest and/or protest policing activities undertaken in a particular place/time). Researchers of diverse phenomena who are interested in diverse areas could easily place the data they collect into the framework.

From these data, individuals attempt to figure out where the conflict was, who was winning, who was losing, what the trajectory of engagement was, and so forth. What is important here is that it is believed from the evaluation that one is directly and explicitly studying the conflict of interest. In this work, the conflict is "proxied" by the source material and through these one has a general sense of what happened. Developing upon a theme addressed in my earlier work, referred to as the "Rashomon Effect,"[19] researchers need not presume that all individuals hold the same opinions about state–challenger interactions. It is possible and, indeed, likely that distinct actors maintain different opinions about what is

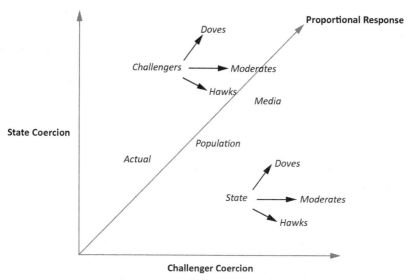

FIGURE 10.5. States versus challengers and the Rashomon effect.

taking place.[20] For example, the state might believe and/or convey that it is under siege and that it is under-responding to the behavioral challenges with which it is confronted. This could allow it to secure popular support and reduce criticism about what is being done. Similarly, challengers, within the same conflict, might believe and/or convey that they are under-responding to state action. This will be done for the same reasons. The traditional media, with its interest in "balanced" reporting, might describe a more proportional conflict, with each side contributing to the outcome. This does not reflect the reality of the situation, but instead reflects the type of narrative the source wishes to provide. The population might believe that the conflict resides at a point distinct from all of those identified here. Moreover, the reality of the situation might be completely different from any of the actors' portrayals. One could complicate matters further, identifying that the state is split with doves, moderates, and hawks each maintaining a slightly different view of the situation. The challenger itself could be split in its opinions, as well as the population and media (not shown). I consider this complexity in Figure 10.5.

These differences are important because they likely influence how conflicts are fought by influencing perceptions of combatants and their recruitment efforts. It could influence bystanders – especially their willingness to get involved, as well as which side would acquire support (e.g., as suggested by Kalyvas).[21] The distance between the different actors' perceptions could be crucial for understanding likely outcomes – adopting either bargaining or prospect theories. In short, the differences would influence the likelihood of conflict onset, escalation, termination, and recurrence – things that conflict scholars want to study. Work has been undertaken on specific aspects of this problem. For example, researchers have compared coverage of different newspapers against one another within a complex situation (Davenport), or newspapers against NGO and state reports (McCarthy et al.; Davenport and Ball), but not within the relative perspectives maintained in the SvC framework whereby different actors are viewed relative to one another.[22]

Indeed, what is discussed here represents a very different way of viewing the problem away from what is currently framed as a "bias" in our source material and invoking an evaluation of what is better considered "perspective."

To adopt this approach, researchers would have to stop pooling their source material or simply comparing sources against one another in order to ascertain similarities. Rather, they would have to take sources seriously, evaluating who is creating them and for what purposes as well as who is reading them and for what purposes. This more nuanced approach would allow research to better evaluate what information is being created and how it is being used in conflict situations.

What is important about the work is that while it allows for the possibility that distinct data sources may differ in precisely where they place a particular conflict in the two dimensions, it is still believed that these different sources reference the same underlying reality – that is, there is some latent conflict. Here, it is presumed that sources are "trying to get the conflict right." In this context, the state's work of maintaining political order is revealed through the source material, indicating how well it is doing at surveillance, protest policing, counterterrorism, and counterinsurgency. If sources over- or underestimate anything, it is presumed that they did not have the resources to do the background research or that they were prevented from getting the story.

This is not the only view, however. It is possible that sources are not trying to capture some latent conflict. They just might be trying to portray the reality that they wish others to adopt. In this latter view, sources are not "trying to get the conflict right." Rather, they are trying to provide a performance (i.e., the characterization of repression and dissent) in order to persuade some audience. Here, state work regarding political order is revealed through the source material but it does not necessarily have anything to do with actual governance – at least, not as it relates to identifying and countering actual behavioral challenges/challengers in the relevant territorial domain. Rather, it captures the stories of resistance and subjugation, which in turn can influence perceptions, attitudes, behavior, and outcomes.

PERFORMING ORDER

I find the performance argument compelling because it incorporates a reality that has long influenced conflict studies but that has not generally been included specifically in this research: that, although different sources exist, states have a predominate influence over information collection as well as distribution.[23] As a result, states end up significantly influencing the performance of order that is projected to the mass citizenry. For example, state agents can overtly restrict the media or feed it stories, or the media could simply do as state officials say because it acknowledges that, insofar as the generation of "news" goes, political authorities are the best "meal ticket" in town. State actors could restrict challenger ability to distribute information through bans, harassment, or investigations. Officials could feed information to film and television directors, magazine editors, blog posters, or other conveyers. They could restrict, threaten, or make access difficult for ordinary citizens. Finally, state agents could restrict, threaten, or make access difficult for members of states who might disagree with the most favored position. In short, states wield influence over most of the actors in the conceptual model, rendering most of what we come to understand about conflict from the purview of existing authorities. A version of the state's role is provided in Figure 10.6 with the lines signifying the influence that more aggressive political hawks affiliated with the government could have on diverse actors.

The implications of this conception are important to identify. First, we should expect certain types of characterizations of state–dissident interactions to emerge from the materials distributed and consumed throughout a nation-state. For example, states might appear to be much less aggressive and/or responsive than they actually are, whereas challenging behavior might appear to be much more frequent or violent relative to what states do toward challengers. Second, revelations about where state–dissident interactions actually are (compared with where they are reported to be) could be amazingly devastating for states if they significantly deviate from what individuals otherwise understand. Revelations that the state is something other than what is projected

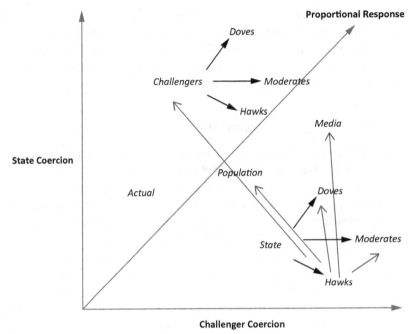

FIGURE 10.6. States versus challengers and state control.

could thus result in mass outrage and defection as individuals feel betrayed. Alternatively, these revelations might actually have a hard time changing opinion because they are so widely different from what people believe to be true (i.e., that which is reported elsewhere). Third, if the argument here is correct, then there should be some wider outcry about the death of an independent media. Most acknowledge that newspapers are generally going the way of the dodo, but there has been no discussion of what this means for citizens or for the assessment of interactions between states and dissidents. Some would counter my concerns by citing the increasing influences of social media, but it is yet to be established if social media reports events better than does investigative journalism. It is also not clear, given the difficulties of source as well as event verification, if social media is easier or more difficult for states to infiltrate and influence. Perhaps with the proliferation of everyone's perspectives over the internet, we end up with what Stephen Colbert refers to as "Truthiness," a situation in which everything exists and there is no truth (i.e., actual facts that would be agreed upon if known), only the truth that one opts to believe.

This argument is relevant to the state and the current volume in diverse ways. First, it is relevant to the state-building literature in that it provides us with a way to understand how political authorities engage in what Tilly refers to as domestic "pacification" (i.e., the systemic elimination of domestic armed political rivals). Rather than simply characterize this period in behavioral terms, however, my approach also suggests that observers be attentive to narratives about contestation across sources. Indeed, one would expect that sources close to political authorities (or rather potential political authorities) would generally characterize contentious interactions as clearly indicating that they are beginning to monopolize the use of violence. This victory then signals to opponents and bystanders (at home or abroad) that they are legitimate. Clearly these two interact in some capacity. Rivals can each say that they are winning the battle, but some victories must be taking place. For example, in the French Revolution it appears to some that the only battle that mattered was the Bastille and after it fell, the conflict was over. Of course, there were violent exchanges before this time as well as after it, but the *story* of the conflict simplifies and focuses the discussion – most likely, however, only on one side of the conflict (i.e., government or challengers). The other side (i.e., challengers or governments, respectively) probably keeps trying until they cannot push their claims-making effort any longer.

After the state is initially taken, then a different period emerges: one in which new authorities essentially purge themselves of potential challengers. Again, this is done both behaviorally (i.e., through bans, restrictions, arrests, and executions) and narratively (i.e., as the story of the victorious revolution/regime change is crafted and distributed). To be clear, I do not anticipate that this period would be all repression, all the time. Rather, I would expect that political authorities allocate repression, both behaviorally and narratively, against those that challenge or appear to challenge them. Authorities deploy accommodation, cooptation, and favorable narrative depictions toward those who either have already adapted to the new regime or could potentially adopt an acceptable position toward it. This is how states are made and reproduced, as those within the population begin to put themselves into surviving categories.

State survival here is in both the contentious and narrative realms. For example, political authorities may claim a position of domination but behaviorally not have the wherewithal to back it up. At the same time, civil society might not (yet) have the capacity to test this and thus the appearance/performance of order takes place. It is also possible that authorities actually defeat behavioral challenges but do not properly communicate this to the relevant citizenry.

Now, given what was stated earlier, states are not all powerful and what has taken place at one period does not carry over to all periods. Indeed, it is the ability to continue to vanquish potential challengers behaviorally as well as narratively that reveals the state's capacity to maintain order. For example, it is possible that states fail to monitor what Verta Taylor calls "abeyance structures" – that is, underground organizations where individuals maintain networks that can be later utilized to go aboveground and engage in behavioral challenges. States may not properly continue the job of communicating their victory, subsequent domination, and citizen acquiescence to newer generations who might realize that it is within their power to "test the waters" and see what governments are capable of. Interestingly, my approach suggests that the contestation would be both behavioral and narrative. Concerning the latter, if one were to consult sources emerging from the different communities, they would come to very different conclusions regarding the possibilities for change. Indeed, this would explain why individuals would rise up in seemingly "impossible" situations (i.e., contexts where political opportunity structure appears closed with authoritarianism and state repression). This would also explain why many states appear to collapse so quickly once mass resistance begins – something that existing research has found generally puzzling.

Again, however, this is where state capacity to perform order is revealed. If political authorities can respond to the upstarts behaviorally as well as narratively, revealing the futility of resistance, then the government can survive. This refers not just to protest and protest policing, terrorism and counterterrorism, and insurgency and counterinsurgency, but also to stories about these contests that emerge from distinct communities that may or may not follow one another.

Although the argument identified earlier is believed to be applicable to all states, I do not believe that observers would be equally capable of examining the topic across contexts in precisely the same way. For example, the behavioral and narrative battle in political democracies would be much more complex in the sense that there would likely be a tremendous amount of material available. Here, we would find publicly accessible government documents, NGO reports, newspapers from diverse communities as well as private memoirs, letters, novels, songs, and so on. Within more authoritarian contexts, the situation is different. Here, one is likely to find only government documents or simply government declarations, directives, and speeches that are distributed by state-sanctioned media. In addition to this, one would have to excavate and explore the subaltern – the private reflections perhaps told in cafes or homes, and one would have to use the methods of James Scott to decipher messages of subversion in everyday language. Regardless of where one conducts such work, however, one must be attentive to the fact that what took place and the stories about what took place are not the same thing.

In the following, I explore some of the implications of the argument outlined earlier and show how it reveals state dysfunction and functionality as well as how states deal with movements from the former to the latter as well as the reverse.

ORDERING PERFORMANCES

Functional Order: A Success Story

Between 1919 and the late 1950s, the Communist Party of the United States of America (CP-USA) engaged in a wide variety of challenges to the U.S. state and its economic system. Bent on overthrowing capitalism in general and the United States in particular, the Party attempted to raise awareness regarding the evils of the American political–economic system and supported all struggles against it. The activities put forward toward these ends were as numerous as they were diverse, from editorials to unionization to political campaigns to mass protests. The magnitude of the challenge presented cannot be underestimated. Focused initially on major cities, these efforts began to emerge everywhere. While the methods were somewhat conventional (e.g., creating legal trade unions), however, the objectives were not: the Communists sought nothing less than complete radical transformation. At the same time, the magnitude of the challenge should not be overstated. Although the challenge and objective were significant in their scope, the organizational capacity to enact the desired change was limited. Nevertheless, one would not know this from looking at newspapers or state reports of the day. According to these sources, America was under assault. The scare that was "Red" was pervasive.

In response to the activities mentioned earlier, the U.S. state engaged in a similarly wide variety of repressive strategies to identify, constrain, and destroy the "commies." By most accounts, this was the most thorough initiative of its kind in U.S. history.[24] In the 1940s, the American Communist Party was officially banned and state agents throughout the country assembled lists of members as well as their activities (real and imagined). In turn, suspected activists were harassed, detained, questioned, arrested, beaten, and deported. Interestingly, and directly in line with the arguments identified earlier, these activities were not hidden from the U.S. population. Rather, they were placed on the front pages of the most important newspapers as well as in the prime-time programming of some of the most important radio and television stations at the time. The balance of the coverage and thus the perception of order emerging was abundantly clear.

The outcome of the search and destroy mission undertaken by U.S. political authorities was seemingly no less than a devastating removal of all things Communist in American life.[25] Over time, membership in the Party dwindled to a small number. This number then increased only to later decline. A similar path was followed by associated newspapers. If one was "Red" by the 1960s, then one was as good as dead – jobless, friendless, shunned, and scorned. In this context, repressive behavior appeared to work exactly as planned: upon being targeted by the American state, the challenged organizations basically ceased to exist along with the activities, individuals, and many elements of the ideology associated with them. By the end of the period, there were few if any Communists left and few contentious events or repressive acts to be reported (at least, those that responded to challenging activities). What was left was a series of repressive laws; over time, these were removed or redirected against new challengers.

From Dysfunctional to Functional Order

"Bloody Sunday" – the mass killing of civil rights activists in Derry, Northern Ireland, that occurred on January 30, 1972 – signaled a major shift in the conflict, commonly known as "the Troubles," between the British (who wished to continue to govern/influence the politics of Northern Ireland), Loyalists (who wished to stay associated with the British), and Republicans (who wished for independence). Indeed, this event is generally believed to be singly responsible for escalating the conflict from a small civil rights protest into a full-blown violent struggle led by the then much smaller Irish Republican Army.[26]

Why is this the case? The argument outlined in this chapter seems to be instructive. On Bloody Sunday there was an incident at a peaceful civil rights march that resulted in the British army killing twenty-six individuals, some activists and some innocent civilians/bystanders. An investigation immediately after the events in question (the Widgery report in

April 1972) exonerated the soldiers involved, largely placing the blame on young "hooligans." This narrative legitimated the shooting of the twenty-six, which was portrayed as broadly proportional. Here, the events started off straightforwardly enough, with protestors advancing their demands for enhanced civil liberties without much incident. After a wrong turn in the march, things went sour with ever-increasing hostility. Some violence ensued and in its wake individuals were killed.

The disagreements with this characterization of the Bloody Sunday events are now legendary, revealing divergent opinions about what had transpired in particular, as well as what this meant for the overall political struggle in general. Indeed, it is frequently maintained that support for the IRA and terrorism were the direct result of the debate about this single state–dissident interaction.[27] The legacy of this disagreement was so profound that, in January 1998, Prime Minister Tony Blair initiated the "Bloody Sunday Inquiry" (the Saville report), which took twelve years and 5,000 pages to complete, at a cost of roughly 200 million pounds. The report that emerged from this effort acknowledged that British para-troopers fired the first shot and fired at those fleeing. Here, recognizing some of the claims made by alternative narratives as legitimate, individual soldiers were blamed, but not the army as a whole. In a sense, the few were "tossed under the bus" to save the reputation of the many and the overall legitimacy of the state.

Although it has been criticized by some, others find the report highly satisfactory. Indeed, in many respects, it seems as if Bloody Sunday might finally be put to rest, and with it one of the worst human rights violations of the Troubles as well as perhaps the single most important event in establishing, and perhaps maintaining, IRA mass support.

From Functional to Dysfunctional Order and Back Again

While significant attention has been given to Rwanda in 1990–1994, there is little discussion of the pre-1990 era. The current regime aims to establish its own legitimacy as being intricately connected to the events in 1990–1994 (especially the last year). But considering the period from 1970 through the present proves to be quite informative for the current discussion of performing order.

Prior to 1990, Rwanda appeared to be a relatively well-functioning autocracy. Clearly one group (Hutus) and, more specifically, one group from one geographic region (the North), appeared to be in power for quite some time. Indeed, there did not appear to be any domestic opponents.

In many ways, the state seemed to have vanquished its internal enemies (the Tutsi population of 1994) and also its external enemies (the German and Belgian colonists). Behavioral instances of violence were relatively low but repression was fairly high as civil liberties were limited. The Tutsi were especially restricted as they were largely excluded from both the political and the economic realms they used to dominate. At this point, the state was seemingly functioning – albeit repressive.

This changed in 1990. In this year, the Rwandan Patriotic Front (RPF), principally composed of Tutsi exiled decades earlier, mounted attacks from Uganda and very quickly pushed into Rwanda itself, revealing a significant weakness of the Rwandan state. Indeed, had it not been for the French and Belgians, it is likely that the RPF would have taken the whole country. This period was one of high contestation – less behavioral than narrative, as the RPF and the Rwandan army held their positions while the Arusha Accords were being worked out. Indeed, it is during this time that extremist Hutus began to discuss how tenuous the situation was for the Hutu population, claiming that their community was existentially threatened. This resulted in not only discussion but also military preparation, as militias filled with hate began to be trained and armed throughout Rwanda. Interestingly, it turns out that while this was taking place, the RPF was setting up weapons caches throughout parts of Rwanda as well.

After the downing of the Rwandan president's plane in April of 1994, the behavior and narratives of the extremist Hutu were unleashed. Here, as violence was enacted it was maintained that the Hutu community was threatened by the Tutsi from *without* (as the RPF came from Uganda) as well as *within* (as Tutsi neighbors and sympathizers lived right next door). At the same time, the RPF unleashed their version of events in the form of accusations of genocide accompanying their rapid acquisition of territory. Some events were more reported than others – in part mirroring the magnitude of deaths. By the end of the conflict (three months by most estimations), the RPF had been victorious behaviorally, having easily defeated the Rwandan (Hutu extremist) military. Additionally, the RPF had been victorious narratively as people (around the world) began to accept their characterization of the violence as being exclusively genocidal. Initial discussions identified an ethnic cleansing/genocide as well as mass killing of those who opposed the extremists. Over time, however, the former was the only form of violence discussed.

This characterization of events helped the RPF. It allowed them to distance themselves from the prior Rwandan state. It allowed them to resubjugate the majority Hutu population, which now had even fewer claims on the current government since the story of their victimization during the 1990–1994 period had been removed from public discussions. It also allowed the RPF to portray themselves in a sympathetic way to the international community, facilitating their receipt of extensive economic assistance and fueling the so-called Rwandan economic miracle. Indeed, given the subsequent pacification of all domestic challengers (i.e., all rival political parties and behavioral challenges) as well as international challengers (through repeated incursions and occupations into the Congo), Rwanda by 2010–2012 looks more functional than ever before.

That said, the state is ever guarded about trying to maintain its image as a survivor of political violence and a functional provider of political order. For example, the International Criminal Tribunal on Rwanda investigating events of 1994 was compelled by the Rwandan state to only focus on events concerning the victimization of the Tutsi. All other forms of violence were ignored and, indeed, to discuss them could result in claims of "divisionism" and "genocide denial" – both punishable under Rwandan law. Additionally, invasion and violence in the Congo has repeatedly been ignored and covered up by the Rwandans even after major disclosures by the UN were put forward. Indeed, following each disclosure, the Rwandan state has revealed itself more than capable of blocking additional discussion. At present, Rwanda seems to be one of the most functional, domestically peaceful (i.e., the only violence is covert), and prosperous countries in Africa, while simultaneously being one of the most domestically repressive (in terms of restricted civil liberties) and internationally violent. At the same time, with 85 percent of the population being forcibly restrained and intimidated, as well as the Hutu population being effectively written out of all discussions regarding the new Rwanda, it is clear that the situation on the ground might be very different from the view emerging from the international media. In fact, I doubt that many would be surprised if the three-term political autocrat Kagame were attacked and the country collapsed once again into violence.

CONCLUSION

This chapter has attempted to identify a relatively novel way for evaluating one aspect of what states do – countering behavioral challenges – as well as some of the ways in which this process develops – where states are capable, where they are largely incapable, where they shift from capable to incapable, and where they shift from incapable to capable. Although the general argument is believed to be generalizable, within this chapter,

I have focused on the United States, Northern Ireland, and Rwanda. Subsequent work will apply this argument to other cases as well as diverse aspects of the process. There are numerous implications of this work.

First, researchers need to acknowledge that there is a conflict between those attempting to bring forth change as well as those attempting to sustain the status quo that is distinct from the conflict that exists regarding what individuals know about this conflict. Sometimes the former is more important but sometimes the latter is more important. Researchers need to start figuring out which is which.

Second, scholars should reflect upon how the growth of specific forms of communication, such as social media, and the death of other forms of communication, such as newspapers, influence the awareness of political conflict. Scholars have long relied upon sources such as newspapers and integrated information about their limitations and strengths into the topics under discussion, but this is not consistently done. It is necessary to, in as rigorous a manner as possible, acknowledge that this is a limitation with prior work and prepare for an evaluation of how newer forms of communication are different from or similar to older sources.

Third, many of the claims identified here are in need of more detailed systematic analysis. This would involve a combination of source material regarding what information exists as well as who has done what to whom, when, and where. These endeavors are frequently viewed independently but this division must end. For example, with regard to the U.S. case alone, questions abound. What will finally make the U.S. state fully restore the civil liberties taken by the Patriot Act? What disclosures about repressive practices without challenges would be sufficient to provoke the U.S. population to demand changes and/or the U.S. state to reduce repressive action? Revelations from the Snowden affair have identified even more repressive behavior, but these were largely contained within the criminalization of the messenger rather than a wholesale reform of state coercive practices. Other questions exist as well. Exactly how long does it take for a challenging event to dissipate in the memory of the population, the legal as well as security apparatus put in motion to address it, and the politicians who were elected to contend with it? Additionally, exactly why do we expect states to stop this repression when their mandate to govern, their ability to control information, and their access to extensive resources are built on the fiction of behavioral challenges as well as their ability to counter them? Research needs to address these topics in the future if awareness of contentious performances and their connection with political order are to improve.

Notes

1 Of course, this fight is not a straight one. States have access to surveillance equipment to monitor individuals, places, and behavior; they have access to informants and agents provocateur to provide information about challengers as well as to prompt said challenger into the realm of illegality facilitating a legitimate coercive response; they also have access to the military, police, national guard, intelligence organizations, courts, and national legislature to enact/authorize activities they require to keep society from "getting out of hand."

2 Max Weber, "Part II: Power," in *From Max Weber: Essays in Sociology*, ed. H.H. Gerth and C. Wright Mills (New York: Oxford University Press, 1946). Note that the literature summarized in this section does not represent everything written on the topic. In particular, I have highlighted research that specifically defines and operationalizes relevant concepts as well as subjects, and compiled information through some form of rigorous examination while controlling for diverse factors and considering alternative explanations. As this involves several hundred pieces of scholarship over forty years, I invite someone to conduct a parallel examination of literature that employs more historical and ethnographic approaches.

3 Eckhart Zimmermann, *Political Violence, Crises, and Revolutions: Theories and Research* (Boston: G.K. Hall, 1983).

4 Mark Lichbach, "Deterrence or Escalation? The Puzzle of Aggregate Studies of Repression and Dissent," *Journal of Conflict Resolution* 31, no. 2 (1987): 266–97.

5 Edward Muller, "Income Inequality, Regime Repressiveness and Political Violence," *American Sociological Review* 50, no. 1 (1985): 47–61; Eduard Ziegenhagen, *The Regulation of Political Conflict* (New York: Praeger, 1986); Ron Francisco, "Coercion and Protest: An Empirical Test in Two Democratic States," *American Journal of Political Science* 40, no. 4 (1996): 1179–204; Will Moore, "Repression and Dissent: Substitution, Context and Timing," *American Journal of Political Science* 45, no. 3 (1998): 851–73; Will Moore, "The Repression of Dissent: A Substitution Model of State Coercion," *Journal of Conflict Resolution* 44, no. 1 (2000): 107–27.

6 Christian Davenport, "Multi-Dimensional Threat Perception and State Repression: An Inquiry into Why States Apply Negative Sanctions," *American Journal of Political Science* 39, no. 3 (1995): 683–713; Christian Davenport, Sarah Soule, and David Armstrong, "Protesting While Black? The Differential Policing of American Activism, 1960 to 1990," *American Sociological Review* 76, no. 1 (2011): 152–78; Will Moore, "The Repression of Dissent: A Substitution Model of State Coercion," *Journal of Conflict Resolution* 44, no. 1 (2000): 107–27.

7 Douglas Hibbs, *Mass Political Violence: A Cross-National Causal Analysis* (New York: Wiley, 1973); Stephen Shellman, "Process Matters: Conflict and Cooperation in Sequential State-Dissident Interactions," *Security Studies* 15, no. 4 (2006): 563–99.

8 James Fearon and David Laitin, "Ethnicity, Insurgency and Civil War," *American Political Science Review* 97, no. 1 (2003): 75–90; Quan Li, "Does Democracy Promote or Reduce Transnational Terrorist Incidents?," *Journal of Conflict Resolution* 49, no. 2 (2005): 278–97; Benjamin Valentino, Paul Huth, and Dylan Balch-Lindsay, "Draining the Sea": Mass Killing and Guerrilla Warfare," *International Organization* 58, no. 2 (2004): 375–407.

9 James Fearon and David Laitin, "Ethnicity, Insurgency and Civil War," *American Political Science Review* 97, no. 1 (2003): 75–90.

10 See, for example, Hibbs, *Mass Political Violence*; Steve Poe and C. Neal Tate, "Repression of Human-Rights to Personal Integrity in the 1980s – a Global Analysis," *American Political Science Review* 88, no. 4 (1994): 853–72; Christian Davenport, "Multi-Dimensional Threat"; *Christian Davenport, State Repression and the Domestic Democratic Peace* (New York: Cambridge University Press, 2007); Linda Keith Camp, "The United Nations International Covenant on Civil and Political Rights: Does It Make a Difference in Human Rights Behavior?" *Journal of Peace Research* 36, no. 1 (1999): 95–118; Emilie Hafner-Burton, "Right or Robust? The Sensitive Nature of Repression to Globalization," *Journal of Peace Research* 42, no. 6 (2005): 679–98.

11 Stathis Kalyvas, *The Logic of Violence in Civil Wars* (Cambridge: Cambridge University Press, 2006).

12 Kalyvas, *Logic of Violence*, 51.

13 Karl-Dieter Opp and Wolfgang Roehl, "Repression, Micromobilization, and Political Protest," *Social Forces* 69, no. 2 (1990): 521–47.

14 Lotta Harbom, Erik Melander, and Peter Wallensteen, "Dyadic Dimensions of Armed Conflict, 1946–2007," *Journal of Peace Research* 45, no. 5 (2008): 697–710; Halvard Buhaug, Scott Gates, and Paivi Lujala, "Geography, Rebel Capability and the Duration of Civil Conflict," *Journal of Conflict Resolution* 53, no. 4 (2009): 544–69; David Cunningham, Kristian Skrede Gleditsch, and Idean Salehyan, "It Takes Two: A Dyadic Analysis of Civil War Duration and Outcome," *Journal of Conflict Resolution* 53, no. 4 (2009): 570–97.

15 David Cunningham and Douglas Lemke, "Beyond Civil War: A Quantitative Analysis of Sub-State Violence," (2011) http://papers.ssrn.com/sol3/papers.cfm?abstract_id=1900695.

16 One could employ a different aspect for example frequency or scope but I maintain that lethality is the topic that most individuals are interested in across fields, places, and times. This is also the dimension that has been examined the most as well as one with the clearest operationalization.

17 Barbara Harff, "No Lessons Learned from the Holocaust: Assessing Risks of Genocide and Political Mass Murder Since 1955," *American Political Science Review* 97, no. 1 (2003): 57–73.

18 Charles Tilly, *From Mobilization to Revolution* (Reading, MA: Addison-Wesley, 1978).

19 Christian Davenport, *Media Bias, Perspective and State Repression: The Black Panther Party* (New York: Cambridge University Press, 2010).

20 Ontologically, this is different from Chapter 2. I do not presume that there is one unified reality with different actors perceiving distinct elements. Rather,

I maintain that there are different realities as reflected from the partial way that actors conceive and seek out evidence regarding the world. If the assumption of stability in Maryl and Quinn's chapter is relaxed, however, then we are generally discussing the same thing except that my focus extends beyond just the state to challengers as well.

21 Kalyvas, *Logic of Violence.*

22 Davenport, *Media Bias, Perspective and State Repression*; John McCarthy, Clark McPhail, and Jackie Smith, "Images of Protest: Dimensions of Selection Bias in Media Coverage of Washington Demonstrations, 1982 and 1991," *American Sociological Review* 61, no. 3 (1996): 468–99; Christian Davenport and Patrick Ball, "Views to a Kill: Exploring the Implications of Source Selection in the Case of Guatemalan State Terror, 1977–1996," *Journal of Conflict Resolution* 46, no. 3 (2002): 427–50.

23 Lucy Salmon, *The Newspaper and Authority* (New York: Octagon Books, 1976).

24 Robert Goldstein, *Political Repression in Modern America: From 1870 to the Present* (Cambridge: Schenkman Pub. Co., 1978).

25 Goldstein, *Political Repression in Modern America*; Ellen Schrecker, *Many Are the Crimes: McCarthyism in America* (New York: Little, Brown & Company, 1998); Elizabeth Pontikes, Giacomo Negro, and Hayagreeva Rao, "Stained Red: A Study of Stigma by Association to Blacklisted Artists during the 'Red Scare' in Hollywood, 1945 to 1960," *American Sociological Review* 75, no. 3 (2010): 456–78. William T. Walker, *McCarthyism and the Red Scare: A Reference Guide*, ABC-CLIO, 2011. Don E. Carleton, *Red Scare: Right-Wing Hysteria, Fifties Fanaticism, and Their Legacy in Texas* (Dallas: University of Texas Press, 2014); Landon Storrs, *The Second Red Scare and the Making of the New Deal Left* (Princeton: Princeton University Press, 2015).

26 Robert W. White, "On Measuring Political Violence: Northern Ireland, 1969 to 1980," *American Sociological Review* 58, no. 4 (1993): 575–85; Hrag Balian and Peter Bearman, "Pathways to Violence: Dynamics for the Continuation of Large-Scale Conflict," working paper (2011), http://faculty.chicagobooth.edu/workshops/orgs-markets/past/pdf/Balian.pdf.

27 Robert W. White, "On Measuring Political Violence: Northern Ireland, 1969 to 1980."

11

Fiscal Forearms

Taxation as the Lifeblood of the Modern Liberal State

Ajay K. Mehrotra[*]

Most scholars today would agree that the state is not a single, unified entity. Pierre Bourdieu's metaphor that helped launch this volume presumes that the modern liberal state contains mainly two parts or hands, with the left hand encompassing the fiscal ministerial cabinets and the right hand representing the spending ministries responsible for ensuring the public good.[1] Although this anthropomorphic metaphor is insightful, its bi-modal nature obscures the many facets and functions of the modern state. Perhaps a more appropriate image is a Hindu deity with multiple arms and hands. As the many chapters in this book attest, scholarly conceptions of the modern state have moved well beyond the classical characteristics regarding a monopoly over the legitimate use of physical force, or sovereignty over a well-defined geographical territory, or even administration by a hierarchical, professional bureaucracy.[2] All of these traditional, Weberian markers of the modern state have, in recent years, come under increased scholarly scrutiny.

Yet regardless of how we depict the many functions or institutional arrangements of national governments, the modern state cannot exist without an effective and permanent process of generating significant public revenue. For nearly all advanced industrialized nation-states, taxation is the one policy area without which nearly all of the other functions and aspects of the state would be impossible.[3] Conversely, most failed states can frequently trace their dysfunction to an inability to generate public revenues in a fair and effective manner – an inability, that is, to provide for a legitimate form of revenue raising.[4] Moreover, one of the defining distinctions between liberal states and their autocratic counterparts is their sources of public revenue and the manner in which it is generated. Thus, to continue the Bourdieusian metaphor, the administration of fiscal policy may represent the forearms of the body politic with taxation as the lifeblood of the modern liberal state.

But, like blood itself, taxation does much more than provide material support for the modern polity. Because taxation is one of the most widely and persistently experienced relationships that individuals have with their government, it helps define the social and cultural meaning of citizenship. The process of paying taxes helps forge civic identity; it validates the financial responsibilities of being part of a broader political and social community. This notion of fiscal citizenship institutionalizes a social contract between the state and its citizens, between the sovereign and its subjects, formalizing our obligations to each other as members of an "imagined community." It also signifies who is a member of such a community, or how wide we draw the circle of "we."[5] At times, in U.S. history, that circle has been narrowly drawn, as in the use of poll taxes or property qualifications to deny the franchise to disfavored groups. Fiscal citizenship has thus been a malleable concept. It has been used both to coerce elites into contributing their fair share to the commonwealth and to marginalize nonelites from the democratic process. Yet, as this chapter will show, U.S. progressive-era reformers deployed the idea of fiscal citizenship to promote graduated income taxes by stressing the ethical duties and social obligations of wealth.

A historical study of taxation also reminds us that the public and private realms are inextricably intertwined, rather than separate or distinct. "Private liberties have public costs," Holmes and Sunstein have written. "Individual freedom is both constituted and bolstered by collective contributions."[6] As the public sector has grown in size and importance, so too has the blurring of the line between public and private. Whether we refer to the result as a "symbiotic state," as Clemens does in Chapter 1, or call it a delegation of public authority to private parties, as Morgan and Campbell have noted elsewhere, there is no denying the increasing interpenetration of the public and private realms.[7] This is certainly evident in the ways that most modern liberal states administer their tax systems. By relying on the process of third party reporting and tax withholding, these states have harnessed the organizational power and capacity of private actors to help generate public revenue.

Because the extraction of collective contributions often entails potentially conflicting interests between the state and its citizens, debates about taxation in liberal democracies are also continually reproduced rather than resolved. Like many social contracts, taxes are regularly renegotiated. Whereas autocratic nations may demand revenues from their citizens or unilaterally sell national resources to fund their activities, liberal democracies rely on the consent of the governed to determine their tax laws and policies. The process of revenue extraction must be considered fair and legitimate by ordinary citizens in order for a liberal democratic nation-state to govern effectively. That was certainly the case at the turn of the twentieth century when the United States and other modern democracies turned to direct and progressive taxes to fund the increasing activities of their respective central states. Then and now, taxes were the linchpin in the development and maintenance of modern democratic institutions. Investigating the precise role that taxation has played in both responding to and quelling democratic pressures can help us see how modern statecraft, as Novak, Sawyer, and Sparrow (Chapter 9) have suggested, has long been embedded in a broader social context.

Given all that taxation embodies, it is a critical, yet understudied, element in comprehending the evolution of state power and democratic authority. This chapter thus explores the central role of taxation in the development of modern liberal states. It begins by briefly reviewing some of the classic scholarly literature linking taxation to war and state formation, but then turns to some recent studies that reveal these linkages to be more complex and historically contingent than previously acknowledged. The chapter then investigates how scholars have recently begun to go beyond the conventional view of taxation as simply a source of material resources to examine the historical relationship between fiscal policy and citizenship. It also explores how tax laws and policies have facilitated the rise of a hybrid public/private administrative regime.

The adoption of direct and progressive taxation in the United States during the early twentieth century offers a prime example of how taxation has shaped social and cultural conceptions of fiscal citizenship and enabled the emergence of a mixed public/private regime. The late nineteenth-century reform movement for direct and progressive taxation began with social democratic pressures from ordinary working-class citizens and their populist representatives in Congress who were protesting the inequities of the late nineteenth-century tax regime and its reliance on indirect and highly regressive taxes such as the protective tariff. When the U.S. Supreme Court stymied these protests, a group of public intellectuals, social activists, and progressive lawmakers harnessed the social demands for a more democratic fiscal order and advanced a new conception of the fiscal state. These leading historical figures stressed how changing notions of taxation could shape the common interests of society and construct new beliefs about the state. The historical U.S. case study thus shows how progressive reformers deliberately deployed a particular vision and language of taxation to help lawmakers and ordinary Americans reimagine the financial basis of government programs.[8]

The beginnings of the U.S. system of direct and progressive taxation also shed light on other significant aspects of state-building. To understand the process of institutional change that is required to instantiate a new fiscal order, one must explore the actual, concrete workings of state power. "The State," as institutional economist John Commons acutely and succinctly noted, "is what officials do."[9] In this sense, this chapter joins those state-centered studies that move beyond overly theoretical or abstract analyses of the state to explore "real-world governance practices," or what Morgan and Orloff refer to in their introductory essay as "implementing states." By investigating what state officials actually do with their power – such as how they can coerce private-sector actors to collect and remit taxes through the process of withholding – we can better understand what the modern fiscal state actually is.

WAR, TAXATION, AND STATE-BUILDING

Social theorists have long recognized the importance of taxation to modern state formation. Weber focused mainly on the coercive nature of state power over nonstate actors and how the accepted social legitimacy of such power provided the modern state with its central authority. Although the success of legitimate coercion had many causes, for modern states it was rooted in the ability of state institutions and actors to remain independent of the individuals and groups they were charged with regulating, policing, and, of course, taxing. An effective civil bureaucracy was, for Weber, a key component to the autonomy of the state. And, in turn, securing and maintaining an effective source of funding for administrative authority was equally important. "A stable system of *taxation*," he wrote, "is the precondition for the permanent existence of bureaucratic administration."[10]

If Weber was attuned to the important links between effective taxation and public administration, it was Schumpeter who recognized the more consequential aspects of what he referred to as "fiscal sociology." Building on the work of Rudolf Goldscheid, Schumpeter contended that the roots and consequences of nearly all social, political, and economic developments could be understood by a careful analysis of a state's tax and spending programs.[11] "The budget," Schumpeter maintained, "is the skeleton of the state stripped of all misleading ideologies." He was particularly aware of how the history of fiscal policies reflected the social and cultural development of a particular people. In a once-forgotten, but now somewhat clichéd, passage, Schumpeter bombastically claimed that a nation-state's fiscal history held the secrets of macro-social development itself. "The spirit of a people, its cultural level, its social structure, the deeds its policy may prepare – all this and more is written in its fiscal history, stripped of all phrases" wrote Schumpeter in 1918. "He who knows how to listen to its message here discerns the thunder of world history more clearly than anywhere else."[12]

For Schumpeter, war was a pivotal factor in understanding the fiscal sociology and history of nation states. Writing in the wake of World War I, Schumpeter was concerned mainly about the debt burdens of his native Austria, but his broader objective in studying the origins of the "tax state" was to identify the critical variables that led modern nation states to develop abundant and stable sources of funding that were autonomous from the powers of the Crown.[13] Chief among these variables was war. Unlike the princely households of premodern times, which had drawn their funds coercively from personal dues owed to the prince as individual or from the exploitation of royal lands, the modern nation-state, Schumpeter argued, rose to prominence as a result of military conflicts. The growing expenses of waging war required princes to turn to nobles and burghers – the estates – for funds. In exchange for granting princes the right to levy taxes to underwrite military conquests and defenses, the estates won the right to administer the taxes. A public bureaucracy independent of the princely household began to emerge, and when the public purse eventually became institutionally severed from the prince's private claims, Schumpeter concluded, "the tax state had arrived – its idea and its machinery." In short, war was the handmaiden of the tax state.[14]

Modern scholars also have stressed the importance of war to state formation, generalizing Schumpeter's logic across place and time to create a kind of Darwinian explanation for the rise of the "fiscal–military" state.[15] "A state that wished to survive had to increase its extractive capacity to pay for professional armies and/or navies," explained historical sociologist Michael Mann. "Those that did not would be crushed on the battlefield and absorbed into others." In the long run, surviving states converged – through the process of military competition – toward efficient and productive tax systems.[16] Working mainly in the area of Western European history, other historical social scientists have persuasively demonstrated how wars and the effective extraction of tax revenues have been instrumental to the creation of modern states; how rulers and lawmakers throughout time have sought to maximize revenue given certain rational constraints; how differing cultures, values, and political systems have determined the variation of tax regimes across place and time; and how social resistance to modern industrialization and state centralization has determined comparative differences in the origins of tax regimes. Indeed, in many of these accounts, the social and political responses to international conflicts have come to define nation-states. As Charles Tilly has succinctly put it, "war makes states."[17]

War as the primary force behind state formation has also been explored in other contexts beyond Western Europe. More recent studies of Africa, Latin America, and China have similarly stressed how the strains of conflict have shaped statecraft.[18] These broad, comparative studies have also begun to influence the interdisciplinary subfield of American Political Development (APD), which had mainly been preoccupied with the development of the U.S. welfare state and the expansion of bureaucratic authority.[19] It is only recently that scholars have begun applying the models of comparative state formation to the U.S. experience to reveal the underappreciated ways in which taxation was, and continues to be, an essential component of modern American social, political, and economic development. For instance, Pollack has stressed the importance of war to the development of a "fiscal–military" state in the United States. "State building in America was stimulated during periods of sustained warfare," he writes, "and both state building and war making required that political leaders adopt more aggressive revenue strategies to finance their expanded activities." While Pollack notes that the United States at its founding began with a decentralized system of statecraft that set it apart from its European counterparts, he contends that ultimately military demands forced the United States along a remarkably similar path.[20] Thus, even within the new APD literature, war and its demand for revenue continues to be a critical – perhaps *the* critical – variable in understanding modern state formation.

Although the work of comparative historical social scientists and the more recent APD literature have been tremendously instructive, these accounts frequently elide the importance of human agency in developing the social and cultural legitimacy of public power. The rich and complex process of American state formation – or, indeed, the formation of any state – cannot be explained solely with reference to changes in broad structural forces or functional needs, such as the demands of war.

The strains of war were certainly vital to the development of the American fiscal state, but there was little that was natural, neutral, or necessary about how these forces specifically shaped the new order. Powerful social movements, political activists, public intellectuals, lawmakers, and key government administrators all engaged in highly contested, contingent, and uncertain battles over the ideas, laws, and institutions that would come to define the development of the American polity. In other words, historical actors made choices and took actions that altered the course of history. They seized the opportunities provided by the changing forces of modernity to shape the implementation of the modern American state according to their various ideals and visions.[21]

In recent years, a new historiography about the rise of the American fiscal state has emerged to complement, and in some cases challenge, the conventional accounts. From the founding era's calls for "no taxation without representation" to the Union Army's Civil War experiment with graduated income taxes to World War II's transformation of the class income tax into a mass tax, historians have once again returned their focus to the central actors and events that have shaped the development of the American fiscal state.[22] Some celebrate, for instance, the important role that Franklin D. Roosevelt played in bolstering the modern, U.S. income tax regime and its focus on progressivity.[23] Others lament the way that liberal reformers in the 1940s, including FDR, made steeply progressive taxes highly salient to Americans, while burying tax benefits as indirect and hidden subsidies to the middle class.[24] Still others have revisited the importance of war to show how the funding needs of World War II were the crucial pivot for the social and cultural legitimacy of a powerful and durable central state.[25]

While the New Deal and World War II eras were important, the story about the rise of the modern American fiscal state begins in the late nineteenth and early twentieth centuries when the intellectual, legal, and administrative foundations of this new polity first took shape. The late nineteenth-century system of indirect, hidden, partisan, and regressive national taxes – associated mainly with the highly partisan tariff and regressive excise taxes on alcohol and tobacco – was eclipsed in the early twentieth century by a direct, transparent, professionally administered, and progressive income tax that soon accounted for more than half of all federal tax revenue. This fiscal revolution was a watershed in the development of modern American public finance. The move from taxing goods toward taxing people and processes underscored the modern and radical nature of this tectonic shift. Despite modest beginnings, the early-twentieth-century tax laws were, as Friedman has observed, "the opening wedge for a major transformation in American society."[26]

The rise of this new fiscal polity had enormous implications for modern American economic, social, and political life. First, the new fiscal regime reallocated across both income classes and national regions the economic responsibility of financing the growing needs of a modern industrialized democracy. Second, this fiscal reordering redefined the social meaning of modern citizenship. Third, it facilitated the beginnings of a fundamental change in political arrangements and institutions. And fourth, the new fiscal order helped underwrite the subsequent expansion of the American liberal state. Though some of these aims would not be fully realized until much later, it was between the end of Reconstruction and the onset of the Great Depression that the central intellectual, legal, and administrative foundations of the modern American fiscal state first took shape.[27]

THE HISTORICAL IMPORTANCE OF FISCAL CITIZENSHIP

Given the material aspects of taxation, American historians have long recognized that changing tax obligations and responsibilities invariably affected the economic distribution of fiscal burdens.[28] Less noticed is how changing the structure of taxation also influenced social and cultural conceptions of citizenship. Indeed, the turn-of-the-century transformation in American public finance was, first and foremost, an intellectual revolution – a cultural shift in thinking about how taxes shaped social relations. A group of reform-minded intellectuals, drawing on the raw social experiences of the modern industrial age and responding to social protests against the massive inequalities of the time, directed a dramatic change in the way educated Americans and policymakers imagined the financial basis of government programs.

The progressive-era theorists and activists who led this conceptual transformation were a historically unique group of social critics and reformers that included Henry Carter Adams, Richard T. Ely, and Edwin R. A. Seligman. These leading historical figures underscored the common interests that brought citizens together in a modern industrial nation-state. They advanced a fundamental change in the way that ordinary Americans and elite policymakers thought about the relations between state and society. At the heart of this consequential epistemic shift was the idea that a citizen owed a debt to society in proportion to their "ability to pay." This curt yet crucial phrase encapsulated the idea that individuals who had greater economic power also had a greater obligation to contribute to the public good – to contribute not only proportionally more, but progressively more. Influential thinkers and political leaders used the key words of "ability to pay" as a cognitive map, as a type of mental frame, to illustrate the widening circle of modern associational duties and social responsibilities.[29]

They also used "ability to pay" and similar terms as political tools to galvanize support for the progressive tax reform movement. "Each word has its practical cash value," pragmatist philosopher William James noted. We do things with words. And what these progressive political economists sought to do with their words, as well as their actions, was to convince lawmakers, government administrators, and ordinary Americans that a new fiscal system based on the notion of taxing a citizen's "ability to pay" could transform American state and society.[30] Revenue reformers understood that "fairness" and "ability to pay" were protean concepts with multiple meanings. Their goal was to use these words and ideas to energize a social and political movement that reflected the growing antipathy toward the prevailing fiscal order.

These new notions of taxation were, of course, a product of their times. The progressive political economists who led this intellectual campaign harnessed increasing social frustrations to challenge the fundamental assumptions of an earlier age. Recognizing how the forces of modernity had created a more interdependent society, these thinkers stressed the need for greater cooperation and bureaucratic authority.[31] In doing so, reformers were reflecting how the U.S. central state by the turn of the twentieth century was already exercising its power in a variety of new areas. The Interstate Commerce Commission and the Federal Trade Commission presaged the rise of the regulatory state.[32] The earlier emergence of Civil War veterans' pensions, likewise, denoted the public sector's increasing commitment to social welfare spending.[33] And the efforts to build an American civil service consisting of professional bureaucrats dedicated to public service, rather than private profit, signaled the early stages of a modern administrative state.[34] Although the federal government in the early years of the twentieth century was still spending most of its revenue on military expenditures and national defense, other areas of government spending would soon become increasingly prominent. To fund the rise of the modern regulatory, administrative, social welfare state, economic experts understood that the prevailing national system of regressive excise taxes and the tariff were woefully insufficient.

The progressive political economists leading the charge for direct and graduated income taxes understood that they needed to challenge the ideas and beliefs that supported the existing fiscal order. They thus sought to discredit the Victorian theories of atomistic individualism and laissez-faire political economy that underpinned the late nineteenth-century tax system. Chief among these outdated theories was the so-called "benefits theory," the principle that an individual's economic obligations to the state were limited to the benefits that such individual received from the polity. Reform-minded social scientists worked to supplant this principle, and its attendant vision of the state as a protector of private property, with a more equitable principle of taxation based on one's "faculty" or "ability to pay" — a principle that promoted an active role for the positive state in the reallocation of fiscal burdens, the reconfiguration of civic identity, and the rise of administrative authority. For these reformers, the state was, as Ely once noted, "an ethical agency whose positive aid is an indispensable condition of human progress."[35]

Proponents of the progressive tax movement also believed that with a fundamental restructuring of American public finance, citizens would begin to reimagine their civic duties and democratic obligations. In an age when the social dimensions of American democracy became paramount – when "the identification with the common lot," as the social reformer Jane Addams explained, was "the essential idea of democracy" – new forms of taxation based on rejuvenated egalitarian principles provided a new way of thinking about fiscal citizenship.[36] Belonging to a broader political and social community meant that taxes were no longer simply the price paid for government services and benefits. Instead, the new democratic meaning of civic identity was based on the idea that each citizen owed a debt to society in proportion to his or her "ability to pay."[37]

There was perhaps no greater evidence of how the progressive political economists attempted to shift the conceptual basis of taxation than the way they attacked the benefits principle. Columbia University political economist Edwin R. A. Seligman, the leading authority on progressive taxation, maintained that the benefits doctrine was based, at its core, on an outdated and obsolete conception of citizenship. In a now-famous passage, Seligman summarized the progressives' view of taxation:

It is now generally agreed that we pay taxes not because the state protects us, or because we get any benefits from the state, but simply because the state is a part of us ... In a civilized society the state is as necessary to the individual as the air he breathes; unless he reverts to stateless savagery and anarchy he cannot live beyond its confines ... To say that he supports the state only because it benefits him is a narrow and selfish doctrine. We pay taxes not because we get benefits from the state, but because it is as much our duty to support the state as to support ourselves or our family; because, in short, the state is an integral part of us.[38]

Tax reform, simply put, was used to reconfigure the relationship between citizens and the state, to reinvigorate the "imagined community" of the modern American polity.

As a result of these reform efforts, the 1913 peacetime income tax was targeted at the country's wealthiest citizens. The law set a "normal" tax rate of 1 percent on all incomes above $3,000 ($4,000 for married couples) and a graduated set of "surtax" rates ranging from 1 to 6 percent on incomes above $20,000. Consequently, only about 2 percent of U.S. households were affected by the first, peacetime income tax, and they faced top marginal tax rates that varied from 1 to 7 percent.[39] Thus, at least initially, the income tax was essentially a "class tax" aimed at the nation's richest citizens.[40] The 1913 law's narrow base of taxing elite citizens was precisely what reformers had in mind: to use a moderately progressive income tax to counterbalance the regressive incidence of the prevailing regime's consumption taxes, namely alcohol and tobacco excise taxes and the tariff, which affected nearly all of the "necessities of life."[41] As Tennessee Congressman Cordell Hull, one of the chief architects of the 1913 income tax, explained, "I have no disposition to tax wealth unnecessarily or unjustly, but I do believe the wealth of the country should bear its just share of the burden of taxation and that it should not be permitted to shirk that duty."[42]

If the 1913 income tax began the process of spreading the tax burden, the World War I experience heightened the obligations of fiscal citizenship. The ethical duty placed on America's wealthy elite by the 1913 income tax became more urgent and pronounced during the war emergency, especially when the federal government began conscripting young men to participate in the war effort. Paying taxes had always been seen as a form of shared sacrifice, but that sacrifice took on new meaning when ordinary Americans were risking life and limb. Indeed, the "conscription of men" led to greater social demands for "the conscription of wealth," particularly when the wartime economy was generating tremendous, though uneven, economic prosperity among the country's leading business corporations and their owners and managers.[43] Lawmakers responded directly to these social demands. In a series of wartime revenue acts, Congress lowered income tax exemption levels, dramatically increased marginal rates, and adopted novel and controversial business levies such as the excess-profits tax – all in an effort to demonstrate that the fiscal sacrifices of war would be shared by all Americans. As a result, nearly 20 percent of American households paid income taxes, and the robust wartime tax regime underwrote roughly 30 percent of the total costs of World War I.[44]

Yet, while direct and progressive taxes could be used to stress the social obligations of affluent citizens to give back to the community, taxation at this time was also used for more illiberal aims. In the American South, the rampant use of poll taxes and other voting requirements disfranchised poor and illiterate African-Americans and set in motion voting patterns that have had long-lasting implications.[45] Similarly, many states and localities at the turn of the century required citizens to hold property and pay property taxes in order to vote. Though property tax requirements, like the poll tax, were meant to exclude citizens from voting, the lawful payment of taxes was also used strategically by early feminists and suffragettes to fight for the right to vote. The relationship between taxation and voting thus cut two ways. Like many other laws, taxation could be used both as a sword to advance and maintain illiberal objectives and as a shield to defend individual rights and civic ideals.[46]

Because of the malleable use of tax laws, early-twentieth-century fiscal statebuilders understood that the state could be a cultural force in reconfiguring civic identity and beliefs about public power. Yet at the same time, many progressive-era tax reformers did not lose sight of how the tax collection process went well beyond ideational or cultural constructs. Implementing the ideas and visions of elite economic and political thinkers meant embedding the new fiscal order in law, one of the central vehicles of articulated and coercive state power.[47] Although in its more formal articulations law may appear to be an exclusive exercise of public power, in reality law frequently requires the melding of public and private authority. The use of tax laws to extract public revenue is no exception.

COERCION, TAXATION, AND BLURRING THE PUBLIC/ PRIVATE DISTINCTION

There were many ways that the modern American fiscal state deployed its coercive legal powers. One of the most significant was the way it delegated duties to the private sector through the early use of withholding to collect and remit income taxes. From the beginning, the U.S. income tax used a crude form of information reporting and withholding that was referred to at the time as "stoppage at the source." The Civil War income tax, for example, required corporations to remit portions of interest and dividend payments to the federal government before transferring the after-tax returns to certain bond and stock holders.[48] This system of public/private tax collection was used again when the first permanent, peacetime income tax was adopted in 1913. Building on the Civil War system and borrowing from the British experience, the new collection method required institutions that were making disbursements to individuals to withhold and remit a portion of high salaries, dividends, interest, and rents as partial tax payments.[49]

In the congressional debates surrounding the adoption of the 1913 income tax, progressive lawmakers drew upon Edwin Seligman's income tax treatise to argue that the United States was particularly well-suited to adopting a "stoppage at the source" system of tax collection. Reading directly from Seligman's income tax treatise, Alabama Congressman Oscar Underwood, the primary sponsor of the 1913 law and an early advocate of withholding, explained that the accelerating rise of American corporate capitalism had made information reporting or "stoppage at the source" particularly appealing in the United States:

> In the United States the arguments in favor of this method are far stronger than in Europe, because of the peculiar conditions of American life. In the first place, nowhere is corporate activity so developed and in no country of the world does the ordinary business of the community assume to so overwhelming an extent the corporate form. Not only is a large part of the intangible wealth of individuals composed of corporate securities, but a very appreciable part of business profits consists of corporate profits.[50]

Quoting Seligman again, Underwood concluded that withholding could be particularly effective in the United States. "The arguments that speak in favor of a stoppage-at-source income tax abroad hence apply with redoubled force here," Underwood declared. "The stoppage-at-source scheme lessens to an enormous extent the strain on the administration; it works, so far as it is applicable, almost automatically; and where enforced it secures to the last penny the income that is rightfully due."[51]

Underwood's invocation of Seligman's research proved effective. As part of the 1913 tax law, Congress enacted a "stoppage at the source" system of withholding that required any person or organization making payments of more than $3,000 in salary, interest, or other fixed income to withhold and remit tax payments on behalf of the individual taxpayer. Yet, because the 1913 statute itself was ambiguous about how this early form of withholding would be implemented, Congress granted the U.S. Treasury Department tremendous latitude in developing the necessary bureaucratic details and machinery. Treasury officials did not hesitate in using their newfound powers, and soon the 1913 income tax law became the vanguard for the growth of the proto-administrative state.[52] During World War I, this legally delegated authority to the executive branch would be critical in consolidating the growing powers of the wartime fiscal state.

Well before the war began, however, the U.S. Treasury Department was attempting to establish the legal and regulatory foundations of the new tax regime by ensuring that the income tax would be an effective tool for raising revenue, strengthening trust between citizens and the state, and bolstering the legitimacy of expanded public power and authority. Less than a month after the enactment of the 1913 income tax law, the Treasury Department issued two detailed regulations outlining the specific requirements of the new withholding system. These regulations provided precise guidance on which financial institutions in the chain of fiduciary agents had the legal duty to collect and remit taxes. They also stressed the significance of ascertaining accurate tax information and using institutions such as large-scale, industrial corporations as deputized tax-collecting agents.[53]

The importance of these administrative developments did not escape the notice of legal experts. Garrard Glenn, a New York commercial lawyer and Columbia Law School Lecturer, saw "collection at the source" as "the new law's most salient, if not its most popular feature."[54] What caught Glenn's attention was how the regulations empowered a form of private, third-party reporting and remittance by which "the Government ends by not only getting the tax, but by knowing whom it is taxing."[55] In the case of interest payments, for example, the regulations required debtor corporations and financial institutions to remit withheld taxes along with certificates of ownership identifying the taxpayer/creditor. Similar rules were established for dividends, rents, and other annual fixed charges. The process of collecting taxpayer information thus facilitated greater social control and surveillance by state actors. Just as the poll tax was used in the post-Reconstruction South as a pernicious tool to reestablish racial domination and subordination, the greater "legibility" of national taxpayers through withholding and information reporting gave federal officials unprecedented social knowledge and power.[56] Conservative critics, after all, had long opposed the income tax on similar grounds as an "inquisitorial" levy.[57]

Greater tax information gathering and knowledge production were essential to fulfill the conceptual aspirations of the new fiscal polity. A progressive income tax based on an individual's "ability to pay" could not exist without some method of accurately measuring an individual's income or taxpaying faculty. "We might as well face the fact," Glenn conceded, "that the Government cannot go very far with taxation of incomes without being forced to adopt an inquisitorial system for discovering objects of taxation."[58] For many ordinary Americans, who were expressly exempt from the income tax and who supported it as a means toward recalibrating the fiscal equilibrium, a robust system of third-party remittance and information reporting could also give the new fiscal state greater social, cultural, and political legitimacy. If quotidian workers and farmers, who paid their share of national taxes through excise taxes and other regressive consumption taxes, could be assured that federal tax authorities were monitoring and collecting income taxes from the wealthier classes, these ordinary working-class Americans were more likely to support the new fiscal regime.[59]

The process of collecting income taxes at the source also blurred the line between public power and private rights. Because large-scale corporations were frequently the source of annual payments subject to withholding – namely managerial salaries and interest and dividend payments to individual bond and stockholders, respectively – these private corporate entities, in effect, became quasi-public tax collectors. As Glenn explained, the Supreme Court had long upheld the use of a business corporation as "an agent of the Government for the collection of the tax."[60] But the new regulations went a step further. They "laid upon this citizen turned tax gatherer the additional duty of collecting from the creditor a statement identifying himself as such."[61] The new industrial corporations were certainly up to this important information-gathering task. With their rational and routinized systems of accounting, business corporations contained a surfeit of financial information.

In many ways, the rise of managerial capitalism facilitated the development of the fiscal state. By becoming deputized tax collectors and third-party reporters, private businesses thus became central arenas for the mutual and reciprocal constitution of state and society.[62] Present-day tax experts have continued to recognize the importance of the modern corporation to tax collection. "The key to effective taxation is information, and the key to information in the modern economy is the corporation," the public finance economist Richard M. Bird has written. "The corporation is thus the modern fiscal state's equivalent of the customs barrier at the border."[63]

The harnessing of private authority for the purposes of public tax collection proved relatively effective. Although the individual income tax by itself only generated roughly $40 million, or less than 6 percent of total revenue, in fiscal year 1915, Treasury officials and lawmakers remained optimistic about the subsequent development of the levy. Indeed, over time, salaries and dividends withheld by business corporations became leading sources of personal income tax revenue. Historians have estimated that during the early years of the tax, "businessmen ... accounted for about eighty-five percent of the income reported, and almost ninety percent of the tax paid." Contemporary estimates corroborate that salaries and dividends accounted for 44 percent of personal income tax revenue in 1916, with those figures jumping to nearly 80 percent by 1920.[64]

All businesses did not readily acquiesce to the blurring of public power and private rights, to be sure. While the income tax in its infancy remained relatively modest in scale and scope, most business corporations and elite individual taxpayers resigned themselves to complying with the new tax system, though not without some legal protests.[65] Yet when the WWI tax regime significantly altered the reach of the federal government's tax powers, businesses successfully lobbied to limit the use of tax withholding but not third-party information reporting. Because the wartime tax laws, with their highly progressive rates and novel levies, had substantially complicated the calculation of tax liabilities, business leaders were able to convince the Treasury Department that they could not comply with the administrative burdens of tax withholding. Although many tax advocates were skeptical of these business claims, the use of "stoppage at the source" was temporarily suspended during World War I, and it did not make a full-fledged return until decades later when World War II radically transformed the American fiscal order from a "class tax" to a "mass tax."[66]

CONCLUSION

The "fiscal–military" state has long been the historical paradigm of effective public power – and for good reason. The exigencies of waging war, as Weber, Schumpeter, and Tilly have explained, required central governments to procure private resources quickly and efficiently in the name of self-preservation and the public good. Yet, while the quantifiable benefits of taxation are critical to the origins and maintenance of state power, taxation does much more than merely provide sustenance for the body politic. It also structures the polity. An effective system of revenue extraction lends greater social and cultural legitimacy to state authority. It helps define who is included in the political and social community and who can be excluded. Taxation is, in short, an instantiation of the social contract.

At the turn of the twentieth century, as scholarly and popular understandings of modern society began to change in the United States, so too did the rationales for taxation as a social pact. In the late nineteenth century, the prevailing "benefits" theory of taxation commoditized the fiscal relationship between individuals and the state, limiting state power to the quid pro quo of protecting private property and individual security in exchange for tax payments. By contrast, the new notion of taxation based on "ability to pay" stressed the importance of ethical duties and social solidarity. Creating progressive income and wealth-transfer taxes based on an individual's taxpaying abilities became one way for progressive reformers and policymakers to use new tax laws to change the conceptual basis of public financing. These new laws provided opportunities to forge a new sense of civic identity and fiscal citizenship.

Implementing these new tax laws and forging this new sense of identity required expanded administrative capacity. For a nation-state with limited bureaucratic autonomy, at least relative to other advanced industrial nation-states, this meant turning to private entities to help with the process of collecting and remitting tax revenues. Through the process of income tax withholding and third-party reporting, the U.S. Treasury Department came to rely on private businesses, mainly large-scale corporations, to provide the information and organizational knowledge to help implement the new "inquisitorial" tax laws. In the process, the new fiscal state further blurred the already indistinct line between public power and private rights.

Studying the rise of progressive taxation in the United States is only one way to learn more about the broad and multiple implications of taxation. As scholars continue to grapple with the many hands, fingers, and fiscal forearms of the state, more research needs to be done, particularly on the relationship between ineffective systems of revenue extraction and failed states. New studies on the converse of statebuilding, for instance, can shed further light on important questions about what states are and what they do or do not do effectively. Such investigations could help us better understand not only how and why taxation is the lifeblood of modern statecraft, but also how taxation helps us refine our conceptual understanding of what the modern liberal state actually is.

Notes

* Earlier versions of this chapter were presented at the annual meetings of the Social Science History Association and the University of Chicago's Neubauer Collegium. Thanks to the participants of those meetings for their useful feedback and to Kimberly Morgan and Ann Orloff for their leadership and editorial guidance. Thanks also to Rian Dawson, Jayce Born, and Jessica Laurin for their outstanding research assistance.

1 "Un entretien avec Pierre Bourdieu: 'Il n'y a pas de démocratie effective sans vrai contre-pouvoir critique,'" *Le Monde*, January 14, 1992.

2 Max Weber, "Politics as a Vocation" in *From Max Weber: Essays in Sociology*, ed. H.H. Gerth and C. Wright Mills (New York: Oxford University Press, 1958); *Economy & Society*, vol. 1, eds. Guenther Roth and Claus Wittich (Berkeley: University of California Press, 2013).

3 Philip T. Hoffman, "What Do States Do? Politics and Economic History," *Journal of Economic History* 75, no. 2 (2015): 303–32.

4 Ashraf Ghani and Clare Lockhart, *Fixing Failed States: A Framework for Rebuilding a Fractured World* (New York: Oxford University Press, 2009); Jeffrey I. Herbst, *States and Power in Africa: Comparative Lessons in Authority and Control* (Princeton: Princeton University Press, 2000).

5 Benedict Anderson, *Imagined Communities: Reflections on the Origins and Spread of Nationalism* (London: Verso Books, 1983). For more on "fiscal citizenship," see generally Richard A. Musgrave, "Clarifying Tax Reform," *Tax Notes*, 70 (1996): 731, 732.

6 Stephen Holmes and Cass R. Sunstein, *The Cost of Rights: Why Liberty Depends on Taxes* (New York: W.W. Norton, 1999); Charles Tilly, *Democracy* (New York: Cambridge University Press, 2007), 143–45; Charles Tilly, "Extraction and Democracy," in *The New Fiscal Sociology: Taxation in Comparative and Historical Perspective*, eds. Isaac William Martin, Ajay K. Mehrotra, and Monica Prasad (New York: Cambridge University Press, 2009), 173–82.

7 Clemens, Chapter 1; Kimberly J. Morgan and Andrea Louise Campbell, *The Delegated Welfare State: Medicare, Markets, and the Governance of Social Policy* (New York: Oxford University Press, 2011).

8 This case study is drawn mainly from Ajay K. Mehrotra, *Making the Modern American Fiscal State: Law, Politics, and the Rise of Progressive Taxation, 1877-1929* (New York: Cambridge University Press, 2013).

9 John R. Commons, *The Legal Foundations of Capitalism* (New York: Macmillan, 1924), 122.

10 Max Weber, "Bureaucracy," in *From Max Weber*, eds. Gerth and Mills, 208 (emphasis in the original).

11 Rudolf Goldscheid, "A Sociological Approach to the Problems of Public Finance," in *Classics in the Theory of Public Finance*, eds. Richard Musgrave and Alan T. Peacock (New York: Macmillian, 1967), 205–10.

12 Joseph A. Schumpeter, "The Crisis of the Tax State," in *Joseph A. Schumpeter: The Economics and Sociology of Capitalism*, ed. Richard A. Swedberg (Princeton: Princeton University Press, 1991).

13 Thomas K. McCraw, *Prophet of Innovation: Joseph Schumpeter and Creative Destruction* (Cambridge, MA: Harvard University Press, 2007), 94–97.

14 Schumpeter, "Crisis of the Tax State," 105.

15 Colleagues and I have elsewhere referred to this modern strand of Schumpeterian fiscal sociology as "military theory." See Isaac William Martin, Ajay K. Mehrotra, and Monica Prasad, "The Thunder of History: The Origins and Development of the New Fiscal Sociology," in *The New Fiscal Sociology*, 1–28.

16 Michael Mann, "State and Society: 1130–1815: An Analysis of English State Finances," *Political Power and Social Theory* 1 (1980): 165–208.

17 Charles Tilly, ed., *The Formation of National States in Western Europe* (Princeton: Princeton University Press, 1975); Charles Tilly, *Coercion, Capital, and European States, AD 990–1990* (New York: Basil Blackwell, 1990); Margaret Levi, *Of Rule and Revenue* (Berkeley: University of California Press, 1988); Carolyn Webber and Aaron Wildavsky, *A History of Taxation and Expenditure in the Western World* (New York: Simon and Schuster, 1986); Sven Steinmo, *Taxation and Democracy: Swedish, British and American Approaches to Financing the Modern State* (New Haven: Yale University Press 1996); Kimberly J. Morgan and Monica Prasad, "The Origins of Tax Systems: A French-American Comparison," *American Journal of Sociology* 114, no. 5 (2009): 1350–94. See also Richard Bonney, ed., *The Rise of the Fiscal State in Europe, c. 1200–1815* (New York: Oxford University Press, 1999); John Brewer, *The Sinews of Power: War, Money, and the English State, 1688–1783* (London: Century Hutchinson, 1988). For a recent reappraisal of the importance of war to the global development of progressive taxation, see Kenneth Scheve and David Stasavage, "The Conscription of Wealth: Mass Warfare and the Demand for Progressive Taxation," *International Organization*, 64 (Fall 2012): 529–61.

18 See, e.g., Herbst, *States and Power in Africa*; Miguel Centeno, *Blood and Debt: War and the Nation-State in Latin America* (Philadelphia: Pennsylvania State University Press, 2002); Cameron Thies, "War, Rivalry, and State Building in Latin America," *American Journal of Political Science*, 49, no. 3 (2005): 451–65; Victoria Tin-bor Hui, *War and State Formation in Ancient China and Early Modern Europe* (Cambridge: Cambridge University Press 2005); Wenkai He, *Paths Toward the Modern Fiscal State: England, Japan and China* (Cambridge: Harvard University Press, 2013).

19 Theda Skocpol, *Protecting Soldiers and Mothers* (Cambridge: Harvard University Press, 1995); Stephen Skowronek, *Building a New American State: The Expansion of National Administrative Capacities, 1877–1920* (New York: Cambridge University Press, 1982); Daniel P. Carpenter, *The Forging of Bureaucratic Autonomy: Reputations, Networks, and Policy Innovation in Executive Agencies, 1862–1928* (Princeton: Princeton University Press, 2001). For a general overview of the APD literature, see Karen Orren and Stephen Skowronek, *The Search for American Political Development* (New York: Cambridge University Press, 2004).

20 Sheldon D. Pollack, *War, Revenue, and State Building: Financing the Development of the American State* (Ithaca: Cornell University Press, 2009), 293. See also, Bartholomew H. Sparrow, *From the Outside In*; Bensel, *Yankee Leviathan*.

21 For a recent critique of the standard accounts and their obsession with war, see generally Steve Pincus and James Robinson, "Wars and State-Making Reconsidered: The Rise of the Interventionist State" *Annales. Histoire, Sciences Sociales* 1:2016, 5-36; Hoffman, "What Do States Do?" Notable exceptions that attend to the importance of human agency and historical contingency include Brewer, *The Sinews of Power*; W. Elliot Brownlee,

Federal Taxation in America: A Short History (New York: Cambridge University Press, 2004).

22 Max Edling, *A Revolution in Favor of Government: Origins of the U.S. Constitution and the Making of the American State* (New York: Oxford University Press, 2003); Calvin Johnson, *Righteous Anger at the Wicket States: The Meaning of the Founders' Constitution* (New York: Cambridge University Press, 2005). On the significance of slavery to the antebellum fiscal system and American democracy, see Einhorn, *American Taxation/American Slavery*.

23 Joseph J. Thorndike, *Their Fair Share: Taxing the Rich in the Age of FDR* (Washington DC: Urban Institute Press, 2013). For a contrasting account of New Deal tax policy, see generally Mark Leff, *The Limits of Symbolic Reform: The New Deal and Taxation, 1933–1939* (New York: Cambridge University Press, 1984).

24 Molly Michelmore, *Tax and Spend: The Welfare State, Tax Politics, and the Limits of American Liberalism* (Philadelphia: University of Pennsylvania Press, 2012).

25 James T. Sparrow, *Warfare State: World War II Americans and the Age of Big Government* (New York: Oxford University Press, 2011). On the post–WWII period, see generally Julian Zelizer, *Taxing America: Wilbur D. Mills, Congress, and the State, 1945–1975* (New York: Cambridge University Press, 1998).

26 Lawrence Freidman, *History of American Law*, 3rd ed. (New York: Simon & Schuster, 2005), 430.

27 Mehrotra, *Making the Modern American Fiscal State*.

28 Brownlee, *Federal Taxation in America*; Sidney Ratner, *American Taxation: Its History as a Social Force in Democracy* (New York: W.W. Norton, 1942); Randolph E. Paul, *Taxation in the United States* (Boston: Little, Brown & Co., 1954).

29 Daniel Rodgers, *Contested Truths: Keywords in American Politics since Independence* (New York: Basic Books, 1987).

30 William James, *Pragmatism: A New Name for Some Old Ways of Thinking* (New York: Longmans, Green, and Co., 1907).

31 Thomas L. Haskell, *The Emergence of Professional Social Science: The American Social Science Association and the Nineteenth Century Crisis of Authority* (Urbana: University of Illinois Press, 1977); Robert H. Wiebe, *The Search for Order, 1877–1920* (New York: Macmillan, 1966).

32 Thomas W. Gilligan, William J. Marshall, and Barry R. Weingast, "Regulation and the Theory of Legislative Choice: The Interstate Commerce Act of 1887," *Journal of Law and Economics*, 32, no. 1 (1989): 35–36; Gerald Berk, *Louis D. Brandeis and the Making of Regulated Competition, 1900–1932* (New York: Cambridge University Press, 2009).

33 Skocpol, *Protecting Soldiers and Mothers*.

34 Skowronek, *Building a New American State*; Nicholas R. Parrillo, *Against the Profit Motive: The Salary Revolution in American Government, 1780–1940* (New Haven: Yale University Press, 2013).

35 Richard T. Ely, "Report of the Organization of the American Economic Association," *Publications of the American Economic Association* 1 (1886): 6–7.

36 Jane Addams, *Democracy and Social Ethics* (New York: Macmillan Co., 1902), 11.

37 Anderson, *Imagined Communities*. American intellectual historians have identified the significance of taxation to the general reform impulse of the time period. "The graduated income tax," James T. Kloppenburg has written, "was perhaps the quintessential progressive reform." Kloppenberg, *Uncertain Victory: Social Democracy and Progressivism in European and American Thought, 1870–1920* (New York: Oxford University Press, 1986), 355.

38 Edwin R.A. Seligman, *Essays in Taxation* (New York and London: Macmillan, 1895), 72.

39 Act of Oct. 3, 1913, ch. 16, §§ II.A, II.C, 38 Stat. 114, 166, 168

40 Brownlee, *Federal Taxation in America*, 52–57.

41 Mehrotra, *Making the Modern American Fiscal State*.

42 Congressional Record, 61st Cong., 1st Sess. (1909), 44:536, 533.

43 Mehrotra, *Making the Modern American Fiscal State*, ch. 6; Scheve and Stasavage, "Conscription of Wealth."

44 Hugh Rockoff, *America's Economic Way of War: War and the US Economy from the Spanish-American War to the Persian Gulf War* (New York: Cambridge University Press, 2012), 125; Brownlee, *Short History of Taxation*; Steven A. Bank, Kirk J. Stark, and Joseph J. Thorndike, *War and Taxes* (Washington DC: Urban Institute, 2008).

45 Alexander Keyssar, *The Right to Vote: The Contested History of Democracy in the United States* (Philadelphia: Basic Books, 2000), 89–90.

46 Linda Kerber, *No Constitutional Right to be Ladies: Women and the Obligations of Citizenship* (New York: Hill & Wang, 1999).

47 As socio-legal scholars Bryant Garth and Joyce Sterling have put it, law is the "traditional language of the state." Bryant Garth and Joyce Sterling, "From Legal Realism to Law & Society: Reshaping Law for the Last Stages of the Social Activist State," *Law & Society Review* 32 (1998): 409–71.

48 Revenue Act of 1862, Act of July 1, 1862, ch. 119, 12 Stat. 432, § 81, 12 Stat. at 469.

49 Act of Oct. 3, 1913, ch. 16, §§ II.A, II.C, 38 Stat. 114, 166, 168.

50 *Congressional Record*, 62nd Cong., 2nd sess. (1912), 48:3587 (Underwood quoting Seligman, *The Income Tax*, 661–62).

51 Ibid.

52 Section II, subsection D, Underwood Tariff Act, 38 Stat. 114 (1913).

53 U.S. Treasury Department, "Regulations of the United States Treasury Department Regarding the Deduction of the Income Tax at the Source..." (1913).

54 Garrard Glenn, "The Income Tax Law and Deduction at the Source," *Columbia Law Review* 13 (1913): 714–26.

55 Ibid., 721.

56 James C. Scott, *Seeing Like a State: How Certain Schemes to Improve the Human Condition Have Failed* (New Haven: Yale University Press, 1998).

In this sense, tax compliance was a means of creating model taxpaying citizens. Assaf Likhovski, "'Training in Citizenship': Tax Compliance and Modernity," *Law & Social Inquiry* 32, no. 3 (2007): 665–700.

57 Stanley, *Dimensions of Law in the Service of Order*, 283.

58 Glenn, "Income Tax Law," 723.

59 Braithwaite and Levi, *Trust and Governance*.

60 Glenn, "Income Tax Law," 725. Although he mistakenly attributed this language to Justice Field, Glenn correctly cited to the Civil War income tax case that upheld the B&O Railroad's withholding of interest and dividends. *United States v. B. & O.R.R.* 84 U.S. 322(17 Wall. 322) (1872).

61 Ibid.

62 Ajay K. Mehrotra, "American Economic Development, Managerial Capitalism, and the Institutional Foundations of the Modern Income Tax," *Law & Contemporary Problems* 73, no. 1 (2010): 25–62.

63 Richard M. Bird, "Why Tax Corporations?" *Bulletin for International Fiscal Documentation* 56 (2002): 199.

64 U.S. Treasury Department, *Annual Report of the Secretary of the Treasury on the State of the Finances for the Fiscal Year Ended June 30 1915* (Washington DC: Government Printing Office, 1916), 53; Buenker, *Income Tax and Progressive Era*, 14; U.S. Treasury Department, U.S. Internal Revenue, *Statistics of Income Compiled from the Returns for 1916* (Washington DC: Government Printing Office, 1918); U.S. Treasury Department, U.S. Internal Revenue, *Statistics of Income Compiled from the Returns for 1920* (Washington DC: Government Printing Office, 1922).

65 *Brushaber v. Union Pacific Railroad*, 240 U.S. 1 (1916).

66 Carolyn C. Jones, "Class Tax to Mass Tax: The Role of Propaganda in the Expansion of the Income Tax during World War II," *Buffalo Law Review* 37 (1988): 685.

The State and the Revolution in War

Meyer Kestnbaum

September 1792 – France was embroiled in revolution for almost two and a half years. Roughly five months before, France had declared war on Prussia and Austria and it had not gone well. Only the prior month, popular insurrection erupted violently in Paris and culminated in a direct attack upon the Crown, leading to insistence upon the removal of Louis XVI and setting in motion the dissolution of the Legislative Assembly and its subsequent replacement by the National Convention.

Amidst the rapid radicalization of the Revolution, as France was beset by instability, Prussia launched an invasion. Fielding the most powerful professional standing military in all of Europe, King Frederick William II directed the Duke of Brunswick to crush the armies assembled by the Revolutionary state, drive on to Paris, rescue King Louis XVI, and bring an end to the Revolution. The army traveled with a host of onlookers, enlarged by anticipation of the rapid collapse of French forces, which it was believed could stand up to neither the cannonades nor the infantry assaults of the Prussians. In this group was Johan Wolfgang von Goethe – poet, novelist, philosopher, scientist, and counselor to members of the high nobility. Ever the perspicacious observer, Goethe shared the expectations of Prussia's easy advance, fueled by the representations of French émigrés. But not long after the Prussians' opening artillery barrage proved indecisive and the dust began to settle, Goethe took stock.

Thus the day had passed away: the French stood immovable ... Our people were withdrawn out of the fire, and it was exactly as if nothing had taken place. The greatest consternation was diffused among the army. That very morning they had thought of nothing short of spitting the whole of the French and devouring them; nay, I myself had been tempted to take part in this dangerous expedition from the unbounded confidence I felt in such an army and in the Duke of Brunswick. But now every one went about alone; nobody looked at his neighbor; or if it did happen, it was to curse or to swear.[1]

Something wholly unexpected had taken place, shattering the army's morale as well as the prevailing understandings of the state at war. As Goethe recounts,

[N]ight was coming on ... I was called upon to say what I thought of it; for I had been in the habit of enlivening and amusing the troop with short sayings. This time I said, "From this place and from this day forth commences a new era in world history, and you can all say you were present at its birth."[2]

In the days that followed, Prussian forces crumbled and fell into disarray. The challenge to revolutionary might abandoned, Brunswick withdrew beyond his borders to recover from the stunning humiliation.

The Battle of Valmy was one critical point of inflection in a broader revolution – a revolution in war stretching across the Atlantic world that began with the new United States during its War of Independence,[3] and, within fifteen years of the epochal duel with the forces of the French Revolution, included even a reformist Prussia struggling with its own war of liberation.[4] Eclipsed were the professional armies of the old regime, replaced by widely varying popular militias and standing armies composed of citizen-soldiers. This was a revolution that transformed the state as war-maker not simply because states gained greater bureaucratic and technical capabilities, but because they became enmeshed with new forms of social power. In the memorable words of Carl von Clausewitz, thinking back upon Revolutionary France at the end of a career spanning this tumultuous period of change in war: "Suddenly war again became the business of the people – a people of thirty millions, all of whom considered themselves to be citizens."[5]

THE STATE AND REVOLUTIONS IN WARFARE

For sociologists, political scientists, and many historians, the work of Charles Tilly provides the point of departure for analyzing war and statemaking.[6] Underlying research following from Tilly is the notion that "the political" and "the military" are inextricably intertwined, if distinct, and that making sense of the development of the state involves specifying how these domains intersect.[7] For Tilly, the key lies in how the pressures of preparing for and making war drive both the subordination of rival claimants to political power under central rule and the construction of organizational structures distinct to the state. Tilly contends these are interrelated processes, characterized by the concentration of coercive might in organizations over which the state gains control, and supported by the development of civil administration and tax collection under central administrative direction. State formation, in this view, is a contested process, seen from the center as one of consolidation of authority and control over the means of coercion, and from beyond as one of pacification and subordination.[8]

Warfare drives state formation owing to a monumental shift in war-making identified by a substantial interdisciplinary academic community as "the military revolution."[9] The notion of "the military revolution" highlights a set of dramatic changes in warfare unfolding in Western, Northern, and Central Europe between roughly 1550 and 1650, but harkening back to the late fifteenth century and in some renditions continuing to the late eighteenth century. The key lies in the development of professional armies, employing drill and discipline and equipped with gunpowder weapons, maintained by the state on a standing basis year round. The military power of this set of arrangements was stark, and because of the requirements it imposed on political authorities attempting to field, maintain, and oppose such forces, it ultimately served to remake armed conflict into an enterprise of engagements among state-led standing militaries. In conjunction with the development of the Westphalian system of competing states to which this form of war helped give rise, "the military revolution" inaugurated an era of state-organized warfare.[10]

Such a view of warfare defines the broad context and underlying assumptions with which much of the Tilly-inspired line of scholarship operates. After the formation of standing military forces increasingly under central state control, warfare is understood to assume a more or less fixed form, shifting mainly in terms of the availability of human and material resources given the prevailing organization of the economy, the technology of production and weaponry, and the construction of a central administration. Analytic attention is directed away from shifts in the state as war-maker that might unfold according to alternative logics than through concentration and centralization, pacification and disarming. And what is more, in these accounts war itself remains largely a black box, leaving changes in the way warfare works and in the capacity of war to drive shifts in the state as war-maker largely unexamined.

To move beyond the productive if unintended narrowing of the study of war and the state, we must bring the social organization of warfare to the center of analysis. Only then can we begin to understand Goethe's claim to have observed a world-historical shift in war. This shift was another revolution in war-making, momentous in its own right, unfolding *within* the framework of state-organized warfare produced by the earlier "military revolution." But in fundamental ways, the transformation observed by Goethe challenged core assumptions of that earlier shift and remade the state as war-maker. Following the work of noted historian Peter Paret, I identify this dramatic break as "the revolution in war at the end of the eighteenth century."[11] It erupted suddenly in the last decades of the 1700s amidst widespread popular political uprisings and then unfolded over roughly the next one hundred years, emerging first in Europe and North America and ultimately diffusing across the globe by the first decades of the twentieth century.

Analytically, we can specify "the revolution in war at the end of the eighteenth century" most clearly if we focus on who is implicated in the state's war-making. With the creation of standing military forces in Western, Northern, and Central Europe at the end of the fifteenth century, state-building princes and monarchs began to usher ordinary people out of interstate war. Statebuilders and military commanders neither solicited the involvement of civilians or nonstate personnel in armed conflict nor made them its target. At the end of the eighteenth century, however, ordinary people were brought back to the center of war among states. The state turned to the broad expanse of those it ruled to find persons to arm, to provide the resources necessary for armed conflict, to support war efforts, and ultimately to endure dislocation and devastation. And this was the case just as the state transformed the ordinary people over whom *other* states ruled into casualties and victims of intentional attack.

The military revolution of the sixteenth century had begun a process in which warfare was brought under state control and extrastate ties and concerns were minimized, with war waged increasingly by state agents and supported by state organizations. The revolution in war at the end of the eighteenth century, instead, began a process in which the state as a distinct set of organizations surrendered its exclusivity in the domain of war. The state continued to organize war but became bound into a host of new and complex relationships with ordinary people in an enormous range of social locations, both those over whom it ruled and those of other states – relationships that broke down the clear distinctions between state and nonstate in the domain of war that had been so carefully built across the period of the military revolution and destroyed even the pretense that state organizations and agents alone prosecuted war or bore its burdens. The result was a state at war remade – refashioned by the forging of a host of administrative, authoritative, and coercive linkages across the boundary between state and nonstate and rendering such boundaries and their salience fluid in the domain of war.[12] The expansion of state power through intensified linkages with social forces would also occur in other domains, including taxation (Chapter 11), welfare (Chapter 1), and, more broadly, the production of public quiescence (Chapter 10). It would also shape the heavy imprint – both material *and* symbolic – of states upon the peoples they ruled and fought against.

THE REVOLUTION IN WAR AND REMAKING THE STATE

To understand the revolution in war at the end of the eighteenth century and begin to explain its transformative effects on the state as war-maker, it is necessary to unpack and then better situate the social organization of war-making. The first step is to distinguish analytically between state-led mobilization for war and the definition and treatment of the enemy as the two primary ways people are drawn into state-organized armed conflict. The former is an issue of how belligerents produce coercive force. It entails the formation of coercive organizations, including but not limited to standing armed forces, as well as the mobilization of human, material, and moral or political resources. It also establishes the "we" who are brought together to make war, allowing the analyst to identify the institutions and cultural idioms with which those mobilized are bound together. The latter is an issue of how belligerents direct and apply force versus a foe. It centers on the category of "the enemy," understood as those persons political and military elites deem may be legitimately subject to the intentional use of coercion,[13] and specifies the form that coercion is to take. The notion of "the enemy" performs two important pieces of work: it identifies a potentially plastic category of persons, varying over time and by belligerents; and it focuses analytic attention squarely on those whom the state deems are appropriate to attack. Who may be legitimately targeted and attacked, in turn, is closely linked to the prevailing laws of war distinguished as the *jus in bello* – the set of conventions and rules governing the actual conduct of war on the ground that sharpen or blur distinctions between combatants and noncombatants.

State-led mobilization and definition and treatment of the enemy may each influence the other for any particular belligerent over time. The key to understanding their transformation, however, is to place these interacting features of the social organization of war in relation to both the politics of war-making and what I will call the logistical uses of coercion. The politics of war-making highlight the relationship between how the state mobilizes for war and that state's organization of social stratification, distribution of political power, and logic of political inclusion. Shifts on either side alter the fit between war-making and the society making war, inducing a specific politics. The logistical use of coercion specifies how the state employs organized coercive force on the ground and highlights considerations at the level of what Hans Delbruck has called strategy – what kinds of engagements military forces enter into, with what allocation and concentration of force, in an effort to produce what kind of result by force of arms.[14] Attending to these considerations allows the analyst to capture how the manner in which force is actually employed against a foe plays a part in the transformation of state-organized coercion.

With these distinctions in place, it is possible to describe the contours of the account I offer in this essay. The revolution in war in North America and Western Europe unfolded in two waves across much of the long nineteenth century. The initial break came in the early years, during the American War of Independence (1775–1783) and the French Revolutionary and Napoleonic Wars (1792–1815), and was organized around shifts in state-led mobilization. In these conflicts, we see the development of state-directed military mass mobilization centered on mass armies of citizen-soldiers serving short periods in the ranks. We also see the cobbling together of state and nonstate organizations to raise, assemble, and direct the vast range of personnel, material resources, and political support from the general population required to wage war with such a force, as well as the initial emergence of self-armed guerrillas on the margins of war. The second wave, then, unfolded more than two generations later, during the U.S. Civil War (1861–1865) and the Franco-Prussian War (1870–1871) with an expansion of state-led mobilization and the efflorescence of guerrillas and partisans in interstate conflicts. It is at this moment that we see the beginnings of a new set of practices and understandings regarding the enemy in interstate war among Europeans or their descendants. For the first time since the mid-seventeenth century in Europe or in conflicts among those of European extraction, state-raised armed forces employed direct coercion as a matter of design against unarmed civilians in a war between states.

How can we make sense of this pattern of transformation across the long nineteenth century? It is a story of the breaking apart of a well-established set of military arrangements in the midst of armed conflict and the emergence of new ways of war-making; the consolidation of change during interludes of peace; and the eruption of further change during armed conflict, powerfully shaped by the prior consolidation, which has patterned war-making in profound ways ever since. It is a story of novel, disruptive politics of war-making spurring changes in state-led mobilization or treatment of the enemy, changes that are subsequently reinforced by new strategies guiding the use of coercive force on the ground. And it is a story of how state-led mobilization of the people as citizens into armed conflict ultimately precipitated the targeting and attacking of even unarmed civilians, but only after the passage of many years, and only because the state's mobilization of the citizenry somewhat paradoxically led others to take up arms and enter war without state authority, undermining prevailing understandings of "the enemy" in interstate conflict.

The Culmination of "the Military Revolution": War in the Old Regime

To fully appreciate this story, we must begin with the stable synthesis out of which the revolution in war emerged. By the last decades of the seventeenth century in Europe and subsequently North America, the politics, social organization, and distinctive use of coercion that typifies the military revolution had gelled to form a coherent whole. Characterized by monarchical, princely, or urban oligarchic control, dynastic or familial concerns, and popular exclusion from both politics and war-making, warfare was the province of the professional standing army equipped with gunpowder weapons. Due to the tremendous cost of forming and maintaining this force, its political significance in securing the Crown or mercantile oligarchy from challenges and threats both within and outside its borders, and limits on the raising of public funds and tax extraction, expansive war ran the risk of forcing a devolution of political power through the granting of rights of political representation in exchange for resources, or else throwing the state into fiscal crisis. If indeed the armed forces were truly put in jeopardy, war threatened collapse of the state itself. The result was a professional army under state control that waged a distinctly limited variety of war, reliant on substantial but judicious mobilization of men and resources and dominated by a concern over maintenance of forces as they stood and protection from loss.[15]

With respect to treatment of the enemy, we observe something parallel. Conventions limiting intentional coercion in interstate war only to those armed by another state became more or less firmly institutionalized in Europe after the conclusion of the Thirty Years' War, codified in theory and customarily applied in practice among warring states. The effect was profound, producing powerful constraints on the actual conduct of military operations through a twofold logic of self-restraint. Conventions protecting unarmed civilians and other noncombatants from intentional coercion were widely shared, and insofar as they were identified with religious and ethical systems considered morally binding they carried substantial weight. However, that weight would not have been enough to counterbalance the lure of potential military advantage were it not reinforced by a very real fear: any state violating conventional restraints on treatment of noncombatants embraced by their adversaries could expect brutal reprisals, shifting the calculus of what was to be gained by war. Only as states enforced adherence to the principle of noncombatant immunity in practice could war remain something they could afford to wage, politically and militarily.[16]

The relations between the politics of war-making up to the late eighteenth century and the logics of mobilization and treatment of the enemy were expressed in the dominant military strategy of the era. With great but tightly circumscribed coercive capacity in the professional army, the use of force was organized around two poles: giving battle, but only under favorable circumstances; and maneuver, in which battle was avoided so as to draw out the enemy and compel them to exhaust themselves as they moved to meet forces, or in which siege was laid in an attempt to exhaust a foe's resources, especially food. The object of battle was to defeat an opponent's forces and thus dictate strong conditions to the foe in a settlement, among them the yielding of territory. The object of maneuver, including siege, was to gain control over territory and erode the opponent's capacity to continue on, making the end of hostilities preferable to continuing and creating pressure to submit to conditions in the ensuing peace. Pursuing either pole, armies themselves were rarely if ever committed in significant portions in one location. Rather, they were routinely broken into multiple detachments in an effort to shield forces from loss in any one location and gain or maintain control of territory through the holding of strong points and the control of strategic locations. Battle promised a direct route to results, but ran the tremendous risk of loss of forces as well as enormous and unrecoverable outpouring of effort and expense with little or no lasting effect – precisely because engagements among detachments of professional forces in the field rarely if ever proved decisive. The costs of war were so great, and the risks so substantial to the state, that the *indecisiveness* of battle made it relatively unattractive. Ironically, however, just as avoidance of battle dominated what frequently became a war of position, the longing for battle sufficiently decisive that it might justify its costs grew in equal measure.[17]

In this variety of warfare, there was no appeal to increasing the size of armed forces dramatically or altering the basis of their service.[18] Their size, strictly speaking, was not the source of their military power, as understood by military commanders and theorists as well as state-builders – their training and discipline were. Untrained soldiers were useless in themselves and a military threat, spreading indiscipline and likely compromising the cohesion of military organization. Long service – ten, twenty, or thirty years or more in the ranks – and insulation from civilian society were the key to training and discipline, and they ensured political reliability of ranks that were drawn primarily from urban and rural laborers. The political fear of arming large numbers of propertyless laborers who might not be subject to the control of military life for protracted periods, especially if they might overwhelm those already in service, only compounded the militarily suspect nature of any shift in mobilization of the ranks. In the years and even months before the beginnings of the revolution in war at the end of the eighteenth century, military commanders and statesmen alike had great confidence in the stability and superiority of their way of organizing warfare – and it faced no serious challenge.[19]

THE EMERGENCE OF MILITARY MASS MOBILIZATION

The coherence of this old regime synthesis broke apart during the American War of Independence and the French Revolutionary and Napoleonic Wars, for several belligerents involved. The break was dramatic, unfolding fairly swiftly during armed conflict and in entirely unforeseen ways for those states that experienced it. The transformation involved four interconnected causal processes: the emergence of a popular politics around newly instituted national citizenship and expressed in taking up arms; the collapse and reconstitution of organized force under state control; the instituting of citizen conscription and a shift in the mobilizing frame for war; and the eclipse of maneuver in favor of battle alone. While precise sequences and forms varied across different cases, the move toward military mass mobilization was set in motion by a highly contingent shift in the politics of war-making; this in turn created new relations between these politics and state-led mobilization in terms of "the national citizen," shaping the reconstitution of standing force and leading to a transformative institutional fusion of citizenship and soldiering in the form of conscription; ultimately, this was expressed in how military commanders elaborated ways to summon and direct mass force so as to achieve decision in battle.

The point of departure lies in the emergence of a popular politics bound up with national citizenship. In contrast to the particularistic, corporative citizenship of a society of legal privilege, national citizenship is defined with respect to an individual's unmediated and political relationship to the state as sole legitimate ruler whose authority derives from the people as sovereign, a relationship that extends without distinction in principle among its members across the territory ruled by that state, and excludes those beyond.[20] Although formally egalitarian, national citizenship excluded many within the territory of the state, based, for example, on property, gender, or race. National citizenship crystallized out of a series of reforms or acts of institutional creation – extending formally egalitarian constructions of citizenship across a territorial frame and corresponding to a single political authority. These unfolded alongside and in interaction with an actual popular politics of resistance to prevailing authority, whose participants appropriated the newly emerging category "national citizen" and understood themselves in this idiom, in contradistinction to subjects of the prevailing authority they challenged. In the revolutionary instances of the newly formed United States and France, this popular politics of resistance expressed itself in the forming of citizen militias as a means to enact resistance as well as appropriate and symbolically dramatize the citizen's status. Even Prussia followed suit, although reforms were instituted from above, by the absolutist monarch and through *Standisch* bodies, and were informed by events abroad. In turn, the popular politics organized around national citizenship resulted from the Prussian Crown's call to form citizen militias as a way to throw off the yoke of imperial French rule during their own War of Liberation.

This popular politics of national citizenship intersected, in turn, with the breakdown and reconstitution of state-controlled coercion in ways that would prove critical for the revolution in war. In several respects, the eruption of a popular politics of national citizenship intertwined with and was conditioned by the collapse of state-controlled force. In the newly formed United States, repudiation of British rule amounted to the demise of the British system of waging war in the New World, based on regulars from the metropole fighting alongside mobilized colonial militia regiments maintained almost on a standing basis. In France, the revolutionary opening was created by the collapse of the old royal army, many of its elements turning to the side of revolutionaries. In Prussia, devastating defeat at the hands of the French in the Napoleonic Wars led to the formal subordination of Prussia to French Imperial rule and the partial dismantling of the Prussian army, which in conjunction with the subsequent collapse of French imperial forces after 1812 created the circumstances of the War of Liberation.

As revolutionary challengers captured the state in the United States and France, and the Prussian Crown and reformers tried to bring the state out from under French domination, internal political and external military threats drove state elites to reconstitute state-controlled coercion.[21] In the new political environment, fear of arming the people at large and concerns over indiscipline became secondary. All three states considered patterning a rebuilt state-directed force after the citizen militias that had exploded onto the scene. The militia as a military instrument remained suspect in the eyes of military men, however, and this alternative was ultimately rejected in favor of enfolding the militia within the structure of a regular, standing force clearly under state control and with unitary command. Reconstituting state-controlled coercion in this manner drew on the abundant organizational resources of the former professional standing armies, but explicitly incorporated the citizen militia in varying ways – forming the standing force from militiamen in the United States, amalgamating *gardes nationales* units beside holdover units of the old army to revolutionize it in France, or making the militia formally subordinate to and a reserve for the standing army in Prussia.[22]

These two streams of an emergent national citizenry taking up arms and the reconstitution of state coercion around newly armed citizen militias were brought together powerfully and dramatically with the conscription of national citizens in the standing army. Facing a powerful military threat from abroad, under pressure to consolidate a polity in the midst of extensive popular political mobilization, and confronted by the tenuousness of the link between political partisanship in support of the regime and military service among its newly defined citizenry, reformers in the newly formed United States, France, and Prussia instituted conscription of national citizens into the line army.[23] From the perspective of reformers, the chief virtue of conscription lay in the way it bound those armed by the state to a political community, transforming military service into a patriotic act. It promised a way to foster and channel the mobilizations of the popular classes while consolidating state control over force. From the perspective of the newly defined citizenry, conscription meant a heavy burden many resisted, especially at first, before the successive waves of its implementation dramatized the authority with which the state imbued the obligations of citizens and began to alter expectations of citizens to more closely align them with the state's demands. Beyond enthusiastic volunteers who immediately embraced service as a citizen, conscription offered the masses political recognition if not a say in political life, a way to participate in at least one of the state's chief endeavors and – perhaps only symbolically – to appropriate part of the state as their own.[24]

The effects of conscription on warfare were dramatic and far-reaching. The obligatory service of citizens formed the foundation of a new regime of war-making – state-led mass military mobilization within the national frame – extending beyond the raising of troops to the mobilization of resources and political support for war. The new way of war relied on compulsion, yes, but also appeals for voluntary assistance in the idiom of national citizens doing their duty in times of war, strengthened by the claim that the state could rightly exact such assistance if it were not willingly offered. This amounted not merely to a repudiation of the old regime's politics of popular exclusion, but the institutionalization of popular inclusion at the heart of war-making. However, inclusion was far from uniform, as conscription produced a strongly differentialist variety of mass incorporation into war. Mass mobilization rejected distinctions based on privilege and was broadly inclusive in terms of social class, but hardened categorical distinctions along gender lines, for example, just as it specified exactly how different categories of persons should contribute to the state's war effort.[25]

Mass military mobilization within the national frame was made possible, in turn, by cobbling together state administrative and extractive organizations with politically engaged, locally rooted organizations that emerged as part of the politics of popular mobilization – from citizen militias to revolutionary committees, to political clubs and popular societies, to fraternal and other voluntary associations, to town councils and political coordinating committees. This array of state offices, quasi-public bodies, parties, voluntary associations, and militias formed the organizational infrastructure of the state's mobilizing efforts, bound more or less loosely together at the center and reaching down to the locality.[26]

Even as state-led mass mobilization first emerged around the institution of conscription, it was still far from obvious how to use an army of inexperienced and ill-trained citizens. In their initial engagements, citizen armies were employed as old regime forces had been, but citizen forces were revealed to be peculiarly able to absorb the onslaught of opposing forces and remain functional. Incorporating the people in war-making augmented both human and material resources, and the resilience of the force grew as the ranks of operational units could be kept close to full and those units were formed into armies capable of recombining components as needed, offering internal support, and providing a reserve. Although raising men to serve was always difficult, this challenge was mitigated in part by conscription and a strong organizational backbone, provided at least initially by experienced commissioned and especially noncommissioned officers, as well as the development of tactics that relied less on skill than on organizational coherence.

Taking advantage of the organizational resilience of mass citizen armies and no longer plagued by concerns over force protection, commanders explored assembling larger armies in the field. Within scant months, an entirely unexpected result became apparent: properly organized, these expanded forces were able to march across substantial territory, bypass cities and towns as well as strong points, resupply as they went, and avoid leaving behind strong detachments as a way to control territory, instead relying on their own force to protect their rear. When they arrived at the end of their march, furthermore, they were ready to give battle – and not just any battle. For these resilient, enlarged forces, drawing on an expanded pool of resources and able to replenish themselves, acquired the capacity yearned for but elusive under the old regime: the capacity to engage an opposing army directly and subject it to such sustained and intense destructive power that it could disrupt and disorganize that force. In Clausewitz's terms, these new citizen armies could actually disarm the enemy, not merely wear the enemy down or make the end of hostilities preferable. This was battle that held the prospect of being truly decisive. And in this way, battle quickly became the cornerstone of a new strategy of coercion, in which states at war assembled and directed force almost exclusively against opposing armies in the field.[27]

These new coercive capacities had one apparently paradoxical consequence, which brings our focus back to the question of the definition and treatment of the enemy. Citizen armies represented a substantial concentration of force, and their military power, when paired with the apparatus of mass mobilization, was terrific, even when their size remained moderate. By forming such a force, the potential contribution of ordinary people to an opponent's war effort became readily imaginable, and no doubt the ordinary people on whom another state might draw held out some kind of allure as a potential target. However, the prevailing laws of war that reserved the intentional use of force only for those armed by an opposing state still held firm. As historian Gunther Rothenberg has gone to pains to document, there is no evidence in these conflicts of systematic, state-directed campaigns of coercion directed at civilians or other non-combatants, with most exceptions in line with what we observe in the period of limited war waged by professional forces across the earlier eighteenth century.[28] Indeed, the firmness of the prevailing laws of war was initially buttressed by the turn taken in newly emergent military strategies. For as the new capacities of citizen armies were harnessed and channeled into war against opposing armies in the field, they tended to shield civilians and other noncombatants from precisely this tremendous concentration of force.[29] In this way, the very means by which coercive capacity was realized on the ground reinforced prevailing ways of defining and treating the enemy.

Aftermath of the Military Mass Mobilization of Citizenries

Mobilizing the people into war as national citizens had profound consequences. Of those particularly important for the revolution in war, we can distinguish among them in terms of their primary impact on the politics of war-making, the social organization of war-making, or the use of force.

Waging war organized around the institutional fusion of national citizenship and soldiering had three interrelated effects on the politics of war-making. First, mobilizing the masses into armed conflict around the politically resonant idiom of citizen obligation gave rise to a nationalization of warfare – both among and within states. Political authorities and ordinary people alike increasingly came to understand wars and their parts in them in national terms.[30] Second, this nationalization of war became linked to the issue of honor. Citizen conscription transformed duty and sacrifice into a privilege of men as citizens, detached from exclusionary, aristocratic constructions. Such honor – and its converse, dishonor and humiliation – became defining concerns for men as citizens simply by virtue of their potential relationship to the state as soldiers. In turn, because honor was democratized and bound to public performance and estimation, personal and national honor became tightly interconnected. Both the individual soldier's contribution to the defense of the honor of his nation and the way the humiliation of the nation in war reflected negatively upon the honor of the soldier make this relationship clear. As a consequence, it is also possible to see how war itself became an issue of national honor – so that the outcome *as well as the conduct of war* mattered in terms of whether a nation was deemed honorable. Last, these considerations of nationalization and honor point toward a third set of consequences: not only did the obligation to serve in the armed forces become increasingly accepted,[31] but beyond those touched by military service, we observe a profound *popular appropriation* of war. Mobilizing the people into war as citizens, underscoring the shared obligation to serve, meant that increasingly large segments of the citizenry came to see the state's wars as their own.[32]

The combined military power and political implications of mobilizing the masses via conscription meant several things for the organization as well as the use of coercion. Perhaps most importantly, the model of the citizen military and the mobilized nation at war became explicit, elaborated in strategic theory and the subject of political debate. Largely as a consequence, the model and its attendant institutional underpinnings – including national citizenship – began to diffuse. However, even in those states where it first emerged, it underwent a revision of sorts in times of peace. There, the citizen military was put on narrower footing – relying no longer on the short service of the very many, but rather on the long service of a somewhat smaller cohort – while the officer corps became self-consciously more professional through the formation of military academies and a general staff. At the threat of war, such citizen militaries could be expanded to draw on the citizenry at large, as required, directed by a cadre of experienced commissioned and noncommissioned officers, where new citizen-soldiers were incorporated alongside experienced soldiers in the ranks. Such extensibility went hand in hand with, and indeed was elicited by, the parallel diffusion of the new coercive strategy of pursuing battle with armies able to yield decision.

THE TREATMENT OF THE ENEMY

The outbreak of war in the last third of the nineteenth century tested the stability of this new synthesis, in a fairly short period yielding a substantial change not in state-led mobilization but rather in the definition and treatment of the enemy. In the opening phases of both the U.S. Civil War and the Franco-Prussian War, we see the continuation of a way of defining and treating the enemy in war characteristic of the mid-eighteenth century and early years of mass military mobilization. War routinely subjected to assault only those who bore arms for a state. Alongside this, however, there crystallized a powerful, even corrosive set of new practices – campaigns of intentional destruction of private property – directed with little regard to whether persons were armed by the state or even directed expressly at those who did *not* bear arms. The first reflected the principle of noncombatant immunity, which in the domain of the enemy expressed the primacy of those men whom the state arms in war – in this instance, as its chief and only legitimate target. In the second, bearing arms for the state lost its salience. These new attacks on civilians, and the way in which they were rendered legitimate even as they deviated from longstanding custom, require explanation.

Two distinct sets of practices emerged that were striking less in their novelty per se than in the fact that it had been centuries since such things were done by design and with state authorization outside armed rebellion in European wars or colonial conquest.[33] The first was broadly characteristic of both the U.S. Civil War, accelerating across 1863 and 1864, and the Franco-Prussian War, from the first months all the way until its close. The core of this set of practices lies in direct attacks on towns and villages in the vicinity of the invading army, in which inhabitants were allowed to flee, but the military leveled homes, destroyed farms, and forcibly dislodged residents, oftentimes leaving the town or village in ruins. This was accompanied periodically and even routinely by the Prussians in France, with forced requisitions or fines imposed on the town leadership either to avoid destruction or as an additional burden placed on the locality seeking to strip as much as possible from the area. Such attacks were carried out one at time, in serial fashion, none of which was extensive and with no particular effort to coordinate across them; but they numbered in the dozens and covered large sections of the territory passed through by invading armies.[34]

The second set of practices involved a small number of significantly larger-scale attacks, organized and orchestrated over weeks or even longer, employing major concentrations of coercive force with much greater material and symbolic impact. Toward the end of the U.S. Civil War, beginning in the summer of 1864, the Union army initiated several such campaigns against southern civilians. Perhaps the most famous was Sherman's capture of Atlanta and his subsequent march to the sea through Georgia to the coast, where he captured Savannah. Having turned out the inhabitants of Atlanta, Sherman proceeded to burn sections of the city, notably the industrial and warehouse districts, and laid waste to a corridor over 300 miles wide along the path of his soldiers' march. Sherman went on to do much the same in South Carolina. These marches were anticipated by Sheridan's campaign in the Shenandoah

Valley, an invasion route for the Confederacy up to Washington, D.C. Having defeated Confederate forces in the area, Sheridan and his men despoiled 400 square miles of some of the most fertile agricultural land on which the Confederacy could draw. In both campaigns, the effort was expressly to destroy property – including property in slaves, which amounted to their liberation – seizing or destroying crops, livestock, and provisions; burning barns, mills, factories, and railroads; and destroying homes and the means of earning livelihoods.[35]

When the Franco-Prussian War erupted in 1870, such scorched earth policies were not systematically pursued across large swaths of land, although Sheridan himself instructed the German staff on his methods. Instead, the siege – which had disappeared as a centerpiece of war across the eighteenth century – returned with stunning effect, in which the Prussian encircling of Strasbourg, Metz, and then Paris led to near starvation. More importantly, in Strasbourg and then more famously still in Paris, the siege included bombardment by heavy field guns, directed toward industrial and other manufacturing areas, and as much as possible away from densely inhabited sections of the city or occurring when residences would be less likely to be occupied.[36]

These new attacks on civilians were the product of three intertwined causal processes: conflicts came to be defined by engagement between similarly organized, large, citizen militaries backed by a mobilized political community; self-armed fighters – guerrillas and partisans – destabilized conventions limiting the use of force and precipitated attacks on civilians that could be justified and deemed legitimate; and wars characterized in these terms provided little opportunity for any one battle to prove decisive, inducing a new coercive strategy organized around attrition in war that transformed attacks on civilians and noncombatants into a linchpin of a new way of using military force. This was a shift built on the intensification of the political effects of mass-mobilizing citizenries into war that not only served to redefine the enemy in expansive, homogenous terms but also transformed attacks on noncombatants into an acceptable and even central part of the new reality of waging interstate war.

The basic contours of each conflict were set by the state's expansion of existing standing forces through appeals to volunteers and then conscription, backed by extensive mobilization of the national citizenry in economic as well as political terms. From the perspective of ordinary people, mass war against similarly organized adversaries both heightened a sense of national membership and intensified the popular appropriation of armed conflict – so that increasingly the military crisis at hand was something in which they as citizens had a stake, and to which they could, and should, contribute. Under these conditions, when massed forces met in deeply contested territory, large numbers of local men took up arms on their own and entered the war as guerrillas or partisans. These guerrillas drew on the historical legacy of revolutionary citizen militias decades before, but, critically, had the opposite valence in terms of state-led coercion. Rather than offering a new basis on which the state reconstituted armed force, they remained a force apart: citizens expressly *not* armed by the state, fighting for their state and often in the area of regular forces, but without the state's authority or organizational involvement.

When guerrillas entered war being waged by state-led mass forces, the distinction between combatants and noncombatants began to lose its clarity in a harrowing and ultimately destabilizing fashion. Once the people at large did not require the state's mediation to take up arms in war, but instead armed themselves and entered the fray, the threat faced by an invading and occupying power swelled precipitously. This threat was not merely strategic, in the sense of military losses or dissipation of resources, but also political, since guerrillas threatened to pry war-making out of the hands of the state.[37] The sense of threat was joined moreover to a sense of normative violation, for the organization of guerrilla forces and their particular conduct – refusing to identify themselves by wearing uniforms or openly carrying weapons, hiding among civilians, using sneak attacks – constituted a breach of the laws of war.[38] For those who adhered to and fought by the prevailing *jus in bello* – notably statesmen and professional military officers, for whom these conventions formed a cornerstone of what they deemed honorable conduct in military operations – the emergence of guerrillas was a testament that the opponent did not intend to fight a fair fight and served to justify a swift and generally lethal response toward guerrillas themselves.

What is critical here, however, is not the treatment of guerrillas per se, but rather their broader impact. In an environment fueled by the military and political fear of irregulars, as well as the repudiation of long-standing rules of conduct they represented, guerrillas taking up arms on their own without state authority implicated the breadth of the civilian population in the opposing state's war-making. Anyone at any time could bear arms, emerging from the shelter of civilian society and disappearing again within it. And by virtue of their role as source and refuge, not only the state making war but also the people at large could be held to account. Invading and occupying powers responded to the blurring of the lines between combatants and noncombatants by lumping all segments of the opposing political community into an increasingly undifferentiated enemy. Gone was the primacy of being armed by the state, replaced instead by a more or less homogenous construction of the mobilized citizenry as enemy.

Campaigns of intentional coercion launched against civilians therefore became reasonable – not merely corresponding to threat and violation, but also a matter of fitting response. Although such attacks produced civilian casualties, what defined them was the way they inflicted significant privation, hardship, and even terror upon civilians as a tool of war. In a conflict of extensive mobilization, their strategic purpose was to drain away resources and break the will of the people to fight, both critical to their opponent's efforts to wage mass war.[39] Such attacks represented a major shift in military practice, in which the target of intentional coercion was no longer only the opposing state's chief instrument of war – the armed forces – but instead included the opponent's *capacity* to make war, rooted in this moment in a mobilized civilian population.

This targeting of an opponent's capacity to make war contributed to the formation of a new approach to the use of coercion. Although the process played out differently in the U.S. Civil War and the Franco-Prussian War, an unintended consequence of mass mobilizing militaries confronting one another in war was that no one battle could prove decisive. Instead, only the cumulative effect of several battles could hope to disarm the enemy. Even then, the prospect of rebuilding the armed forces on the fly meant that only the capture of the political center of the opponent could guarantee decision. Across the course of both of these wars, therefore, we see a new logistical use of coercion: a form of war of attrition built around serial battle, defined by prolonged and continuous engagement, ending only with complete exhaustion of a nation's resources supporting its forces in the field or with the capture of a capital. A defining component of this new kind of war was the targeting of the human, material, and political resources on which the state depended to wage mass war. The door to making war in this way had been opened by targeting economic infrastructure, but the direct attack on civilian property threw open that door, bringing with it the prospect of undermining the political support, morale, and will of a people at large to go on. The crystallization of this new approach, in turn, helped render state attacks on civilians and noncombatants intelligible and even legitimate, spurring a process by which even international congresses organized to reformulate the laws of war came to include provisions for determining which kinds of attacks on noncombatants were unacceptable.

CONCLUSION

To this day, we live with the legacies of the revolution in war at the end of the eighteenth century. Without reference to the reintroduction of ordinary people into the state's war-making, it would be difficult to make sense of total war, revolutionary conflict, or wars of liberation and independence. In the present, we observe the continuing legacy of this revolution in the centrality of armed nonstate actors and trans-border mobilizations in conflicts that embroil the United States in Iraq and Afghanistan, in the threat of large-scale terrorism mounted by groups such as al-Qaeda, as well as the quasi-state ISIL in Syria and Iraq. For the state as war-maker, the revolution in war leaves its lasting imprint, even after a move away from military mass mobilization and a turn to more professional forces, as can be seen, for example, in the current United States. Not only does the prior history of mass war leave the question of popular support for entering, continuing, and ending war absolutely central to national politics, but as sociologist Michael Mann has underscored, this prior history of mass war waged by citizens in the creation and defense of democratic nations continues to shape popular perceptions and expectations of what the state's wars are for, what they can achieve, and what makes them worthwhile.[40]

The revolution in war also has powerful implications for theorizing the state. Like several other essays in this volume, my account of statebuilding places symbolic processes at the center. The deployment of state authority is critical to making sense of both the mass mobilization of citizenries into war and the intentional targeting of unarmed civilians. The key to both lay in whom the state armed and in what terms. In the domain of mobilization, reconstituting state forces around citizen militias and then fusing citizenship to soldiering through conscription drove the shift to state-led mass war and fashioned the politically salient category around which the state reorganized armed conflict. In turn, this yielded a strongly differentialist incorporation of the citizenry into the state's war-making, distinguishing roles people were called upon (or allowed) to fill in terms of gender, age, race, and even civilian employment. In the domain of the enemy, alternately, those who entered war without state authority as guerrillas or partisans drove a process by which the category "armed by the state" began to lose its salience from the point of view of the adversary facing self-armed fighters. As a consequence, the state homogenized those mobilized against it into an increasingly undifferentiated enemy, subjecting even unarmed civilians to intentional attack. That mass mobilization of citizenries and intentional targeting of civilians were causally linked by a process of popular appropriation – where the extension of state authority to create an obligation of citizen service led civilians to embrace the state's wars as their own and enter conflicts on their own initiative – only serves to underscore further the centrality of the symbolic in statebuilding.

Notes

1 Johann Wolfgang von Goethe, *Campaign in France*, trans. Robert Farie (Middletown: Ricardo Cunha Mattos Portella, 2012), 45.

2 Ibid.

3 Meyer Kestnbaum, "Citizenship and Compulsory Military Service: The Revolutionary Origins of Conscription in the United States," *Armed Forces and Society* 27 (Fall 2000): 7–36.

4 Meyer Kestnbaum, "Citizen-Soldiers, National Service and the Mass Army: The Birth of Conscription in Revolutionary Europe and North America," *Comparative Social Research* 20 (2002): 117–44.

5 Carl von Clausewitz, *On War*, ed. and trans. Michael Howard and Peter Paret (Princeton: Princeton University Press, 1976), 592.

6 Charles Tilly, "War-Making and State-Making as Organized Crime," in *Bringing the State Back In*, eds. Peter Evans, Dietrich Rueschemeyer and Theda Skocpol (Cambridge: Cambridge University Press, 1985), 169–191; and Charles Tilly, *Coercion, Capital and European States, AD 990–1992* (Cambridge: Blackwell, 1992).

7 See Peter Paret, *Understanding War: Essays on Clausewitz and the History of Military Power* (Princeton: Princeton University Press, 1992); and Peter Horne, ed., *State, Society and Mobilization in Europe during the First World War* (Cambridge: Cambridge University Press, 1997); Michael Mann, *The Sources of Social Power, vol. 1, A History of Power from the Beginning to AD 1760* (Cambridge: Cambridge University Press, 1986); Michael Mann, *The Dark Side of Democracy: Explaining Ethnic Cleansing* (New York: Cambridge University Press, 2005).

8 Norbert Elias, *The Civilizing Process* (New York: Pantheon Books, 1978, 1982).

9 See Geoffrey Parker, *The Military Revolution: Military Innovation and the Rise of the West, 1500–1800* (Cambridge: Cambridge University Press, 1988); and William McNeill, *Age of Gunpowder Empires, 1450–1800* (Washington, DC: American Historical Association, 1989).

10 Meyer Kestnbaum, "Mars Revealed: The Entry of Ordinary People into War among States," in *Remaking Modernity: Politics, Processes, and History in Sociology*, eds. Julia P. Adams, Elisabeth S. Clemens, and Ann Shola Orloff (Durham: Duke University Press, 2005), 249–85; and Meyer Kestnbaum, "Organized Coercion and Political Authority: Armed Conflict in a World of States," in *The New Wiley-Blackwell Companion to Sociology*, ed. George Ritzer (New York: Blackwell Publishing, 2012), 588–608.

11 Paret, *Understanding War*; and Peter Paret, "Napoleon and the Revolution in War," in *Makers of Modern Strategy: From Machiavelli to the Modern Age*, ed. Peter Paret (Princeton: Princeton University Press, 1986), 123–42.

12 For illustrations of linkages between state and nonstate organizations in war, see Theda Skocpol, Ziad Munson, A. Karch A, and Bayliss Camp, "Patriotic Partnerships: Why Great Wars Nourished American Civic Voluntarism," in *Shaped by War and Trade: International Influence in American Development*, eds. Ira Katznelson and Martin Shefter (Princeton: Princeton University Press, 2002), 134–80.

13 Carl Schmitt, *The Concept of the Political* (Rutgers: Rutgers University Press, 1976).

14 Hans Delbruck, *The Dawn of Modern Warfare*, trans. Walter J. Renfroe, Jr. (Lincoln: University of Nebraska Press, 1985).

15 Michael Howard, *War in European History*, (New York: Cambridge University Press, 1976); Gunther Rothenberg, *The Art of Warfare in the Age of Napoleon* (Bloomington: Indiana University Press, 1978); Geoffrey Best, *War and Society in Revolutionary Europe, 1770–1870* (New York: St. Martins, 1982); Christopher Duffy, *The Military Experience in the Age of Reason* (London: Routledge, 1987); Parker, *The Military Revolution*; Jeremy Black, *European Warfare, 1660–1815* (New Haven: Yale University Press, 1994); and Jeremy Black, *Western Warfare, 1775–1882* (Bloomington: Indiana University Press, 2001).

16 Geoffrey Parker, "Early Modern Europe," in *The Laws of War: Constraints on Warfare in the Western World*, eds. Michael Howard, G. Andreopolous, and M. Shulman (New Haven: Yale University Press, 1994), 40–58. See also Geoffrey Best, *Humanity in Warfare* (New York: Columbia University Press, 1980); and Best, *War and Law since 1945* (Oxford and New York: Clarendon Press of Oxford University Press, 1994).

17 Delbruck, *Dawn on Modern Warfare*; and Russel F. Weigley, *The Age of Battles: The Quest for Decisive Warfare from Breitenfeld to Waterloo* (Bloomington: Indiana University Press, 1991).

18 Kestnbaum, "Citizenship and Compulsory Military Service."

19 Kestnbaum, "Citizen Soldiers, National Service and the Mass Army."

20 Rogers Brubaker, *Citizenship and Nationhood in France and Germany* (Cambridge: Harvard University Press, 1992).

21 See Theda Skocpol, *States and Social Revolutions: A Comparative Analysis of France, Russia and China* (Cambridge: Cambridge University Press, 1979); and Skocpol, "Social Revolutions and Mass Military Mobilization," in *Social Revolutions in the Modern World* (Cambridge: Cambridge University Press, 1994), 279–98.

22 Kestnbaum, "Citizenship and Compulsory Military Service." See also Katharine Chorley, *Armies and the Art of Revolution* (Boston: Beacon Press, 1973); Paret, *Understanding War*; and Roger Chickering and Stig Forster, eds., *War in the Age of Revolution, 1775–1815* (Cambridge: Cambridge University Press, 2010).

23 Kestnbaum, "Citizen Soldiers, National Service, and the Mass Army."

24 Ibid; and Kestnbaum, "Organized Coercion and Political Authority."

25 Meyer Kestnbaum and Emily S. Mann, "Arms and the Man: War and Hegemonic Masculinity," manuscript.

26 Kestnbaum, "Organized Coercion and Political Authority."

27 Delbruck, *Dawn of Modern Warfare*; David G. Chandler, *The Campaigns of Napoleon: The Mind and Method of History's Greatest Soldier* (New York: Scbribner, 1966); Weigley, *The Age of Battles*; and Robert M. Epstein, *Napoleon's Last Victory and the Emergence of Modern War* (Lawrence: University Press of Kansas, 1994).

28 Gunther Rothenberg, "The Age of Napoleon," in *The Laws of War: Constraints on Warfare in the Western World*, eds. Michael Howard, G. Andreopolous, and M. Shulman (New Haven: Yale University Press, 1994), 86–97. Cf. David A. Bell, *The First Total War: Napoleon's Europe and the Birth of Modern War as We Know It* (Boston: Houghton Mifflin, 2007), on civil war and state attacks on popular opponents of the revolutionary regime.

29 Delbruck, *Dawn of Modern Warfare*.

30 Brubaker, *Citizenship and Nationhood*; Omer Bartov, *Murder in our Midst: The Holocaust, Industrial Killing, and Representation* (New York: Oxford University Press, 1996); and Elaine Scarry, "The Difficulty in Imagining Other People," in *For Love of Country: Debating the Limits of Patriotism*, J. Cohen, ed. (Boston: Beacon Press,1996), 98–110.

31 Paret, *Understanding War*.

32 Kestnbaum, "Citizen Soldiers, National Service and the Mass Army," and "Organized Coercion and Political Authority."

33 This qualification is absolutely essential, since such practices were much more common in protracted rebellions in which control of the state by the rebels (or the formation of a second state after secession) was not achieved, as well as in situations of colonial conquest and domination involving the subordination of ethnically or religiously differentiated opponents, which often acquired a racialized character. The important issue analytically here is how such practices became commonplace in interstate wars among not merely similar states but, loosely, Western powers.

34 Mark Grimsley, *The Hard Hand of War: Union Policy toward Southern Civilians 1861–1865* (New York: Cambridge University Press, 1997); Michael Howard, *The Franco-Prussian War: The German Invasion of France, 1870–1871*, 2nd ed. (London: Routledge, 2001); John Horne, "Defining the Enemy: War, Law and the Levée en masse from 1870 to 1945," in *The People in Arms: Military Myth and National Mobilization Since the French Revolution*, eds. Daniel Moran and A. Waldron (Cambridge: Cambridge University Press, 2002), 100–23; Isabel V. Hull, *Absolute Destruction: Military Culture and the Practices of War in Imperial Germany* (Ithaca: Cornell University Press, 2005); and Daniel E. Sutherland, *A Savage Conflict: The Decisive Role of Guerrillas in the American Civil War* (Durham: University of North Carolina Press, 2009).

35 James M. McPherson, "From Limited War to Total War in America," in *Road to Total War*, eds. Förster and Nagler, 295–309.

36 Howard, *The Franco-Prussian War*; and Best, *Laws of War*.

37 Förster and Nagler, eds, *Road to Total War;* Eric J. Hobsbawm, *Bandits,* rev. ed. (New York: The New Press, 2000).

38 Horne, "Defining the Enemy"; and McPherson, "From Limited War to Total War."

39 Forster and Nagler, *Road to Total War.*

40 Michael Mann, "The Roots and Contradictions of Militarism," in *States, War and Capitalism: Essays in Political Sociology* (London: Blackwell, 1988).

PART IV

STATES AND EMPIRES

The Transnational/Global Turn

13

Imperial States in the Age of Discovery

Julia Adams and Steve Pincus

If the original transition to modernity and the associated state formation took place in Europe between the sixteenth and nineteenth centuries, how did colonialism and empire figure in? The almost simultaneous discovery of sea routes to the East and the existence of large land masses in the West marked a fundamental turning point in European and global history. These discoveries almost immediately transformed the economic and political horizons of Europeans. Did European empire-building then reconfigure European states?

Nowadays scholars give an enormous range of answers to these closely related questions and observations, and define the questions themselves in distinctive ways. At times this involves the usual challenge of scholars reaching across far-flung specialties and disciplinary abysses. There are also gaps between scholarly generations, with some earlier scholars of transitions to modernity sidestepping empires as emblems of a more distant past. More recently, however, discussion of empires has rebounded, and with a vengeance. Thinking through the relationship between early modern empire-making and transitions to modernity is an ongoing collective challenge.

The question of how colonialism and empire changed early modern Europe was explicitly on the table during World War II, posed in brilliant, and quite restricted, politico-economic terms. It first appeared then in the guise of debates over the role – if any – of long-distance trade, including the slave trade and colonial trade more generally, in European economic development. Eric Williams's *Capitalism and Slavery* forcefully high-lighted the impact of the capital created and amassed in the West Indies on the rise of industrial capitalism in England.[1] Other scholars pushed the question still earlier than Williams's emphasis on the late eighteenth and early nineteenth centuries: what, they typically asked, was the preeminent cause of the original transition from feudalism to capitalism? In a set of lively exchanges that became known as the Dobb-Sweezy and then the Brenner Debates, the proposed answers boiled down to returns from trade, including coerced exchange, versus endogenous changes in metropolitan-based forms of production.[2] A later iteration, invoking the role of the state in the revolutions that divided the old regimes from the new, asked whether war (re)made states. In particular, did political engagement in expensive overseas adventures weaken the tax base of old regime state elites and therefore promote state breakdown and revolution?[3]

These arguments and debates cut across academic disciplines, stretching across sociology, history, radical economics, political theory, anthropology, English literature, and beyond. At the time, there was a sense of a broadly shared theoretical language that spanned academic disciplines. The arguments were fierce, and had perceived political stakes, because to many the possibility still loomed of a contemporary transition out of capitalism to another, more highly evolved form of political economy, whether that be socialism or a reformed welfare capitalism. The stories of transition from feudalism to capitalism were therefore also interpreted by many as parables of present possibilities, and of springboards to rosier futures.

Empire was not always explicitly theorized in these arguments over the causes of early modern European development, but it was there, even if occluded. Did the original or "primitive" accumulation (to use Karl Marx's language in *Capital*) derive from colonial spaces? If so, they were generally not conceived as colonial *per se* but as spatially separated economic modes of production.[4] Or did the developmental engine instead derive its power from contiguous capitalist and even proto-national dynamics?[5] Under what conditions did the processes that were unleashed by the geographical expansion of Europeans to the East and West, mediated through early modern states, dislodge old regime elites, culminating in great revolutionary upheavals?[6] These far-reaching questions were understood as belonging to the realm of political economy, about the transition from one mode of production, feudalism – in which peasant labor was not separated from the landed means of production, and lords exercised extraeconomic pressure to extract surplus labor from the peasantry – to another, capitalism – in which peasants became proletarians who sold their labor-power on the market and lords or seigneurs were displaced by capitalists who did not consume goods but instead accumulated and reinvested capital. Empire was in the deep background – an undertheorized and even potentially embarrassing context in which the real changes were taking place.

For many reasons, both worldly and academic, the coherence and indeed purchase of the postwar paradigm eroded by the 1990s; over a half-century, it ran its course.[7] Yet the knotty empirical problem articulated here – why the original European transformation took place – persists, as does the question of the impact of processes deemed outside of Europe on that epochal change.

In what follows, we first argue that recent intellectual developments that together challenge the emergence of the nation-state as the inevitable modern state form, undermine – where they do not outright abolish – the division between early modern states and empires. We then show that imperial state formation played a decisive role in the theorization of the rise of modernity. Finally, we argue that the racialization of political discourse in the heart of these imperial states in the late eighteenth and nineteenth centuries did much to obscure the unity of imperial state formation. By highlighting the differences between the white metropole and the dark colonial periphery, racializing discourses made it hard to see empires as coherent and unified state forms. State agents no longer understood their political obligations to subject groups equally. The consequences continue to bedevil us today.

IMPERIAL STATES AND STATIST EMPIRES

It is now established – if not completely recognized as such – that the iconic period of early modern European state formation was actually in large part an era of *imperial* state formation. Whereas most scholars used to assume that a profound gulf separated empires from modern states, scholarly research on the early modern era has pointed in the opposite direction. There is little if anything to distinguish the extension of states into neighboring provinces from their extension into distant territories in the great period of European statebuilding (ca. 1400–ca. 1800). The reach of French power into Brittany or Languedoc was not fundamentally different from the development of French sovereignty in Canada or Martinique.[8] Contemporaries in Britain drew explicit parallels between the state's increasing power in the Highlands of Scotland and in the Southern and Western extremities of British North America. In both British cases, for example, the state extended its influence with violence, absorbed or otherwise threatened local kinship structures, impinged upon local cultural traditions, reoriented local economies, and invested heavily in infrastructure. Indeed, in both Scotland and North America, contemporary commentators referred to the locals as "aboriginals."[9]

While today's scholars refer to the extra-European manifestations of European power in the early modern world as empires, contemporaries referred to them as states. While scholars often refer to the consolidation of territory in the early modern period as the making of nation-states, contemporaries more often called this consolidation, even internal to Europe, the making of empires. Indeed, in the early modern period, the very notion of a core and a periphery, in whatever language, was politically contested rather than taken as natural or inevitable. Recall that Saint Domingue (Haiti) sent representatives to the National Assembly in 1789. Recall, too, that Adam Smith followed a long line of British patriots when, in 1776, he argued for giving all of the British colonies, not just the North American ones, full representation in an imperial parliament in Westminster.[10] Much of eighteenth-century discussion in political economy focused on whether or not the colonies or the European heartlands were the most economically dynamic. Adam Smith along with Benjamin Franklin thought it was likely that the British capital would move to North America, just as the Roman capital had moved from Italy to Byzantium. Indeed, the seat of the Portuguese monarchy in the nineteenth century was in Brazil, not Iberia.

The central tension, it could be said, was as much competition among empires as it was imperial state strategies within empires. In this era, "territorial" as opposed to "nonterritorial" served to indicate not two types of states, but rather two strategies that had proponents within each and every imperial state. In each European state, therefore, there were advocates of commercial extension who warned against the fiscal and social costs of territorial control pitted against defenders of territorial empire who lambasted the fragility of commercial ties and their socially revolutionary consequences. These groups were not spatially determined, though they may well have been tilted by the local economies that emerged. The most energetic defenders of the territorial expansion of the British Empire in the third quarter of the eighteenth century were the great Maryland land owner George Chalmers and the Georgian William Knox, while the British Prime Minister William Pitt and the Scottish-born Presbyterian minister John Witherspoon were two of the most powerful advocates of commercial empire.[11]

The networks and communities that had initially established these early modern empires were gradually institutionalized in the seventeenth and eighteenth centuries. This increasingly meant that discussions of competing state strategies might begin in the Americas and quickly gain political and social allies, and traction, in Europe. In the French, Dutch, Spanish, Portuguese, and British empires, major political, commercial, and social players moved across their imperial spaces, while communication networks helped ensure that humbler members of the empire could imagine themselves as part of a singular unit. There were deep cleavages, to be sure, but those cleavages were more often social, economic, cultural, religious, or political than they were in any simple sense spatial. The French and Spanish Bourbon Empires of the eighteenth century were increasingly centralized and integrated.[12]

But perhaps the rhetoric and behavior of the American Revolutionaries best highlights the general point. Instead of defending their actions as a necessary colonial revolt against imperial oppression, as one might expect, the signers of the Declaration of Independence chose to narrate the ways in which one particular vision of imperial rule had ousted an earlier and more inclusive version. The initial impetus toward revolution in the American colonies is best understood as a civil war between defenders of competing imperial visions[13] – loyalist commitment to a territorial empire in which the colonies were subservient to the mother country and the patriot ideal of an economically and politically integrated empire devoted to commercial expansion.[14] The Americans who declared independence from the British Empire did not see their actions as anti-imperial. Indeed they immediately insisted that they were creating a new imperial state.[15]

Thus the European empires of the early modern era were part and parcel of state formation projects and vice versa. The many hands of the state were vested in empire.

MERCANTILISM AND THEORIES OF MODERNITY

Not only did the making of European imperial states play a significant and underappreciated role in the transitions to modernity, but imperial state formation has played a decisive role in the theorization of the coming of modernity. The origins of historical social science or social science history itself lay in the debate over the thoroughgoing effects of global expansion on European states. So fundamental were these global transformations that a range of Enlightenment thinkers pointed to the Age of Discovery as *the* turning point in European and global history. They understood these transformations as the key to the creation of the modern world. "No event has been so interesting to mankind in general, and to the inhabitants of Europe in particular, as the discovery of the New World and the passage to India by the Cape of Good Hope," insisted the Abbé Raynal in his classic *Philosophical and Political History of the Settlements and Trade of the Europeans in the East and West Indies.* "It gave rise," he explained, "to a revolution in commerce, and in the power of nations; and in the manners, industry and government of the world in general."[16] "The discovery of America, and that of the passage to the East Indies by the Cape of Good Hope, are the two greatest and most important events in the history of mankind," maintained Adam Smith in 1776. "Their consequences have already been very great: but, in the short period of between two and three centuries which has elapsed since these discoveries were made, it is impossible that that the whole extent of their consequences can have been seen."[17]

Scholars, politicians, clerics, and writers have offered a bewildering array of explanations for Europe's transition(s) to modernity. Often it is difficult to distinguish among causes, processes, and consequences of that transition. What is remarkable, however, is that so many eighteenth- and nineteenth-century commentators emphasized the central role played by the extension of European empires and trade to the east and west. Why did so many in the eighteenth and nineteenth centuries believe that these discoveries were so important? Contemporaries offered a wide variety of explanations, of course. Some highlighted the cultural and social-psychological consequences for Europeans of encountering different cultures, strange religions, and unfamiliar ways of life.[18] We return to this point in the next section.

Many commentators, particularly those who were most insistent on the fundamental nature of the transition, underlined the political and economic consequences of the "age of discovery." European commercial and political expansion east and west initiated new discussions about the nature of empire and its relationship to trade. In just this vein, Karl Marx and Friedrich Engels endorsed Adams Smith's assessment. "The discovery of America, the rounding of the Cape, opened up fresh ground for the rising bourgeoisie. The East-Indian and Chinese markets, the colonization of America, trade with the colonies, the increase in the means of exchange and in commodities generally, gave to commerce, to navigation, to industry, an impulse never before known, and thereby, to the revolutionary element in the tottering feudal society, a rapid development ... Modern industry has established the world market, for which the discovery of America paved the way."[19]

This strikingly new ideological terrain has been obscured for a long time because scholars assumed that until the modern era most Europeans believed in a backward-looking conception of the relationship between state and economy. The preponderance of scholars since the mid-nineteenth century have offered variants of the same story: that Europeans were equipped with a single agreed-upon theory of political economy – mercantilism – that shaped their responses to the new global opportunities in a similar manner. Europeans sought and gained empires in the East and West. Because Europeans believed that the amount of property in the world was finite, we are told, they scrambled to seize and defend as much territory as they possibly could. Gaining territory allowed Europeans to extract precious raw materials from the West – Jonathan Swift recommended items such as "gold, silver, sugar or tobacco" in Book IV of *Gulliver's Travels* – and exchange them for calicoes and spices in the East. European mercantilists needed extractive empire to support economic, political, and cultural expansion in Europe. They needed colonies that were economically subservient and politically dependent on the European mother countries to advance their struggle for property, since that struggle was necessarily a zero-sum game.[20]

Later commentators were not wrong to assert that some Europeans described early modern economic activity in those terms: many did do so. But they are wrong to see an early modern mercantilist consensus and to describe an age of mercantilism that preceded an era of free trade. The apparent consensus, which does not hold up to sustained historical research, was actually the product of late nineteenth- and early twentieth-century political contestation. For many early modern Europeans argued against those who maintained that the amount of property was finite and delimited by the amount of territory in the world. These early moderns argued that property could be infinitely expanded by human labor. Labor, not land, held the key to prosperity. John Locke maintained that "if we will rightly estimate things as they come to our use, and cast up the several expenses about them, what in them is purely owing to nature, and what to labour, we shall find, that in most of them ninety-nine hundredths are wholly to be put on the account of labour." "The enjoyment of all societies will ever depend upon the fruits of the earth and the labour of the people," argued the Dutch political economist Bernard Mandeville. Raw materials mixed with labour, insisted Mandeville, "are a more certain, a more inexhaustible and a more real treasure than the gold of Brazil, or the silver of Potosi."[21] Adam Smith similarly began his *Wealth of Nations* with the observation that labor created property.

Even in economic terms, however, it was not labor alone that created the conditions for infinite growth. Only when producers rewarded their laborers with high wages were there possibilities for a demand-driven economy. Only the creative interplay between production and consumption generated the crucible of infinite growth. It was in this sense that Mandeville argued that private vices created public virtue.[22] It was only luxurious tastes supported by high wages, in the view of John Trenchard, that could induce people to believe "that other things are necessary to their happiness besides those which nature has made necessary." In this sense, he reasoned, "the luxury of the rich becomes the bread of the poor."[23] Adam Smith deployed the same logic in arguing in favor of high wages against the illicit collusion of employers to keep the working-men poor.

Those who believed in a labor-based high wage economy came to very different conclusions about empire than their land-based, raw material-fetishizing opponents. Whereas the latter – Tories and neo-Tories in the British context – argued for territorial expansion and extractive empire, the former – Whigs in Britain and British North America – argued in favor of opening markets and political and economic integration. The value of European expansion, in their view, was not the extraction of raw materials but the creation of a wider world of capitalist consumers. This, of course, was a key point advanced by Marx and Engels in *The Communist Manifesto*,[24] echoing the conclusions of Adam Smith. "The discovery of America, however, certainly made a most essential" change in the state of Europe, Smith maintained. "[B]y opening a new and inexhaustible market to all the commodities of Europe, it gave occasion to new divisions of labor and improvements of art, which, in the narrow circle of the ancient commerce, could never have taken place for want of a market to take off the greater part of their produce. The productive powers of labor were improved, and its produce increased in all the different countries of Europe, and together with the real revenue and wealth of the inhabitants." This reasoning led Patriot politicians in the British Empire to argue in favor of colonial development rather than colonial extraction. And this orientation explains why Britain spent a much larger percentage of its revenue than its European rivals on developing the colonies where the land-based theory held political sway.

Both the proponents of the land-based theory of wealth and those who felt that labor alone (and not the interplay of production and consumption) created property were great advocates of chattel slavery. Slaves offered an ostensibly inexpensive way to extract raw materials. But Patriot Whigs who defended a high-wage theory of wealth creation were always fierce critics of slavery. Slaves made poor consumers, they believed. From the 1710s onward, as W. E. B. Du Bois catalogued long ago, Whigs in colonial assemblies sought to limit the influx of African slaves while Patriot polemicists in England and across the Empire argued against the creation of slave-based extractive economies. Adam Smith was only one in a long list of Patriot political economists who argued that the Empire would be better off without slavery.[25]

Patriots did not, for the most part, set the political agenda for the British Empire after 1760. Nor did those with similar ideas about political economy triumph in other European countries. Slavery was not abolished in the British Empire until the nineteenth century. Nor did the Patriots achieve the full political integration of the Empire. Those who argued for authoritarian and extractive empire did not triumph in mid-century because they had the better arguments. Why did the Patriots lose out? This strikes us as a central question in investigating the relationship among empire, states, and European capitalism. One cannot begin to grapple with the question without understanding that there were competing political imperial projects in the eighteenth century. To explain why one party lost and the other one won – if only briefly – requires integrating studies of the economies, language, and politics of empire. Indeed if Karl Marx was right to claim that "the modern history of capital dates from the creation in the 16th century of a world-embracing commerce and a world-embracing market,"[26] we need to better understand the way that the actors themselves understood the economics of that commerce and the politics of that market.

Nevertheless, as should now be clear from the foregoing analysis, throughout the eighteenth and nineteenth centuries Europeans from every walk of life grappled with the profound implications of European imperial expansion east and west. There was no consensus about what kind of *polity* could embrace and shape the new opportunities and new challenges. There was no uniform answer to the question of how Europeans could best respond to the issues raised by trying to incorporate new peoples, new goods, new territories, and completely new understandings. But the vast majority in the eighteenth and nineteenth centuries thought that European imperial expansion had permanently changed their world. They believed that there had been a fundamental transformation. The challenge felt in the emerging social sciences was, then, to explain and account for that transformation, and ultimately to grapple with it.

CONCLUSION

Transitions to modernity are increasingly – or, rather, once again – understood to rest on the force of culture, on people's taking part in specific meaningful and consequential interactions. The very idea of modernity registers this social fact; it is incontestably a more expansive one than the development of a new economic mode of production and the states that accompanied it. It encodes a new sense of the "now" – the shared notion of a perpetually open present and all the unprecedented opportunity and insecurity that that implies – and a linked series of specifically cultural characteristics, such as instrumental rationality, calculation, disenchantment, and bureaucratic discipline, that are "inseparable from the advent of the 'spirit of capitalism'"[27] and modern political organization and forms of association but not reducible to them.

The question of the impact of colonialism and empire on European transitions has been gradually and insensibly recast by the massive conceptual "cultural turn" of the twentieth century. And among the array of culturalist theories of European transitions to modernity, several highlight extra-European manifestations of cultural power that reshape, root and branch, both European social worlds and what it meant to be European.[28]

The story we have been telling – one aspect of the whole, but an important and neglected one – is one in which both the imperial state formations and the cultural understandings that both helped shape and resulted from those imperial states were central to the genesis of modernity. It is one in which actors saw their world in increasingly global and potentially integrated terms – even if that integration involved new strategies of oppression and domination. Our account differs from earlier stories in that we highlight what could be termed material *and* cultural elements. Neither was in any sense prior to the other. Neither would or could, without the other, have generated the epochal transition. Imperial statemakers believed that contact with the hitherto unknown worlds, east and west, fundamentally transformed the contours of politics, and they were correct. Similarly, it was the transformation of global commerce that made the broadest patriarchal patrimonial strategies plausible and sustainable in the early modern world.

Nevertheless, it is unsettling that so much earlier thinking both about the transitions to modernity and about states and empires themselves refuses this integration. Core and periphery, mother country and colony, "the West and the Rest": these and other binaries still dominate the academic literature. How and why did these come to be so entrenched? One key dimension resides in a nineteenth-century rewriting that has since recast the early modern foundations of our modern political imaginations: the "racial recognition" mechanism and analysis of the transition to modernity, which devolved from appropriations of Georg Hegel and the Hegelian intellectual lineage.[29] The historical collision of European colonialism and empire, the claim is, initiates a distinctive kind of large-scale transformation. Europeans became "modern," it is argued, only when they recognized themselves as such in contrast to what they saw as the "not modern" – the so-called primitive or traditional peoples, societies, and territories. This split understanding eventually penetrated both modern society and its "Other" via the construction of states, economies, laws, and all manner of institutions and new imperial relations.

One original cause of the advent of modernity was the dialectical encounter among European explorer–colonialists and the colonized peoples in the New World and the global South. In the centuries-long era after the initial colonial contact, the recognition relation became a core mechanism by which both European and subaltern elites negotiated a fractious yet interdependent relationship that involved political sovereignty over, and economic exploitation of, the colonial masses. The array of consequences of this repeated encounter include but are not limited to, within this theoretical approach, the racialized character of modernity – notably specific conceptions of slavery and genocide, as well as the creativity of colonized peoples brought into harsh contact with western cultural forms; the formation of European imperial states; the extraction of surplus from colonial economies; and, more particularly, the revolutionary discourses of America and Haiti – as well as the later nationalist revolutionary movements in Africa and Latin America.

It is equally important, however, that the perceptual and cultural transformation reached a tipping point at a particular moment: the late eighteenth century.[30] Those responsible for the racialization of political discourse increasingly demanded and constructed a sharp distinction between European and overseas spaces. Racial ideologies, we now know, tended to harden in the late eighteenth and early nineteenth centuries. This meant that state agents, for example, no longer understood their political obligations to their various subject groups equally. Whereas Highland Scots and the Iroquois were both coded as aboriginals in the early eighteenth century, the Highlanders "became white" in the nineteenth century whereas the Iroquois were defined as indigenous.

Comparative work on disaster relief in the Caribbean has demonstrated that European elites, via states, increasingly treated white and nonwhite population groups differently. Whereas the British Treasury had devoted a huge part of its revenue to colonial infrastructural development in the eighteenth century, the nineteenth-century state never devoted the same level of resources to India that it had to Georgia or Nova Scotia. Canada and Australia were treated very differently from Britain's African and South Asian colonies. The centrality of race to American state formation – to what became the United States – was therefore a direct consequence of its being a late eighteenth- and nineteenth-century imperial polity.

Raynal, Marx, Smith – all wrote that the expansion into the New World completely transformed the questions that Europeans needed to ask about their own development, about not whether but *why* Europe was fundamentally transformed in political, economic, social, and moral terms by contact with new worlds, plural. This fundamental transformation did not only take place at the same time as the classic period of state formation, it was both a necessary precondition and ultimately a consequence of those projects of state formation. The transition(s) to modernity intimately related to imperial state formation. While empires have been the most common state form throughout human history, early modern imperial states were different in two fundamental ways. Structurally, they were able to marshal resources, human labor, and institutions of quantitative and spatial levels that were heretofore unthinkable. Culturally, these new imperial states were forced to confront difference in new and important ways. It was this dual transformation that fundamentally shaped the world we live in. It was this dual transformation that infinitely expanded the horizons of human possibility. It was also this dual transformation that left us with concepts of difference that have led to unprecedented scales of human suffering.

Notes

1 Eric Williams, *Capitalism and Slavery* (Chapel Hill: University of North Carolina Press, 1944).
2 For the Dobb-Sweezy debate, see Rodney Hilton, ed., *The Transition from Feudalism to Capitalism* (London: New Left Books, 1976). See also Robert Brenner's "The Origins of Capitalist Development: A Critique of Neo-Smithian Marxism," *New Left Review* 1, no. 104 (1977): 25–92.
3 The classic statement of this thesis is J.F. Bosher, *French Finances 1770–1795: From Business to Bureaucracy* (Cambridge: Cambridge University Press, 1970). In essence, modern scholars are following on from arguments advanced in the eighteenth century about the consequences of burgeoning national debts;

see Richard Price, *A Preface to the Third Edition of the Treatise on Reversionary Payments* (London: T. Cadell, 1773), 24. Theda Skocpol, *States and Social Revolutions: A Comparative Analysis of France, Russia and China* (Cambridge: Cambridge University Press, 1979); Charles Tilly, *Coercion, Capital, and European States, AD 990–1992* (Oxford: Blackwell, 1992).

4 Pierre Philippe Rey, *Colonialisme, Néo-Colonialisme et Transition au Capitalisme*, vol. 15 (Paris: F. Maspero, 1971); Pierre Philippe Rey, *Les alliances de Classes: Sur l'articulation des Modes de Production: Suivi de Matérialisme Historique et Luttes de Classes* (Paris: F. Maspero, 1973); Immanuel Wallerstein, *The Modern World-System I: Capitalist Agriculture and the Origins of the European World-Economy in the Sixteenth Century*, vol. 1 (New York: Academic Press, 1974).

5 Brenner, "Origins of Capitalist Development"; Perry Anderson, *Lineages of the Absolutist State* (London: New Left Books, 1974).

6 Skocpol, *States and Social Revolutions*; and Tilly, *Coercion, Capital, and European States*.

7 Julia Adams, Elisabeth S. Clemens, and Ann Shola Orloff, "Social Theory, Modernity, and the Three Waves of Historical Sociology," in *Remaking Modernity: Politics, History, and Sociology* (Chapel Hill: Duke University Press, 2005), 1–72.

8 James Given, *State and Society in Medieval Europe: Gwynedd and Languedoc under Outside Rule* (Ithaca: Cornell University Press, 1990).

9 This point is being developed by Justin Brooks in his Yale doctoral dissertation.

10 Adam Smith, *An Inquiry into the Nature and Causes of the Wealth of Nations*, vol. 2, ed. R. H. Campbell and A. S. Skinner (Indianapolis: Liberty Fund, 1982 [1776]), 622–23.

11 George Chalmers, *Estimate of the Comparative Strength of Great Britain* (London: C. Dilly and J. Bowen, 1782); George Chalmers, *An Introduction to the History of the Revolt of the Colonies*, vol. 1 (London: Baker and Galabin, 1782); William Knox, *The Claim of the Colonies* (London: W. Johnston, 1765); William Knox, *Three Tracts Respecting The Conversion And Instruction Of The Free Indians And Negroe Slaves In The Colonies* (London, 1768); William Knox, *Present State of the Nation*, 4th ed. (Dublin: R. Acheson, 1769); William Knox, *The Interest of the Merchants and Manufacturers of Great Britain* (London: T. Cadell, 1774); John Witherspoon, *An Address to the Natives of Scotland Residing in America* (London: Fielding and Walker, 1778); John Witherspoon, *The Dominion of Providence over the Passions of Men* (Philadelphia: R. Aitken, 1776); *South Carolina Gazette*, 9 June 1766, no. 1609; Dennys de Berdt (London) to Colonel White, 16 January 1766, Library Of Congress, MSS 18036; Charles Garth (London) to South Carolina Committee of Correspondence, 19 January 1766, William Clements Library, Charles Garth Letterbook, f. 163v; William Pitt, 14 January 1766; Richard Simmons and Peter Thomas, *Proceedings and Debates of the British Parliaments Respecting North America: 1754–1776*, 6 vols. (Millwood: Kraus International Publications, 1982), vol. 2, 81. For similar arguments in France, see Francois-Joseph Ruggiu, "India and the Re-Shaping of the French Colonial Policy (1759–1789)," *Itinerario*, 35, no. 2 (Aug. 2011): 25–43.

12 There is a vast literature on the Bourbon reforms, among the most recent
Allan J. Kuethe and Kenneth J. Andrien, *The Spanish Atlantic World in the
Eighteenth Century* (Cambridge: Cambridge University Press, 2014). See also
Jean Tarrade, *Le Commerce Colonial de la France à la fin de l'Ancien Regime*
(Paris: Presses Universitaire de France, 1972).

13 On civil war: Resolves of Frederick County, 8 June 1774, *Revolutionary
Virginia: The Road to Independence*, vol. 1, ed. Robert L. Scribner
(Charlottesville: University of Virginia Press), 136; Daniel Hulsebosch,
*Constituting Empire: New York and the Transformation of Constitutionalism
in the Atlantic World, 1664–1830* (Chapel Hill: University of North
Carolina Press, 2005), 145; Lords Dissenting to Address on the King's Speech,
26 October 1776, Simmons and Thomas, *Proceedings and Debates*, vol. 6, 73;
John Wilkes, 26 October 1775, Simmons and Thomas, *Proceedings
and Debates*, vol. 6, 97; James Duane (Philadelphia) to Peter Van Schaak,
2 October 1774, *Letters of Delegates to Congress, 1774–1789*, eds. Paul H.
Smith et al., 25 vols. (Washington: Library of Congress, 1976–2000), vol. 1,
136; Catherine Macaulay, *An Address to the People of England, Scotland and
Ireland*, 3rd ed. (New York: John Holt, 1775), 14; Jonathan Shipley to
Benjamin Franklin, June 1775, Benjamin Franklin Papers Online; Ezra Stiles
(Newport) to Isaac Karigal, 7 July 1775, Beinecke, MS Vault Stiles, Corresp.,
box 12; *Crisis*, no. LI, 6 January 1776; Temple Luttrell, 26 October 1775,
Simmons and Thomas, *Proceedings and Debates*, vol. 6, 112; Samuel
Johnson, *Taxation no Tyranny: An Answer to the Resolutions of the American
Congress* (London: Thomas Cadell, 1775), 68–69; Richard Rigby, 27 October
1775, Simmons and Thomas, *Proceedings and Debates*, vol. 6, 139; Thomas
Jefferson (Virginia) to William Small, 7 May 1775, *The Papers of Thomas
Jefferson Digital Edition, Main Series*, eds. Barbara B. Oberg and J. Jefferson
Looney (Charlottesville: University of Virginia Press, Rotunda, 2008–2016),
vol. 1, 165; Thomas Paine, *Common Sense*, 3rd ed. (London: J. Almon,
1776), 15–16, 23; George Washington (Philadelphia) to George William
Fairfax, 31 May 1775, *The Papers of George Washington Digital Edition,
Colonial Series*, ed. Theodore J. Crackel (Charlottesville: University of
Virginia Press, Rotunda, 2008), vol. 10, 368; Samuel Adams (Philadelphia)
to James Warren, 16 April 1776, *Letters of Delegates to Congress*, vol. 3, 530;
Richard Henry Lee (Philadelphia) to Landon Carter, 2 June 1776, *Letters of
Delegates to Congress*, vol. 4, 117; Abraham Clark (Philadelphia) to Elias
Dayton, 4 July 1776, *Letters of Delegates to Congress*, vol. 4, 376.

14 On Patriot political economy of empire in the later 1770s, in addition to
Smith, see, among others, Alexander Hamilton, "Full Vindication of the
Measures of Congress," 1774, p. 14; Richard Henry Lee, "Draft Address to
the People of Great Britain and Ireland," 11–18 October 1774, *Letters of
Delegates to Congress*, vol. 1, 177; Arthur Lee, *An Appeal to the Justice
and Interests of the People of Great Britain* (London: J. Almon, 1776), 39;
Benjamin Franklin, in *Public Advertiser*, 9 March 1774; Benjamin Franklin, in
Public Advertiser, 29 January 1770. "Our" in this sentence refers to
the British. Richard Price Observations, 1776, pp. 17, 27–29; Matthew
Robinson-Morris, Baron Rokeby, *Considerations on the Measures Carrying*

on with Respect to the British colonies in North America (London: R. Baldwin, 1774), 79; Steve Pincus, "1776: The Revolt against Austerity," *New York Review of Books: NYR Daily*, 20 May 2015, www.nybooks.com/daily/2015/ 05/20/1776-revolt-against-austerity/; Steve Pincus, *The Heart of the Declaration* (New Haven: Yale University Press, 2016), chaps. 2–3.

15 Washington, Circular, 8 June 1783, *The Writings of George Washington*, ed. John C. Fitzpatrick (Washington: Government Printing Office, 1938), vol. 26, 485; Ezra Stiles (Newport) to Philip Furneaux, 12 April 1775, Beinecke, MS Vault Stiles, Corresp., box 12; William Hooper (Philadelphia) to James Iredell, 6 January 1776, *Letters of Delegates to Congress*, vol. 3, 45. Here we take issue with the claims advanced in David Armitage, *The Declaration of Independence: A Global History* (Cambridge: Harvard University Press, 2007).

16 Guillaume Thomas François Raynal, *A Philosophical and Political History of the Settlements and Trade of the Europeans in the East and West Indies*, vol. 1, trans. J. Justamond (London: T. Cadell, 1776).

17 Smith, *Wealth of Nations*, vol. 2, 626.

18 The range of consequences of extra-European encounters has long been debated. See, for example, J.H. Elliott, *The Old World and the New, 1492–1650* (Cambridge: Cambridge University Press, 1970); Anthony Grafton, *New Worlds, Ancient Texts: The Power of Tradition and the Shock of Discovery* (Cambridge: Harvard University Press, 1992), and Stephen Greenblatt, *Marvelous Possessions: The Wonder of the New World* (Chicago: University of Chicago Press, 1992).

19 Karl Marx and Friedrich Engels, *The Communist Manifesto* (London: Penguin Classics, 2002 [1848]).

20 This mercantilist consensus has been described and criticized in a rash of recent publications: Istvan Hont, *Jealousy of Trade: International Competition and the Nation-State in Historical Perspective* (Cambridge: Harvard University Press, 2005); Philip J. Stern and Carl Wennerlind, eds., *Mercantilism Reimagined: Political Economy in Early Modern Britain and Its Empire* (New York: Oxford University Press, 2014); Sophus A. Reinert and Pernille Roge, eds., *The Political Economy of Empire in the Early Modern World* (Basingstoke: Palgrave Macmillan, 2013); Sophus A. Reinert, *Translating Empire: Emulation and the Origins of Political Economy* (Cambridge: Harvard University Press, 2011); Abigail Leslie Swingen, *Competing Visions of Empire: Labor, Slavery, and the Origins of the British Atlantic Empire* (New Haven: Yale University Press, 2015); Steve Pincus, "Rethinking Mercantilism," *William and Mary Quarterly*, 3rd ser., 69, no. 1 (Jan. 2012): 3–34.

21 John Locke, "Second Treatise of Government," in *Political Writings of John Locke*, ed. David Wootton (New York: Penguin Books, 1993), 281–82; Bernard Mandeville, *The Fable of the Bees* (London: J Roberts, 1714), 178–79.

22 Mandeville, *Fable*.

23 John Trenchard and Thomas Gordon, *Cato's Letters*, 5th ed. (London: T. Woodward et. al., 1748), 24 Feb. 1722, no. 67, 1748, 307; 8 Dec. 1722, no. 106, 1748, vol. IV, 6.

24 Marx and Engels, *Manifesto.*

25 W.E.B. Du Bois, *The Suppression of the African Slave Trade to the United States of America 1638–1870* (New York: Longmans and Co., 1896), 10. For more recent discussions of this theme, see Pincus, *Heart of the Declaration*; John Blanton, *This Species of Property: Slavery and Subjecthood in Anglo-American Law, 1619–1783*, PhD Thesis, CUNY (2015).

26 Karl Marx, *Capital: A Critique of Political Economy*, vol. 1, trans. Ben Fowke (New York: Penguin Classics, 2002 [1867]), part II, chap. 4.

27 Michael Löwy and Robert Sayre, *Romanticism against the Tide of Modernity* (Chapel Hill: Duke University Press, 2001), 18, quoted in Adams, Clemens, and Orloff, "Social Theory, Modernity, and the Three Waves of Historical Sociology," 13.

28 For a review and analysis of these seven sociological models, one of which is "racial recognition theory" condensed in the following, see Isaac Ariail Reed and Julia Adams, "Culture in the Transitions to Modernity: Seven Pillars of a New Research Agenda," *Theory & Society*, 40, issue 3: 247–72.

29 Ibid.

30 Silvia Sebastiani, *Scottish Enlightenment: Race, Gender and the Limits of Progress* (New York: Palgrave Macmillan, 2013); Tzvetan Todorov, *The Conquest of America: The Question of the Other*, trans. Richard Howard (New York: Harper & Row, 1984).

14

Making Legibility between Colony and Empire

Translation, Conflation, and the Making of the Muslim State

Iza Hussin

What does it mean to see like a state? James Scott's important and powerful *Seeing Like a State* locates the vantage point of the high modernist state far above those it seeks to order, govern, and alter, and makes clear that seeing like a state begins not with the act of seeing, but with efforts to render legible the incomprehensibility and unpredictability of everyday life. "Legibility is a condition of manipulation," and making legibility has long been at the core of the modern state.[1] Yet, looking beyond the totalitarian and monolithic panoramas of the high modernist state, it is possible to see that the effort to render legibility has not only been a top-down project, but is also an effort undertaken from below; legibility may indeed be a condition of manipulation, but it also confers benefits for those positioned to receive them. Through the lens of British colonial law, this chapter explores the making of legibility from two perspectives: that of Indian Muslim judges positioned between the colonial state and Indian Muslim society, seeking to deliver justice within the local context, and that of the imperial system, seeking to make sense of Islam and Muslim life at the end of the nineteenth century. The first rearticulated the place of Islam within colonial law; the second located Islam within a hierarchy and logic of imperial law in which elements of life seen as religious would be relegated to the realm of the private and the family. To see like a state, this chapter shows, more often than not involves translative and comparative work at many levels of abstraction. The ubiquity of translative and comparative dynamics in the work of the state suggests a need to envision the many hands of the state as informing the ways in which the state produced information, interpreted concepts and categories, and pronounced justice – many eyes, many optics, many voices.

Scholarship on the colonial state has long grappled with the question of the colonial state's ability to project its power from metropole to colony, seeking to understand the extent to which the colonial project imposed order, hierarchy, and difference from the center, despite its basic insufficiencies of military force, administrative capacity, and political legitimacy.[2] In the arena of colonialism and religion, where these insufficiencies were particularly dire, scholars have tended to emphasize the way in which the colonial state produced order and subjectivity, with religion itself becoming one department of the state among many.[3] Scholars working on secularism and the state have recently argued that when states define religion, they necessarily also order and confine it.[4] In these accounts, the state's ability to define, label, arrange, and order has generally been understood as an established part of its toolkit.[5] These tools, it is also understood, tend to have been applied toward the building of a unified vision and pattern extending uniformly across its domains, subservient to state ideological and political–economic concerns.[6] The state's unity of purpose, as well as its ability to enforce conformity to this purpose among the human actors and institutional complexes that comprise the state, remains a largely underexamined assumption.

This chapter seeks to examine the work of the British colonial state as it passed through the hands of its "native" middlemen in India – agents chosen to do the work of the state whose utility lay precisely in their position between state and subjects, whose local knowledge was undisputed, and whose positions "in between" required them to do crucial translative and comparative work between British and native societies. The work of these actors, both part of the colonial state and critically apart from it, unsettles the idea that the colonial state was able to seamlessly deliver policy outcomes as articulated at the top of the imperial hierarchy. Not only that, native middlemen such as the Indian Muslim judge at the center of this story worked to rearticulate the goals and meaning of colonial law to itself. In other words, the state's ability to define, label, arrange, and order – to make legibility – came not simply from the top or from the metropole, but was conditioned and altered from within the processes by which it ruled, and the strategic choices of the actors upon which it relied to rule. The colonial state, heavily dependent on the role of intermediaries and middlemen, presents many opportunities for empirical study of these dynamics, but these dynamics are omnipresent in state structures, and indicate rich ground for further exploration (see Chapter 4 for a study of how contemporary nonstate actors render economies legible to investors).[7]

The second half of the nineteenth century saw epistemic and political processes through which both local and colonial elites sought comparability and ubiquity, processes with trans-regional and trans-imperial reach. The late nineteenth century saw the emergence of newly capacious categories of law, not just in India, but across empires and continents – personal status law, family law, religious law, customary law. These became indispensable components of the modern state's tool chest, but were neither wholly state inventions nor durable legacies from the past. In concluding, I present an argument for further exploration and investigation – that the dynamics of translation, comparison, and mediation that we see in cases such as *Ramzan*, in the following, lent themselves to powerful and productive imperial conflations – between Islamic law and personal status law, between family law and the law of the private sphere, among others – whose legacies endure in the contemporary state.

TRANSLATION AND CONFLATION: FROM THE COLONIAL TO THE IMPERIAL

The two perspectives on legibility offered in this chapter – that of native judges in colonial courts, and that of developing categories of law across the British Empire – highlight differences between the ways that the colonial and the imperial state worked toward making legibility. The role of native intermediaries in multiple domains of the state marks the existence and importance of spaces of difference within empires and colonies. As Steinmetz observes, critical analytic and empirical questions remain as to the "distinct species of symbolic capital" involved in these spaces, the struggles they engendered, and the particularities of each of these micro-fields.[8] Steinmetz argues, "even where native authorities controlled some aspects of decision making they operated according to customary legal codes approved by the foreign authorities";[9] this chapter suggests that the symbolic economy of colonial legal spheres required the presence of native judges, whose position in between led to systematic and iterated renegotiations of the very rules of the colonial game. Yet the nature of the symbolic capital controlled by these native actors – not functionaries of the state, not executors of policy, but active interpreters and makers of the rules of the colonial state – was over time to quite radically alter the workings and meanings of Islam in colonial law, and networks and strategies among actors across the empire would contribute to the redefinition of "Muslim" and Islamic law.

As Morgan and Orloff argue in the Introduction to this volume, the state project is multiple and contradictory; these spaces of difference and the agents whose work defined and bridged them were many, even common, in the colonial state. The binding of "subjects into their own subjection," to which Morgan and Orloff refer, involves give and take by both the state and its subjects, and this essay seeks to further explore the agency of the state by thinking about the work its agents do as interlocutors between communities and the state.[10] In the colonial courts of British India, for example, a key element of this work was to *translate* local particularity into idioms recognizable to the British legal system. One outcome of this translative work was to describe Indian Muslims in terms familiar to Anglican Christians. The work of achieving imperial legibility, on the other hand, while relying upon knowledge gained from colonial settings, also involved abstracting beyond particular local contexts, toward a more comprehensive view. In the imperial sphere, a key element of legal reasoning was to seek out ways in which Muslim subjects of empire could be seen as a group comparable to Anglicans, Hindus, and others. One outcome of this work was *conflation*: making previously different areas of life and law equivalent and making possible a regime of law labeled "personal status," covering newly defined domains of marriage, the family, and private life. Here, too, critical roles were played by Muslims seeking to make themselves legible to imperial states and here, too, the effort at legibility was driven also by the varied interests of Muslim actors, not all of them aligned with the interests of the state.

Noting the indispensability of interlocutors, interpreters, and translators in the work of the state allows a rethinking of sovereign state acts, and of institutional change, that shows evidence of institutional borrowing, echoes of past forms and logics, and hybrid discourses of legitimacy. Against the totalizing vision that Scott attributed to the high modern state, therefore, is another way of seeing like a state, by necessity as well as by design: rather than state logic imposed from above, projecting a nonhuman scale onto political and social life, there is the more common pastiche cobbled together out of the reality of state projects built piece by piece, moment by moment. Political scientists and sociologists have discussed these phenomena under different headings: Streeck and Thelen have focused on "displacement" and "layering" in institutional change;[11] Espeland and Stevens refer to the political work of commensuration, on its ability to "refract power in many ways," and on its key role in the making of modern subjects and states.[12] The anthropologist Susan Gal has commented on the phenomenon of "apparent familiarity" across institutions that comes into being through processes of standard-ization and fractal recursion along hierarchies and "axes of differenti-ation."[13] Morgan and Campbell's exploration of delegated governance seeks to more precisely delineate the boundaries of the state between public and private actors.[14] In the case of British India, but also in nation-states that govern religious and cultural minorities, delegation delineated spaces of difference within the public sphere as well. The civil servants who served in these spaces were often privileged members of subject groups as well as state agents, part of the state because of their utility as middlemen, but subject to scrutiny and suspicion because of their status as members of target communities.

THE BENEFITS OF LEGIBILITY: TRANSLATING ISLAM IN COLONIAL COURTS

Building on the analytic utility of the "many hands" paradigm, this chapter focuses on a legal judgment from British India, *Queen-Empress v. Ramzan & Ors* (March 7, 1885), a case that revolved around questions of how to define a Muslim, and who had the right to do so.[15] This case bears the standard hallmarks of colonial processes of state-making: the work of defining the subjects of colonial authority, labeling the targets of administrative intervention, and arranging them according to a predeter-mined hierarchy of value, aimed at the production of social and political order for the colonial state. Yet here, where the matter at hand was the definition of "Muslim" with respect to worship in mosques, the judge himself – Syed Mahmood – was an Indian Muslim, and his role in deciding the case was explicitly tied to his knowledge of Islam. The judgment argued for a more prominent role for Islamic legal sources and reasoning within the legal system of British India, while at the same time working to make Islam legible in terms of Anglican Christianity. By virtue of their positions between the colonial state and its subjects, intermediary actors such as Mahmood played both a structural and an interpretive role; in doing its work, the state's many hands also routinely question its norms, interpret its knowledge in light of their own, and alter its course.

The original conflict referred to in the *Ramzan* case occurred in a mosque in Benares in 1884: three men, among them Ramzan, entered the mosque and pronounced the word *amin* (amen) during prayer, a practice regarded by some other congregants as heterodox.[16] A heated argument ensued about whether this was permitted during prayers, and the three were expelled from the mosque with the help of police and prohibited from entering again unless they recanted their position on this practice. Ramzan and the others were accused by other members of the mosque of not being Muslim, and of "the offence of insulting the religion of the Hanafia Musalmans" under Sections 297, 298, and 352 of the Indian Penal Code (1860). The Magistrate tried the case and found the three guilty under Section 296 ("disturbing religious assembly") and sentenced them to a fine or a month's imprisonment, based on the interpretation that saying *amin* loudly during prayers in a mosque constituted causing disturbance to religious worship and was therefore a criminal offence. Eventually the case reached the Allahabad High Court and was heard by a bench that included Judge Syed Mahmood (1850–1903). On the face of it, the case turned on whether saying *amin* could be understood to constitute an offence under the Indian Penal Code, of disturbing religious assembly; underneath the facts of the case were issues of congregational politics, of possible financial misconduct, and of doctrinal differences used to draw a line between those who were considered Muslim and those not. Mahmood was ultimately to argue that a Muslim had the right to worship in a mosque "according to his tenets," and that it was not a criminal offence to say *amin* in a mosque.[17]

It would seem a small point, a small case, except that Mahmood built upon the facts of the case a foundation for enlarging the scope of application of Islamic law in British India, based on the argument that "Muhammadan Ecclesiastical Law" needed to be consulted in cases such as these. In fact, he argued, "the Muhammadan Law shall be administered with reference to all questions regarding 'any religious usage or institution.'"[18] The manner by which he made this argument was to render Islam and Muslim worship comparable to Anglican Christianity. Through cases such as *Ramzan*, the "Indian Muslim" was made legible as a category in law comparable to the "Christian," as was the "Hindu"; the mosque and temple were understood as spaces equivalent to churches, and the activities performed in them categorized as "worship." Cases such as these allow a closer look at the involvement of local agents in epistemic and political processes, delineating processes through which the state sought to produce comparability and ubiquity across its domains, and suggesting that these processes were themselves translative and comparative, dialogical rather than unidirectional. This is not to say that the political economy of colonial institutions was balanced between colonizer and colonized, nor that outcomes were egalitarian; it is, however, to see these middlemen as themselves having interests and worldviews that remained important even as they did the work of the state they served.

Further, a closer examination of these cases shows that these middlemen – not merely translators, scribes, and expert witnesses producing raw material for British adjudication but judges and lawyers with delegated responsibility for the making of British justice – played critical roles in making space for "native" sources of law and legal reasoning. In *Ramzan*, the judge argued against the established hierarchy and practice of English common law in British India, in favor of a broader application of Islamic law. Intrinsic to the making of British colonial law were Indian judges whose positions between colonizer and colonized gave them the legitimacy and knowledge to perform their functions, an interest in expanding the space allowed for certain "native" institutions beyond what the colonial state envisioned, and a desire to make these institutions legible and credible within the colonial context. From the perspective of law and its politics, even the state's "projection" of a unified image required a multiplicity of lenses and optics, many hands from the start.[19] Rather than seeing this multiplicity as deviation from the norm of the state, dysfunction, or malfunction, the many hands and eyes of the colonial state helped produce durable transformations in law and society, in what it meant to govern Muslims, and in what it would mean to be Muslim.

By the middle of the nineteenth century, British colonial rule in India depended – more and more openly – upon the participation of Indians in administrative and institutional capacities. This dependence was twofold: first, on the lack of material capacity to administer a huge state with a relatively small number of British officials, and second, on the vision of legitimate colonial governance as proxy and tutelage for native rule. When the British Crown took over the government of India from the East India Company in 1858, the symbolic importance of rule of law, and the need to demonstrate the legitimacy of British rule in India, gave local intermediaries and authorities a critical role to play in indirect rule.[20] With the 1857 revolt clearly in mind, religion was marked out as a domain needing particular care.[21] The role of Indians in the British colonial state machinery was critical, and their difference from the colonial administrator was a key component of their utility and visibility in the state.

The aftermath of the revolt removed many aristocrats, religious leaders, and elites associated with long-standing institutions of Indian Islam from positions of influence in British India. This cleared the field for a rising class of British-educated men such as Syed Ahmad Khan (1817–1898), Faiz Badruddin Tyabji (1844–1906), Syed Ameer Ali

(1849–1928), Abdur Rahim (1867–1962), and Asaf Ali Asghar Fyzee (1899–1981) to become interlocutors between the colonial state and Indian Muslims.[22] Judge Mahmood was the son of Syed Ahmad Khan, a close ally of the British in India as well as a fierce proponent of the advancement of the Indian Muslim community. The first Indian Muslim appointed to a High Court judgeship in British India, Mahmood studied in schools established by the British in India before receiving a scholarship from the British to study law in England. Mahmood was admitted to Lincoln's Inn in 1869 and soon after became the first non-European member of the Allahabad Bar.[23] The institutionalization of Islamic law within the ambit of state courts and the increasing reliance on the logics and language of colonial legality meant that Muslim lawyers trained in European law, such as Syed Mahmood, began increasingly to play important intermediary roles in interpreting Islamic law within the legal idiom of the colonial state. These lawyers performed their functions assured of the basic unassailability of English legal logic, largely untrained in matters of *fiqh* (Islamic jurisprudence) and Islamic legal practice, yet they saw the courts and legal processes themselves as venues for the advancement of Muslim identity and strategy.

Muslims newly incorporated into the legal hierarchy of British India were not only called upon to judge matters of the law relating to religious usages and institutions, they were also often pressed to define who a Muslim was, and what the proper conduct of Muslim worship and religious observance should be. In *Ramzan*, as in other cases, Judge Mahmood was called into the case because he was Muslim and knew the "Muhammadan Ecclesiastical Law." When the case reached the Allahabad High Court, Mahmood noted, "in view of the peculiarities of the question with regard to the right of worshipping in mosques possessed by Muhammadans, my learned brother referred the case to a Division Bench, of which, at his suggestion, and with the approval of the learned Chief Justice, I was to be a member."[24] Once on the Bench, at several points, Mahmood questioned or steered the process of the trial. From the Division Bench, the case was referred to the Full Bench "to obtain an authoritative ruling on the question"; from the Full Bench, Mahmood reserved his order, refusing to either concur in or dissent from the decision to uphold the conviction.

For Judge Mahmood, the Bench ruling was problematic not only because of the absence of "the authorities of Muhammadan Law" in the details and reasoning of the judgment, but because of the general principle upon which this absence was justified. "If it is conceded that the decision of this case depends (as I shall presently endeavor to show it does depend) upon the interpretation of the Muhammadan Ecclesiastical Law, it is to my mind the duty of this Court, and of all courts subordinate to it, to take judicial notice of such law."[25] He finally provided a written dissenting opinion that was printed in the India Law Report of 1885. After 1875, cases published in the India Law Reports were binding on all subordinate courts in British India; the Reports published about 300 of Judge Mahmood's opinions, lengthy pieces of legal scholarship that also included, translated, and interpreted Arabic jurisprudential sources, thereby making them usable throughout British India as sources of law.[26] His opinion in the *Ramzan* case was a separate ruling, dissenting from the judgment made by the full bench, but became one of the most-cited and influential rulings about the use of mosques, disputes over the diversity of Muslim conduct, and the right of Muslims to worship according to their conscience. In later years, this judgment would also be cited to defend the rights of members of minority sects of Islam to claim their right of access to mosques, and their rights to be treated as Muslims under the law.[27]

Judge Mahmood argued that the matter of the case, which was "the right of a Muhammadan being able to pray in a mosque according to his tenets," required reference to the "express guarantee given by the Legislature in Section 24 of the Bengal Civil Courts Act (VI of 1871), that the Muhammadan law shall be administered with reference to all questions regarding 'any religious usage or institution.'" Mahmood argued that, by this reasoning, even courts applying criminal law should take notice of the interpretation of "Muhammadan Ecclesiastical Law" as part of "the rules of civil law":

That the application of some of the sections of the Indian Penal Code depends almost entirely upon the correct interpretation of the rules of civil law, cannot, in my opinion, be doubted ... but for this principle, the rules of the Penal Code would in many cases operate as a great injustice.[28]

Further, Judge Mahmood argued that Muhammadan law should not be equated with foreign law in cases such as these, providing a potentially expansive rationale for reference to Islamic legal sources more generally:

I hold therefore that in a case like the present ... Muhammadan Ecclesiastical Law ... is not to be placed upon the same footing with reference to this matter as any foreign law ... and it follows that I can refer to the Muhammadan Ecclesiastical Law for the purposes of this case, notwithstanding the absence of any specific evidence on the record regarding its rules.[29]

Mahmood used the institution of precedent and the citational practices of British law to bring Islamic legal logic and texts back into the legal system of British India. His legal legacy sheds some light on how Muslim elites navigated colonial institutions of law to bring shar'i content back into the system. Whereas the earlier replacement of *fiqh* experts with legal texts in colonial law courts served to reify Islamic law into a limited and somewhat static domain, Muslim lawyers and judges working in the colonial law courts in the late-nineteenth and early-twentieth centuries found ways of turning this reliance on text and precedent to their advantage.[30] These elites actively participated in the new institutions of colonial law, and their presence provided a visible signal of the legitimacy and justice of the colonial state, at the same time that their actions within these institutions continued to negotiate the state's boundaries. In particular, despite their acceptance of the forms of colonial rule, its logics, and its jurisdiction, they continued to negotiate the boundaries of Islamic law and struggled to retain shariah content and logics, using the new institutional avenues of the colonial law system.

THE EFFECTS OF TRANSLATION: "SCRIPTURALIST ISLAM"

Yet the participation of British-trained lawyers and judges in the courts of British India also profoundly altered the content and meaning of Islam in the legal system. It is here that a focus on the *many hands* of the state also allows deeper exploration into its *many optics* – the institutional inclusion of Indian Muslims in the legal system of British India made possible a renegotiation of the place and content of Islam in the law, but their inclusion also transformed the ways in which Islam would be understood, both by the state and by Muslims themselves. The optics of the state depend upon the perceptions and strategies of its key agents: here, Judge Mahmood translated the case of *Ramzan* according to the vernacular of British India, that included a value system based upon Anglican Christianity and a legal hierarchy of canonical texts, all the while acknowledging an underlying tension with the methods and logic of Sunni Islamic jurisprudence. Ultimately, the work of British-trained lawyers and judges such as Mahmood, working within the system to enlarge the jurisdiction of Islamic law, would bring about a system of law that prioritized canonical text over learned debate, precedent over judicial reasoning, and located the proper domain of Islam over the narrower arena of family law and ritual matters. This "scripturalist Islam"[31] translated Islamic legal institutions, logics, and texts into the idiom of Anglican Christianity, and Islamic law into the language and order of common law, and would in time help to answer an expectation among British judges and jurists that Islam in a Muslim state could occupy the same place as Christianity in England.

Mahmood was neither a scholar of *fiqh* nor a lawyer trained in Islamic adjudication, rather, he was "an Islamic modernist committed to individual interpretation of sacred texts with limited attention to the historical traditions of commentators."[32] Instead of *fiqh* experts serving as advisors and witnesses, increasingly, British-trained Muslim judges functioned as knowledgeable arbiters of Islamic legal issues in the courts of British India and generated a significant amount of authoritative law in multiple arenas – including who should be considered a Muslim, how worship in a mosque should be conducted, and how to understand the relationship between Muslim practice in India and the authoritative texts of Islamic law. Like Judge Mahmood, they brought with them a new orientation toward the sources and logic of the shariah and an acceptance of the jurisdictional divisions and some of the assumptions of British law in India. This new orientation included a reliance on textual sources, a preoccupation with making Islamic law legible in British terms, and an interest in articulating the logic of Islamic jurisprudence in ways that would endure in the British system. A primary element of the reorientation of the practice of Islamic law in the courts of British India was the demonstration of a methodology for determining the content of Muslim practice, tradition, and orthodoxy, and to make that methodology both usable in the courts and relatable to other sources of colonial law. To this end, having made an argument that the Muhammadan Ecclesiastical Law must be referred to in cases of this type, it remained the task of the judge to determine which texts and practices mattered. Mahmood determined that "orthodox" in this case referred to Sunni practice and the schools of Sunni jurisprudence, despite the presence of non-Sunni Muslims in India. Within this orthodoxy, he arranged an order of authoritative legal texts, situating particular texts of the Sunni Hanafi school of jurisprudence, the British translation and compilation of the *Hidaya* primary among them, at the top of the hierarchy of jurisprudential sources to consult.[33]

A second element of this reorientation was translation, making Islam and the content of Muslim religiosity fully legible in Anglo-Christian terms. Mahmood's arguments about the relationship between authoritative Islamic texts, Muslim practice, and orthodoxy were based on an assumption that Islam is comparable to Christianity, Anglicanism in particular, and that his audience would be persuaded to his point of view more readily if they understood this comparability. He referred from the beginning of his judgment to "the Muhammadan Ecclesiastical Law,"[34] which in his argument means the "Koran," "Sunna" and the teachings of the four schools of Sunni *fiqh*; at other points he referred to four "orthodox schools of Muhammadan Ecclesiastical Law," thereby equating Sunni *fiqh* with church law. He referred to mosques as having "congregations" and being "consecrated"; in attempting to determine whether the alleged offences were actually committed during worship, he compared Muslim prayers with the reading of the Nicene creed. The word *amin* itself "has been adopted in prayers by Muhammadans as much as by Christians."[35] The only point of distinction he drew was to comment that unlike "an ordinary Christian church," mosques were also places for "religious and moral teaching and discussion."[36]

Mahmood was careful in his jurisprudence to preserve some elements of divergence between Islamic jurisprudence and British – he acknowledged the prevalence of debate in Islamic jurisprudence and the need for consensus on matters not clearly enunciated in the Koran, and went on to list the opinions of jurists in the Hanafi and Shafi'i school, noting that while the Malikis and Hanbalis would concur on this issue, their opinions were not pertinent because "their followers do not exist in British India."[37] Mahmood also referred to the wider world of Muslim practice, tying the Muslims of India to a hinterland beyond British control, referring for example to the practices of Muslims at the Kaaba ("the greatest mosque in the world") and "all the Muhammadan countries like Turkey, Egypt, and Arabia itself," where the practice of saying *amin* was varied but not controversial. Finally, and with prescience, Mahmood's judgment made clear that determinations as to the proper and lawful conduct of Muslim worship needed to be sensitive to the rights of the minority *within* a religious group. He argued that the Public Prosecutor's opinion that "the mere fact of the disturbance being caused to the religious assembly is sufficient to constitute the offence"[38] placed undue emphasis on Section 296, valuing maintenance of peace above the right of individuals to worship according to their tenets.

Mahmood's arguments and his method of reasoning the case show a keen awareness of the potential breadth of his audience, and they allow a glimpse into the "intimate interaction of legal administration and indigenous identity formation" that helped inscribe "scripturalist Islam" in the Muslim state.[39] In doing so, they help show that indigenous identity formation was a process in which particular local elites played critical mediating roles, and they reveal the logic by which scripturalist Islam appealed to both Muslims and British actors in the late nineteenth century.[40] They also show that this translative logic was seen to be enormously important for communicating the content and meaning of Islamic jurisprudence to a common law audience. In Mahmood's words, "I have mentioned all this in order to render intelligible what I am going to say presently," with regard to the content of the case, but the need for intelligibility, when articulated within the medium of the law, also had far-reaching effects for Islamic law itself.

IMPERIAL CONFLATIONS: PERSONAL STATUS LAW AS "RELIGION"

British-trained Muslim lawyers such as Judge Mahmood, working within the colonial state, helped to redefine the shariah as Muslim personal law through the legislation and precedential systems of the courts of British India.[41] This had the effect of turning a colonial domain of governance into an arena for the assertion of a distinct Indian Muslim community interest; however, it also fundamentally altered the scope and meaning of Islamic law in British India.[42] From a wide-ranging system of laws and institutions with jurisdiction over politics, society, and the state, the shariah redefined as laws of Muslim personal status came to govern only matters of marriage, divorce, religious endowments, and ritual observance. Cases such as *Ramzan* show how, from a narrowly prescribed realm of colonial law, Muslim judges and lawyers worked through common law processes and reasoning to expand the jurisdiction of Islam. They did so, however, in ways that were legible to the colonial state, and translatable within the idiom of colonial law. Across the British Empire, Muslims attempting to make themselves legible to the colonial state were using the vehicle of law to assert a Muslim interest; by the end of the nineteenth century, in India, Egypt, Malaya, and elsewhere, diverse regimes of local and Islamic legal practices were rendered legible to the empire as "Muslim personal status law."

From the perspective of the rising class of Muslim administrative and political elites in British India, the codification and regularization of laws governing Muslim life represented a number of opportunities: to widen the space allowed for native practices within British law in India, to give some shariah practices the status of established law, to clarify and regularize that law, and to make possible their own participation and intervention in this legal sphere – as lawyers, authoritative interpreters, advocates, and members of a rising "Indian Muslim" community. From the perspective of British colonial administrators and judges in India, the codification and regularization of laws relating to Muslims reduced confusion in the courts and made the administration of justice more regular and reliable, in particular by removing the amount of leeway provided to expert witnesses and to interpretation of Islamic jurisprudential sources. Codification and regularization also carried the added benefit of reducing the complexity and diversity of practices and authoritative rules that might have applied to native subjects, by applying one marker of identity above all others – religion. The Muslims of India would have one kind of law applied to them, regardless of their differences of language, region, sect, or traditional practice; a similar unification would apply to the Hindus and Christians of India. British conceptions of "communities" divided by religious affiliation after 1857 in India prompted law reforms based on legal pluralism; after the 1880s, in particular, claims for political representation by Indians came to be articulated in terms of communal representation.[43]

As conflicts in the courts over the proper interpretation of Islam continued, the effort to communicate Islamic law and Muslim practice as comparable to, and legible in terms of, Christianity also contributed to an understanding of the religions of British India as occupying similar spheres of life and representing equivalent confessional communities. The administration of justice in the courts and the legislative process reinforced the understanding that Indians were divisible into two fundamental communities – Hindu and Muslim – and that politics could not but be structured along these lines. Legal reforms in the early twentieth century (1909 Indian Councils Act, known as the Morley-Minto reforms), articulated as giving over more power to natives in government, also responded to concerns among Muslim elites that their interests be protected as minorities through electoral representation. The colonial category of personal status law – law applying to subjects based upon confessional identity – therefore became conflated, in British India, with a domain of Islamic law first defined by the colonial state, but later taken on and expanded by Muslim elites themselves – laws of marriage, the family, and ritual observance. This conflation further reinforced delineations of public and private domains in the administration of law and the governance of religion, such that the private would overlap with the religious, and the religious with the communal. From the end of the nineteenth century onward, moves to increase Indian participation in government also further entrenched the dichotomy and tension between Hindu and Muslim communities.

Looking beyond India also helps make clear how colonial understandings of Islam and Muslim subjects were shaped by imperial experiences and concerns, and how empires learned from other empires how Muslims were defined and how to govern them. At the same time Britain's Muslim subjects in India were working to make themselves legible to the colonial state as a community based on confessional identity, in Egypt, Muslims who had previously been governed by Ottoman and French law were coming under the rule of the British Empire. The meeting, in Egypt, of British common law approaches to the governing of Muslims with Ottoman and French civil law practices and institutions contributed further to the conflation of personal law with personal status.[44] The movement of colonial officials between British India and Egypt in the later decades of the nineteenth century was also a significant network for the importation of "Indian" ideas into the administration of Egypt.[45] In Egypt, all this resulted, at the end of the nineteenth century, in efforts at legal reform in which Islamic legal content would largely be elaborated within the confines of *"al-Ahkam al-Shar'iyya fi al-Ahwal al-Shakhsiyya,"* "shari'ah laws in matters of personal status," referring largely to family law.[46]

In Egypt, the French state inherited an Ottoman system that differentiated among imperial subjects by confessional identity, drawing from the Ottoman imperial system of *millet* (in which recognized minority groups in the Ottoman Empire, such as Christians and Jews, could govern according to their own laws) and from the system of mixed and native courts imposed by European powers upon Egypt. Egyptian elites redefined a realm of Islamic legal practice that would overlap with these inherited legal classifications and, like their counterparts in India, sought to define this realm in order to preserve the latitude of Islamic legal reasoning while negotiating the boundaries of the colonial state. By the time the British took over the administration of Egypt, they inherited an evolving imperial consensus that communities were divided by religious identity, that at the heart of religious identity were matters of ritual and the family, and that both ritual and family matters were to be understood as private matters.

Across the British imperial world during this period, in fact, there were increasing similarities within Muslim communities in response to the encroachment of British law.[47] These strategies were twofold: local Muslim elites often accepted, and at times expanded upon, colonial categorizations of Islamic law as pertaining only to a narrow private domain of family, personal status, and ritual worship, but at the same time they continued to assert and renegotiate the proper division between matters of Islam and matters of the state, including the meaning and scope of Islam as articulated by British colonial law.[48] They mark a convergence between previously quite separate logics and institutional bases, due to the assumption by imperial officials that the principles for governing Muslims in India would translate to the Muslims of Egypt or Malaya, and to an increasing interest among varied Muslim elites to articulate Islam in ways that would be legible to the British, and translatable across multiple domains. Over the *longue durée* of British colonialism and imperialism, the religious and the private realm were co-constituted over the Muslim family, in the institutionalization of personal status law.[49] In British India in the 1770s, personal law referred to differential jurisdictions, as laws applied depending upon membership in religious communities: Hindu laws for Hindus, Muslim laws for Muslims. By the time the formulation was instituted in Egypt as al-Ahkam al-Shar'iyya fi al-Ahwal al-Shakhsiyya, the "personal" in personal law carried two meanings – the first tied to communal affiliation, the second to the individual as a unit of administrative control, recognizable across the empire by the signifier "Muslim."[50] This understanding of Islamic law as centrally focused on family and private matters, and of religious identity as centrally located in the domains of marriage, gender, and ritual observance, endures in the legal systems of many contemporary Muslim and non-Muslim states.

TRANSLATIONS AND CONFLATIONS IN THE MAKING OF THE MUSLIM STATE

The routinized and iterated work of making legibility at various levels of the state, made possible and ubiquitous through the translative and comparative functions of courts and jurisprudence, contributed to the making of the Indian colonial state as well as the British imperial state, and on the way contributed to a radical transformation of Islamic law and its relation to Muslim life. A closer look at legal institutions, often understood as the linchpin of state power and sovereignty, reveals the work of middlemen whose roles were indispensable to the legitimacy, authority, and functioning of the state precisely because of their positions as part of the communities they helped govern. Yet these middle positions also provided state actors with the resources and interest to advocate for and realize change in state institutions, toward the incorporation of alternate (and sometimes conflicting) sources and logics of law and practice. The agency of the state, when the work of middlemen such as Muslim judges in British India is taken into account, is complex, working to change state logics at the same time that it reaches toward the extension of state power. State agency, enacted through networks of law, religion, and culture, also extends beyond its borders, articulating areas of contrast and familiarity across imperial, regional, and global polities and further reinforcing categorical conflations such as that between religious law and personal law, family law and private law.

Rather than assuming either the vision of the colonial state or its hierarchies, this chapter has sought to explore the implications of *many eyes, many optics, many voices* of the state, in the making of information, rules, and law. The preoccupation of the state has, by and large, not been to suppress these multiplicities, but to translate and compare among them. To see like a state, this chapter has argued, especially like a colonial and imperial state, is to seek out comparison and translation, areas of legibility that may then become bases for manipulation as well as extrapolation. While it is often assumed that the state dictates a vision from above that its agents seek to realize, a closer exploration of the work of middlemen and intermediaries suggests that this drive for comparison was also generated by the need for legibility from below. Further, this drive for legibility was itself motivated by interests to renegotiate the knowledge, norms, and mission of the state. When the imperial state is held distinct from the colonial state, it also becomes clear that states often see through each other's eyes, inheriting institutions, languages, and practices from each other and reworking them in multiple venues. The many hands of the state do not merely point us in the direction of rethinking the state's agency or its unity as an actor; they also indicate the work of multiple interpreters, interlocutors, and agents *as* the work of the state.

Notes

Thanks are due to Ann Orloff and Kimberly Morgan for their comments on a number of drafts of this chapter, and to Kapil Raj, Sanjay Subrahmanyam, and colleagues at the École des Hautes Études en Sciences Sociales (EHESS, Paris) for their very constructive and helpful comments on portions of this work, presented as part of my tenure as Professeur Invitée at EHESS (Spring 2015).

1 James Scott, *Seeing Like a State: How Certain Schemes to Improve the Human Condition Have Failed*, (New Haven: Yale University Press, 1999), 183.
2 Ranajit Guha, *Dominance without Hegemony: History and Power in Colonial India* (Cambridge: Harvard University Press, 1998).
3 Talal Asad, *Genealogies of Religion: Discipline and Reasons of Power in Christianity and Islam* (Baltimore: Johns Hopkins University Press, 1993).

4 Winifred Sullivan, *The Impossibility of Religious Freedom* (Princeton: Princeton University Press, 2005); Elizabeth Hurd, *The Politics of Secularism in International Relations* (Princeton: Princeton University Press, 2008); Wael Hallaq, *The Impossible State: Islam, Politics, and Modernity's Moral Predicament* (New York: Columbia University Press, 2013).

5 Discussing contemporary religion and fundamentalisms, Olivier Roy has referred to the process in which the state standardizes religions as "formatting." *Holy Ignorance: When Religion and Culture Part Ways* (New York: Columbia University Press, 2010), 187–91.

6 See Chapter 15. Exceptions include Lauren Benton, *A Search for Sovereignty: Law and Geography in European Empires, 1400–1900* (Cambridge: Cambridge University Press 2010).

7 Michel de Certeau, *The Practice of Everyday Life* (Berkeley: University of California Press, 1984); Joel Migdal, *State in Society: Studying How States and Societies Transform and Constitute Each Other* (Cambridge: Cambridge University Press 2001); Bruno Latour, *The Making of Law: An Ethnography of the Conseil d'Etat*,(Cambridge: Polity Press 2009); James Mahoney and Kathleen Thelen, eds., *Explaining Institutional Change: Ambiguity, Agency, and Power* (Cambridge: Cambridge University Press 2010).

8 Chapter 15.

9 Chapter 15.

10 Philip Abrams, "Notes on the Difficulty of Studying the State," *Journal of Historical Sociology* 1, no. 1 (1988 [1977]): 68.

11 *Beyond Continuity: Institutional Change in Advanced Political Economies* (New York: Oxford University Press 2005), 19–24.

12 "Commensuration as a Social Process," *Annual Review of Sociology*, 24 (1998): 332, 339.

13 "Sociolinguistic Regimes and the Management of 'Diversity,'" in *Language in Late Capitalism: Pride and Profit*, eds. Alexandre Duchene and Monica Heller (New York: Routledge), 22–42.

14 Kimberly J. Morgan and Andrea Louise Campbell, *The Delegated Welfare State: Medicare, Markets, and the Governance of Social Policy* (New York: Oxford, 2011).

15 *Indian Law Reports Allahabad series* (Government Press, 1885), 461.

16 Alan Guenther, "A Colonial Court Defines a Muslim," in *Islam in South Asia in Practice*, ed. Barbara Metcalf (Princeton: Princeton University Press, 2009), 293–304.

17 *Indian Law Reports Allahabad series* (Government Press, 1885), 461, at 13.

18 *Indian Law Reports Allahabad series* (Government Press, 1885), 461, at 7.

19 Migdal, *State in Society.*

20 Karuna Mantena, *Alibis of Empire: Henry Maine and the Ends of Liberal Imperialism* (Princeton: Princeton University Press, 2010).

21 Iza Hussin, *The Politics of Islamic Law: Local Elites, Colonial Authority and the Making of the Muslim State* (Chicago: University of Chicago Press, 2016).

22 Asaf Fyzee, *Outlines of Muhammadan Law* (Delhi: Oxford, 1974), 51.

23 The Honourable Society of Lincoln's Inn, through which barristers would be called to the English Bar. Guenther, "Colonial Court," 294.

24 *Indian Law Reports Allahabad series* (Government Press, 1885), 461 at 1.

25 *Indian Law Reports Allahabad series* (Government Press, 1885), 461 at 7.

26 Guenther "Colonial Court," 295. Guenther argues convincingly that the Law Reports Act of 1875 had the unintended consequence of creating a new source of Muslim law.

27 *Ata-Ullah v. Azim-Ullah, Indian Law Reports Allahabad series* (Government Press, 1890), 494; *Hakim Khalil Ahmad v. Malik Israfi, Patna Law Journal* (1917), 108.

28 *Indian Law Reports Allahabad series* (Government Press, 1885), 461 at 7.

29 Ibid.

30 Guenther, "Colonial Court," 293–304.

31 Michael Anderson, "Islamic Law and the Colonial Encounter in British India," in *Institutions and Ideologies: A SOAS South Asia Reader*, eds. David and Peter Robb Arnold (London: Curzon, 1993), 165–85.

32 Guenther, "Colonial Court," 294.

33 The *Hedaya* was Charles Hamilton's (d. 1792) translated and truncated version of a key compendium of jurisprudence from the Hanafi school of law, *al-Hidaya* [The Guide], used as an authorized source of Islamic law in the courts of British India. Mahmood cited Hamilton's preface to his "translation of the Hedaya," which Mahmood defines as "the most celebrated textbook of the Hanafi school of law," (13) before discussing the conflicting opinions of commentators found within the hadith collections of Bukhari and Muslim.

34 *Indian Law Reports Allahabad series* (Government Press, 1885), 461 at 1.

35 Ibid., 461 at 11.

36 Ibid., 461 at 17.

37 Ibid., 461 at 13.

38 Ibid., 461 at 18.

39 Anderson, "Islamic Law."

40 Cf. Ebrahim Moosa, "Colonialism and Islamic Law," in *Islam and Modernity: Key Issues and Debates*, eds. Masud, Salvatore, and van Bruinessen, 166.

41 Hussin, *Politics of Islamic Law.*

42 Scott Kugle, "Framed, Blamed and Renamed: The Recasting of Islamic Jurisprudence in Colonial South Asia," *Modern Asian Studies* 35, no. 2, (May 2001): 257–313.

43 Hussin, *Politics of Islamic Law.*

44 Guido Tedeschi, "Personal Status and Statut Personnel," *McGill Law Journal* 15, no. 3 (1969): 452–64.

45 Robert L. Tignor, "The 'Indianization' of the Egyptian Administration under British Rule," *The American Historical Review* 68, no. 3 (April 1963): 636–61; Thomas Metcalf, *Imperial Connections: India in the Indian Ocean Arena, 1860–1920* (Berkeley: University of California Press, 2008).

46 Hussin, *Politics of Islamic Law.*

47 Ibid.

48 These similarities mark an increase in exchanges between South Asia, the Middle East, and Southeast Asia, facilitated by technological change and the

colonial peace, but also by the opportunities these afforded to existing Muslim networks of learning, pilgrimage, and trade.

49 Hussein Agrama, writing about Egyptian law, relates the formulation of personal status to the problem of public order in Egypt, describing the 1897 reform of the Shariah courts as having "brought into affinity a new set of concepts and affects – family, intimacy, publicity, secrecy, and public order – through which the domains of public and private could be mutually entailed and authorized by the state." *Questioning the Secular* (Chicago: University of Chicago Press 2012), 100.

50 Hussin, *Politics of Islamic Law*.

15

The Octopus and the *Hekatonkheire*

On Many-Armed States and Tentacular Empires[1]

George Steinmetz

This chapter asks how we can best theorize states, and how the study of states can be integrated with the analysis of empires without collapsing the two. States and empires may seem at first glance to be two distinct topics. Although the two were brought together in the work of many of the founders of social science, such as Franz Oppenheimer, Max Weber, Karl Haushofer, Carl Schmitt, and Raymond Aron, the state–empire relationship has vanished as a social scientific concern in recent decades.[2] The entire debate in U.S. social science during the 1980s and 1990s between neo-Marxist and neo-Weberian state theory failed to theorize empires or indeed even to acknowledge their existence.[3] The second volume of Michael Mann's *Sources of Social Power*, which deals with the historical period in which the world's largest colonial empires were forged, 1760–1914, ignores imperial phenomena altogether (except for the Austro-Hungarian empire).[4] Mann's 1983 *Macmillan Student Encyclopedia of Sociology* carried no entries on empires or colonies, although there was an entry on "economic imperialism."[5] This blindness to empires and amnesia about colonialism was a nearly universal feature of social scientific writing in this period,[6] with the exception of a small group of colonial historians who were relatively marginal in their respective disciplines.[7]

Of course, this situation has changed in the past decade, with more and more empirical studies of colonies and empires. But this resurgence of interest in empire across the human sciences has not been accompanied by much interest in the theoretical discussions about the state. Empires and states have been discussed in separate scholarly literatures since the 1960s and this has largely continued up to the present. A second tendency has been to collapse the two objects and to analyze empires as enormous states (or states as empires), or to relegate empires to the ancient or non-Western world. The conflation of state and empire is usually found in the work of nomothetically oriented social scientists, but the same reasoning crept into the thinking of Bourdieu, who spoke in his lectures on the state of "ce type d'empire, d'état" ("this sort of empire or state") and of the "vast and weakly controlled states ... that other theorists call empires."[8] There is also a well-established genre in which European state formation is shown to have certain features associated with colonial conquest and domination. The best work explores differences as well as similarities between European states, colonies, and empires.[9]

An additional set of problems with extant state theories came into focus once scientific interest in empires was reawakened after 2000 by the resurgent American empire and the reinvigoration of colonial historiography and theory. While the differences between the American state and the overseas American "empire of bases" are fairly obvious to an immediate observer, the boundaries between states and empires become blurrier once we reexamine colonial history. Were overseas colonies simply extensions of national states? If so, could they be understood with the same concepts used to make sense of France or Belgium? Or was the colonial state *sui generis*, requiring a separate theoretical model? What about the anomalous polities that do not immediately fit into the categories of state or colony, such as the Princely States of the British Raj, the Dominions of the British Commonwealth, or the semi-sovereign reservations of the American Indians? Each of these polities seems to violate standard definitions of state and colony, suggesting the need for a more variegated typology of political forms. And finally, how does the supervenient category of empire fit into this? Are empires simply assemblages of states and colonies, or do they have emergent properties? This entire problem of scaling "up" geopolitically from the state can be compared with an earlier discussion of the need to scale "down" the idea of the unitary state into different political levels. As I argued in *Regulating the Social*, we need to investigate whether the same model of political process operates at each scale. I discovered there that completely separate models were required for making sense of the municipal and national levels of social policy formation.[10]

This brings us to a further point. Even when we have made the proper typological distinctions we are still faced with the problem of explaining political processes and policies. Here again the leading theories of states – whether Marxist, neo-Marxist, Weberian, neo-Weberian, realist and geopolitical, Foucauldian, or culturalist – fall short. None of these approaches comes to grips with a basic metatheoretical premise of all social science: that social practices are constructed relationally, conflictually, and hierarchically. The realist and geopolitical literatures define the state relationally but turn it into a black box. The best neo-Marxist theories open up this black box but restrict themselves to analyzing the state's internal divisions in terms of representatives of different factions of economic social classes. Max Weber and historians of Cameralism and the Prussian bureaucracy analyze the practices and mentalities of political administrators and civil servants, showing that their interests are often irreducible to economic ones. But they do not theorize the state as a field of relational and hierarchical differences among holders of various kinds of resources.[11] Foucault, Lefebvre, and James C. Scott interpret states as ordering space and regulating individuals and groups,[12] but these thinkers describe a state that is even more monolithically unified than in the most reductionist Marxist accounts.[13]

Beyond the work of Bourdieu and the Bourdieusians, little analytical effort has been invested in understanding states as multifaceted, evolving fields, or congeries of fields riven by internal divisions and axes of domination. The Bourdieusian field approach has other salutary effects, such as seeing states as congeries of individual agents and groups and as realms that are interesting in their own right, without being pulled toward a rigid focus on the "outcomes" of public policy. I will argue that a close engagement with Bourdieu's ideas can greatly benefit this area of study. Although Bourdieu is the originator of sociological field theory, he is not usually seen as a theorist of empire, despite the fact that his lifelong research program began in late colonial Algeria (1955–1960),[14] and even though he traced the genealogy of his other main concepts (habitus, and symbolic, social, and cultural capital) to this very context.[15] Nor has Bourdieu been fully integrated into English-language discussions of state theory, even though he spent several years lecturing on the state at the Collège de France and devoted part of his time to research projects in that area (including his well-known studies *The State Nobility* and *The Social Structures of the Economy*).

Bourdieu dealt with colonialism and the state in two separate periods and never tried to integrate his thinking from these two moments.[16] Nor did Bourdieu think systematically about the distinctive features of colonial as compared to noncolonial states. Bourdieu's work on French Algeria did not foreground competition among different groups of colonizers, even though this would be an obvious concern from the standpoint of his mature theory. Given Bourdieu's aversion to playing the role of the Sartrian "total intellectual" it is not surprising that he rarely intervened in discussions of geopolitics, for example during the first Gulf War.[17] His *theoretical* abstinence in these topical areas is perhaps more surprising. Yet it would be unfair to criticize him for this, since Bourdieu was carrying out research on dozens of topics and was also subject to the same retrenchment onto the space of the nation state that characterized nearly all European sociology (and American sociology, with limited exceptions[18]) in the decades after the end of colonialism.

My contention here is that we can gain enormously by bringing together Bourdieu's thinking on these different topoi, and that colonialism, states, and empires should not be thought of as separate tracks of inquiry. Bourdieu's mature theoretical approach provides a fruitful resource for reinvigorating state theory. It also helps to solve some of the main analytic puzzles raised by colonialism and empires and sheds light on the classic problem of the relations between "society" and the state.

BOURDIEU ON THE STATE AS A COMPLEX FIELD OF FIELDS

Bourdieu argues that the state is a meta-field, a "space of agents and institutions that have [a] kind of meta-power, power over all powers."[19] If we stayed at this level, Bourdieu's theory of the state might seem to identify a sort of *deus ex machina* conceptualized at the same level of generality as the cruder state theories he repeatedly criticizes. The plurality of "agents" and "institutions" points to one of the general features of Bourdieusian fields, which is that they are always arenas of struggle, permeated by differences. At the level of particular acts of public policymaking there is often a wide array of contending actors endowed with differing resources and "unusual strengths,"[20] and pushing very different agendas. Like any field, the state has to be analyzed relationally as an array of positions whose identities are defined in relation to other positions. Positions are filled by (or aligned with) persons, of course, and this poses a whole set of additional problems. The structure of positions inside the state field tends to be homologous to the structure of the field of power, without being reducible to the latter. Bourdieu asks us to focus on how state offices and parastatal fields are staffed and to ask about "the properties that are needed to be effective in this field."[21] Agents' habituses and social properties are transformed in preparation for their entry into the state, and they continue to be remade once they are inside the state field. Bourdieu encourages us to ask about the specific habitus of state officials and different groups of officials in different branches of a state. He asks how bureaucratic dispositions evolve as individuals circulate in these spaces and "successively occup[y] various functions," coming to carry "their whole itinerary in their habitus."[22] As officials begin to accumulate field-specific "administrative capital," their positioning in the field may change correspondingly.

The state is not just a field or set of fields, but also a *formal* organization or a congeries of formal organizations. Most of its structural positions are statutorily defined posts. Even if the state is a formal organization, however, analysts cannot ignore the less empirically obvious question of defining field-specific "statist capital." There is no reason to assume that the formal, legally defined structure of organizational positions, the array of offices and job descriptions, corresponds to the distribution of bureaucratic capital. Indeed, the relationship between the statutory level and the deeper sociological levels of power should be an object of social-historical investigation.

Bourdieu gave a very schematic answer to this question in his suggestion that the state's functions are divided into a "left hand" and a "right hand." The former includes welfare policies, education, the lower courts, and so on. This sector tends to recruit primarily from what Bourdieu calls the "minor state nobility," those richer in cultural capital than economic capital. At the state's "right hand" we find financial functions and ministerial cabinets that recruit mainly from the "upper state nobility," a group that displays "considerable amounts of both cultural and economic capital."[23] This analysis points to a *homology* between the field of power and the state's functions and departments. Rather than simple "instrumental" control of the state by nonstate elites, Bourdieu suggests an elective affinity between certain state offices and bureaucratic roles and actors with particular social properties.

If we take Bourdieu's more sustained empirical work seriously, however, and use Bourdieu to further elaborate his ideas, we should also look for points of *disjuncture*, places where social properties do *not* map readily onto the grid of state offices and jobs. For example, it would be more consistent with Bourdieu to argue that the polarization between cultural and economic capital might be further divided in both the right-hand and the left-hand sectors of the state field into autonomous and heteronomous poles.[24] A subfield of "left-hand" state activity such as education or social insurance also will be similarly subdivided. Government experts on higher education nowadays, for example, are split between defenders of market-based approaches and corporate practices and others who insist that universities should be defined by autonomous criteria of excellence. While both groups are located at the "left hand" of the state, the former are closer to the temporal powers. Bourdieu suggests that these heteronomous officials may be richer in economic and generic social capital than in field-specific symbolic or cultural capital, and vice versa.

Another place in which we can use Bourdieu to refine Bourdieu concerns his language of "state field," "bureaucratic field," and "administrative field." His use of these phrases interchangeably is misleading, and not simply because state activities often take a nonbureaucratic form. Put simply, historical and sociological studies of states need to undertake a much more systematic analysis of the political apparatuses or formal institutions that make up a state, as well as the different departments into which these apparatuses are sorted, and indeed, as Bourdieu insists, to study "the actual structure of [the state's] mechanisms."[25]

Bourdieu also neglects to clearly make a basic distinction between the sectors of the state involved in *formulating* policy – through decrees, parliamentary legislation, court decisions, or administrative elaboration by bureaucracies or committees – and the lower-level sectors involved in *implementing* policy. This distinction is familiar to students of public administration and "street level bureaucracy" or "*la politique au guichet*."[26] Just as social policies continue to be transformed at the "street" level as they are implemented, so colonial native policies were sometimes revised at the point of contact with their addressees.[27] Bourdieu does allude to the distinction between policymakers and policy implementers and he insists that the state "is not an *apparatus* ... capable of converting every action into the simple *execution* of a rule," but he does not sufficiently attend to the outer circles or bands of the state field where policies are put into practice.[28] At the same time, these adjustments and revisions do not bring policy implementers into the heart of the administration where policies are being made, any more than action at the point of production by industrial workers on the shop floor means that workers are part of a firm's key decision making.

This suggests that we need to distinguish at the very least between the wider state field, which includes lower-level public employees, and the administrative field or narrower state field, which consists of policymakers – heads of state, upper-level officials and bureaucrats, judges, and legislators. Bourdieu does distinguish between the state field and the *political field* of parties, interest groups, lobbies, elections, and parliaments.[29] Bourdieu defined the political field as "the site in which, though the competition between the agents involved in it, political products, issues, programmes, analyses, commentaries, concepts and events are created – products between which ordinary citizens, reduced to the status of consumers, have to choose."[30] The political field is "the relatively autonomous world within which struggle about the social world is *conducted only with political weapons*"[31] – as opposed to administrative weapons, for example, or scientific ones.

This paves the way toward a systematic sociology of dynamics within the core of the state meta-field and its various subfields, the various outer reaches of the state (policy implementation), and the surrounding fields of power and politics. We also need to push Bourdieu's distinction between the political field and the bureaucratic field inside the state, distinguishing between career civil servants, elected officials, appointed officials, and actors mandated to sit on temporary commissions. Elected officials may bring a species of political capital into the state that sometimes can stand up to accumulated bureaucratic capital. We should also begin distinguishing among different subfields within the state, each governed by different rules of entry and perhaps by subfield-specific stakes and varieties of symbolic capital. These subfields may correspond to different ministries or departments.

Bourdieu's approach also needs to be made more specific in *spatial* terms. After all, the state is the ultimate territorialized social object.[32] With the exception of ancient "marcher empires" and nomadic politics, states have always been defined by their location in a specific place. There are other social objects that resemble states in this respect, including cities, regions, and empires, as well as buildings and other parts of the built environment.[33] Fields also differ in their degrees of territorialization. We can find references to spatial processes throughout Bourdieu's work, and, indeed, his entire theoretical approach is sometimes characterized as a fundamentally spatial one.[34] But field theory needs to ask how fields and other social spaces are actively produced.

BOURDIEU AND EMPIRES

If the state can be understood as a kind of meta-field, as Bourdieu argues, then it also makes sense to extend the field concept to colonial states and entire empires.[35] Field theory provides a theoretical and methodological framework for analyzing metropolitan states and their colonial offices, overseas colonial states, and the relations among different colonies within a single empire.[36] Bourdieu's concepts help to explain shifts and variations in colonial native policies.[37]

In addressing these problems I will suggest a series of extensions of Bourdieu's approach, the most important of which involves expanding the notion of field to the scale of empires. I will also draw a distinction between imperial *social spaces* and imperial *fields*. Systems of colonial states were often configured as coherent fields. This meant that imperial officials could move back and forth among different colonial states. In other respects, however, empires were *not* unified fields but congeries of fields that coexisted in less integrated formations that I will call imperial *spaces* (following Bourdieu's distinction between social space and social field). The clearest division between imperial field and imperial space can be seen in instances where mobility between metropolitan colonial offices and the overseas colonial service was limited. Particular colonial states sometimes walled themselves off in ways that prevented penetration by officials from other colonies. In the twentieth-century British empire, the Colonial Office and Administrative Service was responsible for the colonies in West, East, and Central Africa; India was the exclusive responsibility of the India Office and Indian Civil Service; Sudan was dealt with by another distinct branch, the Sudan Political Service; and the Dominions Office (1925–1947) dealt with the semi-independent dependences, including Canada, Australia, New Zealand, and South Africa. Each of these offices guarded its own prerogatives for selecting officials to send out to their respective colonies or dominions. Given the limits on a civil servant's career mobility between, say, Kenya and India, and the separate legislation and informal official culture pertaining to each colony, the British Empire cannot be characterized as a single field. The British settlers and officials in this Empire can be described as participating in a unified *social space*, however, as I will argue in the following.

The state's extensions can also be followed beyond its borders into overseas colonies, foreign consulates and embassies, military installations, and extraterritorial zones and bases. The fields and spaces of colonial officialdom spanned entire empires, with individuals circulating not just between metropole and colony but also among colonies, or holding different offices within a single colony or zone of imperial influence. Imperial science also produced fields with extremely complex shapes and with octopus-like tentacles reaching in all directions. Like colonial traders, scientists moved among colonies and sometimes among empires.[38] Other imperial careers never entered the metropole at all but were pursued entirely within the colonies or Commonwealth countries.

Connected to this rescaling of social fields and social spaces, we need to specify that modern colonial empires consisted of a multiplicity of states, or state fields. There was at least one state – a European one – in each of the colonies. In colonies organized around *indirect rule*, one or more indigenous states coexisted with the conquering power's state. Finally, there was a state in the metropole – the states that have been the main concern of so-called state theorists. The metropolitan state was further divided into semiautonomous administrative departments, one or more of which was responsible for colonial affairs. Most colonial states were also subdivided into separate departments, which tended to expand in number over time as new functions were invented. The British colonial state in Ceylon had fifty-four different departments in 1931, for example.[39] One example is labor departments, which were introduced as colonial governments began to acknowledge the existence of indigenous workers. Thirty-three of the thirty-five British colonies had labor departments by 1946, with 200 employees; the French Empire had sixty-five colonial labor inspectors by 1952.[40]

Construed as a whole, this combination of metropolitan colonial offices and overseas colonial states constitutes an *imperial administrative space*. Why call this an imperial *space* rather than an imperial *field*?[41] Recall that all members of a field share a common illusio and recognize one another as qualified members of the field, even as they compete for a specific form of symbolic capital. Movement from one field to another is therefore by no means assured. And indeed, the metropolitan colonial office and overseas colonial state fields usually operated with distinct species of symbolic capital. For example, the German colonial state field before 1914 was governed by competition for a kind of ethnographic capital, unlike the German metropolitan state and colonial office, where displays of ethnographic sagacity would be irrelevant at best, and could even be awkward or damaging.[42] There were also distinct state fields in each colony, or in particular groups of colonies, which hindered lateral movement by colonial officials. Entry into the British colonial service in India was controlled by competitive examination, while selection into the African service was governed by less formal qualifications connected to social class habitus.[43] Thus while there was some career mobility at the highest levels between the Indian administration and African governorships, the incommensurability of recruitment practices limited movement at the lower levels of administration.

Similar limits on the circulation of imperial agents existed in the other modern colonial empires. Different departments of the French state were responsible for the "old" colonies in the New World, the sub-Saharan African colonies, and each of the three North African colonies. Although the French Colonial Ministry centralized some colonial professions between the two world wars, enabling colonial agrarian engineers and laboratory scientists to circulate more freely among colonies, the "de facto decentralization" of French colonial administration was intensified and explicitly "theorized" by the professors at the Parisian École Coloniale.[44] A different kind of limit existed in the German imperial and diplomatic space in China before WWI. On the one hand, career diplomats with no special knowledge of China could be posted to German legations in China, as part of a trajectory that dispatched them to different countries across the globe. The *Governor* of the German colony in Qingdao had to be a Navy officer. The corps of German translators in China, finally, were more mobile within German and European fields, working for the German legations and the colonial government and also for various private businesses; some even worked for the Chinese state.[45] In sum, while the diverse institutional extensions of a given empire might express certain common features, this did not mean that they congealed into a singular field.

A further revision of Bourdieu concerns the definition of *empires* as opposed to *states* and *colonies*. This is not a minor point, since empires have prevailed over mere states throughout world history. Bourdieu focused on the historical genesis of the modern state, and this led him to study the transition from what he saw as the *dynastic* state to the *bureaucratic* state in modern Europe. Empires figured in Bourdieu's discussion only as precursors of modern states – as the "vast and weakly controlled states" that "other theorists call empires" and that are located at the "peripheries."[46] Bourdieu argued that the Russian, Chinese, Ottoman, Roman, and other large land empires differed from European states insofar as they did not integrate their subjects into political or economic "games" beyond their narrow localities. These empires were a sort of "superstructure" that "allowed social units with a local base to remain relatively independent." To the extent that this was true, Bourdieu would have been justified in differentiating empires from states.[47] But he ignored the existence of empires that do indeed integrate their subjects into various kinds of "games" – including the scientific games into which Bourdieu enticed his own Algerian research assistants and students around 1960. He ignored the distinguishing features of empires – their expansiveness and their asymmetrical power relations between core and conquered peripheries. As noted earlier, Bourdieu sometimes used the words "empire" and "state" interchangeably. But empires are more than giant states, and are more than the forerunners of modern states. They are also different from federations, hegemonies, and entities such as the European Union, whose member states are not formally unequal in power. The twentieth century empires I am considering here were asymmetrically structured assemblages of multiple states and other geopolitical forms, such as extraterritorial zones, military bases, and legations and embassies.

A final revision of the model concerns Bourdieu's analysis of the political field as the domain of electoral politics, parties, interest groups, lobbies, and so on, as distinct from the state. He argues that the political field is much more permeable to the outside.[48] Political fields and even legislative councils existed in many twentieth-century colonies, but their influence on policymaking was much more limited than it was in the metropole, due to the autocratic character of colonial states. The basic distinction (discussed earlier) between the sectors of the state involved in formulating policy and those sectors involved in implementing policy is especially important to keep in mind when analyzing modern colonial empires, because of the severe limits on entry into the narrower state field by the colonized. The colonized were almost entirely excluded from the colonial state's policymaking, even though they were deeply involved in implementing policy. This exclusion applied even to native leaders or chiefs whose *local* authority over their own people was recognized by the colonial government. To the extent that the colonized were allowed to run some of their own affairs, this self-governance was effectively part of a parallel, dominated state. The fact that this native state was supposed to remain subordinated to the European state is indicated by the name for this sort of governance – indirect rule. A complete study of the functioning of indirect rule would need to examine the semiautonomous native state fields alongside the European colonial state fields.

THE MODERN COLONIAL STATE

If empires can be distinguished from states by their expansiveness and asymmetrical power relations, we can differentiate colonial and noncolonial states according to the *foreign sovereignty* criterion and *rule of hierarchical difference* criterion. The *foreign sovereignty* criterion specifies that colonies are territories in which political sovereignty has been seized by a foreign political power and where these outside conquerors govern in the place of territorial natives. This criterion allows us to distinguish a state that discriminates against immigrants or slaves from one that discriminates against the autochthonous population. The second criterion specifies that the conquering state treats the conquered as fundamentally inferior – as barbarians, savages, heathens, a lower race, a stagnant civilization, or as needing to be "developed" before they can qualify for self-government. Taken together, these two criteria distinguish modern colonial states from most instances of state formation in modern Europe. Although most European states were created through continental conquest, the conquerors' typical goal was to turn the conquered into nationals. Where a rule of difference was applied after continental conquest, as in the Nazi annexation of Poland or the English conquest of Ireland, it seems appropriate to speak of colonialism even within Europe. And in settler nations such as postcolonial Australia, New Zealand, Palestine/Israel, Canada, the United States, and most of the Latin American states, there have been *internal* colonial conditions insofar as territorial autochthons have been treated legally as second class citizens.

Colonial governments were states: they were perpetually operating, compulsory institutions that exercised a *relative* monopoly of violence within defined territories.[49] European colonies had explicit rules about replacement and the chain of command when the top officials – usually governors – were absent or unable to perform their duties.[50] Colonial states had clearly bounded geographical territories. Even the most remote colonial borders were typically defined through international negotiations and marked off physically in the landscape to show where one colonizer's sovereignty gave way to another's.

To count as a state, a colonial governing apparatus also needs to assert its partial independence from the metropolitan state as well as indigenous polities. Autonomy from the native state or indigenous field of power is already contained within the idea of the colonial state's monopoly of violence. Even where native authorities controlled some aspects of decision making, they operated according to customary legal codes approved by the foreign authorities.[51] Customary law was trumped by the colonizer's law when it violated European precepts held to be universal or inviolable (as in the so-called repugnancy standards in British colonial law). Colonial historians have shown that indigenous chiefs were allowed to control only a limited subset of policy issues and were usually under European supervision.

Most colonial governors had a great deal of independence from the metropole; district officials were similarly free from much interference by the colony's headquarters. Laws within each colonial territory were enacted by the governor, sometimes with the advice of a legislative council. In normal times in the French colonial empire, overseas governors could "ignore, or seriously modify, orders emanating from Paris."[52]

The governor in British colonies was legally defined as the "single and supreme authority responsible to, and representative of, Her Majesty," and as being "second only to the sovereign should she decide to visit her colony."[53] In the words of one colonial office official, the position of colonial governor combined "the functions of King, Prime Minister, Speaker, and permanent head of the civil service. In his Colony his word is law and his decisions are final."[54] British governors were required to listen to advice from members of their executive councils, but they were "in no way obligated to heed [that] advice."[55] British colonies were so autonomous from the colonial office that they could usually "resist London's best efforts towards even [a] minimal measure of unity."[56] Even major shifts in metropolitan colonial policy, such as the British colonial office's attempt to replace indirect rule with "local government" after 1945, had to proceed by persuading individual governors.[57]

Colonial governors enjoyed a great deal of freedom from their metropolitan superiors. The governor of German Kiaochow was required to obtain approval from the navy office in Berlin only for "the most important and far-reaching regulations," and, in fact, none of his regulations were ever overturned. Lothar von Trotha, the acting governor of German Southwest Africa in 1904, was able to initiate a genocidal campaign against the Herero without consulting the chief of the general staff, von Schlieffen, or anyone else in Germany.[58] Colonial officials were also independent enough from European economic interests in their colonies to do quite the opposite of what settlers, planters, and investors demanded of them. In German Samoa, for example, the government refused settlers' demands that Samoans be compelled to work on European plantations and banned the sale of native-owned land to foreigners. In Southwest Africa the colonial army exterminated the settlers' principal labor force, creating a labor shortage in the colony that lasted for years. In German Togo and Cameroon, colonial officials opposed "the very European merchants whose interests they presumably represented."[59] In the French Ivory Coast, the governor refused to mobilize additional forced labor for European employers in 1942, warning of the "grave consequences" to indigenous society.[60]

Several factors enhanced the independence of colonial officials from Europe. Officials in the colonies insisted that it was impossible to understand the local situation from Europe. Thus the Nigerian Governor Grigg insisted that the colonial office had no "knowledge of the colony" and had "made suggestions so impractical as to appear ridiculous."[61] The German colonial department informed the Samoan governor in

1900 that "it would not be appropriate for the foreign office to determine the further details of native policy given that conditions are really only visible on the spot."[62] Most colonies before WWII were required to generate their own revenues locally, giving them further leverage in resisting central control. Before 1945, every colonial officer in the British Empire was "employed and paid by one or the other of the territorial governments."[63]

In systems of indirect rule, chiefs dominated tribal *micro-state fields*. The relationship between indirectly ruled chieftainships and the colonial state was an asymmetrical relationship between two overlapping but distinct fields. Tribal authorities were usually paid a salary by the European state. The colonized could ensure the success of the colonial state's "native policies" by playing their assigned roles, and by the same token they could undermine European policy by withholding their cooperation or revise state policy through more indirect forms of resistance. This gave the colonized some influence over policies, and sometimes even veto power, but it did not give them the ability to participate directly in colonial-level lawmaking. For the most part, then, indigenous subjects' political participation was limited to native states, whose powers were highly circumscribed by foreign overrule, or as appointed civil servants, where they were involved in carrying out laws but not making policy (see Chapter 14 for a discussion of how indigenous officials performed important translative work for colonial rulers, rendering subject populations legible to those who governed them).

All of this slowly began to change in the 1940s, when legislative bodies with indigenous representatives started to gain more power in European colonies, even if the final word still rested with each colony's governor. After 1945, subjects of the French empire were represented in the assembly of the French Union in Paris. Africans gained some electoral representation at the local level of government in the British colonies. Indigenous subjects were trained to fill positions in the colonies' administration and not simply allocated to native states. The Parisian École coloniale graduated an increasing number of indigenous students.[64] The graduating classes at the Oxford training program for colonial "cadets," which were entirely white before WWII, became somewhat more diverse afterwards (Figures 15.1 and 15.2).

Beneath the level of the colonial governor, effective sovereignty in overseas colonies resided with the legendary "men on the spot," the "real chiefs of the empire,"[65] who were in direct daily contact with indigenous leaders and local communities. Many of these district officials had as

FIGURE 15.1. Oxford University Colonial Services Club, June 1939.
From album containing group photographs of the Oxford University Colonial Service cadets, Rhodes House Library, Oxford.

FIGURE 15.2. Oxford University Colonial Services Club, 1949 (close up).
From album containing group photographs of the Oxford University Colonial Service cadets, Rhodes House Library, Oxford.

much autonomy from their colony's central headquarters as governors had from the metropole. One district official in German Togo replaced 544 chiefs during his twenty years in office.[66] The district commissioners in German Kiaochow adjudicated most legal cases involving Chinese defendants. They needed the governor's authorization only when recommending the death penalty, but even a death sentence could be summarily imposed by a German district commissioner "in the case of an uprising, a surprise attack, or some other state of emergency."[67] In the British and French empires, "formal policy impinged gently" on district commissioners, providing them with an "immense scope for freedom of action."[68]

ELITE CLASS STRUGGLE WITHIN THE METROPOLES AND IN OVERSEAS COLONIAL ADMINISTRATIONS

Native policy was the centerpiece of modern European and U.S. colonial governance, often trumping economic, missionary, and other concerns.[69] But native policy was just one element of the overall policy interventions by a colonial state. Modern colonial states developed a full panoply of separate ministries, one of which was typically focused on native administration. In a colony such as German Southwest Africa, three different groups of officials dominated the state field between 1884 and 1914.[70] In British Tanganyika after WWI, native policy had its own separate ministry, which drew on the services of full-time "Government Sociologists" and "Government Anthropologists" to investigate various aspects of native life.[71] It was these functionally differentiated colonial states that Ernest Gellner had in mind when he wrote that "a colonial administration tended to be a genuine bureaucracy."[72] Before the 1930s, British officials in Tanzania who were focused on native administration were able to assert their paramountcy vis-à-vis other factions within the colonial state field. The economic crisis of the 1930s strengthened the hand of other officials who were more oriented toward economic growth.[73]

This example of a shift in the dominant subfield or ministry within the overall field of the colonial state points to a further specification of the field theoretical model. Bourdieu's approach requires that the researcher identify the specific form of symbolic capital operating in a given field. In the case of the state, Bourdieu referred to this form as "state" capital (*capital étatique*). It would follow that the colonial state field is governed by competition for colonial state capital (*capital étatique coloniale*). Before the 1920s, colonial state fields were usually structured by an *ethnographic* definition of colonial statist capital, but other criteria emerged during the Great Depression and with the post–WWII turn to developmentalism.[74] Specialists in economic development were sometimes able to impose their preferred definition of distinction on the local state field and force others to compete on that terrain, or at least to unsettle the local field's definition of the dominant principle of domination. The key point is that struggles erupted constantly within colonial state fields, and that they were often organized along lines corresponding to actors' social properties, including their holdings of generic and field-specific symbolic capital.

What exactly were the pertinent "social properties" of colonial officials? A brief comparison of the German and British colonies and colonial offices illustrates the need to combine concepts that are transportable across historical and spatial boundaries – concepts such as field and symbolic capital – with attention to the uniqueness of each geo-historical context. The British and German fields of power differed significantly, as did the place of their respective colonial offices in the overall field of the metropolitan state. These differences shaped recruitment into the overseas colonial states and therefore influenced colonial policy. Such national differences mean that the social properties represented inside the colonial offices and colonial states also varied across empires.

One historian argues that "the only real unity" in the British colonial service was the "common ground of class and educational background, contributing as it did to similarity in attitude and response."[75] A different picture has emerged from more detailed research on the class background of the colonial service. Among the governors of British Africa, there were "less than a dozen scions of the landed gentry."[76] There was a "falling off, after the First World War, of interest in a colonial service career shown by the products of the "best schools in England," with the majority coming from either "public schools of the second or third rank" or "state secondary schools."[77] The focus of university study for colonial officials shifted from "greats" to more modern disciplines.[78] Struggle within the overseas British colonial state fields now took place mainly among a "lesser nobility" consisting of the sons of professionals and clergymen, with few Etonians, noblemen, or sons of capitalists.[79]

The German metropolitan field of power before WWI was divided between businessmen, an older nobility, and an educated professional middle class, the so-called Bildungsbürgertum. The economic bourgeoisie increasingly dominated the field of power, but the state field remained unsettled: the nobility continued to control the army and foreign service, while the Bildungsbürgertum extended its influence from the scientific and educational realms into the offices of the state's "left hand" and into municipal government. The ranks of German colonial governors before WWI were distributed among noblemen, businessmen, and Bildungsbürger. Colonial policymaking inside the central German state was the purview of the army, navy, and foreign office, but the Reichstag had the capacity to approve or refuse colonial budgets, which meant that political parties had some influence on policy too. As a result, colonial policy in the metropole was forged in a turbulent process in which the same elite class fractions that competed with one another in overseas colonial state fields struggled not just with one another but also with representatives of the working class and the German Catholics. The ongoing production of colonial policy was not elaborated in the Reichstag, however, but in the colonial department/office and in the various colonial states. The prestige of the colonial department was lower than that of other national and Prussian ministries. As a result, the colonial office was dominated by social groups that had less power in the state field and in the field of power as a whole. It is telling that the colonial office was the only national ministry during the colonial era with a Jewish secretary of state, Bernhard Dernberg (1907–1910). The third secretary of state for the colonies was Wilhelm Solf (1911–1918), a Bildungsbürger with university degrees in Sanskrit and law whose father was an industrialist. In short, as colonial affairs consolidated into a separate subfield of the German state it became a stronghold for the dominated sectors of the dominant class. This process came to an end with WWI, which saw a military takeover of the state field and Germany's loss of its colonial empire.

CONCLUSION: FROM "SUR L'ÉTAT" TO "SUR L'EMPIRE"

I am not suggesting that field theory can make sense of every aspect of modern colonialism, much less the history of all states and empires. Field theory is premised on a differentiation of society into separate realms, and therefore tends to be restricted to the modern era. As for empires, they are shaped not just by state fields but by the interimperial meta-field of competing empires and the international states system,[80] as well as non-fielded processes. Every policy, whether it exists at the level of an empire, a colony, or a nation-state, is the product of an overdetermined conjuncture of causal series. This much is clear even from the standpoint of a metatheory such as critical realism or even a garden-variety historicism. What needs further clarification is the idea of the state as a complex metafield whose internal dynamics codetermine policy. Because states are fields, they are battlefields. It is those battles, as well as the struggles between rulers and the ruled, and among the ruled, to which theorists of politics, states, and empires must attend. Some of the more significant turning points in modern history, including the decision to annihilate indigenous populations or religious minority groups, can only be explained by paying close attention to elite struggles inside state and imperial fields. Dynamics within overseas colonial administrations can help explain, for instance, why the Germans in Southwest Africa launched a genocidal campaign against the Herero and Nama, while the German government in Samoa attempted to preserve the colonized in an aestheticized condition of precapitalist traditionalism. They can explain why settlers in colonies such as German Samoa were unable to impose their vision on the colonial state, while settlers in French Algeria or British Kenya were more successful, at least until the end of colonial rule. Presumably, a field-analytic approach would shed new light on the Nazi state's turn to genocide.

What about the metaphor of the state's left and right hands? I have argued that this imagery is too simple even for Bourdieu's own analysis of the metropolitan state. And if states are octopus-like, empires would seem to be veritable Hekatonkheires. Since indirect rule is the default approach to native governance in modern empires, the political space of the conquering imperialists will typically be superimposed on additional indigenous fields. Mapping the complex relations between and within the subfields that make up a state or an empire should be the foremost task of political historians. Empires have been a more common form of political organization than nation-states throughout most of human history. This means that we should not be tempted to leave empires unanalyzed, or to reduce them to a single analytic dimension such as capitalism, atavism, or the will to power.

Notes

1 The Hekatonkheires of Greek mythology were hundred-handed and fifty-headed monsters.
2 George Steinmetz, "Major Contributions to Sociological Theory and Research on Empire, 1830s–present," in *Sociology and Empire*, ed. George Steinmetz (Durham, NC: Duke University Press, 2013), 1–50; Ibid., "The Sociology of Empires, Colonialism, and Postcolonialism," *Annual Review of Sociology* 40 (2014): 77–103; Ibid., "Empires, Imperial States, and Colonial Societies," in *Concise Encyclopedia of Comparative Sociology*, eds. Masamichi Sasaki,

Jack Goldstone, and Eckart Zimmermann (Leiden: Koninklijke Brill NV, 2014), 58–74.

3 Julia Adams and George Steinmetz, "Sovereignty and Sociology: From State Theory to Theories of Empire," *Political Power and Social Theory* 28 (2014): 269–285.

4 Mann, of course, corrected this oversight in the subsequent two volumes, reanalyzing some of the same time periods in terms of empires.

5 Michael Mann, *The Macmillan Student Encyclopedia of Sociology* (London: Macmillan, 1983). This was republished as *The International Encyclopedia of Sociology* (New York: Continuum, 1984).

6 I have been able to determine that between a third and half of all British and French sociologists worked in the colonies between 1949 and 1960, but that sociologists in both countries turned inward toward the metropolitan nation-state after independence. By the end of the 1960s, the colonial object had vanished. Historians of sociology in both countries proceeded as if colonial sociology had never existed in the postwar period, for reasons of shame and anachronism. Steinmetz, "A Child of the Empire: British Sociology and Colonialism, 1940s–1960s," *Journal of the History of the Behavioral Sciences* 49 (2013): 353–378; "Sociology and Colonialism in the British and French Empires, 1940s–1960s," *Journal of Modern History* (forthcoming).

7 Daniel Rivet, "Le fait colonial et nous: histoire d'un éloignement," *Vingtième siècle* 33 (1992): 127–138.

8 Pierre Bourdieu, *Sur l'état. Cours au Collège de France 1989–1992* (Paris: Seuil, 2012), pp. 126, 213.

9 On the *differentia specifica* of empires, see Jane Burbank and Frederick Cooper, *Empires in World History: Power and the Politics of Difference* (Princeton, NJ: Princeton University Press, 2010); on the peculiarities of the colonial form of state, see Steinmetz, "The Colonial State as a Social Field," *American Sociological Review* 73, no. 4 (2008): 589–612. American state formation is a thing apart, given the legacies of settler colonialism. It is best compared to state formation in the former British, Spanish, and Portuguese settler colonies.

10 Steinmetz, *Regulating the Social: The Welfare State and Local Politics in Imperial Germany* (Princeton, NJ: Princeton University Press, 1993).

11 "I will not deal separately with neo-institutionalist field theory, since it is derived almost entirely from Bourdieu's field theory even while erasing some of Bourdieu's main insights, such as the definition of fields as arenas not just of consensus but more signally of conflict around specific stakes; see David L. Swartz, "Theorizing Fields," *Theory and Society* 43 (2014): 675–682. Fligstein and McAdam make the misleading claim that "the relationship between states and fields has never been systematically theorized" and that "no one has conceived of states, as we do, as complex systems of interdependent fields in their own right." As Swartz reminds us, Bourdieu "clearly was there earlier." Bourdieu's recently translated lectures on the state from 1989 to 1991 demonstrate this to anyone who does not have access to the original French version, but some of Bourdieu's articles on the state were long available even in English. Bourdieu, "Rethinking the State: Genesis and Structure

of the Bureaucratic Field," in *State/Culture*, ed. Steinmetz (Ithaca, NY: Cornell University Press, 1999): 53–75; Neil Fligstein and Doug McAdam, *A Theory of Fields* (Oxford: Oxford University Press, 2012), 2–6; Bourdieu, *On the State* (Cambridge: Polity, 2015), abbreviated hereafter as *OTS*.

12 Graham Burchell, Colin Gordon, and Peter Miller, eds., *The Foucault Effect: Studies in Governmentality* (Chicago, IL: University of Chicago Press, 1991); Henri Lefebvre, *De l'État*, 4 vols. (Paris: Union générale d'éditions, 1976–1978); James C. Scott, *Seeing like a State* (New Haven, CT: Yale University Press, 1998).

13 Pluralist political sociology took seriously the role of social divisions in shaping policy but did not leave any analytic room for analyzing the state as an arena with some autonomy from the environing social space. Indeed, pluralist political theory understood the state as a continental European phantom; see Steinmetz, "Culture and the State," in *State/Culture*, ed. Steinmetz, 1–49.

14 Kamel Chachoua, ed., *L'Algérie sociologique, En hommage à Pierre Bourdieu (1930–2002)* (Alger: CNRPAH, 2012); Pierre Bourdieu, *Algerian Sketches* (Cambridge: Polity, 2013); Amín Pérez, *Rendre le social plus politique. Guerre coloniale, immigration et pratiques sociologiques d'Abdelmalek Sayad et de Pierre Bourdieu*, doctoral thesis, École des Hautes Études en Sciences Sociales, 2015.

15 Bourdieu, *The Social Structures of the Economy* (Cambridge: Polity, 2005), 2. As I demonstrate elsewhere, the intellectual impetus for Bourdieu's field theory can also be traced to Algeria, specifically to his relations with the French Army's Information Service, for which he worked, and to the local branch of the French statistical service, for which Bourdieu carried out a series of studies in 1960. Steinmetz, "Sociology and Colonialism in the British and French Empires."

16 Bourdieu mentioned the colonial context fleetingly in his lectures on the state; *Sur l'état*, 354, 233.

17 On Bourdieu's political reserve, see Kamel Chachoua, "Pierre Bourdieu et l'Algérie," in *Chachoua*, ed., *L'Algérie sociologique*, 9–23; on Bourdieu's critique of the traditional role of intellectual political engagement, see Bourdieu, "Recherche et action," in *Forschen und Handeln. Vorträge am Frankreich-Zentrum der Albert-Ludwig-Universität Freiburg (1989–2000)*, ed. Joseph Jurt (Freiburg i. B.: Rombach Wissenschaften, 2004), 85–92.

18 Michael Kennedy and Miguel A. Centeno, "Internationalism and Global Transformations in American Sociology," in *Sociology in America: A History*, ed. Craig Calhoun (Chicago, IL: University of Chicago Press, 2007), 666–712.

19 *OTS*, 367.

20 *OTS*, 32.

21 *OTS*, 18.

22 *OTS*, 18.

23 David Swartz, *Symbolic Power, Politics, and Intellectuals: The Political Sociology of Pierre Bourdieu* (Chicago: The University of Chicago Press, 2013), 143.

24 Contrary to a more mechanistic versions of structuralism, however, there is no reason to expect such binaries or other relational divisions to reproduce themselves *tous azimuts*, like fractals, or at each hierarchical level.

25 *OTS*, 5.

26 Vincent Dubois, *La vie au guichet: relation administrative et traitement de la misère* (Paris: Economica, 1999).

27 George Steinmetz, *The Devil's Handwriting: Precoloniality and the German Colonial State in Qingdao, Samoa, and Southwest Africa* (Chicago, IL: University of Chicago Press, 2007); Chapter 14.

28 *OTS*, 11.

29 Bourdieu, *Propos sur le champ politique* (Lyon: Presses universitaires de Lyon, 2000), 379.

30 Bourdieu, "Political Representation: Elements for a Theory of the Political Field," in *Language and Symbolic Power* (Cambridge, MA: Harvard University Press, 1991), 172.

31 *OTS*, 335, my emphasis. As Dezalay argues similarly, law should be defined sociologically as whatever lawyers do, and as the place where battles are fought with legal weapons. Yves Dezalay, *Marchands de droit: La restructuration de l'ordre juridique international par les multinationales du droit* (Paris: Fayard, 1992), 3.

32 See, for example, the excellent study of Gabonese state formation as the production of space by Roland Pourtier, *Le Gabon*, vol. 2: *État et développment* (Paris: Harmattan, 1989).

33 Bourdieu mentions the spatial structure of the state in his first lecture (*OTS*, 9), distinguishes between "State 1" and "State 2," and refers to the way a national space is created by the state. *OTS*, 223.

34 Jean-Louis Fabiani, "Theory and Practice in French Sociology after Pierre Bourdieu," unpublished paper given at the World Congress of Sociology, Brisbane, July 2002.

35 Steinmetz, "Social Fields and Subfields at the Scale of Empires: Colonial States and Colonial Sociology," *Sociological Review* (forthcoming).

36 Alternatives to the theoretical approach presented here include Michael W. Doyle, *Empires* (Ithaca, NY: Cornell University Press, 1986); Carl Schmitt, *The Nomos of the Earth* (New York: Telos Press, 2003 [1950]); and Immanuel Wallerstein, *The Modern World-System*, 4 vols. (Berkeley: University of California Press, 2011).

37 Steinmetz, *The Devil's Handwriting*.

38 On these sorts of careers, see Steinmetz, "A Child of the Empire"; D. Lambert and A. Lester, eds., *Colonial Lives across the British Empire: Imperial Careering in the Long Nineteenth Century* (Cambridge: Cambridge University Press, 2006).

39 A. H. M. Kirk-Greene, *On Crown Service: A History of HM Colonial and Overseas Civil Services, 1837–1997* (London: I. B. Tauris, 1999), 54.

40 Frederick Cooper, *Decolonization and African Society: The Labor Question in French and British Africa* (Cambridge: Cambridge University Press, 1996), 275–276.

41 On the usefulness of this distinction, see Lilian Mathieu, *L'espace des mouve-ments sociaux* (Bellecombe-en-Bauges: Éditions du croquant, 2012), who suggests that one should speak of a *space* rather than a *field* of social move-ments, even though each specific movement may constitute a distinct field.

42 Steinmetz, *The Devil's Handwriting*.

43 Ralph Austen, " The Official Mind of Indirect Rule: British Policy in Tangan-yika, 1916–1939," in *Britain and Germany in Africa: Imperial Rivalry and Colonial Rule*, ed. Prosser Gifford and William Roger Louis (New Haven, CT: Yale University Press, 1967), 594; Sir Ralph Furse, *Aucuparius: Recollections of a Recruiting Officer* (London: Oxford University Press, 1962).

44 Christophe Bonneuil, *Des savants pour l'empire: La structuration des recherches scientifiques coloniales au tems de 'la mise en valeur' des colonies françaises 1917–1945* (Paris: Editions de l'ORSTOM, 1991), 52; Pierre Singaravélou, *Professer l'Empire: Les sciences coloniales en France sous la IIIe République* (Paris: Publications de la Sorbonne, 2011), 322.

45 E.g., Otto Franke, *Erinnerungen aus zwei Welten. Randglossen zur eigenen Lebensgechichte* (Berlin: Walter de Gruyter & Co., 1954).

46 OTS, 133.

47 OTS, 297.

48 Bourdieu, *Propos sur le champ politique*.

49 There is a legalistic objection to the notion of the colonial state, namely, that colonies lacked autonomous status in international law. Wolfgang Knöbl, "Imperiale Herrschaft und Gewalt," *Mittelweg 36*, 21, no. 3 (2012): 19–44. This objection is overruled by the reality of colonial state's autonomous activities in most practical instances, many of them documented in my *Devil's Handwriting*.

50 In addition to Weber, see especially Charles Tilly, *Coercion, Capital, and European States, AD 990–1990* (Cambridge, MA: Blackwell, 1990). In the British colonies the most senior official acted as governor in the latter's absence; in the German colonial empire, such absences were regulated by the law on "the substitute representation of civil servants." Kirk-Greene, "On Governorship and Governors in British Africa," in *African Proconsuls: European Governors in Africa*, eds. H. Gann and Peter Duignan (New York: Free Press, 1979), 234; Steinmetz, *The Devil's Handwriting*, 32.

51 As Hussin (Chapter 14) demonstrates, colonial legal spheres often "required the presence of native judges, whose position in between led to systematic and iterated renegotiations of the very rules of the colonial game," and this resulted in quite radical transformations over time in "the workings and meanings of Islam in colonial law." I show similar reworkings of colonial policy by colonized actors in German Qingdao and Samoa in Steinmetz, *The Devil's Handwriting*.

52 William B. Cohen, "The Colonial Policy of the Popular Front," *French Historical Studies* 7, no 3 (1972): 368–393, 377.

53 Kirk-Greene, "On Governorship," 224, 227.

54 Sir Charles Jeffries, *Partners for Progress: The Men and Women of the Colonial Service* (London: Harrap, 1949), 108.

55 Kirk-Greene, "On Governorship," 233.

56 Robert Heussler, *Yesterday's Rulers. The Making of the British Colonial Service* (Syracuse, NY: Syracuse University Press, 1963), 15–16.

57 Arthur Creech Jones, "The Place of African Local Administration in Colonial Policy," *Journal of African Administration* 1 (1949): 3–15. The Colonial Office's postwar program of local government was rejected by some governors of African colonies. R. D. Pearce, *The Turning Point in Africa: British Colonial Policy, 1938–48* (London: Frank Cass, 1982), 180.

58 Steinmetz, *The Devil's Handwriting*, ch. 4.

59 Ralph Austen and Jonathan Derrick, *Middlemen of the Cameroons Rivers* (Cambridge: Cambridge University Press, 1999), 130.

60 Cooper, *Decolonization and African Society*, 151.

61 Gregory, *Sidney Webb*, 125.

62 Auswärtiges Amt to Governor Solf, May 31, 1900, New Zealand National Archives, Archives of the German Colonial Administration, XVII.A.1, vol. 1, p. 90.

63 Charles Jeffries, *A Review of Colonial Research 1940–1960* (London: H.M.S.O, 1964), 32.

64 Archives nationales d'Outre-mer (Aix-en-Provence), École coloniale/École nationale de la France d'outre-mer, collection "Fonds de l'École." The École coloniale had actually started as a training school for Cambodians who would go home to participate in governing their own country, now a French protectorate.

65 Robert Delavignette, *Les vrais chefs de l'Empire* (Paris: Gallimard, 1939); Trutz von Trotha, *Koloniale Herrschaft* (Tübingen: J. C. B. Mohr, 1994), 109–110.

66 Von Trotha, *Koloniale Herrschaft*, 268.

67 Georg Crusen, "Moderne Gedanken im Chinesen-Strafrecht des Kiautschou-gebietes," *Mitteilungen der Internationalen kriminalistischen Vereinigung* 21 (1914), 134–42; Von Trotha, *Koloniale Herrschaft*, 110.

68 John Smith, "Foreword," in Kirk-Greene, *Symbol*, ix. For another example, see Cooper, *Decolonization and African Society*, 46.

69 Native policy can be defined as encompassing all colonial state policies aimed at producing a stable, uniform definition of the character and culture of the colonized and urging them to act in accordance with this definition. Steinmetz, *The Devil's Handwriting*.

70 Steinmetz, *The Devil's Handwriting*.

71 H. A. Fosbrooke, "Government Sociologists in Tanganyika. Part II. A Sociological View," *Journal of African Administration* 4 (1952): 103–108.

72 Ernest Gellner, "Sociology and Social Anthropology," *Transactions of the Sixth World Congress of Sociology* (Geneva: International Sociological Association, 1967), vol. 2, 76. Gellner carried out fieldwork in Morocco at the end of the French colonial period.

73 Austen, "The Official Mind"; Margaret L. Bates, "Tanganyika under British Administration, 1920–1955," PhD diss., Oxford University (1957).

74 In my study of the German colonial state I found that all state officials, no matter what their position and properties, framed their interventions as if they were competing for a sort of *ethnographic capital*. The pressure on the

colonial state to stabilize the colonized through native policy put a premium on the colonizer's alleged ability to understand his subjects; colonizers were therefore led to frame their interventions as stemming from a profound grasp of the natives' true culture and character. A study of policymaking in British Malaya and the American Philippines between the 1880s and the 1930s confirmed this theory: Daniel Pei Siong Goh, *Ethnographic Empire: Imperial Culture and Colonial State Formation in Malaya and the Philippines, 1880–1940*, PhD diss., University of Michigan (2005). Rather than arguing that ethnographic capital is *always* the main stake of competition within modern colonial state fields, however, I now believe it better to speak of *colonial statist capital* as the generic form of symbolic capital common to these fields.

75 Heussler, *Yesterday's Rulers*, 53.

76 I. F. Nicolson and Colin A. Hughes, "A Provenance of Proconsuls: British Colonial Governors 1900–1960," *Journal of Imperial and Commonwealth History* 4 (1975): 81.

77 Nicolson and Hughes, "A Provenance," 79, 91; Kirk-Greene, "On Governership," 249.

78 A. H. M. Kirk-Greene, *A Biographical Dictionary of the British Colonial Governor* (Brighton: Harvester Press, 1980), 19.

79 Nicolson and Hughes, "A Provenance."

80 International relations theory can also benefit from a field theoretical perspective; see Rebecca Adler-Nissen, ed., *Bourdieu in International Relations* (London: Routledge, 2013).

Index

ability to pay, as taxation philosophy,
     291–92
ACLU Women's Rights Project, 144
Adams, Henry Carter, 291–92
Adams, Julia, 255
Addams, Jane, 293
administrative people exchanges, 83–86,
     93–96
adult worker model, 139
AFDC. *See* Aid to Families with Dependent
     Children; Personal Responsibility
     and Work Opportunity
     Reconciliation Act; Temporary
     Assistance to Needy Families
     program
affirmative action
   in Brazil, 214–15, 217–18
   for whites, in U.S., 183–92
African-Americans. *See also* race, racism
     and; segregation
   incarceration of, 194–95
   people exchanges and, 98
   poll taxes and, 285, 295
   racial democracy for, 184–85
   under VRA, 185–86
Afro-Brazilians, 211–13, 221. *See also* race,
     racism and
Agamben, Giorgio, 231–35
Agrama, Hussein, 368
Aid to Families with Dependent Children
     (AFDC), 60, 141–42, 145–46,
     148–49

Ali, Syed Ameer, 355–56
Alves dos Santos, Ivair Augusto, 216
American Political Development (APD),
     289–90
anthropogeography, 114–15
anti-formalism, in American law,
     232–38
   Emerson on, 237
APD. *See* American Political Development
Aron, Raymond, 369
associational activity, 35–38, 40. *See also*
     non-governmental organizations;
     non-profit sector; Red Cross
   in administrative state, 41
   contract theory and, 40–41
   general will influenced by, 40–41
   liberal theory and, 40–41
   state projects and, interdependence
     with, 37
   suppression of, 40–41
   symbiotic state and, 42
attribution, of statecraft, 63–64
Australia, VAW policies in, 159, 169
authoritarianism, 246, 274–75. *See also*
     totalitarianism
   subnational forms of, 14–16, 182–83,
     195
autogestion, 41–42
autonomous feminism, 21
   VAW and, 160–61, 168–72
autonomy of states, 2, 14, 245, 287,
     380

Bairros, Luiza, 217–19
Baltimore People's Unemployment League,
    36, 44
bankruptcy. *See* sovereign bankruptcy rules
Barker, Ernest, 239
Basel II rules, 117, 126
Battle of Valmy, 307
Bauer, Michael, 67
Beauvoir, Simone de, 158–59
benefits theory, of taxation, 293
Bird, Richard M., 298
Black, Hugo (Supreme Court Justice),
    234–35
Blair, Tony, 277
Bloody Sunday, 276–77
boundaries, of states, 4–5, 7, 9, 13,
    18–19, 47, 52–53, 106, 120, 135,
    310, 353. *See also* Mitchell,
    Timothy
  Bourdieu on, 10
  internal, 39–42
  location of, 9–10
  public-private hybridity for, 9
  sociocultural influences on, 10
  street-level bureaucracy and, 10
Bourdieu, Pierre, 12, 284
  on boundaries of states, 10
  on classification, 61, 64–65, 230
  on colonialism, 371–72
  on cultural capital, 373–74
  on empires, 375–79, 388–89
  on field theory, 208–9, 371–75
  on hands of the state, 7–8, 41, 284
  on public bureaucracy, 373–75
  public choice theory and, 85
  on state as meta-field, 371–75
  on state capabilities, 41, 103
  on symbolic power of states, 81, 83–86,
    103, 114–15
Brady restructuring plan (1990), 123
branding, of nations, 122
Brazil. *See also* Cardoso, Fernando
    Henrique
  capital development in, 106
  color consciousness in, 204–5
  colorblindness in, 204–6, 220
  as raceless state, 205–6
  as racial democracy
    Freyre and, 205–6, 210
    myth of, 204–10
    promotion of, 210–12

racial equality in, 204–5, 208–12
  through affirmative action programs,
    214–15, 217–18
  Afro-Brazilians and, 211–13, 221
  black NGOs and, 213–15
  under Law of Quotas, 217–18
  National Policy for the Promotion of
    Racial Equality, 209
  reconfiguration of state orientation for,
    215–19
  Santiago Regional Conference of the
    Americas and, 212–15
  SEPPIR, 215–18, 225
  as racial state, 220–21
  conception of, 205–8
  racial order and hierarchy, 206–7
  through state practices, 207
  in subnational government policies, 206
  whitening of population, 206
  racism in, 179
  Campaign Reaja o Sera Morto against,
    179
  rolêzinhos in, 218–19
  state repression in, 218
Brenner Debates, 333–34
BRIC economies, 106. *See also* Brazil;
    China; India; Russia
Bringing the State Back In, 2–3, 8
British Empire, 340–41. *See also* colonial
    states; colonialism; India, as British
    colony
  sociologists within, 388–89
  symbolic capital of, 351–53
bureaucracy, of state, 14, 140, 167. *See also*
    Brazil
  Bourdieu on, 372–75
  colonialism and, 384
  Schumpeter on, 288
  in U.S., 180–81, 192–93, 230, 292
  Weber on, 36, 229–30, 244, 287–88
Burnham, James, 250

Cameralism, 371
Campaign Reaja o Sera Morto (React or
    Die), 179
Canada, VAW policies in, 159, 169
capital. *See also* cultural circuit of capital
  in BRIC economies, 106
  ethnographic, 392–93
  metacapital, 12
  symbolic, 351–53

capitalism. *See also* mercantilism;
  neoliberalism
  corporate, 296
  feminist critiques of, 137, 139–40
  financial, 106
  Foucault on, 81
  imperialism and, 334–35, 340–41
  managerial, 298
  nation-states as force against, 6
carceral state, 194, 230
Cardoso, Fernando Henrique, 204,
  213–16
caregiver model, 144–45, 157
care-giving, full-time. *See also* male
  breadwinner model
  in Sweden, 142
  in U.S., 145
Carpenter, Daniel, 180–81
CEDAW, 168
CERD. *See* Convention on the Elimination
  of Racial Discrimination
Chagas, Matevs, 225
Chalmers, George, 336
charities. *See* associational activity;
  Red Cross
Charity Organization Society, 45–46
child care services, 144, 146, 148, 163
China, capital development in, 106
citizen armies, 318–19
citizens
  equal treatment of
    under Federal Emergency Relief Act,
    54
    politics of delegation and, 42–47
    by Red Cross, 42–45
    under social assistance programs,
    48–51
    in symbiotic states, 37
    under Voting Rights Act, 186
  individuality of
    general will and, 40–41
    Red Cross and, 44
    in symbiotic states, 37–38
  military mass mobilization of, 319–20
  state-led coercive behavior of, during
    wartime, 324
citizenship. *See also* equal treatment, of
  citizens
  in Brazil, 206–7
  corporate, 315
  fiscal, 285–87, 291–95

national, 315–16, 319–20
women and, 131–33, 137, 165
citizen-state dyads, 264–65
civil rights, civil rights movement and
  Bloody Sunday and, 276–77
  racial democracy and, 184–85
  in U.S., 179, 184–91
    administrative state and, 186–88
    associational connections for, 190–91
    federal courts' role in, 189
    FEPC and, 186–87
    multidimensional approach to, 191–93
    under New Deal, 192
    policy development history for,
    187–88
    state fragmentation as influence on,
    189–90
    state standardization of, 188–89
    state theory and, 193–95
    under VRA, 185–86
civil society, 14, 36–37, 273–74. *See also*
  associational activity; non-profit
  sector; Red Cross
Civil War (U.S.), 251–52, 311
  income tax during, 295
  treatment of enemies during, 321–22, 328
civil wars. *See also* French Revolution
  conflict-repression nexus and, 262–63
  political order and, 265–71
  violence in, logic of, 263–64
class policies, for gender justice, 160,
  163–65
Clastres, Pierre, 245
coercive behavior, by states
  against citizens, during wartime, 324
  citizen-state dyads and, 264–65
  conflict studies and, 260–65
    data evaluation in, 268–71
    internationally-oriented domestic,
    261–63
    performance argument in, 271–75
    political order in, 265–71
  conflict-repression nexus, 261
    civil wars and, 262–63
    in Northern Ireland, 276–77
  military mobilization and, 316–17
  overproduction of, 259
  in Rwanda, 277–79
  through taxation, 295–99
  types of, 259, 281
  in U.S., 275–76

Colbert, Stephen, 272
colonial states
  elite class struggles in, 384–86
  ethnographic capital in, 392–93
  foreign sovereignty criterion for, 379–80
  formation of, 388
  governing structures in, 380–82
  as imperial administrative space, 377–78
  legalistic objections to, 391
  modern, 379–84
  native policy in, 381–82, 384, 392–93
colonialism. *See also* post-colonialism
  Bourdieu on, 371–72
  expression of state authority and, 350
  globalization and, 16
  Indian Muslim society and, 349
    Islam worship in, 353–58
  indirect rule and, 355, 376–77, 379,
    381
    as default approach, 382
    of microstate fields, 382
  legibility of, 353–58
  modern Europe influenced by, 333–34
  symbolic capital and, 351–53
color consciousness, in Brazil, 204–5
colorblindness
  in Brazil, 204–6, 220
  in U.S., 191, 204–10
commensuration, 48
Commons, John, 287
The Communist Manifesto (Marx and
    Engels), 340
Communist Party of the United States of
    America (CP-USA), 275–76
conflation, 352
conflict studies, 260–65
  data evaluation in, 268–71
  internationally-oriented domestic,
    261–63
  performance argument in, 271–75
  political order in, 265–71
conflict-repression nexus, 261
  civil wars and, 262–63
conscription, military, 89, 100–1
  of citizens, 319–20
  during wartime, 294, 317–18
constructivism, historical social sciences
    and, 3–4
contract theory, 54. *See also* Locke, John;
    social contract
  general will and, 40–41

contracts. *See* labor contract agreements
Convention on the Elimination of Racial
    Discrimination (CERD), 211, 224
corporate capitalism, 296
corporate citizenship, 315
correctional facilities. *See* prisons
CP-USA. *See* Communist Party of the United
    States of America
CRAs. *See* credit rating agencies
credit rating agencies (CRAs), 108. *See also*
    Moody's; Standard & Poor's
  categories for, 118
  country ratings and, 108–13
  economic crises predicted by, 113–15
  history of, 108
  market volatility as influence on, 116
  ratings methodology for, 110, 115–16,
    123–24
  sovereign debt and, 108–13
  state empowerment of, 117–18
  transparency for, 123–24
credit ratings
  after Brady restructuring plan, 123
  downgrades of, 116
  encoding and, 113–15
  for Greece, 116, 123
  hardening of, 115–16
  inflation as factor for, 111–13
  inscription and, 117–18
  loosening of, 115–16
  moral reduction criteria for, 110
  performativity and, 118–19
  political conflict as influence on, 113
  qualitative evaluation dimensions for,
    111–13
  trade liberalization as factor in,
    111–13
  during 2010 Eurozone crisis, 113
  for U.S., 127
criminal justice system. *See* prisons
cultural circuit of capital, 107
cultural turn, in history and social sciences,
    3–4, 10, 13, 259, 342
culture
  evaluation of nations and, 107, 111–16,
    118–21
  gender inequality and, 146–47, 161,
    163–64
  state boundaries influenced by, 7, 10
  taxation and, 285, 288–89, 291, 295
  Weber and, 4–5

daddy politics, in Sweden, 146–47
daily people exchanges, 93–96
"death taxes," 60
debt. *See also* national debt; sovereign debt
  social, 118
decisionism, 246, 252–53
  Dewey on, 255
  Merriam on, 247, 249–50
  Schmitt on, 255
Delbruck, Hans, 311
delegated governance, 42, 353
  after failure of federal assistance
    programs, 47
democracy, democracies and
  Dewey on, 29–30, 243–45
  gender equality, 135–37, 140
  oligarchic tendencies of, 244–45
  private social work and, 50–51
  state and, 14, 40–41, 81–82, 137,
    231–32, 236–37, 243–47, 249
  taxation and, 285–87, 293
  in U.S., state authority and, 14–15,
    181
democratization trap, 184–85
Dernberg, Bernhard, 386
desegregation, 190, 193
de-stateness, 97–98
Dewey, John, 231, 233–34, 241–42
  on decisionism, 255
  on democratic states, 29–30, 243–45
  on state bureaucracy, 244
  on theory of sovereignty, 242–43
dignity, social assistance programs and,
  49–50
direct population exchanges, 87
discrimination. *See* gender, discrimination;
  racial discrimination; sex
  discrimination
Dobbin, Frank, 187–88
Dobb-Sweezy exchanges, 333–34
doctrinal issues, for gender justice,
  162–64
doxa (permanence), 63–64, 74
Dubber, Markus, 235–36
Dubois, W. E. B., 209–10, 224, 341
Durkheim, Emile, on nation-states, 9
  as form of political consciousness,
    12
  legislative functions of, 29–30
  legitimate symbolic violence by, 103
  metrics of, 104–5

Earned Income Tax Credit, 146, 148–49
economic crises. *See also* Eurozone crisis
  CRAs as predictors of, 113–15
  in Greece, 118
EEOC. *See* Equal Employment
  Opportunities Commission
Egypt, in Ottoman Empire, 363, 368
Elias, Norbert, 103
Ely, Richard T., 291–92
Emerson, Ralph Waldo, 231–38
empires. *See also* colonial states; imperial
  states; *specific empires*
  Bourdieu on, 375–79
  definitions of, 16, 378–79
  field theory on, 375–79, 388–89
  global contexts for, 16
  modern Europe influenced by, 333–34
  non-territorial, 16
  statist, 335–37
  territorial, 16
  theoretical approach to, 334–35
  as unified social space, 376–77
employment, maternal, 131, 133–34,
  143–46, 149–51
employment regulation, gendered labor
  policies and, 133, 155
  in Sweden, for maternal employment,
    143–44
  in U.S., 148–49
Engels, Friedrich, 338, 340
Equal Employment Opportunities
  Commission (EEOC), 144–45
equal treatment, of citizens
  under Federal Emergency Relief Act, 54
  politics of delegation and, 42–47
  by Red Cross, 42–45
  under social assistance programs,
    48–51
  in symbiotic states, 37
Ernst, Charles, 48
Esping-Anderson, Gøsta, 6
estate taxes, 60
ethnographic capital, 392–93
European Tigers, 107
Eurozone crisis (2010), 114
  credit ratings influenced by, 113
  financial causes of, 126–27
Evans, Peter, 53–54, 158
exceptionalism, 232–35
exchanges. *See* population exchanges
executive power, in U.S., 181–82

Fair Employment Practices Committee
(FEPC), 186–87
Family and Medical Leave Act (U.S.),
148
Family Assistance Plan (FAP), 145–46
family law, 160–61, 165–68, 351, 365
gender justice and, 160, 165–68
in Malaysia, 167
fiqh and, 167–68
reform of, 165–68
family policies, gendered labor policies and,
133
FAP. *See* Family Assistance Plan
Federal Emergency Relief Act, 35, 54
equal treatment under, racial stratification
and, 54
feminism
autonomous, 21, 160–61
liberal, 136, 143–44
Marxist, 137
radical, 136
second-wave
analytic tools of, 133
historical-institutionalism and,
140–41
in patriarchal welfare states, 137
state hierarchies and, 137
state support for, 136–38
in Sweden, 136–38, 143–46
traditional legal tradition and, 136
in U.S., 136–38, 143–46
socialist, 137
state theory and, 135–41
third-wave, 138–41
historical social science and, 133
"Jane Crow" laws and, 139
fiqh (legal opinion), 167–68, 356, 359
fiscal citizenship, 291–95
fiscal sociology, 287–88
Fitch
ratings methodology, 110
U.S. credit rating, 127
Foucault, Michel, 257
on the administration of lives,
84–85
on capitalism, 81
Nietzsche's view of the state, 230
public choice theory and, 85
on state powers, 2, 82, 371
Fourth World Congress on Women in
Beijing (1995), 169

France. *See also* French Revolution;
Napoleonic Wars
autogestion in, 41–42
national debt management in, 126
socialist regimes in, 41–42
student movements in, 41–42
Franco-Prussian War, 311, 322
Franklin, Benjamin, 336
French Revolution, 273, 306, 311, 314–15
Freyre, Gilberto, 205–6, 210
frontline public workers, 90–94. *See also*
street-level bureaucrats
assessment of, 101
political works of, 90–91
population exchanges and, 90–96
indirect, 92–93
Frymer, Paul, 189
Fugitive Slave Act of 1850, 237
full-time care-giving. *See* care-giving,
full-time
Fyzee, Asaf Ali Asghar, 355–56

Gal, Susan, 352–53
Garth, Bryant, 304
Gellner, Ernest, 384
gender, 159–60. *See also* women
discrimination, 135, 137, 143–45,
148–49, 161, 172–73
division of labor, 131–32, 161–63
"doing gender," 149–50
institutional components of, 159–61,
173–74
institutionalized religion and, 165–68
normative heterosexuality and, 161
redoing gender, 136
states shaped by, 135–41
status hierarchy and, 161
undoing of, 132
welfare states and, 133–34
gender inequality, 136
defined, 161
through gender division of labor, 161
institutionalization of, 151, 161
state action on, 172–73
gender justice
class policies and, 160, 163–65
communist countries and, 177
doctrinal issues for, 162–64
family law and, 160, 165–68
institutionalized religion and, 165–68
Islam and, 167–68

under Islamic Family Law (Federal
Territories) Act, 167
nondoctrinal issues for, 162–64
status policies and, 160, 163–65
under Sudanese Family Law, 168
for VAW, 159
in women-friendly states, 158–59
gendered labor policies
caregiver model and, 144–45
employment regulation as part of,
133, 155
in Sweden, 143–44
in U.S., 148–49
family policies as part of, 133
future challenges for, 150–51
historical development of, 131–32
male breadwinner model and, 139, 142,
144–45, 157
patriarchal states and, 134–35
in Sweden
academic literature on, 152
construction of, 141–49
destruction of, 141–49
employment regulation as part of,
143–44
for fathers, 146–47
full-time caregiving and, 142
for maternal employment, 143–44
neoliberalism and, 146–49
policy reform for, 146
political context for, 134
second-wave feminism and, 143–46
in U.S.
academic literature on, 152
AFDC and, 60, 141–42, 145–46,
148–49
construction of, 141–49
destruction of, 141–49
Earned Income Tax Credit and, 146,
148–49
employment regulation as part of,
148–49
under FAP, 145–46
full-time caregiving and, 145
for maternal employment, 143
neoliberalism and, 146–49
political context for, 134
second-wave feminism and,
143–46
welfare programs and, dismantling of,
142

gendered states, 131–51
historical-institutionalism and, 138
third-wave analyses of, 138–41
General Federation of Women's Clubs, 44
general will, 40–41
German Empire, 277–78, 377–78, 381–86.
See also colonial states
before World War I, 385–86
GGRA. *See* Golden Gate Restaurant
Association
Gibson, Edward, 195
Gilchrist, Jack, 71–72
Ginsburg, Ruth Bader, 144
Glenn, Garrard, 297–98, 305
global ethno-racial politics, 208–9
global south, Western standards in, 6.
See also Brazil
globalization
colonialism and, 16
empires and, 16
nation-states influenced by, 1, 4, 15–17
Goethe, Johann Wolfgang von, 306–7
Golden Gate Restaurant Association
(GGRA), 66
Goldscheid, Rudolf, 287–88
"government out of sight," 42. *See also*
hidden state, in U.S.
Great Britain, national debt policy in,
126
Great Depression
CRAs during, 108
social assistance during
through Baltimore People's
Unemployment League, 36, 44
by Charity Organization Society,
45–46
by private organizations, 45–46
through Red Cross, 35–36
Greece. *See also* PIIGS economies
credit ratings for, 116, 123
economic crisis in, 118
Griggs v. Duke Power Company,
187–88
guerrillas, 322–24. *See also* partisans
Gulliver's Travels (Swift), 339

Hamburger, Philip, 235–36
Hamilton, Charles, 367
Hartz, Louis, 229–30
Haushofer, Karl, 369
Hayek, Friedrich von, 246

Healthy San Francisco (HSF) campaign, 66–69
The Hedaya, 367
Hegel, Georg Wilhelm Friedrich, 238, 343
Hernes, Helga, 140
Hickock, Lorena, 38
hidden state, in U.S., 58–61
  attribution and, 63–64
  classification as part of, 61–65, 70–71, 73–74
    political dimensions of, 63
  cognitive issues with, 60–61
  critique of, 74
  desensitization and, 63–64
  doxa and, 63–64, 74
  dynamics of, 78
  HSF campaign and, 66–69
  invisible-distant policies, 76
  Medicare program as, 65
  misrecognition of government programs compared to, 63–64
  multistability and, 62–63, 65, 75
  paradox of, 60
  through taxation, 60
  visibility campaigns for, 72
  visible-distant policies, 76
  in YDBT campaign, 69–72
hierarchies
  second-wave feminism and, 137
  states and, 104, 118, 132, 136–38, 140, 161, 179, 183, 207, 221, 249–50, 252, 349–50, 356, 365, 371, 379–80
Hinduism, 284, 352, 354–55, 362, 364
historical-institutionalism, 101–2. *See also* institutionalism
  gendered states and, 138
  second-wave feminism and, 140–41
Hobbes, Thomas, 54, 258, 267
Hochschild, Jennifer, 184–85
Holmes, Oliver Wendell, Jr., 231, 233
Hopkins, Harry, 38
HSF campaign. *See* Healthy San Francisco campaign
Hull, Cordell, 294
Huntington, Samuel, 180

IET. *See* Interest Equalization Tax
imperial states. *See also* British Empire; German Empire
  discovery of America by, 338
  formation of, 337–41

historical development of, in Europe, 335–37
  personal status law in, 352
  transition to modernity for, 337–44
imperialism. *See also* colonialism
  continental versions of, 16–17
  mercantilism and, 337–41
incarceration. *See* prisons
income taxation, in U.S., 290. *See also* taxation, in U.S.
India, as British colony, 349
  capital development in, 106
  Islam in
    fiqh and, 356, 359
    legibility of, 353–58
    as personal status law, 361–64
    Queen-Empress vs Ramzan & Ors case, 354
    scripturalist, 358–61
Indian Councils Act, 362
indirect population exchanges, 87–88
  through closure of mental health facilities, 88–89
  by frontline public employees, 92–93
  through military conscription, 89, 100–1
  public choice theory and, 89–90
indirect rule, 355, 376–77, 379, 381
  as default approach, 382
  microstate fields and, 382
individuality, of citizens
  general will and, 40–41
  Red Cross and, 44
  in symbiotic states, 37–38
Ingraham, Patrick, 191
inscription, 117–18
institutionalism, nation-states influenced by, 12
  institutional change and, theories of, 101–2
Interest Equalization Tax (IET), 123
interest rates, sovereign debt and, 126
international lending, modern world system and, 114
internationally-oriented domestic conflict studies, 261–63
invisible-distant policies, 76
Ireland. *See* Northern Ireland; PIIGS economies

Islam. *See also* Shari'a law
 in British India
  fiqh and, 356, 359
  legibility of, 353–58
  as personal status law, 361–64
  Queen-Empress vs Ramzan & Ors
   case, 354
  as scripturalist, 358–61
  gender justice and, 167–68
  The Hedaya and, 367
Islamic Family Law (Federal Territories) Act
  (Malaysia), 167
Italy. *See* PIIGS economies

James, William, 239, 292
"Jane Crow" laws, 139
Jim Crow, 12, 14–15, 181, 190–91, 210,
  237
Jorge, Flavinho, 215–16, 225
justice. *See* gender justice

Katznelson, Ira, 183–92
Kennedy, John F., 189
Kennedy, Robert, 189
Keynes, John Maynard, 116
Khan, Syed Ahmad, 355–56
Knox, William, 336

labor contract agreements, international, 88
labor policy, sexual division of, 161
Law of Quotas (Brazil), 217–18
legal opinion. *See fiqh*
legibility, of modern states
 in colonial courts, 353–58
 purpose and function of, 349
legitimacy
 of colonial rule, 350, 355, 358
 of nation-states, 3–4, 9–10, 17–18,
  21–22, 40, 103–4, 108–10, 236,
  240, 244, 259–60, 297–98
legitimate symbolic violence, 84–85, 103
liberal feminism, 136, 143–44
 in U.S., 143–44
liberal state, 21–22, 39–40, 137–38, 230,
  234, 239, 250, 284–87, 291, 300
liberal welfare state, 133–34
liberalism, 42–45, 51, 133, 136–37,
  230–32, 234, 239, 241, 246,
  251–52. *See also* neoliberalism
 contract theory and, 54
limited statehood, 9

Lippmann, Walter, 246, 250
Little, A. G., 35
Llewellyn, Karl, 233–34
localism, 180–97
Locke, John, 339
Lula da Silva, Luiz Inacio, 214–17

MacKinnon, Catherine, 137
*Macmillan Student Encyclopedia of
  Sociology* (Mann), 369
Mahmood, Syed, 353–54, 356–58, 367
 on *fiqh*, 359
 on personal status law as religion, 361–64
 on scripturalist Islam, 360–61
Malaysia
 family law in, 167
 fiqh in, 167–68
 Islamic Family Law (Federal Territories)
  Act in, 167
 Shari'a law in, 167, 175–76
 SIS in, 167
male breadwinner model, 139, 142,
  144–45, 157. *See also* men,
  breadwinning and
managerial capitalism, 298
Mandeville, Bernard, 339
Mann, Michael, 288–89, 325, 369
market valuations, 105–6. *See also* credit
  ratings
Marshall, John, 236
Marx, Karl, 238, 338, 340–41
Marxist feminism, 137
maternalism, 142, 150
 in Sweden, 150
maternity leave. *See* parental leave
Medicare program, 65
Mehrotra, Ajay, 58
men. *See also* gender
 breadwinning and, 132–33, 139, 141–42,
  146–47
 caregiving and, 132, 134, 143, 145–47,
  150
 conscription and, 294, 317, 319–20
 gender hierarchy and, 137, 140
mental health facilities, closures of, 88–89
mercantilism, 337–41
Merriam, Charles, 231–32, 246–47
 on decisionism, 247, 249–50
 on pluralist states, 248–49
 on totalitarianism, 245–52
 on violence, 251

metacapital, 12
metrics, for nation-states, 104–5
  sovereign debt as, 105–8
Mettler, Suzanne, 58
Michels, Robert, 244
military conscription, 89, 100–1, 294,
    314–15, 317–18, 322–23. *See also*
    military mass mobilization
military mass mobilization
  of citizens, 319–20
  national citizenship and, 319–20
  state coercion and, 316–17
  during wars, 314–20
military revolutions, 308
  revolution in war *versus*, 308–10
Mitchell, Timothy, 10, 36–37, 44–45,
    61–62, 120
modern colonial states, 379–84
modern world system, 114
modernity
  states and, 13, 206, 229–30, 292
  transitions to, 131, 333–34, 337–38,
    342–44
Moody's, 108–10, 123–24, 127
Morley-Minto reforms. *See* Indian Councils
    Act
mothers, employment and, 131, 133–34,
    143–46, 149–51
Mouffe, Chantal, 239
Moynihan, Daniel Patrick, 191
multistability, of hidden statecraft, 62–63,
    65, 75
Muslim clergy. *See* ulama

Napoleonic Wars, 311, 314–16
national citizenship, 315–16
  military mass mobilization and, 319–20
  in Prussia, 315
national debt. *See also* sovereign debt
  financialization of, 117
  in France, 126
  in Great Britain, 126
  institutional supervision of, 119
National Meeting on Racism and Racial
    Discrimination (Brazil), 214
National Policy for the Promotion of Racial
    Equality (Brazil), 209
nation-states. *See also* boundaries, of states;
    legibility, of modern states
  academic study of, 8–17
  boundary between society and, 9

branding and re-branding of, 122
capitalism curbed by, 6
classification of, 120–21
CRAs empowered by, 117–18
defined, 28
for Durkheim, 12, 29–30
evolution of, 5–8
expansion of concept, 3
gender shaping of, 135–41
general will in, 40–41
globalization as influence on, 1, 4,
    15–17
hierarchies within, 104
historical analysis of, in global contexts, 4
institutionalist influences on, 12
intellectual origins of, 5–8
judicial power of, 2
legitimacy of, 3–4
as meta-field, 371–72
metrics for, 104–5
  sovereign debt, 105–8
modes of governance in, 17–18
moral sociology of, 120–21
neoliberalism in, 5
patriarchal, 11, 134–35
phantom, 32
pluralist, 239–40
population management by, 81–82
  public choice theory and, 82, 96–97
  symbolic power in, 82
power in, development of, 13–15
public-private hybridity in, 9
scholarly modifiers of, 2–3
second-wave feminism support in,
    136–38
social sciences and, 17, 29–30
social stratification in, 11–12
strong, 6
structural effects of, 120
symbolic power of, 81
transformation of, 11–12
weak, 6
Weber on, 4–5, 29–30, 258
Westphalian approach to, 1
women-friendly, 132, 149–50
native policy, in colonial states, 381–82,
    384, 392–93
neoliberalism, 117, 142–43
  gendered labor policies and, 146–49
  rise of, 5, 97–98, 117–18
  states and, 15

Nettl, J. P., 180
Neustadt, Richard, 189
New Deal. *See also* social assistance
    programs
  social assistance rehabilitation models
    under, 45–46
  taxation during, 290–91
*The New Democracy and the New
    Despotism* (Merriam), 246–47
NGOs. *See* non-governmental organizations
Nietzsche, Friedrich, 230, 247, 249
Nixon, Richard, 185–86
nondoctrinal issues, for gender justice,
    162–64
non-governmental organizations (NGOs),
    in Brazil, 213–15
  transnational activism by, 214
non-profit sector, 9–10, 44–45, 51. *See also*
    non-governmental organizations
non-territorial empires, 16. *See also*
    imperialism
non-territorial states, 336
normative heterosexuality, 161
Northern Ireland, conflict in, 276–77

Obama, Barack, 69–72. *See also* You Didn't
    Build That campaign
O'Connor, Julia, 133–34
Oppenheimer, Franz, 369
Ottoman Empire, 363

parental leave, 134, 142, 146–47, 158–59.
    See also Family and Medical Leave
    Act (U.S.)
  Daddy quotas, 147, 159
  public funding of, 160, 163, 172
Paret, Peter, 308–9
partisans, 22, 311, 322–23, 325–26
Paschel, Tianna, 179, 195
Pateman, Carol, 137
patriarchal state, 11
  gendered labor policies and, 134–35
  as welfare state, 137
Paul, Rand, 71
people exchanges
  administrative, 93–96
  African-Americans and, 98
  daily, 93–96
  defined, 85–86
  public choice theory and, 83–86
  through state activity, 82–83, 96–97

through state administration activities,
    83–86
  state transformation and, 96–98
  symbolic power and, 83–86
permanence. *See doxa*
Personal Responsibility and Work
    Opportunity Reconciliation Act
    (PWORA) (U.S.), 148
personal status law, 160, 352. *See also*
    family law
  Shari'a law as, 361–64, 368
phantom states, 32
*Philosophical and Political History of the
    Settlements and Trade of the
    Europeans in the East and the West
    Indies* (Raynal), 338
PIIGS economies, 107
Pitt, William, 336
pluralist states, 239–40, 248–49. *See also*
    democracy
police power, in U.S., 234–36
*Police Powers: The Law of Overruling
    Necessity* (Prentice), 234–35
political authority. *See* state authority
political order, in conflict studies, 265–71
Political Theology (Schmitt), 231, 234,
    239–40
poll taxes, 285, 295
population exchanges. *See also* people
    exchanges
  direct, 87
  by frontline public employees, 90–96
  by frontline public officials, 90–92
  indirect, 87–88
    through closure of mental health
      facilities, 88–89
    by frontline public employees, 92–93
    through military conscription, 89,
      100–1
    public choice theory and, 89–90
    through international labor contract
      agreements, 88
  state administration of, 86–90
  target populations in, 100
population management, by nation-states,
    81–82
  public choice theory and, 82, 96–97
  symbolic power in, 82
Portugal. *See* PIIGS economies
post-colonialism, anthropogeography and,
    114–15

Prentice, William Packer, 234–35
prisons, 81, 194, 354
progressive taxation, 287, 290, 293, 304
Prussia, 306–7. *See also* Napoleonic
    Wars
    national citizenship in, 315
    War of Liberation in, 315–16
PRWORA. *See* Personal Responsibility and
    Work Opportunity Reconciliation
    Act
The Public and Its Problems (Dewey),
    241–42
public choice theory
    Bourdieusian analysts and, 85
    Foucauldian analysts and, 85
    indirect population exchanges and,
        89–90
    people exchanges and, 83–86
    population management and, 82,
        96–97

Queen-Empress vs Ramzan & Ors, 354

race, racism and. *See also* segregation
    in Brazil, 179, 210–15, 218–20
        Campaign Reaja o Sera Morto against,
            179
        myth as racial paradise, 203–4
        U.S. comparisons with, 203–4
    in U.S., 183, 209–10
racial classification, in U.S., 183
racial democracy, 184–85
    Brazil as
        Freyre and, 205–6, 210
        myth of, 204–10
        promotion of, 210–12
    civil rights and, 184–85
    state standardization of, 188–89
racial discrimination, 38, 186–93, 204, 209,
    211–16, 218–19
racial equality
    in Brazil, 204–5, 208–12
        through affirmative action programs,
            214–15, 217–18
        Afro-Brazilians and, 211–13, 221
        black NGOs and, 213–15
        under Law of Quotas, 217–18
        National Policy for the Promotion of
            Racial Equality, 209
        reconfiguration of state orientation for,
            215–19

Santiago Regional Conference of the
    Americas and, 212–15
    SEPPIR, 215–18, 225
    global discourse and international policies
        on, 209–10
    in global ethno-racial politics, 208–9
    UN and, 209–10
        CERD, 211
    in U.S., 186–88, 193
racial state, 220–21
    as political concept, 205–8
    racial order and hierarchy in, 206–7
    through state practices, 207
    in subnational government policies, 206
    whitening of population, 206
radical feminism, 136
Rahim, Abdur, 355–56
Rashomon Effect, 268–69
rating agencies. *See* credit rating agencies
Raynal, Abbé, 338
React or Die Campaign. *See* Campaign
    Reaja o Sera Morto
re-branding, of nations, 122
Red Cross, 35
    equal treatment of citizens by, 42–45
    hybrid role of, 42–43
    individuality of citizens for, 44
    after World War I, 36
reification, of state, 7
religion. *See also* Islam
    colonialism and, 349–50, 355–56,
        361–64
    gender justice and, 162–63, 165–68,
        172–73
religious doctrine, gender justice and,,
    162–63
representative politics, state power and, 14.
    See also democracy, democracies and
repression, by states. *See also* coercive
    behavior, by states
    in Brazil, 218
    control of information about, 260
    dissent and, 261
    in U.S. of political parties, 275–76
reproductive rights, 163
revolutions. *See* French Revolution; military
    revolutions
Ribeiro, Matilde, 217, 225
rights. *See* civil rights; reproductive rights
Road to Serfdom (Hayek), 246
Roland, Edna, 212–13, 225

rolêzinhos (non-violent gathering of youths), 218–19
Romney, Mitt, 69–72. *See also* You Didn't Build That campaign
Roosevelt, Franklin Delano, 186–87, 231
  Federal Emergency Relief Administration under, 35, 54
  income tax regimes under, 290
  as progressive, 290
  New Deal policies, 45–46
Rothenberg, Gunther, 319
Rousseff, Dilma, 217–18, 225
RPF. *See* Rwandan Patriotic Front
Rube Goldberg state, 42, 52, 58, 62
rule-makers, 93–94
rule-takers, 93–94
ruling classes, 244–45
Russia, capital development in, 106
Rwanda, conflict in, 277–79
Rwandan Patriotic Front (RPF), 278–79
Ryan, Paul, 70–71

Salzinger, Leslie, 114
Santiago Regional Conference of the Americas, 212–15
Schmitt, Carl, 231, 234, 238–45, 369
  on decisionism, 255
  on pluralist states, 239–40
Schumpeter, Joseph A., 245, 287–89
Scott, James, 11–12, 208, 349, 371
scripturalist Islam, 358–61
second-wave feminism
  analytic tools of, 133
  historical-institutionalism and, 140–41
  legal tradition and, 136
  in patriarchal welfare states, 137
  state hierarchies and, 137
  state support for, 136–38
  in Sweden, 136–38
    gendered labor policies and, 143–46
  in U.S., 136–38
    gendered labor policies and, 143–46
Seeing Like a State (Scott), 349
segregation
  denial of voting rights through, 186
  in U.S., 183–84
    through "separate but equal" policy, 188–89
Seligman, Edwin R. A., 291–93, 296. *See also* taxation, in U.S.
"separate but equal" policy, 188–89

SEPPIR. *See* Special Secretariat for the Promotion of Racial Equality
sex discrimination, 137, 145–46, 148, 161, 172–73
sexual division of labor. *See* gender, division of labor
sexuality. *See* normative heterosexuality
Shari'a law
  in Malaysia, 167, 175–76
  as personal status law, 361–64, 368
Shaver, Sheila, 133–34
Shaw, Lemuel, 236
Shweder, Richard, 114
Silva, Benedita da, 213–14
Silveira da Luz, Robson, 221
Simmel, Georg, 51
Sisters in Islam (SIS), 167
Skocpol, Theda, 6
Skowronek, Stephen, 178, 180
Skrentny, John, 187
Smith, Adam, 336, 338–41
social assistance programs
  Baltimore People's Unemployment League and, 36, 44
  dignity and, 49–50
  federal expansion of, 46–47
  under New Deal, rehabilitation models for, 45–46
  by private organizations, 45–46
  through Red Cross, 35–36
  standardization of, 45
  state actions and, 53–54
  volunteers for, 50
social contract
  government interventions as, 13, 40, 69
  sovereign debts and, 123
  taxation as, 299–300
social debt, 118
social democracy. *See* Sweden
social insurance programs, 46–47, 49, 373–74
  categorization of citizens and, 48–51
  commensuration and, 48
  gender and, 139–42, 144
social sciences, historical, 5
  constructivist influence on, 3–4
  cultural influences on, 3–4, 259, 342
  nation-states and, 17, 29–30
  second wave of, 5
  third-wave feminism and, 133

Social Security Act of 1935 (U.S.), 47
Social Security program, 157
social work, 47–50
socialist feminism, 137
socialist regimes, in France, 41–42
society, boundary between state and, 9, 13,
    19. *See also* boundaries, of states
society-centered state theory, 2
Solf, Wilhelm, 386
Sources of Social Power (Mann), 369
sovereign bankruptcy rules, 120–21
sovereign debt, 105–8
    asset collections as response to,
        120–21
    under Basel II rules, 117, 126
    CRAs and, 108–13
    diversified returns and, 118–19
    encoding and, 113–15
    IET and, 123
    institutional supervision of, 119
    interest rate increases and, 126
    social contract between nations and,
        123
sovereignty, 18, 234, 242–43, 249–50
    colonial rule and, 379–80
Special Secretariat for the Promotion of
    Racial Equality (SEPPIR) (Brazil),
    215–18, 225
Standard & Poor's (S&Ps), 108
    adjustment factors for, 113
    ratings methodology, 110
    U.S. credit rating, 127
state actors, 6–7
state authority
    colonialism and, 350
    development of, 13–15
    masculinity and, 137
    recognition of, 72–73
    Schmitt on, 238–45
    as symbolic, 13
    in U.S., 14–15, 58–61
        complexity of, 58
        delegation of, 58
        under democracy, 14–15
        development of, 14–15
        fragmentation of, 181–82, 189–90
        localism and, 180–97
        standardization of, 181, 188–89
state capacity
    assessment of, 6
    performing order as part of, 274

scholarship on, 53–54
    in U.S., 39, 42–43, 47
state formation. *See* statebuilding
State of Exception (Agamben), 232–35
state power. *See also* state authority
    development of, 13–15
    representative politics and, 14
    strength confused with autonomy, 14
state theory, 17–18, 74. *See also* nation-
    states
    Bourdieu and, 371–72
    Dewey's, 239
    empires and, 369
    feminism and, 135–41
    society-centered, 2
    state-centered, 2
    U.S. civil rights and, 193–95
statebuilding
    through taxation, 287–91
    in U.S., 1–2
        as administrative state, 180–81
        APD and, 289–90
        as bureaucracy, 180–81
        through taxation, 287
        war and, 288–90, 299, 307–14
statecraft, 63–64, 72–74
states. *See also* boundaries, of states;
        imperial states; nation-states;
        repression, by states
    non-territorial, 336
    strength and autonomy of, 14
    symbiotic
        associational activity in, 37
        dynamics of, 51–53
        equality of treatment in, 37
        individuality of citizens in, 37–38
        state capture and, 42
        state projects in, 37
        voluntary organizations in, 35–36
    territorial, 336
    weak, 6, 178–81, 183–84, 187–88, 240,
        278, 370
status hierarchy, gender and, 161
Steinmetz, George, 16, 255, 351
Sterling, Joyce, 304
street-level bureaucrats, 10, 93. *See also*
        frontline public workers
strong nation-states, 6
student movements, in France, 41–42
submerged state. *See* hidden state, in U.S.
Sudanese Family Law, 168

Sutton, John, 187–88
Sweden
  daddy politics in, 146–47
  gender inequality in, 136
  gendered labor policies in
    academic literature on, 152
    construction of, 141–49
    destruction of, 141–49
    employment regulation as part of,
      143–44
    for fathers, 146–47
    full-time caregiving and, 142
    for maternal employment, 143–44
    neoliberalism and, 146–49
    policy reform for, 146
    political context for, 134
    second-wave feminism and, 136–38,
      143–46
  maternalism in, 150
  neoliberalism in, 147, 150
  social democrats in, 143–44, 147
Swift, Jonathan, 339
symbiotic states
  associational activity in, 37
  dynamics of, 51–53
  equality of treatment in, 37
  individuality of citizens in, 37–38
  state capture and, 42
  state projects in, 37
  voluntary organizations in, 35–36
symbolic capital, 351–53
symbolic power, of states
  Bourdieu on, 81, 83–86
  defined, 83–84
  Foucault on, 84
  people exchanges and, 83–86
  through population management, 82
  as violence, 103
symbolic violence. *See* legitimate symbolic
  violence

Taft, Charles, 56
TANF. *See* Temporary Assistance to Needy
  Families program
target populations, 100
taxation
  coercive behavior by states and, 295–99
  conflicts of interest as result of, between
    state and citizens, 285–86
  hidden state and, 60
  as social pact, 299–300

state functions of, 284–85
statebuilding and, 287–91
  public administration as part of,
    287–88
in U.S.
  "ability to pay" philosophy and,
    291–92
  benefits theory, 293
  during Civil War, 295
  as coercive state behavior, 295–99
  direct, 287
  as fiscal citizenship, 291–95
  historical development of, 286–87,
    291–95
  of income, 290
  marginalization of non-elites and, 285,
    295
  modern reform of, 294, 297–98, 304
  during New Deal era, 290–91
  with poll taxes, 285, 295
  private business authority and, 298–99
  progressive, 287, 290, 293, 304
  public power and private rights with,
    conflicts between, 298
  statebuilding and, 287
  during World War I, 294
  during World War II, 290–91
  after World War I, 288
Taylor, Verta, 274
Temporary Assistance to Needy Families
  (TANF) program (U.S.), 148
territorial empires, 16. *See also* colonialism
territorial states, 336
Third World Conference against Racism,
  Racial Discrimination, Xenophobia,
  and Related Tolerance in Durban,
  209–11, 220
third-wave feminism, 138–41
  historical social science and, 133
  "Jane Crow" laws and, 139
Thirty Years War, 312–13
Thoreau, Henry David, 237
Thurmond, Strom, 185–86
Tilly, Charles, 5, 13, 273, 288–89, 307–10
Tocqueville, Alexis de, 55, 182–83
Tomlins, Christopher, 235–36
totalitarianism, 245–52
transparency, for credit rating agencies,
  123–24
Trenchard, John, 340
Tyabji, Faiz Badruddin, 355–56

ulama (Muslim clergy), 167–68
UN. *See* United Nations
Underwood, Oscar, 296
United Nations (UN)
    CERD and, 211, 224
    racial equality policies, 209–10
United States (U.S.). *See also* Civil War;
        gender, discrimination; racial
        discrimination; sex discrimination;
        War of Independence
    as associational state, 182–83
    civil rights in, 179, 184–91
        administrative state and, 186–88
        associational connections and, 190–91
        federal courts' role in, 189
        FEPC and, 186–87
        multidimensional approach to, 191–93
        under New Deal, 192
        policy development history for, 187–88
        state fragmentation as influence on,
            189–90
        state standardization of, 188–89
        state theory and, 193–95
        under VRA, 185–86
    Civil War in, 251–52
    colorblindness in, 191, 204–10
    corporate capitalism in, 296
    credit rating for, 127
    desegregation in, 190, 193
    executive power in, 181–82
    Family Leave and Medical Act in, 148
    Federal Emergency Relief Act in, 54
    gender inequality in, 136
    gendered labor policies in
        academic literature on, 152
        AFDC and, 60, 141–42, 145–46,
            148–49
        construction of, 141–49
        destruction of, 141–49
        Earned Income Tax Credit and, 146,
            148–49
        employment regulation as part of,
            148–49
        Family Assistance Plan and, 145–46
        full-time caregiving and, 145
        for maternal employment, 143
        neoliberalism and, 146–49
        political context for, 134
        second-wave feminism and, 143–46
    hidden state in, 58–61
        attribution and, 63–64

classification as part of, 61–65, 70–71,
        73–74
    cognitive issues with, 60–61
    critique of, 74
    desensitization and, 63–64
    doxa and, 63–64, 74
    dynamics of, 78
    Health San Francisco campaign, 66–69
    invisible-distant policies, 76
    Medicare program as, 65
    misrecognition of government
        programs compared to, 63–64
    multistability and, 62–63, 65, 75
    paradox of, 60
    taxation and, 60
    visibility campaigns for, 72
    visible-distant policies, 76
    in You Didn't Build That campaign,
        69–72
liberal feminism in, 143–44
as multidimensional state, 180–84
New Deal in, 45–46
    civil rights and, 192
police power in, 234–36
PWORA in, 148
racial classification in, 183
racial democracy in, 184–85
repression of political parties in,
        275–76
as Rube Goldberg state, 58, 62
second-wave feminism in, 136–38
segregation in, 183–84
    affirmative action for whites and,
        183–92
    through "separate but equal" policy,
        188–89
Social Security Act of 1935 in, 47
Social Security program in, 157
state authority in, 58–61
    complexity of, 58
    delegation as part of, 58
    democracy and, 14–15, 235–38, 243,
        245–46, 249
    development of, 14–15
    fragmentation of, 181–82, 189–90
    localism and, 180–97
    standardization of, 181, 188–89
statebuilding in, 1–2
    as administrative state, 180–81
    American Political Development and,
        289–90

as bureaucracy, 180–81
through taxation, 287
TANF program in, 148
taxation in, 290
    "ability to pay philosophy" of,
        291–92
    benefits theory, 293
    during Civil War, 295
    as coercive state behavior, 295–99
    direct, 287
    as fiscal citizenship, 291–95
    historical development of, 286–87,
        291–95
    marginalization of non-elites through,
        285, 295
    modern reform of, 294, 297–98, 304
    during New Deal era, 290–91
    with poll taxes, 285, 295
    private business authority and,
        298–99
    progressive, 287, 290, 293, 304
    public power and private rights with,
        conflicts between, 298
    statebuilding and, 287
    stoppage at the source, 295–99
    during World War I, 294
    during World War II, 186–87, 192,
        290–91
VAW policies in, 148, 168–69
as weak state, 178–79

VAW. *See* violence against women
violence. *See also* legitimate symbolic
        violence
    in civil wars, logic of, 263–64
    Merriam on, 251
violence against women (VAW)
    autonomous feminism and, 160–61,
        168–72
    gender justice for, 159
    international policies for, 148, 159,
        168–69
    state action against, 169–73
    in U.S., 148, 168–69
visibility campaigns, for statecraft, 72
visible-distant policies, 76
voluntary organizations. *See* non-
        governmental organizations;
        non-profit sector; Red Cross
volunteers, for public social assistance, 50
von Clausewitz, Carl, 307

von Trotha, Lothar, 381
Voting Rights Act (VRA) (U.S.), 185–86
vulture funds, 119

Wall Street Journal, 67–68
Wallerstein, Immanuel, 114
War of Independence, in U.S., 307, 311,
        314–15
War of Liberation, 315–16
Warren, Elizabeth, 69–70
wars. *See also* civil wars; *specific wars*
    enemies during
        definition of, 310–11
        treatment of, 320–24
    guerrillas during, 322–24
    military conscription during, 317
    military revolutions and, 308–10
    object of maneuvers in, 313–14
    partisans in, 311, 322–23, 325–26
    revolution in, 312–14
    statebuilding and, 288–90, 299, 307–14
    state-led mobilization of, 310–12
weak states, 6, 178–81, 183–84, 187–88,
        240, 278, 370
Wealth of Nations (Smith), 339
Weber, Max, 103, 180–81, 369, 371
    definition of nation-state for, 4–5, 29–30,
        258
    on public bureaucracy, 36, 229–30, 244,
        287–88
Webster, Daniel, 237
welfare. *See* Aid to Families with Dependent
        Children
welfare states. *See also* social assistance
        programs; social insurance
        programs; Social Security Act of
        1935
    defined, 131
    gender regimes of, 133–34
    gendered labor policies in, 142
    patriarchal, 137
Westlye, Kevin, 66
Williams, Eric, 333–34
Witherspoon, John, 336
women. *See also* feminism; gendered labor
        policies; violence against women
    employment and, 131, 133–34, 143–46,
        149–51
    political exclusion of, 136–37, 140
    political mobilization of, 131–32,
        140–41, 168, 173

women. (cont.)
  racial differences among, 142, 145,
      149–50
  the state and, 137
women-friendly states, 132, 134–35,
      149–50, 158–59
Women's Rights Project (ACLU), 144
world society, 104
World War I
  German Empire before, 385–86
  Red Cross volunteers after, 36

taxation development after, 288
  U.S. taxation rates during, 294
World War II
  CRAs during, 108
  FEPC during, 186–87
  U.S. taxation rates during, 290–91
Worthen, Ben, 67–68

You Didn't Build That (YDBT) campaign,
      69–72
Young, Iris Marion, 161